2016

D1013136

THE STEAMER

BUD FURILLO AND THE GOLDEN AGE OF L.A. SPORTS

Andy Furillo
Foreword by **Tommy Lasorda**

SANTA
MONICA
PRESS

Published by:
Santa Monica Press LLC
P.O. Box 850
Solana Beach, CA 92075
1-800-784-9553
www.santamonicapress.com
books@santamonicapress.com

Printed in the United States

Santa Monica Press books are available at special quantity discounts when
purchased in bulk by corporations, organizations, or groups. Please call our
Special Sales department at 1-800-784-9553.

This book is intended to provide general information. The publisher, author,
distributor, and copyright owner are not engaged in rendering professional
advice or services. The publisher, author, distributor, and copyright owner are
not liable or responsible to any person or group with respect to any loss, illness,
or injury caused or alleged to be caused by the information found in this book.

ISBN-13 978-1-59580-088-6

Library of Congress Cataloging-in-Publication Data

Names: Furillo, Andy, author.
Title: The steamer : Bud Furillo and the golden age of L.A. sports / by Andy
  Furillo.
Description: Solana Beach, CA : Santa Monica Press, [2016] | Includes
  bibliographical references and index.
Identifiers: LCCN 2015041923 | ISBN 9781595800886
Subjects: LCSH: Furillo, Bud, 1925-2006. | Sportswriters–United
  States–Biography. | Radio broadcasters–United States–Biography. |
  Sports–California–Los Angeles–History–20th century.
Classification: LCC GV742.42 .F87 A3 2016 | DDC 070.449796092–dc23
LC record available at http://lccn.loc.gov/2015041923

Cover and interior design and production by Future Studio
All photos courtesy of the Bud Furillo collection

CONTENTS

Excerpts from Bud Furillo's Steam Room columns appear throughout the text

To Gail, Jill, Frank, Michael, and Jackie

ACKNOWLEDGMENTS

This book would never have been written unless somebody told me to quit thinking about it and just do it. Thank you, Roger A. Dreyer.

Gary K. Hart offered regular advice and encouragement. So did Bill Enfield. Doug Disney and Betty O'Meara let me know I was on the right track.

I'm deeply grateful to my dad's colleagues who helped me understand his importance to L.A. sports. Melvin Durslag gave me insight and knowledge, as did Steve Bisheff, Jack Disney (R.I.P.), Doug Krikorian, Mitch Chortkoff, Jim Perry, Bob Keisser, Ari Noonan, Larry Stewart, and John Beyrooty. Also: Steve Harvey and John Hall, who broke their maidens at the *Herald*.

Dan Morain is the best political columnist, editorial page editor, and neighbor anybody could have on one street. Thanks to him and his wife, Claudia. I also received terrific encouragement from my friends in the newspaper business, especially Steve Magagnini. Thanks to *Sacramento Bee* publisher Cheryl Dell, executive editor Joyce Terhaar, managing editor Scott Lebar, and everybody else at the paper for their support and encouragement.

Chip MacGregor of the MacGregor Literary Agency rolled the dice on me. So did Jeffrey Goldman, publisher at Santa Monica Press. Thanks also to Kate Murray at Santa Monica Press, a terrific editor.

Thanks to William Randolph Hearst III, Eve Burton, and Shira Saiger at Hearst Communications for the usage of my dad's columns and excerpts, and to Sports-Reference.com for the treasure trove of material it presents to sports researchers.

I enjoyed the smiles and encouragement from supervisor Kathleen Correia and her crew in the California History section at the California State Library.

My aunt, Roberta Ruffalo Johnson Wetherbee, straightened me out on the oral history. Cousin Rich Furillo, too. My great-aunt, Betty "Moogie" Cicchillo (R.I.P.), walked me through the hot spots of 1930s Youngstown.

Thanks to Dale Spalding and all the lifelong friends from Gainford Street.

What a spectacular lineup of brothers and sisters—Gail Furillo, Jill Furillo-Gargano (and brother-in-law Tomas Gargano), Frank Furillo, Michael Furillo, and Jackie Furillo, and all the nieces and nephews.

Special thanks to John and Pat Anderluh and everyone else in the Anderluh and Henning families.

My wife, Deborah Anderluh, a great editor, helped shape this story from the beginning. My son, Andy, is my hero.

My mom, Aline, lives forever in the hearts of all her children.

My dad, Bud Furillo, showed me the blueprint of life—he worked hard, and nobody had more fun.

—Andy Furillo

FOREWORD
by TOMMY LASORDA

Bud Furillo was the kind of guy you could trust immediate-ly. He never let you down, and he built up a reputation for that.

When I first met him, his father lived in my hometown, Norristown, Pennsylvania. His dad found out I was going out to spring training with the St. Louis Browns in San Bernardino. This is 1953. So he called Bud up and told Bud to go and say hello to me and to take care of me. So he walked into our clubhouse one day and wanted to know where Tom Lasorda was, and I said, "Over here." He came over, and that was the beginning of a very long and wonderful friendship.

He always took care of me, just like his father asked him to do. When I became a scout for the Dodgers, he got me a ticket to the first Super Bowl and all the other games. I'd come out and see him in the off-season a lot. He took me out to dinner, everywhere.

This was during the great expansion of sports in Los Angeles, and Bud Furillo was right in the middle of it. You couldn't wait to read the *Herald Examiner* to see what the Steamer was saying. He covered every sport and brought out things nobody else could ever do. And he put together as great a group of writers as you'd ever want to see. You'll never see it like that again.

Bud Furillo was the heart of the media industry that was bringing sports to the people of this great city. You could actually say that I loved Bud Furillo very much. I loved him, and I respected him a great deal, and he was always there for me. He wanted to see me manage the Dodgers. He was always behind me, pushing me, and making people aware of me.

In this book, the Steamer's son, Andy Furillo, makes you aware of Bud and his times—the best in sports that Los Angeles has ever seen.

INTRODUCTION

The last time I saw my dad alive was at the House of Blues on Sunset Boulevard, in Los Angeles.

It was a bright and brilliant January day, and we were there for the Gospel Brunch. My pop wore baggy blue jeans, sneakers, and a loose-fitting T-shirt. Like most everybody in the house, he was dancing in the aisles, fueled by an unbroken pour of mimosas.

A pulsating soul groove electrified the word of the Lord. There were a lot of us there—sisters and brothers and grandchildren and aunts and cousins and nieces and nephews and friends upon friends.

When the show was over, we didn't have much time to talk. Everybody had to go back to somewhere, me to where I lived and worked in the Sacramento area and my pop to Ojai. We hugged goodbye. He kissed me on the cheek and told me he loved me, and I told him I loved him back. Then my sister drove him home to his one-room apartment, where over the past year he'd been pounding the computer, working on a new project.

Bud Furillo—"The Steamer"—was writing his memoirs.

As a sports journalist, my dad had never been much for reflection. He was always an "in the moment" guy, right up to the time they found him dead in his bed.

He had the sports section lying next to him.

At his funeral, the priest said he'd heard that the Steamer had been working on a book, and that one of his sons also was a writer of sorts. The priest asked the scribbler to identify himself, and I meekly raised my hand.

"Finish the book," the priest said.

The command sat around in my head for five years, until one night, at a basketball game in Sacramento, a lawyer buddy grilled me about the old man. I told him about the priest's exhortation, and he told me to get after it, too.

The next morning, I began reading my dad's memoirs. There was some pretty good stuff in them, like the time he covered Florence Chadwick's twenty-six-mile swim across the Catalina Channel in 1952.

"I made it easy," the Steamer wrote, "with a bottle of scotch."

He also mentioned an organized crime trial where a couple mobsters were accused of trying to extort a fighter out of his purse money. One of the witnesses, another mobster named Joey Sica, had some trouble understanding the questions.

"Is there something wrong with your hearing, Mr. Sica?" one of the lawyers asked.

"Yeah," Sica replied. "I got shot in the head once."

I called some of my pop's old friends and colleagues and the sports figures he had covered. I went back to his hometown of Youngstown, Ohio, and walked the neighborhoods where he grew up. I drove around L.A. to trace the streetcar lines he rode as a teenager to attend sporting events all over town.

Searching for my dad's soul, I found it in the scrapbooks kept by his mother and in the library microfilm of everything he ever wrote. The thousands of stories and columns traced the growth of an unvarnished rookie into one of the leading voices of his time, on his subject, in his town.

My dad's career covered seven different decades. It included a lot of time behind the microphone in radio studios and a little bit in front of TV cameras. But he achieved his greatness as a newspaperman.

The years rolled by after his death, and with every day, the public memory of his accomplishment grew more dim. As it faded, so did one of the best accounts of the L.A. sports scene's greatest generation.

It was an era as entertaining as any, ever, in the history of American sports, and nobody knew it, lived it, or told it better than the Steamer.

—Andy Furillo

Chapter 1

FROM YOUNGSTOWN TO L.A.

We have never been able to wash the iron ore out of our T-shirts completely. You can take a boy out of Youngstown, but you can't take Youngstown out of the boy. It doesn't come off.
—January 31, 1973

Bud Furillo was a sharp kid with a feel for the street. Growing up in Youngstown, Ohio, in the 1920s and '30s, he was shaped by an urban, industrial environment that was dominated by steel and made great by the sweat of the working people who produced it. The people of Youngstown hustled to survive and worked double shifts to succeed. Furillo knew what they thought and how they felt, and he listened to what they said. They were his audience, forever.

Later, when he moved away to a big city, where he hung out with the biggest sports and entertainment stars of his day, Furillo always knew—and never forgot—that Youngstown had made him who he was.

When he became a big-shot sportswriter in Los Angeles, Furillo wrote for the people who had come from Youngstown and every other industrial neighborhood in America to resettle on the West Coast after World War II. Too poor to go overboard during the Depression and too determined to have too much fun during the war to defeat foreign enemies, they let the good times roll the minute General Douglas MacArthur signed the armistice with the Japanese on the teak decks of the USS *Missouri*. They celebrated the wars they won, the kids they raised, the steel they molded, and the businesses they created. They loved sports and sports teams. They read the newspaper sports pages and depended on columnists to give it to them straight, from the inside out.

In his years in Los Angeles, the Steamer's readers and listeners expanded to include the lawyers and doctors and politicians and entrepreneurs who shared his hardcore love of sports. Maybe his appeal was that he was a reflection of their own backgrounds and family histories that sprang from the factories and mines of the Rust Belt in places like Youngstown, where the Steamer had gained his own sense of place.

•   •   •   •   •

The Steamer's father, Mike Furillo, came from a family that had emigrated from the mountains of southern Italy in 1901. They came to the United States with organized crime money that they invested in multiple properties in Hubbard, Ohio. They then opened a grocery store and cobbler's shop that fronted one of the more prominent numbers operations in the greater northeastern area of nearby Youngstown.

Angelina Marie Cicchillo, Furillo's hard-working mother, was the oldest daughter of a Benito Mussolini sympathizer who had kept her out of school so she could work on his two-acre, corner-lot farm and in his grocery store, where he sold whiskey for mobsters during Prohibition.

Mike met Angelina through their fathers' arrangement. The Steamer was the first of their two kids, baptized Francis Angelo Furillo—"Frank" on his birth certificate, but it didn't really matter because everyone called him Buddy, anyway.

Amid the double scourge of the Depression and Prohibition, Mike Furillo played his connections and found a gig up by the lake in Cleveland. He hooked onto an organized crime outfit called the Mayfield Road Gang and babysat a still for them. It was easy work, out of the line of fire in the bootlegging wars that bloodied streets from Cleveland to Pittsburgh. Federal authorities eventually found the still and shut it down, "forcing us back to poverty in Youngstown," the Steamer recalled in his memoirs.

The Furillos moved into a rental around the corner from the house where Angelina was born, and where her father still lived.

Unable to pay the gas bill, they once suffered through a winter with no heat, Buddy and his little sister sleeping in the same bed with all their clothes on to stay warm. Thank goodness Buddy's parents had taught him how to sing and play "O Sole Mio" on the accordion; he nailed it in a contest downtown and won the five-dollar first prize, which his folks used to pay the heating bill.

Their neighborhood was called the Sharon Line, named for the streetcar track that ran from downtown Youngstown to the steel mill across the state line in nearby Sharon, Pennsylvania. The community crackled with ethnic diversity. Mostly Italian and Slavic, it became largely African American when the steel companies roamed south in search of strikebreakers. Everybody got along, mostly, except for Angelina's father, who chased black kids off his property with a shotgun.

Corner stores, pool rooms, and a whorehouse on a hill served as centers of the Sharon Line social life. When the weather was good, kids played ball in the streets and cooled off in creeks that their folks had dammed into swimming holes. In the winter, the grown-ups blocked off the streets that sloped into ravines and the kids raced their sleds to the bottom.

Meanwhile, Youngstown had established itself as a major steel production center by the time the Steamer was born in 1925. Coal and canals made the surrounding Mahoning Valley perfect for the part. Big companies like Republic and U.S. Steel moved into the region and built sixteen steel mills there. The steel barons constructed fabulous mansions on the north side of town along Fifth Avenue, above Wick Park. Daniel Burnham, the famous architect who designed modern Chicago, also left his mark on downtown Youngstown, where Federal Street was the home of high-end department stores, nightclubs, lively bars, and fancy restaurants. Before they left for Hollywood, the Warner Brothers opened a theater in downtown Youngstown.

By the time Buddy was five years old, Youngstown had reached its all-time population peak. The 170,002 people who lived there made it the forty-fifth largest city in the United States.

As a kid and all the way into his teenage years, the Steamer played hooky and ran downtown every time the circus came to town. He ditched school another time to wave at the presidential motorcade of Franklin Delano Roosevelt. Bud never missed a Benny Goodman tour, and once stayed up all night talking to Cab Calloway in a downtown bar after the *Hi-De-Ho* man finished a gig. He also saw the great power-hitting baseball star from the Negro leagues, Josh Gibson, hit a monster home run in a barnstorming game at Idora Park. The Steamer flipped burgers at a place called the Petrakos Grill, where he resisted the recruitment efforts of a local Mafioso, a man who ran the local slots and later wound up murdered.

Furillo was never a great athlete, and his father, who loved all sports—especially boxing and Notre Dame football—let him know it, making fun of the kid's lack of foot speed. But the old man did teach Buddy how to box, and the young Steamer once laced up his gloves in the front yard with a tall, lithe kid from the Sharon Line named Tommy Bell. The fight wasn't much.

"He knocked me on my ass," Furillo said.

TRAIN WHISTLE MOANS FOR YOUNGSTOWN
MAY 1, 1962

YOUNGSTOWN, OHIO—The hometown revisited:

It was in 1942 when I last could call this steel-producing town home. Nineteen years of California living failed to erase an attachment for it. This visit might. . . .

The mills are dreary. So are the people, with kind hearts. A melting pot of nations and races. They answered the call for our leading industry with strong backs, which are now bent. A teen-age chum, Spike Rigelsky, whom I would have joined in the mills if my parents hadn't foreseen the future, lamented:

"A lot of guys from the corner are laid off. Automation. The machines chopped me out of a foreman's job. But at least, I'm working."

Most of the publicity the town attracts today isn't good. A hoodlum is blown up in his automobile. Youngstown in headlines for twenty-four hours again.

The night of Easter Sunday, my old parish church was robbed of the holiday collection. . . .

Awaiting gentle Morpheus at the end of a one-day visit, I heard a train whistle blow on a tedious trek by the millyards.

It moaned for Youngstown.

Propelled by his KO of young Bud, Bell turned pro eight years later and went on to fight the biggest names of his era, including Sugar Ray Robinson at Madison Square Garden for the welterweight championship of the world. In the second round, Bell did Robinson the same way he did the Steamer—he knocked the greatest pound-for-pound fighter of all time on *his* ass. Robinson returned the favor in the eleventh and went on to win his first championship.

During a time when Catholicism's strictures on divorce locked unhappy couples into lifetimes of misery, the Steamer's mother untied the knot with Mike when his drinking and abusiveness prompted her to pull a knife on him. Angelina got custody of both children and secured a job mopping floors in downtown barbershops and beauty parlors, where she learned to set hair. After getting her own chair in a beauty shop, she saved her earnings and went on to open her own beauty parlor. She then re-married, this time to a steel mill worker, Robert Ruffalo, who saved his money to buy a gas station and served as a fantastic stepfather. Eventually, the family moved out of the Sharon Line and bought a two-story clapboard house in Youngstown's south side, an emerging middle-class neighborhood of screened-in front porches and big front yards.

The move was the catalyst for a crucial period in the adolescent Steamer's life. The divorce had estranged him from his father's side of the family—a sweet grandfather, a half-dozen aunts and uncles, and more than a dozen cousins. It traumatized him and left him with an emotional void. Bud plugged this emptiness with a passion for sports. Through his love of games and fights and horses, the young Steamer may very well have felt a connection to his absent father.

During the late 1930s, sports became the Steamer's Xanax. He joined a neighborhood sandlot football team that played its home games around the corner from his house on Philadelphia Avenue. They called themselves the Philadelphia Eagles.

"We were the best on the South Side," wrote the Steamer.

He arranged for the Eagles to play a team from the Sharon Line.

"We got beat 20-6," Furillo wrote. "So I quit the Eagles and went back to playing with my buddies in The 'Hood. They were tougher."

Slow, short, and top-heavy, the Steamer eventually realized that his physical limitations were crushing his dreams of becoming the next Joe DiMaggio. Instead, he decided to take on the role of a sports connoisseur. He developed a deep appreciation for sports, seeing them as a testing ground for character, a laboratory for scientific measurement that documented the evolution of the human species.

Sports became his art form. He saw them as drama, as stories to be told. Not only did sports fill the emptiness of his paternal estrangement and help him reconnect to fond feelings from an earlier time, they also became the means for his daily bread and turned out to be the way he would make his mark in the world.

Sports became the basis of all of the Steamer's relationships—with women, family, and friends.

•   •   •   •   •

The move to Los Angeles came in 1940. The Steamer's folks first considered relocating to Florida, but then one of Angelina's sisters, Rose, took up with the scion of a once-prominent Sharon Line bootlegging family, and they ran off to California together. Only problem was, Rose was already engaged to someone else. The fiancé then put together a posse to chase her down that included the Steamer's mother and stepfather. They found Rose and brought her back to Youngstown, but the trip to California had opened their eyes to new possibilities out West. They forgot about Florida and set off for L.A.

The Steamer wasn't sure about this move at all. What fifteen-year-old would be? Yanked from the comfortable familiarities of youth in one of the most uncertain times of his life, young Bud Furillo clung to the only place he had ever known. His apprehensions about the new city were confirmed in his first few innings in Los Angeles, when his folks went bust on an Italian restaurant.

The family settled in the little town of Maywood, on the

industrial southeastern side of the city. They bought a two-bedroom tract house, and Furillo's stepfather found work at a copper tubing plant. Many of their relatives soon followed. Overlooked in the swirl of his family's new beginning, the Steamer got lost in a world dominated by his mother, stepfather, little sister, new baby half-sister, and the aunts and uncles who stayed with them for months at a time. He slept on the couch in the den.

The Steamer found his way around the new city through the Los Angeles streetcar system. Still running strong in 1940, the streetcar line was only six blocks from his folks' overpopulated way-station at Fifty-Third and Carmelita. Furillo's forays into the city led him to the landmarks of the local sports scene, which, like the Steamer, was still in its adolescence. Since it was baseball season when his family moved to L.A., his first stop was the minor-league ballparks.

Wrigley Field, at Forty-Second and Avalon in South-Central L.A., was designed in the image of its famous namesake on Chicago's north side, right down to the ivy-covered walls. The L.A. Angels were the minor-league affiliate of the major-league Cubs, but the quality of the game in the Pacific Coast League was so good that some of the punditry in the West thought it could elevate into a third major league.

Over in the Fairfax District, Furillo discovered Gilmore Field, the wooden ballpark that was home to the Pittsburgh Pirates' farm club, the Hollywood Stars, where gamblers filled the box seats between the bases and shouted suggestions to manager Jimmy Dykes.

"You didn't know which one to listen to because you didn't know which way they were going," Dykes told the Steamer many years later.

During Furillo's first summer in L.A., former Brooklyn Dodgers great Babe Herman was winding down his career with a .307 average for the Stars. The Steamer made it to Gilmore every Sunday, and it seemed like Babe always hit one out for him. But Furillo found himself distracted by another babe at the ballpark. Betty Grable, in her tight yellow sweaters, had a tendency to do that to the male youth of America.

Like everywhere else in the country, boxing was huge in Los Angeles. Two venues offered weekly cards. The Steamer preferred the Hollywood Legion Stadium, where he sat in the balcony for fifty-five cents. Between rounds, he spied on celebrities seated ringside, and he noticed how his favorite actor—George Raft—always seemed in a hurry to leave.

"I got a kick out of Raft whenever a fighter seemed on the verge of a knockout," the Steamer wrote in his memoirs. "Instead of sticking around for the kill, George would grab his topcoat and head for the exits."

The movie tough guy didn't know it at the time, but he set the trend that has forever marked the national image of the Los Angeles sports fan: he was the first to leave early.

Riding the rails around L.A., the teenaged Steamer saw mountains slope into foothills that rolled into the valleys and flatlands that surrendered to the sea. The weather was almost always perfect. It was truly a paradise on a coastal plain.

In the grand beauty of pre-war Southern California, no park, peak, or promontory touched the Steamer's soul more deeply than the stadium inside the green lawns of the exposition grounds south of downtown. The Los Angeles Memorial Coliseum rose to a pinnacle at the point of its Olympic torch. The cauldron flamed the sky atop a fifteen-arch double peristyle that reflected the grandeur of ancient Greece and Rome. Beneath the colonnade, its concourse flowed into a gray-green horizon that climbed nearly a hundred rows toward heaven.

Although baseball in L.A. was strictly minor-league, the city's college football scene was as big-time as anywhere. The city's cathedral of sport housed two major programs. One had already established its national prominence. The other was making moves in the same direction. When the Steamer arrived in Los Angeles in 1940, the University of Southern California had won four national championships in the previous twelve years. Nine years earlier, the Trojans had drawn a quarter of a million people to the train station after their first-ever road win at Notre Dame.

The University of California's Southern Branch, meanwhile, had settled into the hills of Westwood in one of the world's most gorgeous campus settings. A year earlier, the UCLA football team had put itself on the map with an undefeated season that included a 0–0 tie with a USC team that wound up winning a piece of the national championship.

Every weekend, either USC or UCLA played a doubleheader at the Coliseum, with the freshmen opening the show at 11:00 AM. The Steamer always got there early, carrying a brown paper sack stuffed with a submarine sandwich and two bottles of Par-T-Pak root beer. He paid his fifty cents and trudged high into the northeastern corner of the Coliseum, to Section 27. If he had looked backwards from the upper lip of that section, he would have enjoyed a better view of Mount Baldy than the game below. The 10,000-foot peak forty miles away seemed only slightly more distant than the seventy-five yards that separated Section 27 from the back line of the Coliseum's eastern end zone. Lousy seat—no problem. The Steamer was still in the ballpark, and when the crowd size allowed, he snuck toward the goal line to get a better view of his favorite sport's biggest stars.

In UCLA's opener, Furillo watched Jackie Robinson return a kickoff for a touchdown against Southern Methodist University, breaking five tackles seven years before he broke baseball's color barrier. Little left-handed quarterback Frankie Albert brought Stanford into town on its way to an undefeated season and Rose Bowl championship. The Steamer even got to see Bob Dove, a hometown hero from Youngstown who was an All-American lineman on Notre Dame, help the Fighting Irish (the Ohio transplant's favorite team) beat USC.

Three months after the move, the Steamer had found the center of his new city. With its fabulous Coliseum, two college football teams, and appearances by movie stars at fights and baseball games, Los Angeles had certainly cast a spell on young Bud Furillo.

But Youngstown didn't give up without a fight. Twice, its gravity yanked him back into its northeast Ohio orbit. In these extended visits to his old hometown, when he visited his father and stayed at his aunt's farm, the Steamer developed a taste for the finer vices of life—whorehouses, hard liquor, and gambling.

They kept a grip on him to his dying day.

By the time he returned to L.A. for good in his senior year of high school, he was wearing Zoot suits and had developed an ear for jazz. His grades had dwindled so far from his previous B-average that he had to attend summer school to officially claim membership in the Bell High School Class of '43.

Then it was off to war, as a United States Merchant Marine. The Steamer spent most of 1944 below deck on an oil transport in the South Pacific; the ship's captain took him for a wise guy and figured a few months with no sunshine might adjust his attitude. There was nothing to do down there but read, and when Furillo returned to the light of day, he had developed not only a new sense of discipline and determination, but also a lifelong appreciation for the written word.

Later in the war, while on the bridge of an ammunition ship coming out of the Bass Straits off Australia, the Steamer heard a Navy lookout sound the warning: "Two torpedoes off the port bow!"

"I made the fastest three-and-a-half turns possible to starboard," Furillo wrote in his memoirs. "Something whizzed by. The activity sure didn't appear to be that of dolphins playing."

He had another close call at the "Caribbean theater" in Aruba, when he tried to sneak past two Dutch soldiers with a pint of whiskey taped to his ankle. The enemy ordered him to halt, but Furillo made a run for it, hurdling over a ten-foot chain-link fence with a West Side Story vault—head tuck, flip and roll, drop to your feet, and run like hell. One of the guards triggered off a shot. Thankfully, he missed.

During the war and afterward, Furillo's ships dropped anchor at Honolulu, Panama, New Hebrides, New Caledonia, Kwajalein, Eniwetok, Ulithi, Cartagena, Melbourne, Calcutta, Ceylon, Cape Town, Buenos Aires, Trinidad, Manila, Shanghai, and New York City.

"A kid could travel a lot in those days," he wrote in a 1971 column, "even to the Panama slammer in a paddy wagon with some ladies of the evening, from the Villa de Amor at ten o'clock in the morning. The nights were longer then."

While he was at sea, a girl Furillo thought he was going to marry got knocked up by somebody else. This sent him into a deep depression, and he took his blues to the Sunset Strip of southeast L.A.—Gage Avenue in Bell, where a row of nightclubs and bars provided entertainment for surrounding blue-collar towns. One Sunday afternoon, he was hammering down shots in a place called Rex's when a girl took the bar stool next to his. The Steamer recognized her as Aline Rose Newberry, a leggy, good-looking strawberry blonde he'd gone to high school with who was the stepdaughter of a prosperous local bookie. She was the only woman he'd ever met whose passion for sports rivaled his own. By March of 1946, they had gotten married.

Now out of the Merchant Marine, the Steamer found work at a Firestone plant in South Gate and later rolled steel for Bethlehem in Huntington Park. Deciding that he wasn't cut out for manual labor, he searched for a more refined trade to pursue. He first considered working for his father-in-law, who had asked him if he wanted in as an apprentice bookie. Aline had worked for her bookmaking stepfather since high school, taking calls for the business and making $125 a week. Her pop protected the gambling operation with payoffs to the cops. Furillo had some experience in the gambling trade, having dabbled in his family's number-running enterprise on his trips back to Youngstown.

But the Steamer was interested in a different career path, having discovered an inkling of journalistic talent within himself that he had developed over the years. Inspired by the writings of the great Stanley Woodward of the *New York Herald Tribune*, the Steamer had first begun to investigate sports journalism when he was a junior at Woodrow Wilson High in Youngstown. This fire had been stoked in 1942, when he won third prize in a tri-county journalism contest (never mind that there were only five entrants). After his move to L.A., Furillo had been the sports editor of the Bell High School newspaper during his senior year. Later, during shore leaves when he worked in the Merchant Marine, he had covered games as a stringer for the *Maywood-Bell Industrial Post*. Now working the graveyard shift at Bethlehem Steel, he enrolled at East Los Angeles College and became the sports editor of the paper.

In late 1946, he turned pro. One of the Hearst papers in town, the *Los Angeles Evening Herald and Express* (called the *Herald Express* for short), had just settled a three-month strike and announced that they were hiring. Furillo spotted an opening for a copy boy and put in his application at the Herald Express Building on Trenton and Pico, a seedy corner of downtown known for knife fights and knock-down newspaper bars. He landed the job and started working for the paper on December 6, 1946, making twenty-eight dollars and fifty cents per week.

•   •   •   •   •

The *Herald Express* reporters were crackpots and eccentrics, neurotics and drunks, people who did not fit into the corporate culture—then, or in any other era. They had an artistic sensibility, but not at the expense of survival in a real world. They'd met presidents and governors and had even written about them, but they much preferred the company of the wino on the street or the crazy whore on a bar stool next to them. They partied harder than anybody in civil society. They started early and stayed late, and when the day was done, they'd hit the bar to chew over the stories they had covered and the characters they'd met. They went home to wives and husbands and families, to whom they made feeble attempts to explain why they didn't come home sometimes until hours after their promised arrivals.

It was a quarter-century before Watergate, decades before you would need a master's degree from Columbia or Michigan or Berkeley to get through the newsroom door. In 1947, the Steamer's first full year in the newspaper business, the major qualification to become a newspaperman was to want to do it. Then, if you showed hustle and talent and a stomach strong enough to digest chopped-up murder victims and morning whiskey, you were three-quarters of the way to the finish line. Writing ability helped, but it wasn't mandatory. Plenty of rewrite men were always available to make your stuff sing. You just had to get the stuff.

They sat at metal desks in the middle of the newsroom with

earphones wrapped around their heads, in what they called "the bullpen," and banged out paragraphs with clackity typewriters onto half-sheets of brown copy paper. They were the guts of the *Herald Express*, of every newspaper in L.A. and across the country, the heart and soul of an industry at its zenith in Los Angeles. Radio wasn't a news factor yet, and only a couple hundred people owned television sets. Nobody had ever heard of the Internet.

The *Herald Express* reporters and rewrite men sat side by side, in two rows of twelve. They pounded away for seven editions a day that rolled off the presses almost on the hour, starting at nine o'clock in the morning—the *Latest News, Night Edition, Night Final, Stocks Chaser, Eight Star, Sunset* (chased by the minute with the latest results from Hollywood Park and Santa Anita), and finally, the *Predate*, which went to the Southern California outback.

The *Herald Express* slugged it out with four other newspapers in the post-war, pre-information age, spreading tabloid fodder across a broadsheet and winning the afternoon with a circulation of 400,000. It paired with the morning *Examiner*, a slightly smaller Hearst sister also heavy on crime and punishment. The *Times*—which represented downtown business interests and led the market in circulation and advertising—wasn't much for slash and blood, so it created the *Mirror* in 1948 to compete with the *Herald Express* in the afternoon. The *Daily News*, from its own afternoon slot, explained socioeconomic and political dynamics of the day from the perspective of the Democratic left.

The Steamer's first big job as a copy boy was helping with the coverage of the most sensational murder trial in the region—that of Beulah Overell and Bud Gollum, two young lovers who were accused of blowing up the Overell family yacht in Newport Harbor, with Beulah's parents in it. Beulah and Bud beat the murder rap, but the cops still perp-walked them into court every day, where every photographer in town was on hand to pop them with their Speed Graphics. The Steamer sped the photo plates up to the *Herald Express* office in downtown

L.A.–a forty-five-minute, pre-freeway race–to get the pictures into the home edition.

In the office, Furillo jumped from his seat every time a reporter finished a deadline take and yelled, "Copy!" He ran the stories to the city desk, where editors with thick reddish-brown copy pencils checked for spelling and syntax and logical flow and the dreaded informational shortcomings that would send the story back for another phone call, or, in some instances, a plausible imaginary invention inspired by a shot of cheap booze. The Steamer then ran the copy from the city desk to the green eyeshades at the news desk who back-read the stories, dummied pages, wrote headlines, and stuffed everything into a pneumatic tube system that wound overhead and around the newsroom to the composing room next door. In that hot-house din, cigar-chomping men on linotype keyboards transformed molten lead into paragraph magic.

As a copy boy, the Steamer was awestruck by the men who had already gained legendary status in L.A.'s late-1940s newspaper game. Police beat reporter Beverly "Bevo" Means got credit for naming "The Black Dahlia," a woman whose naked body was found cut into pieces in a still-unsolved mystery. Richard O'Connor rewrote feeds from street reporters all day, but still found time on the side to write critically acclaimed biographies on figures such as author Ambrose Bierce, Civil War-era general Philip Sheridan, and sheriff/sports editor Bat Masterson. Rewrite man Jack Smith might have been the best of the bunch. He came to the *Herald Express* from the *Daily News* and then went on to the *Times*, where he wrote L.A.'s best city side column for nearly forty years.

"Those days were the last of 'Front Page' journalism," Smith wrote in the foreword to a 1991 book by Will Fowler, another member of the bullpen. "The *Herald* city room was noisy; there was always a sense of urgency; we worked fast and we worked hard."

These masters of their craft made a huge impression on the twenty-one-year-old kid just getting going in the newspaper business.

"As an office boy, I loved being around those men," the Steamer wrote.

It was a woman, however, who gave the Steamer his first big break in the newspaper business. Agness Underwood began her career as a telephone operator at the *Los Angeles Record*, which had gone out of business and was swallowed up by the *Herald Express*. At her new paper, Underwood established herself in the '30s and '40s as one of the top crime reporters in town. When the Steamer arrived in the city room, "she was on the outs with the city editor," he wrote. "So she sat at her desk and knitted all day."

Aggie liked the new copy boy. She admired his hustle and the initiative he showed coming to work early every day to rewrite stories for the sports section, on his own time. Every afternoon, Aggie sent him out for two bottles of Burgie.

"Kid," she told him, "I'm going to be city editor of this newspaper someday. When that happens, I'll promote you to cub reporter."

Three months into the Steamer's new career, the *Herald Express* promoted Aggie to assistant city editor. She went on to become the first female city editor of a major newspaper in the United States.

She made good on her word to the copy boy. The promotion more than doubled the Steamer's salary to sixty dollars a week. It also entitled him to a bar stool at Moran's every morning at 6:00 AM, when his heroes from the city side tuned up with shots of whiskey and a beer back for the seven editions that lay ahead.

Furillo's job mostly entailed accompanying photographers to the homes of the murdered. While they took pictures of the bereaved, he stole pictures of the slain.

"I didn't feel good about it," he wrote later.

He never got a byline on the news side. His bosses restricted his writing to typing up a calendar of events. But the rookie reporter did claim one front-page opus.

"The price of bread rose today from nine to eleven cents," his piece read.

Pining for a job as a sportswriter, the Steamer stayed late

ADVICE FROM A MASTER: "WRITE LIKE YOU TALK"
JANUARY 28, 1962

One day eight years ago, a young, ambitious sportswriter promenaded around the city room of the newspaper with his nose tilted toward the great beyond as if expecting Damon Runyon to reach down with a congratulatory pat.

"Come here, Jim," beckoned a hard voice from the bullpen. . . . "This word in your story," continued the voice, which belonged to Gene Coughlin. "Prestidigitator, whatinell does that mean?"

"It refers to one skilled in sleight of hand—a juggler," preened the wiseacre.

"Ever use that word in a conversation?" queried Coughlin.

"No," confessed the red-faced rookie.

"Write like you talk, stupid. When a reader has to drop your piece to reach for *Webster*, it's six to five you've lost him forever," Coughlin advised.

Jim, in this case, was me. Coughlin called most of his friends by other names. . . .

He died last week. I cried. Coughlin was an idol of mine.

His lecture was well taken. Nobody goes to the dictionary to figure out the Steam Room, unless they have a tie to press.

What a wonderful upbringing I had, with Coughlin, Dick O'Connor, Lee Ferrero, and Jack Smith to do the teaching. But Coughlin was my leader. . . .

Gene was a two-fisted drinker and a two-eared smoker. In his gay moments, he usually had lighted cigarettes planted in both noise-receivers. . . .

He never duked me in on how to get the publisher's four box seats for a Rose Bowl game, though. When Coughlin was at the [*Daily*] *News*, he once conned the owner:

"Look, I have some important people comin' in for the game from Seattle and your seats would make a lot of points for the paper."

The publisher passed the ducats along to Coughlin. Gene arrived in the Arroyo Seco five minutes before kickoff with three well-known ladies from the world's oldest profession.

The publisher fired him the next day and rehired him for the second edition. . . .

Coughlin never put much stock in Alcoholics Anonymous, but he told me time and again he wished he hadn't been stiff the day Bob Cronin, whom he succeeded as sports editor, was laid away.

"I was a pallbearer. My hand slipped off the casket and we dropped him three times. That shouldn't happen to anybody."

and took scores over the phone. On Friday nights, he covered high school games.

"My goal in life," he wrote, "was to become sports editor of that newspaper."

Aggie Underwood helped boost him to the position. lending him to the sports department when she could. His first byline, under the name "Frank Furillo" on December 15, 1947, led the sports pages under the headline "Herald Express Grid Cup Awarded to Santa Monica."

The lede read: "Coach Jim Sutherland's Santa Monica Vikings' 1947 CIF football champions were awarded the coveted Evening Herald and Express Perpetual Trophy in a Chamber of Commerce luncheon in the Miramar Hotel in Santa Monica."

The Steamer was on his way.

Chapter 2

SPORTSWRITER'S TOWN

It doesn't take much to sum up Aragon's fighting ability. He can be finished off in one column. You could write a serial about his career, yes. For a man who should be recognized as a club fighter, he dominated our scene for more than a decade. He was dramatized as a tremendous puncher, which he really wasn't. His record of knockouts was established against bums for the most part. Maybe the whole part. Art capitalized on the down-hillers or the ones who never could have scaled the fistic peak on a motorcycle. Yet he was our "golden boy."

—January 20, 1960

The Rams were catching on. Major-league baseball was on the way. The Lakers would soon follow. But when Bud Furillo joined the *Herald Express* sports department in December 1947, colleges and club fighters like Art Aragon dominated the scene. Horse racing was huge. Furillo covered it all, and he also picked up a little college basketball about the time UCLA hired a high school coach out of Indiana by the name of Johnny Wooden.

The Steamer's early stuff was rough and unsophisticated, so he read a lot and studied favorites like Jimmy Cannon and Gene Fowler. He learned how to spot a story; he had an inner feel for it. He made connections. His gift of gab got him over with everybody from clubhouse attendants to the owners of the teams. He asked straight questions. He didn't try to trick anybody.

He sought out the biggest names in town and the biggest sports celebrities in the country when they came to L.A. He met coaches at the weekly football writers' luncheons. He backed

up the boxing beat. He hung out at the minor-league ballparks
and broke stories that rippled into the majors.

Furillo's energy made him the protégé of *Herald Express*
sports editor George T. Davis, a fixture in West Coast sports
journalism whose column, For Sake of Sport, led the section
every day. Davis introduced Furillo to Joe DiMaggio and Jack
Dempsey, Casey Stengel and Jim Thorpe. The boss referred
the visiting Pittsburgh Steelers owner Art Rooney to the young
Bud Furillo to get a bet down on a horse. Furillo fed stuff to Davis, and sometimes even ghosted his column. Davis turned him
loose, in search of more fresh and interesting stuff.

At dawn on a Tuesday in September 1952, the Steamer made
his first big hit in L.A. sports journalism when he pulled up to the
curb and parked his car in front of the Crenshaw District apartment of Los Angeles Rams coach Joe Stydahar. The Steamer had
found out that Stydahar—coming off an NFL championship and
just one game into the next season—was about to get fired.

Furillo knocked on the door, and Stydahar invited him
inside.

"There was a bottle of bourbon on the kitchen table," the
Steamer wrote in his memoirs. "He poured me a water glass full
of whiskey and ordered me to drink it. And I did. An hour later,
the telephone rang."

It was team owner Dan Reeves, with the bad news Stydahar
was expecting.

Furillo had the story for the 9:00 AM edition. Reeves spun it
that Stydahar quit, but over a tall glass of bourbon in his kitchen,
the coach told Furillo otherwise.

"This reporter sat with Stydahar when he received the call
from Reeves," the Steamer's story read, "and after talking to his
former boss, said, 'I am through, and as far as I'm concerned, I
was fired.'"

Five years into his career, it was Furillo's biggest scoop, and
it put him on the map as one of L.A.'s top sportswriters, right
when the local scene was about to take off. As the '50s unfolded,
the hunt for the pulse of L.A. sports took him to the Olympic, the
Legion, the minor-league ballparks, and the Coliseum, where

the professionals shared space with the college teams and Bud Furillo made introductions with the legends of their games.

• • • • •

A few years before he sat down at Stydahar's kitchen table, the Steamer's pro football coverage began with his assignment to the L.A. Dons. They played in the old All-America Football Conference that included the Cleveland Browns, the San Francisco 49ers, and the Baltimore Colts, three teams that later merged into the NFL.

Cleveland's AAFC franchise took on the name of its coach. An Ohio football icon, Paul Brown won six state championships at Massillon High School and a mythical national collegiate crown at Ohio State. His pro team monopolized the AAFC championship, winning it all four years of the league's existence.

Bud Furillo first met his northeast Ohio homeboy in October 1949, on an assignment to cover a Browns workout at Brookside Park in Pasadena before a regular season game with the Dons. Furillo wrote that the '49 Browns "had been hailed as the greatest team ever assembled."

This was not hyperbole. The nucleus of the club won three NFL titles after the merger into the more established league. The Browns roster included five future Pro Football Hall of Famers—quarterback Otto Graham, fullback Marion Motley, tackle and place kicker Lou "The Toe" Groza, split end Dante Lavelli, and guard Bill Willis. It also included future pro and college head coaches Ara Parseghian, Lou Saban, Alex Agase, Lou Rymkus, and Mac Speedie. Two Browns assistants, Weeb Ewbank and Blanton Collier, later became head coaches and won NFL championships.

The day Furillo drove to Pasadena to meet Paul Brown, he found the coach in a foul mood. A few days earlier, his team had gotten clobbered in San Francisco, 56–28. It was the Browns' first loss in two years.

"Maybe Connie Mack knew what he was doing when he busted up a championship team," Brown told Furillo, referencing the straw-hat Philadelphia A's skipper who had sold off his

World Series stars in 1913 and built another dynasty that won two more championships.

At practice in lovely Pasadena, Brown berated the future Famers and head coaches.

"If those of you who have fallen down on the job don't bounce back Friday, I'll sell you," Brown screamed, according to Furillo's story the next day. "I don't care who you are or how important you think you may be. I'll get rid of you."

The Browns listened. They beat the Dons, 61–14, and they didn't lose a game the rest of the season on their way to another AAFC championship.

A few Sundays later, the young Steamer wrote the sidebar to a Rams victory over the visiting Chicago Bears in front of 86,000 in the Coliseum. Working the Bears' locker room after the game, he met and interviewed George Halas, the father of professional football in the United States. Over the years, the Steamer watched in amusement as Halas stormed up and down all 100 yards of the Coliseum sideline once a year to intimidate referees, enrage fans, and occasionally attack opposing players.

"Whenever I made a tackle on the Chicago sideline, I always kept an eye on Halas," said Don Paul, the ferocious Rams linebacker of the 1950s, in an interview with the Steamer. "It was not uncommon for him to stick you with one of his rippled soles."

When the Rams played in Chicago, the coach played a few other tricks on them, like selling seats on their bench and tapping the other coaches' phones, according to the Steamer's reporting.

Halas and Furillo grew fond of each other, and every winter, when Papa Bear hibernated at the Arizona Biltmore, he'd ring up the writer to come over for a pop. Once, over poolside drinks, Furillo ordered a Bloody Mary while Halas enjoyed a whiskey sour. Before the waiter had circled the table, the Steamer switched up and asked for a beer instead.

"Please," Halas reprimanded the writer. "No audibles."

Back before the NFL became a multi-billion-dollar empire, Halas sought to save a buck on travel by scheduling the 49ers and Rams one week to the next and finding a spot during the week for the boys to hole up. Mike Ditka once told the Steamer the thrifty Halas "throws nickels around as if they were manhole covers," but pro football's founding father couldn't have been that cheap. One year, in 1959, he bedded the Bears at what is now the Fairmont Sonoma Mission and Inn up in Northern California wine country, a valley over from Napa. These days, rates on the rejuvenation package at the inn begin at $479 a night.

At Sonoma, the Chicago players had an opportunity to bathe in the region's ancient thermal mineral waters, but Halas restricted their nighttime entertainment options. According to the Steamer, he had the television sets removed from their rooms. The tubeless retreat paid off for the rejuvenated Bears, who beat the Rams, 26–21. During the game at the Coliseum, Halas caused a stir when he stepped onto the field of play to grab at a bouncing punt.

"The ball took a funny bounce away from me or I would have had it," Halas told the Steamer. "I'll have to work on that this week."

Papa Bear's players couldn't wait to get back to Chicago after the win so they could return to their favorite shows.

"I couldn't bear to miss *Playhouse 90* again," Chicago linebacker Joe Fortunato told the Steamer.

•   •   •   •   •

On the Rams front, Furillo watched from the sideline the Sunday afternoon of December 23, 1951, when the Stydahars beat the Browns for the NFL championship, 24–17. It was the Rams' only league title in their forty-eight years in Southern California.

A Coliseum crowd of 59,475 watched as Norm Van Brocklin—coming out of the bullpen in the famed dual quarterback system he shared with Bob Waterfield—spotted wide receiver Tom Fears deep over the middle late in the fourth quarter of a tie game and hit him with a seventy-three-yard touchdown pass. Sitting on the bench in the first half, Van Brocklin told the Steamer that he had noticed Fears, a UCLA kid, creating space all day long between himself and Tommy James, the Cleveland DB who was trying to cover him.

"James never could cover Fears, so when I got in there I kept pitching to Tom until we hit the jackpot," the future Pro Football Hall of Fame quarterback told Furillo.

Furillo ran over to the Browns' locker room to hear what Paul Brown had to say about the end of his five-year championship winning streak—four in the AAFC and one in the NFL.

"It was Joseph's turn today," Brown said.

Stydahar's kingly position lasted all of one game. The next year, on September 28, the defending champion Rams lost their opener to the Browns in Cleveland, 37–7, and Dan Reeves had seen enough. Reeves had a thing about the city by the lake. His Rams won the NFL title playing in Cleveland in 1945, but their crowds only averaged 22,000, so he moved the team to L.A.

Enter the new AAFC in 1946, and with it a new franchise in Cleveland, coached by Paul Brown. All of a sudden, Cleveland became a great pro football town. Brown's Browns averaged 57,000 a game in their first season.

Following the Browns' rout of the Rams in the '52 opener, beat writer John B. Old of the *Herald Express* had to blow out of Cleveland to cover the World Series in New York. When word leaked that Reeves wanted Stydahar out, George T. Davis assigned Bud Furillo to the story. The Steamer worked it Sunday into Monday and at 9:00 AM, his paper rolled with his story that Reeves and Stydahar met in Cleveland and that Reeves told the coach he was done. Stydahar put up little fight. He even told Furillo that the shake-up would do the team good.

Rams general manager Tex Schramm, the mastermind behind the construction of the Dallas Cowboys into America's Team in later years, told reporters that Stydahar had offered to resign. That's not how Stydahar saw it. He told Furillo that he couldn't afford to quit.

"I told Mr. Reeves point-blank," Furillo's *Herald Express* story quoted the coach on Monday. "If he thought it would be best for the club and its owners, they could pay me off."

Reeves and Stydahar met again on Monday in L.A. The owner offered the coach a buyout. No deal, Stydahar told Reeves. When everybody went to bed Monday night, Stydahar was still the team's coach.

Very early Tuesday morning, Furillo learned that Stydahar's end was near. He drove to the coach's apartment, and Stydahar invited him in and poured bourbon while they waited for Reeves's call.

The owner's quick hook shouldn't have come as a surprise. He'd already fired three coaches in his first four years in L.A., including Clark Shaughnessy, not long after the popularizer of the T-formation got the Rams into the 1949 NFL title game. Reeves learned in the off-season that Shaughnessy had been sniffing around the Chicago Cardinals job. Out he went.

Neither he nor Stydahar would be the owners' last sack job.

•   •   •   •   •

I don't know how the Steamer found out about the imminent Stydahar firing, but I do know where he got a lot of his story tips. He knew where to hang out.

A bar called Ernie's House of Serfas was located on a hill at La Brea and Stocker, an easy shot to the fashionable Westside and also conveniently located above L.A.'s Crenshaw District, where many of the Rams' coaches and players lived, just a few miles west of the Coliseum.

"The hill was easy to scale, but tough to get down from," Furillo wrote about the place years after he had first visited in 1953. "Sometimes it took days."

Many of the Rams gathered there for refreshments, as did Furillo and other writers, some of whom lived in a motel out back. He became pals with players like Andy Robustelli, Norm Van Brocklin, Tom Fears, and Jon Arnett, and all of them fed him information. Outside the Rams organization, Furillo met the best players in the league when they came to town every year to play in the Pro Bowl, in the years when they actually cared about the game. The Steamer served as something of an L.A. ambassador for the out-of-towners. Somehow, everybody wound up at the House of Serfas.

Management types also hung out on the hill, including one suit who did fairly well for himself. Pete Rozelle and the Steamer

ROZELLE "ONLY LOGICAL CHOICE" FOR NFL COMMISH

JANUARY 27, 1960

Now that it's all over, you wonder why it took twenty-three ballots for National Football League owners to come up with Pete Rozelle as their commissioner to succeed the late Bert Bell.

They should have elected the thirty-three-year-old general manager of the Rams on the first one, instead of boring the nation with their squabbles in Miami Beach for a week.

Rozelle was the only logical choice.

It stands to reason if Pete was able to keep the stormy Rams owners from each other's throats, guiding the rest of the league's executives is an added responsibility which can easily fit into his long stride. The folks who run the other eleven franchises never saw the day they could match the Ram bosses in bickering. . . .

Pete gave the Rams tranquilization without medication. . . .

If you don't mind, I would like to bask in the spotlight of Petey's success just for a moment. It's the closest I'll ever get to $50,000 a year, anyway.

Pete and I sort of started out together in the world. It was obvious that he owned the compass.

Rozelle was sports editor of the Compton Junior College paper at the same time I was sports editor of the East Los Angeles Junior College sheet. That was 1946 . . .

Pete and I kept in close touch throughout his tour of education at the University of San Francisco where he served as athletic public relations director while he was still a student.

When Tex Schramm moved out of the publicity department to assume general managership of the Rams, I wasted no time calling Pete's mother to suggest the Rams as a job possibility.

She called him in S.F. I phoned Schramm.

Needless to say, Pete got the job. . . .

Rozelle will make a fine commissioner because he has everything the job requires—tact, personality, and firmness. . . .

Make the NFL tick like a good watch, Pete.

You will I'm sure. I've been convinced the world is your oyster ever since we went to the track together eight years ago. I took a 3–5 shot.

Your horse won and paid $128.

knew each from junior college, where both had been sports editors of their school papers—Furillo at East L.A. and Rozelle at Compton. While Furillo quit the JCs for his copy boy job at the *Herald Express*, Rozelle stayed in school, transferred to USF and went into public relations.

When Tex Schramm moved up from being the Rams' publicist to general manager in 1952, "I wasted no time calling Pete's mother to suggest the Rams as a job possibility," the Steamer wrote in a later column. "She called him in S.F. I phoned Schramm. Needless to say, Pete got the job."

Rozelle left the Rams for a big-money public relations job in San Francisco before returning to the club as its general manager. Pete was only thirty-three when, in January 1960, George Halas and Paul Brown worked out a way for Rozelle to become the commissioner of the National Football League. And it was Rozelle who worked out the first of the TV deals that made the NFL the richest professional sports organization in world history.

•　　•　　•　　•　　•

The fight game was big everywhere in America when Bud Furillo broke in on the *Herald Express* boxing beat in the early '50s. In a town that celebrated color and flash, the biggest star was a local kid who could hit with either hand and pack the gyms with a guarantee of war every time the bell rang for Round One.

They called Art Aragon "The Golden Boy" because he wore gold trunks and gold robes. He fought lightweight and welter, taking on promising heroes on their way up and the faded names looking to collect on glories of their pasts. He dated starlets, stayed out late, and got in trouble with the law. He thumbed his nose at the booing crowds. He didn't like sportswriters, but he sure loved their ink.

Brylcreemed and suited up in coat and tie, Bud Furillo became a ringside fixture during the Aragon era and helped tell the story as the Golden Boy's pattern became clear. Aragon won controversial decisions, his opponents screamed outrage—and the turnstiles rolled.

"That's the way it goes," fancy southpaw Chuck Davey told

Furillo after losing a decision to Aragon that was so bad it nearly set off a riot.

Like Davey, fight fans in Los Angeles got used to funny business in Aragon's fights. It started as early as May 16, 1950, when the Golden Boy met Tommy Campbell at the Olympic. Aragon came in off a sensational win over Enrique Bolanos, the town's most popular fighter the previous decade. A big-money rematch loomed. In a tune-up, Olympic matchmaker Babe McCoy put the Golden Boy in with Campbell, a journeyman from Rock Island, Illinois. To ensure the outcome, McCoy slipped Campbell a few bucks, with directions to the canvas and instructions to stay there.

In the second round, Campbell came up with a surprise for everybody: he damn near knocked Aragon out. *Herald Express* boxing writer George Main wrote that Campbell "appeared amazed at what he'd done." To the added astonishment of the crowd, Tommy picked Aragon off the deck, stood him up, and waltzed him around the ring until the bell rang. His head cleared, Aragon knocked Campbell out in the third.

Fans booed. They threw trash into the ring. Suspicious state officials held up the fighters' money for a couple days—and two months later, Aragon fought Enrique Bolanos again. Fans packed the Olympic to its 10,400-seat capacity, with 4,000 turned away at the door.

•   •   •   •   •

While California investigators kept notes on suspicious club fighters and the people who controlled them, Bud Furillo expanded his profile to befriend and cover two of the greatest champions of any era.

He first met Sugar Ray Robinson in 1953, when the greatest pound-for-pound fighter of all time was taking a mid-career break to become a song-and-dance man. The Steamer flew to Las Vegas to write a feature on him.

"Fighting was a cinch compared to show business," Sugar Ray told Furillo.

The next year, Robinson's act came to Club Oasis on the

Sunset Strip. Furillo dropped in to say hello. Next thing they knew, Sugar Ray was writing for the *Herald Express*. His byline, "as told to Bud Furillo," offered commentary on heavyweight champion Rocky Marciano's upcoming title defense against Ezzard Charles.

Out of action for nearly two and a half years, Robinson roared back into the ring in 1955 to knock out Bobo Olson in Chicago for the middleweight title. They set the rematch for May 18, 1956, in L.A.'s Wrigley Field. Furillo was a regular at Sugar Ray's Gilman Hot Springs training camp, and he wrote the sidebar on Robinson's fourth-round knockout win.

"It was as if Bobo stuck his chin in a light socket," Furillo wrote, describing Sugar Ray's six-inch left hook that took out Olson.

Tight with Robinson, Furillo was even closer with Sugar Ray's manager, Ernie Braca. Besides managing fighters, Braca was renowned in New York as "the bookie of Broadway." He ran a gambling operation out of Gallagher's Steak House on Fifty-Second Street and "took action from some of the biggest names in show business," the Steamer wrote in his memoirs. When Furillo made regular New York visits through the '50s, Braca introduced him to Toots Shor's, America's all-time greatest sports bar, as well as gamblers and boxing mobsters, top entertainment and sports figures, and the best head waiters in Manhattan.

"He made me feel like a New Yorker, which isn't easy for a yokel from Youngstown," the Steamer wrote about Braca in a 1973 column.

The only fighter Furillo liked more than Sugar Ray was Rocky Marciano, the Italian American hero whose sensational knockout over Jersey Joe Walcott to win the heavyweight championship in September 1953 still ranks as one of the most electrifying moments in U.S. sports history.

The Steamer met Rocky when Marciano came to Los Angeles for plastic surgery after his second fight with Ezzard Charles, when the challenger razored the champ's nose right down the middle. The two hit it off great. For his next defense, in San

Francisco's Kezar Stadium against Don Cockell, Marciano invited Furillo and another L.A. writer, John Hall, into his dressing
room—ahead of the national press—after his destruction of the
British challenger.

"It was so pitiful that many were hoping Rocky would show
mercy and refuse to hit him again," Furillo wrote. "But he didn't.
When Rocky's in the ring, he's in there to belt people out."

Five months later, Marciano came back to L.A. for a rest after
his successful defense against Archie Moore in Madison Square
Garden. Boxing writers speculated about a rematch, but Rocky
told Furillo exclusively that something else was in the works.

"I don't know if I'll fight again," Rocky said.

Marciano, who couldn't stand the gym anymore, said his
wife and mother wanted him to quit. Furillo told *Herald Express*
readers to forget about the rematch, no matter what Rocky told
other writers.

"That's what everyone wanted him to say," Furillo wrote on
October 27, 1955.

Rocky never did fight again. He announced his retirement
six months later.

•   •   •   •   •

In L.A., the fight scene rocked and rolled, with Aragon still at
its epicenter.

In one of the biggest fights of the decade, the Golden Boy
confronted popular lightweight Cisco Andrade in front of 14,000
at Wrigley Field, in a fight that probably wouldn't have come
off had it not been for the intervention of Frank Sinatra. Riding
higher than ever with the release of his new album, *Songs for
Swingin' Lovers*, the singer had recently purchased half of Andrade's contract.

As usual, on the night of April 29, 1956, the Golden Boy
came into the ring slathered in collodion, the solution that cut
men use to close their gashes and make the other guy's punches
slide off their fighters' faces. Andrade's manager, Ralph Gambina, demanded that Aragon wipe the stuff off. When referee
Abe Roth only shrugged, Gambina ordered his fighter back to

the dressing room and announced to the press, "There will be no fight."

Furillo had written a story leading up to the fight about Sinatra's love of boxing and his investment in Andrade. With Gambina threatening a holdout, the Steamer and his sportswriter pal, John Hall, took the issue to Sinatra, who was seated ringside. When he heard that Gambina was refusing to let Andrade fight unless Aragon wiped off the goop, Sinatra walked down to his fighter's dressing room to have a word with the manager.

"Ralph, all our friends are waiting," Sinatra told Gambina, according to John Hall's recollection in an interview fifty-five years later. "Get him into the ring."

Of course, the fight ended in controversy. When Aragon put Andrade down in the ninth round, "The Pride of Cudahy," as Furillo called Cisco, took the count resting on one knee. Andrade got up at nine, but it was too late for referee Roth, whose figures added up to ten. Once again, the fans threw trash into the ring, and once again, Aragon became the object of suspicion. In due time, it caught up with him.

Even before the Andrade fight, California governor Goodwin Knight ordered public hearings on corruption in the fight game. State athletic commission investigator Jim Cox ran the show. He zeroed in on Olympic Auditorium matchmaker Babe McCoy, accusing him of fixing fights and stealing purse money from fighters. Cox called Tommy Campbell to testify about the 1950 fiasco with Aragon. Campbell admitted to the fix.

The commission established a link between McCoy and L.A.'s most prominent organized crime figure, Mickey Cohen, who didn't do McCoy any favors when he told Furillo in the middle of the hearings, "Babe is one thousand percent." Not surprisingly, the athletic commission banned McCoy from the boxing game for life.

Several years later, the Steamer wrote a column on McCoy, who was playing out the string in a dive hotel in downtown L.A. Furillo said it would be wrong to think of McCoy as a complete crook. Of all the fights McCoy put on in L.A., "Ninety percent of them were on the level," the Steamer assured. "Hardly anything's perfect."

Aragon fell later, when an obscure welterweight named Dick Goldstein went public with accusations that the Golden Boy had offered him $500 to lose a fight in San Antonio. Prosecutors filed charges. A jury convicted Aragon, and a judge sentenced him one to five.

In a jailhouse interview, Aragon told Jack Disney of the *Herald Express* that the disgrace had moved him to consider suicide. The Golden Boy's lawyer, Paul Caruso, bailed Aragon out before the fighter could call his own bluff. Caruso appealed the conviction, and a higher court overturned it.

For whatever it was worth, Aragon was back in action. He spent his last years in the ring mostly in places like Tijuana, San Bernardino, and Tucson. He had one last big fight in L.A. and got knocked out by Carmen Basilio. Never a big fan of Aragon, Furillo still recognized his importance to L.A. sports history, and he was on hand to write the Golden Boy's epitaph.

"The old pros who were there knew that Alvaro Gutierrez, a common brawler, would bury the thirty-two-year-old Aragon at the Olympic last night," the Steamer wrote about Aragon's last fight in 1960. "But they came to give him one last rousing cheer and stand in sobbing requiem as referee Tommy Hart held the Golden Boy straight for a second to tell him, 'It's all over,' at 2:22 of the ninth round. Guys who brought their dolls saw a few of them run up to Art's corner during the fight to shriek encouragement. The Olympic ushers and police who refrain from emotion shouted for him as they knelt in the aisles. Every time Art swung the joint rocked. But the cheers weren't enough to spur the 150-pound body in the faded and sagging gold briefs. Nothing was going to help. . . . Between rounds, his seconds fed him pure oxygen from a tank. It reminded me of the neighborhood kids trying to pump up an old football which has sprung a leak."

In his second-day column on Aragon's demise, the Steamer said it was the fighter's personal magnetism that had led the local press to build him into a star, despite his limited ability.

"All of us tried to believe he was something super," the Steamer said. "Good, maybe, but super, never. One thing about him nobody could take away was his heart. Because of it, he survived in the toughest game of all when anybody else with the same limited talents would have been told by a sound manager, 'Kid, go get yourself a job.'"

Aragon's departure deprived L.A. of its biggest home-grown star. With his retirement, the local fight game fell into a slumber until real championship talent woke it up a half-decade later.

•   •   •   •   •

When Red Sanders dropped dead of a heart attack in a hotel room with a hooker, Bud Furillo responded to the death of UC-LA's all-time greatest football coach like every other writer in town: he covered up the truth.

L.A. writers knew right away what had happened at the Hotel Lafayette, but there was no way they'd throw Sanders into a dirty grave. He was their pal, a drinking buddy, and the molder of a UCLA mid-'50s dynasty.

A Nashville native, Sanders's Tennessee charm intoxicated the L.A. press corps sweet as Jack Daniels. Furillo, a college football junkie, drank him in as deeply as anybody, and he emerged from one post-game aftermath with Sanders with one of the greatest sports quotes ever.

It was the afternoon of November 19, 1949, and Sanders sat devastated in the Coliseum dungeon. In his first year on the job, his favored Bruins had lost to their rival, USC, 21-7. Almost all the other writers had departed, leaving the coach alone with a couple of stragglers who weren't on deadline. One of them was the Steamer, to whom Sanders turned and drawled, "Furillo, winning isn't everything, it's the only thing."

More than a decade later, Vince Lombardi said something to the same effect and the national media famously and incorrectly attributed the origination of the quote to the Green Bay Packers coaching legend.

A Vanderbilt grad, Sanders coached his alma mater into the national rankings in 1947 and '48 before UCLA hired him for the '49 season. In a multi-part series in 1953, Bud Furillo portrayed Sanders as a lover of the arts, politics, and diplomacy. It described him as "quiet spoken, a whimsical southerner with a gentle voice," but also as a coach who insisted on doing his job on the practice field from afar, on a tower above and away from his players, both spatially and emotionally.

"I'm too busy coachin' to do any courtin'," he told the Steamer.

Sanders's Bruins dominated L.A. college football in L.A. in the 1950s, winning three conference titles. USC, however, won the biggest game of the decade between the two, 14–12, in the 1952 matchup—the only time the two schools came into the city championship undefeated and untied.

Winning was the only thing for Sanders's Bruins in 1954, when UCLA's best team ever defeated all nine of its opponents by a combined score of 373–40. The accomplishment earned the team the United Press International version of the national championship. The same year, Ohio State won all nine of its regular season games, too, to finish number one in the Associated Press poll. Too bad the two teams couldn't meet at the Rose Bowl, in what might have been that year's college football game of the century. The problem was the no-repeat rule that prevented teams from playing in the Rose Bowl two years in a row. UCLA won the Pacific Coast Conference in 1953, so the '54 team couldn't play in Pasadena.

One of Furillo's favorite assignments in those years was covering the Big Ten Rose Bowl teams. He got a full dose of Wayne Woodrow "Woody" Hayes the year the cantankerous Ohio State coach made his first introduction to the West Coast sporting press with his undefeated Buckeyes of '54. The Steamer, it appeared, was the only L.A. writer whose heart was touched by the abrasive and dynamically successful Hayes, whom the Steamer genuinely liked and admired.

Hayes, in his eight Rose Bowl trips over twenty-one years, prepared his Ohio State teams as if for nuclear war. He hid them out in a monastery in the foothills. He banned the press from his practices, stared down reporters at press conferences, and chastised them for asking stupid questions. He wouldn't let his team participate in the Beef Bowl, a ritual meat-eating contest between the Big Ten and PCC champs. He spiked microphones when writers got under his skin, and once shoved a camera into a photographer's face.

Most of the L.A. writers hated Woody, but Furillo, who loved no class of humans more than head football coaches, was taken by Hayes's determination, sense of history, gruff exterior, and single-minded purpose.

The '55 Rose Bowl had Ohio State playing PCC runner-up USC, but Hayes spent Game Week playing UCLA in the papers. Woody told Furillo he thought Ohio State ran through a much tougher schedule than the Bruins. The Buckeyes did beat six ranked teams to UCLA's two, but the Bruins dominated the two schools' common opponents, USC and Cal, both of which played Woody's guys tougher.

The Buckeyes beat USC easily enough in the Rose Bowl, 20–7, compared to UCLA's 34–0 slaughter of the Trojans. After the game, Hayes rather ungraciously said USC would have finished fifth in the Big Ten. He also ripped the Trojan Marching Band for taking the field at halftime during a downpour that had turned the playing surface into a sea of mud.

If the blunt-speaking Hayes offended anybody, Furillo wasn't one of them. The Steamer even came off as something of an apologist for the coach's crude behavior.

"Hayes came out here to win a football game, and he accomplished his mission," the Steamer wrote afterwards.

Woody returned to California four years later to play in his second Rose Bowl, this time against Oregon in a 10–7 win for the Buckeyes. He made an effort to be nicer, even inviting the press to watch game films of his team. Furillo was the only writer to take him up on the offer, so Woody gave the Steamer a private viewing that the coach personally narrated. The Steamer wrote up a glowing report on Ohio State, with even kinder words for the Buckeye coach.

"[Hayes] just might be the finest collegiate coach in the country," Furillo wrote. He called Woody "refreshing" and direct and honest—a man who "walks, talks, and thinks with trigger-like action."

MEMO TO TROJANS: DON'T DUMP AL DAVIS
January 22, 1959

The rumors persist that Al Davis, able football assistant to Don Clark, doesn't have a chance of staying at SC.

Although both Davis and alumni field secretary Nick Pappas are on probation, it's ten to one that Nick will survive when the faculty committee completes its investigation of recruitment procedures. . . .

But there's a difference in feeling for Pappas and Davis both on and off the campus. As an alumnus, Nick has many friends. Davis, the comparative newcomer from New York, has few.

Most of the writers close to the Trojan scene feel Davis is dead. Trojan alumns have told me the same and so have a few coaches from University Avenue.

I don't think Davis is dead. Because Clark is prepared to go all the way with his hard-working assistant, even if it means walking the plank with him. . . .

But it's Davis they're after. . . .

What is it that makes Davis such a coveted target? Well, the general conclusion of his critics is: "He talks too much."

Al packs the "silly" youthful trait (he's twenty-nine) of not being afraid to say what he thinks, even if it does embarrass an older head. He has done this often.

But since when has it been a "crime" to know your job and do it well? He has performed tremendous jobs for Troy, as a coach and a recruiter.

What more could you want from a man than sincere effort? A sixteen-hour day is routine for Davis. . . .

One national magazine hailed him as "the most inventive young coach in the business," and another called him "a personnel genius." . . .

Troy will never find a harder worker than Davis.

It would be a mistake to get rid of him.

Furillo lauded the Ohio State coach for recruiting and playing more African Americans than any other integrated team in the country and making sure hotels and restaurants accommodated them on the road.

•   •   •   •   •

In 1957, George T. Davis expanded Furillo's college football responsibilities when he handed him the USC football beat—just in time for the Trojans' worst back-to-back seasons in more than fifty years.

They'd been knocked flat in a pay-for-play scandal that took out half the teams in the PCC. Years later, Furillo gave a speech at an Orange County country club that recounted how USC paid its players forty dollars a month. An infuriated man rose from his seat to interrupt the Steamer. His name was George Belotti, and he had played tackle at USC from 1954 to 1956.

"It was seventy-five dollars a month!" Belotti bellowed.

Covering the Trojans, Furillo struck up a friendship with a young assistant on the staff named Al Davis, who had come to Southern California from the Citadel with a reputation for being a recruiting whiz. Furillo once watched Davis work his magic on a big tackle named Dan Ficca from Atlas, Pennsylvania. With Furillo along for the ride, Davis walked Ficca into the Coliseum.

"Think of it, Dan," Davis told Ficca, according to a Steam Room column published many years later. "The Trojans are playing Notre Dame. There are approximately 103,000 people in the stadium and all of them are on their feet screaming, 'Ficca, Ficca, Ficca!'"

Ficca signed with the Trojans.

So did a few other recruits brought in by Davis. It was later learned that some of them received extra benefits, such as free plane rides home for the holidays. A year removed from sanctions, USC found itself in the penalty box once again.

•   •   •   •   •

At UCLA, Red Sanders learned that, while winning may be the only thing, it's not the final thing.

His end came on August 14, 1958. The *Herald Express* story ran that day under the byline of UCLA beat writer Harry Culver. It said Sanders had been paying a visit to an old friend and "athletic trainer" William T. "Pop" Grimes at the Hotel Lafayette "when tragedy struck" in a seedy slice of the Wilshire District near downtown.

Culver's story mentioned that "a friend of Grimes, Ernestine Drake, was present for the visit. Grimes told Culver that Sanders had complained about the muggy heat, so Pop had gone out for soft drinks, leaving Sanders alone with Miss Drake." A lovely blonde, Miss Drake told Culver that while Pop was gone, she and the coach talked football.

"Mr. Sanders asked me if I had seen many games," Drake told the writer. "I didn't even know he was a famous football coach."

"Suddenly," Culver wrote, "the woman said Sanders clutched his chest, gasped, and toppled to the floor."

The heart attack killed Sanders. He was fifty-three years old.

It took a couple news cycles, but the circumstances of Sanders's death were finally forced out of the Los Angeles press corps.

Ernestine Drake, it turned, out, was a prostitute, convicted the previous year in Beverly Hills. Grimes—the old "trainer"— was actually an old pimp. He'd done time in San Quentin.

Did the writers cover up for Red? Of course they did, the Steamer wrote in his memoirs.

"Sanders was a favorite of everybody in the media at the time," he said. "We all went with [the] bogus story."

·   ·   ·   ·   ·

They were cute teams, the minor league Los Angeles Angels and Hollywood Stars. But it was time for them to go. It was time for Los Angeles to become major-league.

The franchise shifts started in 1953, when the Boston Braves bolted for Milwaukee. Baseball impresario Bill Veeck, who had bought the St. Louis Browns in 1951, moved them to Baltimore in 1954 and renamed them the Orioles. *Herald Express* baseball writer John B. Old reported before the 1955 season that the A's would trade Philadelphia for Los Angeles. Old missed it by half a country; Connie Mack moved to Kansas City instead.

Old reported on other possibilities for L.A. He wrote that Phil Wrigley might be interested in dumping his Cubs and starting over in Southern California. Washington Senators officials also told Old that they were interested in Los Angeles.

In 1954, an Old exclusive reported that Brooklyn Dodgers

owner Walter F. O'Malley had grown frustrated with a six-year effort to get a new ballpark. Old said O'Malley "has long eyed Los Angeles as a possible future home for the Dodgers, whose attendance at home games has steadily dropped." Old's sources said another club would likely move to San Francisco if the Dodgers moved to L.A.

On the minor-league circuit, attendance shrunk to mere hundreds at Wrigley and Gilmore. The only time the Angels and Stars drew crowds anymore was when they played each other.

Bud Furillo still found plenty to write about. He hung out at the ballparks and got to know the managers, coaches, and players and stayed in touch with them as they moved up to the majors. He scored a national scoop when he reported that Stars manager Fred Haney would be named skipper of the big-league Pittsburgh Pirates. A couple years later, Haney managed the Milwaukee Braves in two World Series against the Yankees and won one of them.

Furillo met and interviewed Satchel Paige when Veeck signed the forty-two-year-old Negro League legend to play for the Browns in 1951. The Steamer broke the story in 1954 when Paige demanded $21,000 to pitch for the Angels—a raise from the $20,000 he had made in the majors with the Browns. If he didn't get a deal, Paige told Furillo, he'd go back to barnstorming. The Angels didn't come up with the cash, so Paige returned to the traveling circuit, even though "that's awfully hard on us old folks," as he told the star feature writer from the *Herald Express*.

The Steamer palled around with Ralph Kiner in 1950, when the Southern California homeboy and Pittsburgh Pirate slugger was hitting more home runs than anybody else in the National League. But the Pirates couldn't get out of last place, so general manager Branch Rickey cut Kiner's $90,000 salary after the 1952 season, when the Bucs finished in the cellar again, fifty-four and a half games off the pace.

"We finished last with you, we can finish last without you," Rickey famously told Kiner, who had once again led the league with thirty-seven homers.

On February 14, 1953, Furillo reported that "an authoritative source" had told him that "the Mahatma [Rickey's nickname] has made up his mind to peddle Kiner." Rickey proved the scoop true and finalized the deal forty-one games into the regular season, when he sent Kiner to the Cubs.

During the off-seasons of the '50s, Yankees manager Casey Stengel came home to Glendale, where he owned a bank. Introduced to Bud Furillo, "The Perfessor" took a liking to the young sportswriter and invited him to his mansion in the Verdugo Hills for lunch once a year. The two also shared a few belts at downtown drinkeries. Casey preferred Old Grand Dad.

"He'd gaze at the picture on the label and sigh, 'I've never been able to lick this old SOB,'" Furillo wrote in his memoirs.

Another Hall of Famer, Eddie Matthews, whom Furillo had covered as a prep at Santa Barbara High School, hit twenty-five homers as a rookie with the Braves in 1952. In the off-season, he and the Steamer used to run into each other in the L.A. club scene, where Matthews introduced the writer to starlets he strolled around the Sunset Strip. In his second year in the majors, Matthews challenged Babe Ruth's single-season home run record, banging forty-three through the end of August to remain just one off the Bambino's pace.

"I can't understand," Furillo wondered in print, "why Eddie Matthews of Milwaukee isn't deserving of the game kind of raves as Mickey Mantle."

For decades, the Steamer bemoaned the Giants' 1954 World Series sweep of Cleveland. The Indians were the Steamer's team, and he doubled up on them with his bookie on each successive losing game. Despite his horrific losses, he sucked it up and welcomed New York manager Leo Durocher home to Santa Monica after the wipeout, working with *Herald Express* rewrite man Dick O'Connor on a three-part series and coming up with a gem of an historical anecdote that featured two baseball legends.

One time, when he was just starting out with the Yankees, Durocher found himself in a faceoff with the great Ty Cobb. The problem, as Durocher recounted it, was that he hip-checked

Cobb as the Detroit Tigers slasher sprinted from first to third on a single. When Cobb bounced up with his fists raised, Durocher yelled back, "I'll stick the ball down your throat!"

Then there was Tommy Lasorda. In 1953, the future Hall of Fame manager for the Dodgers pitched in the St. Louis Browns organization. The Browns did their spring training in San Bernardino. Furillo walked into the clubhouse once after a game and asked for Tom Lasorda, who waved him over.

"And that was the beginning of a very long and great friendship," Lasorda said.

•   •   •   •   •

Even before his Boys of Summer finally beat the Yankees in the World Series in 1955, Walter O'Malley's restlessness and impatience grew. He announced that the Dodgers would play seven games in Jersey City in 1956. He called hallowed Ebbets Field "obsolete."

L.A. politicians like city council members Roz Wyman and Ed Roybal jumped to arrange meetings with O'Malley. Late in 1956, O'Malley became miffed when New York wouldn't put up the money for a stadium study. New York baseball writer Dick Young reported early in '57 that O'Malley was giving the city six months to come up with a stadium plan. In Los Angeles, John B. Old wrote that the only thing the town needed to land the Dodgers was a new stadium.

The story steamrolled through 1957. On February 21, the Dodgers bought the Angels, along with their ballpark on Forty-Second and Avalon. Councilwoman Wyman told Furillo in a February 27 story, "We'll have those Dodgers here next year." Mayor Norris Poulson told the *Herald Express* on March 9, "They'll be here in 1958." County supervisor Kenny Hahn said on March 11 that O'Malley was looking at Chavez Ravine north of downtown as a ballpark site. On May 3, John B. Old reported on city talks to trade Chavez Ravine to O'Malley straight up for Wrigley Field. On May 29, the National League made it official: the Dodgers and the Giants were moving to Los Angeles and San Francisco, respectively.

DUROCHER INSISTS HE'S NOT LOOKING FOR MANAGER'S JOB

APRIL 4, 1961

PHOENIX—It was with a feeling of good fellowship that I walked onto the sun deck here at the Adams Hotel yesterday to renew a few old Dodger acquaintances and shake hands with Sandy Koufax, Wally Moon, and Leo Durocher.

Leo wasn't glad-handing, however. His opening salvo was hotter than the ninety-six-degree weather. He barked:

"I won't shake your hand. You wrote something about me that's a lie."

Ordinarily, I never lie unless I get in past midnight. And always having felt I have a touch of Durocher in me . . . I responded to his remark. Suddenly there was hi-fi on the sun deck.

Leo claimed I had misquoted him on a matter dealing with the Angels managerial position. . . .

We battled verbally and admirably and it came out a draw. Which made Leo happy because it's better than he usually comes out with umpires. Then we were friends again. And I wanted to know if he could stand being subservient again, which is part of being a coach— and a testy opening question after an argument.

"What's so hard about it?" he came back. "I expected it of my coaches during the seventeen years I was a manager. It's not hard to take orders from [Walt] Alston. In fact, it comes easy for me. I don't second guess him." . . .

Naturally we talked about the numerous managerial jobs in which his name has been dropped. Like in New York and Houston when those two towns join the National League next year. Leo got his Durocher up again. He said:

"Nobody has discussed a manager's job with me. I want to stay with the L.A. Dodgers and I wish they would leave me alone. The only way I would leave this job is if somebody made me an offer too attractive to turn down."

That may be hard to do because as a coach Leo is making more money than he did as a vice president at NBC. . . .

It would take a fantastic offer to get Durocher out of a Dodger suit now that he's wearing one again for the first time since 1948. He likes it and his pals at Hillcrest like him in it.

What the boys at Hillcrest think is very important to Leo.

L.A. wrangled with short-term stadium arrangements—Wrigley, or maybe the Rose Bowl, before the Dodgers worked out a deal to play in a little bandbox called the Coliseum. Its approximately 103,000 seats would hold O'Malley over until he could build in Chavez Ravine.

On October 9, O'Malley told L.A. that he was coming; on October 24, they landed at the airport. Furillo was among the thousands who greeted them.

"Vin Scully, the Dodgers' TV announcer, looked frightened," Furillo wrote, "until he spotted a familiar face which he recognized as having been on the barroom floor at Toots Shor's." The face, of course, belonged to the Steamer.

On their new coast in 1958, the Dodgers were a team in transition, with Jackie Robinson retired and Roy Campanella paralyzed from an off-season car wreck. The Boys of Summer were turning into museum pieces.

The Steamer appreciated the past—after all, Carl Furillo, his first cousin once removed, was the star right fielder in Brooklyn. But at spring training, he focused on the future, touting Tommy Davis, featuring Frank Howard, and detailing Don Drysdale.

The Dodgers broke slowly in their first year in L.A. and fell into the second division and then all the way to last place. They didn't depart the cellar until August, and finished seventh in an eight-team league. Soon enough, things got better for them, and not many writers got over with the new Dodger greats better than Bud Furillo.

•   •   •   •   •

As early as 1952, George T. Davis recognized Furillo's hustle and passion, his sourcing, and his clean and colorful stuff. When he went on vacation, Davis let the kid write his column, For Sake of Sport.

By the middle of 1958, Davis had given Furillo a weekly column. L.A.'s newest voice immediately expressed displeasure that the new major-league baseball team in town wore "Dodgers" instead of "Los Angeles" on its road uniforms. He had Rams running back Tank Younger talking retirement, and the Celtics getting mad at K. C. Jones for signing a contract to play defensive back for the Rams. He declared the House of Serfas "the Toots Shor's of the West." He reported that Reeves—surprise!—had turned up the heat on his coach, Sid Gillman. He welcomed the births of babies born to his bartenders and bookmakers. He told of Cisco Andrade opening a barbershop in Santa Fe Springs, Dodger outfielder and citrus rancher Duke Snider netting four dollars and twenty-five cents on his lemon crop, and USC assistant coach Al Davis correctly picking Iowa and the Baltimore Colts to win the Big 10 and NFL titles. You needed to read Bud Furillo to know that the Dodgers put Junior Gilliam on the trading block, that Gino Cimoli thought he was more than just a late-inning defensive replacement, and that Don Jordan won the welterweight title because his trainer, Eddie Futch, "nursed the hate out of him."

The column went to twice a week. Bavasi ordered new "Los Angeles" road jerseys.

On January 26, 1959, the column went full-time. It came with a name: The Steam Room.

Chapter 3

ENTER THE STEAM ROOM

For the dramatic story of how Al (The Bull) Ferrara broke his ankle at Dodger Stadium, we take you to Room 561 at Daniel Freeman Hospital. It is a private room overlooking Al's money at Hollywood Park. Racing would be dead without his contributions. . . . "It happened in the eighth inning," he said. "I was playing left field"—he can play right, too—"when I charged this smash. I lost it in the lights. I tried to pick it up again and steady my balance. I caught the ball. Me and my body went backwards but my left leg went frontwards." The Bull was interrupted at this stage by the puzzled interviewer. "It says in the book that you did not catch the ball. You are charged with a three-base error." "That hurts more than the pain of the broken bone," he moaned. . . . "The official scorer must have been Ho Chi Minh.". . . Ferrara being out for the season is a terrible loss to the Dodgers, but it is racing's gain.

—April 14, 1968

For fifteen of the most glorious years in Los Angeles sports history, Bud Furillo's Steam Room captured the conversation—of the athletes, the coaches, the owners, the trainers, and the touts. Whether it was from a jockey, fighter, manager, promoter, writer, singer, comedian, or crony, he caught the banter in the clubhouse and in the press box, around the batting cage and on the sidelines, in the gym and at the bar.

The Steamer had an ear for humor and history, and he knew how to crunch it into a style that resonated from the front row to the upper deck. It ran through the watering holes of his home turf in Downey to the social clubs of South Central Avenue. They

spread The Steam Room across the watch sergeant's desk in police stations and mailed it to loved ones doing time on the prison
yard. Politicians took it into smoke-filled rooms, and horse players read it at the rail. They liked him on the streets and in the
suites, and in what he called "the Living Room A.C."—any place
where serious sports fans gathered to watch games or talk about
them afterward.

People liked The Steam Room because Furillo might have
seen something they hadn't, like the time Les Richter—the Pro
Football Hall of Fame linebacker who doubled as long snapper
on the punt team—doubled back to make a game-saving tackle
when a kick was blocked after he had released downfield. Or
when the Steamer captured Jerry West as a collegian in the L.A.
Classic at the Sports Arena blocking a shot, falling down, getting up, running the floor, and jamming the ball home with a
one-handed dunk on the other end after one of his West Virginia
teammates blew the layup. Or the time he saw Jim Fregosi as
a twenty-year-old rookie race into center field to pick up a pop
single, whirl to the plate, and throw out a runner trying to score
from second.

Bud Furillo's column played to the hardest core. Nobody in
town had better sources, in L.A. or across the country. He got
hold of anybody he wanted to, and on deadline if he needed.
He loved characters. He appreciated sports history and celebrated celebrity. He needled, but he didn't burn. He ripped,
but he never stripped anybody of their humanity. He rooted for
his favorites, but he conveyed respect to everybody. Awash in
whimsy, he found humor just about everywhere he looked. He
drew it out of sources as unlikely as George Allen, the obsessive-
ly driven head coach of the Rams with a mania for order who
brought about the team's renaissance of the late '60s. They were
at a party when Allen told the Steamer about the time in 1964
when George Halas stationed Hall of Famers Doug Atkins and
Bill George and Pro Bowl tackle Fred Williams behind the goal
posts whenever the Bears kicked an extra point in the friendly
confines of Wrigley Field.

"Those specialists kept us from blowing a lot of seventeen-dollar footballs," Allen, the one-time Bears defensive coordinator, told the Steamer. "I'll never forget 1964. We only lost eight balls."

Reminded that the Bears finished sixth in 1964 compared to winning the National Football League championship the year before, Allen replied, "True, but the ball retrieving team had a poor record in 1963."

In 1964, Furillo was promoted to sports editor of the paper, two years after it merged with the *Los Angeles Examiner* to become the *Los Angeles Herald Examiner*. In The Steam Room, the emphasis was always on fun. Furillo pursued it the same way Woodward and Bernstein followed the money. When Richie Allen played for the Dodgers, he used to read the *Racing Form* sitting in the stands while his teammates bothered themselves with pregame infield practice. The intransigence convinced club executive Peter O'Malley to trade Allen to Chicago. But it didn't bother White Sox manager Chuck Tanner if Allen didn't want to take ground balls before the game.

"Who is the greatest person you know?" Tanner asked Furillo when the White Sox swung through Anaheim in 1972.

"My mother," the Steamer answered.

"Rich Allen is that great," Tanner countered.

Furillo thought about it for a second, and he had to agree.

"Indeed, there is a striking similarity," he wrote. "Mama Mia never takes infield before the sauce is poured."

The Steam Room could easily pull a gag out of a bench-clearing brawl. One time in Kansas City, A's pitcher Jerry Walker stuck a fastball in the back of the Angels' Leon Wagner. Upset by the pitcher's impertinence, "Daddy Wags"—whose nickname came courtesy of The Steam Room—threw his bat at Walker. The K.C. right-hander then retrieved the ball, turned on Wagner, and plunked him again.

"Awarded first base, Leon actually deserved another," was The Steam Room's position. "After all, Walker did hit him twice."

When the Washington Generals came to L.A. in 1969 carrying a 287-game losing streak to the Harlem Globetrotters, Coach Red Klotz told Furillo exclusively, "We just haven't been able to jell." With Lew Alcindor about to graduate from UCLA, the Steamer suggested that the Generals should get first pick in the draft between themselves, the NBA, and the new American Basketball Association. The idea sounded good to Klotz.

"We need a guy like Alcindor to make us go," he said. "I'd give anything to get him."

Klotz failed to sign Alcindor, who, as Kareem Abdul-Jabbar, later won one NBA title in Milwaukee and five more in Los Angeles.

Lacking a big fella, the Generals failed to figure out the Globies. By early 1972, Klotz's club lost about 5,000 games to Harlem—and the coach was feeling the heat from grumbling Washington partisans. Klotz told the Steamer that he'd had enough. He was retiring.

"This town won't support anything but a winner," he said.

At age sixty-two, Sam Snead stunned the golf world with a second-place finish in the Glen Campbell Los Angeles Open. The fans greeted Snead on the final day of the tournament with a standing ovation at every hole.

"Of course, they had to," the Steamer wrote. "There weren't any seats."

The day Baltimore Colts owner Carroll Rosenbloom hired Don Klosterman to become his general manager, Furillo said he never knew anybody who didn't like the old Loyola quarterback.

"Of course, this might be because I didn't know the Houston player who came into his office and pulled a gun on him during a salary dispute," the Steamer wrote.

Lightweight contender Ruben Navarro, "The Maravilla Kid" from East L.A., made the sign of the cross before each round. It brought to the Steamer's mind a priest's comment when asked if the invocation helped a boxer any.

"Only if he can fight," the holy man had responded.

Earl McCullough was a world-class hurdler who played on the USC national championship football team in 1967. But McCullough was more than just a track guy. Alex Karras, the Pro Bowl tackle on the Detroit Lions and a teammate of McCullough's, told Steam Room readers that Earl was a tough kid who would hit anybody anywhere.

"He would block George Wallace in downtown Montgomery," said Karras, better known as "Mongo," the character in Mel Brooks's *Blazing Saddles* who knocked out the horse.

When the NFL opened bidding in Honolulu to host Super Bowl VI, the city of Houston dispatched civic giant Judge Roy Hofheinz—the construction genius behind the Astrodome, the Eighth Wonder of the World—to represent its interests. New Orleans sent trumpet king Al Hirt. Los Angeles named county supervisor Warren Dorn as its ambassador to the islands.

"Dorn seems overmatched," the Steamer wrote.

He was. League officials gave the game to New Orleans.

On a 1968 fact-finding mission in New Zealand—"a marvelous

NEW ORLEANS FINE TOWN FOR A SUPER BOWL
MARCH 20, 1969

PALM SPRINGS—The gentlemen from New Orleans mapped their plans on the napkins underneath their fettuccine at Perrina's.

"I believe we could offer the nation and professional football something different if we are successful in our bid to get the Super Bowl," said the mayor of that town, Victor H. Schiro. . . .

To beef up his praise for New Orleans, the mayor brought along Al Hirt, the ample trumpet player from Bourbon Street.

"New Orleans is God's town," said Hirt, who knows just about everybody. "There is no city like it in the world." . . .

Also here for the New Orleans presentation was Jim Moran, son of Diamond Jim Moran, and relative of Bobby Brocato, who once won some big races at Santa Anita and Hollywood Park. Naturally, Brocato is Moran's real name.

Moran owns the old Absinthe House on Bourbon Street, where he felt the professional football meetings should have been held in these hours of crisis.

"The old Absinthe House makes strange bedfellows," said Moran. "I remember the night Andy Jackson and Jean Lafitte were able to effect a merger upstairs." . . .

New Orleans deserved to get the Super Bowl. Miami is an AFL town, and the Jets are like the home team, particularly in January when the garment workers go south to get away from Shor's for a decent sandwich at Broadway Joe's.

land where scotch and sodas sell for eighteen cents," Furillo said—the exclusions at the racetrack struck him as curious.

All tracks reported that "bookmakers, moonmakers' clerks, bookmakers' assistants and agents, common prostitutes, idle and disorderly persons, professional tipsters, persons convicted of house breaking, burglary, or pocket picking, forgery, owning or possession of counterfeit coin, theft, false pretenses, receiving stolen goods, mischief, assault or any offense, or crime of any kind" were barred from entering.

He discovered that there were no minimum guaranteed winnings at the New Zealand racetracks, even if you had the winning horse. If the odds were such, you could put two dollars on a big favorite but only get back a dollar and eighty cents if it won.

"This would cause all sorts of complications at Santa Anita," the Steamer wrote, "such as the plant being attacked as if it were an American embassy. It would surely be burned down."

Readers found out from The Steam Room why the Chicago White Sox flopped in 1960 when they tried to repeat as American League champs. Team owner Bill Veeck, tight with the Steamer for years, "convinced me the Sox chose to replace the Yankees as rulers of the nightclub circuit," Furillo wrote.

"Their playing on the other side of the day led to their downfall more than anything else," Veeck told Furillo.

The Steamer reported the time the thuggish defensive back Johnny Sample, as a Baltimore Colt, laid a vicious hit on the New York Giants' Frank Gifford in their epic 1958 NFL championship game. Sample finished off the tackle by planting his knees on Gifford's chest and asking the receiver, who had been chronicling the playoffs on the side for one of the New York papers, "Why don't you write a column about me?"

"I would, son," the stricken Gifford told Sample. "Only I don't know your name."

If you didn't read Bud Furillo, you didn't know that umpire Emmett Ashford sometimes wore French cuffs under his gear when he worked behind home plate "to keep him cool." Or that Leon Wagner, an African American, and his Italian American teammate Rocky Colavito once thought about opening a restaurant when they played together in Cleveland.

"We could have made collard greens scallopini the special-ty of the house," Daddy Wags told the Steamer.

Few Dodger fans knew that Tommy Lasorda once pitched in the minors for manager Ralph Houk in Denver until they read it in The Steam Room in 1966, or that the skipper looked to his fiery pitcher to light a fire underneath the slumbering Bears in a 1956 game against Omaha.

"We've got to shake things up," Houk told Lasorda. "Can you start a fight tonight?"

"What inning?" Tommy asked.

Bobby Fischer may have been a disagreeable, reclusive an-ti-Semite, but Bud Furillo actually made him look human when, during an interview at a celebrity tennis tournament in La Costa, he informed the chess master that former Los Angeles Angels pitcher Bo Belinsky had recently married Playmate of the Year Jo Collins.

"You can't knock that," Fischer replied.

On Bat Day in 1969, The Steam Room reported that the An-gels had received a mistaken shipment of lumber bearing the signature of the Giants' Hal Lanier, a career .228 hitter. This was a club, of course, with sluggers like Willie Mays, Willie McCov-ey, and Bobby Bonds.

"You wonder why the Giants would have even ordered any Hal Lanier models for their bat day," the Steamer wrote—let alone how they wound up in Anaheim.

Furillo rarely used unnamed sources, but when he did, they added to the public's knowledge of the critical issues of the day. Like when the Yankees fired Johnny Keane twenty games into the 1966 season and an unidentified player told the Steamer the reason for the manager's undoing: "He inspired a profound neutrality."

Rodolfo Gonzalez gave the Steamer the scoop on the fight-er's strategy going into his 1972 lightweight championship fight against Chango Carmona.

"I'm going to hit him as hard as I can," Gonzalez said.

"Now that makes sense," the Steamer commented.

Furillo's reporting revealed sports stars in some of their most private settings. Interviewing Yogi Berra in 1964, the Steamer reported that the Yankee skipper "dresses differently than some managers. He opened the door to his Statler Hilton hotel suite in his underwear, shoes, and socks."

Gene Fullmer beat Sugar Ray Robinson and tied him once in their four fights, but the Steamer saw little art in the fighter's clumsy clubbing style.

"Outside his immediate family, I don't know anybody who enjoys his work," Furillo wrote of Fulmer. "He packs all the finesse of a drunk falling off a bar stool."

A stickler for fairness, the Steamer made sure to get both sides of the story when football's Alex Karras and wrestling's Dick "The Bruiser" Afflis laid waste to the Lindell AC in Detroit in one of the greatest bar fights ever.

Karras owned a third of what was one of America's finest sports bars. When NFL commissioner Pete Rozelle suspended Alex in 1963 for gambling, the tackle turned to professional wrestling to make ends meet. He lined up the bout with Dick the Bruiser, but the veteran grappler showed up uninvited at the Lindell a few days before the match and, according to Karras, slugged a bartender. Karras told the Steamer that he stepped in to quell the disturbance.

"I put the Bruiser down and tried to talk some sense to him," Karras said. "I did okay until the cops came. One of them belted me and broke my glasses. That made me mad, so I let the Bruiser up. That's when he wrecked the place. They needed eight cops to take him out of here, in chains, like an animal."

When the Steamer caught up with Dick the Bruiser to get his side of the story, the wrestler disputed Karras's account. He said he was only on his way to the restroom when Karras's boys jumped him. The Bruiser insisted that he took Karras to the ground and was getting the best of the action until a pool hustler took a cue to his head.

"My left eye was nearly hanging out," DTB told the Steamer.

The Steamer didn't beat around the bush when he questioned a sports figure.

"Do you cheat?" he asked Long Beach State basketball coach Jerry Tarkanian, long reputed to be an ethical daredevil.

"I've been accused of it," Tarkanian answered.

"You're a good recruiter," the Steamer said in a follow-up. "Good recruiters cut corners. Do you?"

"I like to have some advantage when I go after an athlete," said Tarkanian, whose cloud of reputed improprieties followed him from Long Beach to Las Vegas, where he won an NCAA title in 1990.

On a Howard Cosell visit to L.A. in 1971, the Steamer asked the broadcaster, "Do you consider yourself abrasive?"

"You won't find young people saying I'm abrasive," Cosell answered. "The disadvantaged don't consider me abrasive, nor do the educated."

"Thus he eliminated everyone but the masses," Furillo commented in The Steam Room.

By the time Sonny Liston finally came through L.A. to fight, he was pretty much finished. He packed the Olympic Auditorium for his easy win over a terrified Billy Joiner, but at age thirty-seven, he didn't fool Bud Furillo. The Steamer got a clue that Liston was nearing the end when he collapsed on his stool between rounds against the ineffective Joiner.

"His legs were stretched out like those of a floorwalker in the five and ten," the Steamer said of Sonny. "His handlers sprayed him and they screamed at him and they prayed for him. Sonny's expression never changed. He always looked old. And wow, did he look fat."

Furillo saw no hope for a Liston comeback, unless Sonny wanted to reboot his career in his old occupation as a labor adjustor for the St. Louis mob.

"There is power in the fists that don't fit an ordinary glove, and they can still destroy most faces," the Steamer said. "So don't challenge him if you see him coming up to the eighteenth hole at the Stardust Country Club in Las Vegas, where he lives, after he's shot a 120 on the first seventeen. There is a meanness there, if he's thirty-six or forty-six. And let me tell you, there are a lot of guys walking around who are forty-six who can take a lot of guys twenty-six."

On a plane ride to Las Vegas, the Steamer got an earful from Los Angeles Angels manager Bill Rigney, who thought the press was being too harsh on another manager in town, Walter Alston of the Dodgers.

"What does Walter have to do to please you guys?" Rigney asked. "Win the pennant every year?"

"That would be nice," the Steamer answered, on behalf of L.A. sports fans everywhere.

An avid fan of professional wrestling, the Steamer shared the shock of all Southern California grappling enthusiasts on the 1971 night when John "The Golden Greek" Tolos reached into a doctor's bag during locker room interviews and threw a poisonous substance into the eyes of the sport's biggest star in town, Freddie Blassie. Television announcer Dick Lane reported that the atrocity blinded the beloved Blassie, who was once a notorious villain until dope-smoking teenagers began to swarm the Olympic Auditorium on Wednesday nights. They implored Blassie, whose signature hold was an incisor to the forehead, with a memorably descriptive chant: "Bite, Freddie, bite!"

Three months after Tolos left Blassie unable to see, it was the Steamer who had the scoop on how the uncle of Freddie's Japanese wife miraculously restored the wrestler's vision, with hushed treatments performed in the island nation's city of Sasebo.

"One morning, I woke up and I could see the light," Blassie told Furillo exclusively. "I cried like a baby."

In front of more than 25,000 fans in the Coliseum, the city's joy was restored when Blassie bloodied Tolos into defeat in their rematch.

Also on the wrestling beat, it was Bud Furillo who reported that Andre the Giant once drank 126 beers during a single-day visit to Los Angeles. The Steamer also welcomed another big man in the sport, Haystack Calhoun, who came to L.A. for a 1972 battle royale at the Olympic. It was Calhoun's first appearance in L.A. in seven years.

"He hasn't changed a bit," Furillo wrote. "He still weighs

620 pounds."

Calhoun claimed he'd never lost a last-man-in-the-ring extravaganza, and the Steamer was not about to question him.

"In wrestling, you take a guy's word," he wrote. "Documentation isn't always reliable."

•   •   •   •   •

One hot summer night in the middle of baseball season, we got a knock on our screen door. Beneath the yellow glow of our front porch light, California Angels relief pitcher Bob Lee stood in the dim evening heat—with the Steamer draped over his shoulder.

We opened the door and Lee, a hard-throwing, six-foot-three, 225-pound right-hander who saved fifty-eight games for the Angels over three years, walked into the house and plopped my passed-out dad onto the living room couch. Lee turned to me, his bloodshot eyes smiling, and said, "Your daddy's had a little too much to eat."

It wasn't an everyday occurrence, relief pitchers bringing the Steamer home when he'd overdone it. But he sure did like to party with them and the other players, coaches, writers, and trainers. He was pretty close to plenty of them, at a time when sportswriters and athletes enjoyed a much closer, far less adversarial relationship.

Money was a factor—you didn't have the Grand Canyon separating the income levels of the two camps. In those days, the players had to work off-season jobs. The Angels even had a pitcher, Danny Osinski, who sold season tickets over the winter—for the White Sox.

In the fifteen years of The Steam Room, Bud Furillo lived and worked in a symbiotic world where the player needed the pub and the scribe need the scoop. Athletes trusted the Steamer and gave him access. He kept their confidences and churned out copy. Journalistic critics later criticized this arrangement. They charged that writers were too close to the players, that they protected them.

True enough. The Steamer did not expose his friends in the sports world as carousers—partly because he was right there with them, chasing women and closing down bars.

Furillo failed to go into investigative detail about the imperfections of the human beings who play sports because he crossed another ethical line: he committed the journalistic sin of liking and admiring many of the people he wrote about. Any court would have convicted him of becoming friends with the people he covered. He shared their joy, like the time when USC tailback Mike Garrett jumped into his arms in the Trojan locker room after the 1964 upset win over Notre Dame and exclaimed, "You said we could do it!" He also commiserated in their defeats, downing vodka in the New Orleans airport with Tommy Prothro after the coach lost his first game with the Rams.

Barriers broke down between my dad and the people and teams he covered. Sometimes, the barriers drew him even closer to his sources, like the night he had Rams head coach Chuck Knox and his staff out to the Lancer Lounge, the Steamer's bar in Downey, on a night that extended beyond closing time. Inexplicably, when the bartender finished his shift at 2:00 AM, he dutifully locked the door from the outside. Nobody inside could get hold of him until six hours later, and the next day, Chuck had a little explaining to do to his wife, Shirley.

In the years he was on the Angels beat, the Steamer played golf with some of the players every once a while. One time, after eighteen holes, he brought first baseman Lee Thomas, shortstop Joe Koppe, and some others over to the house to go swimming. The Steamer regularly brought his kids into the clubhouse to meet the players. Center fielder Jimmy Piersall once gave me one of his old mitts. My older brother, Frank, and I played in an Angels father-son game. My younger brother, Mike, was a ball boy for the Lakers when they won the title in 1972.

Sometimes the Steamer even became part of the story, like in June of 1973, when the disenchanted Los Angeles Rams quarterback Roman Gabriel wanted out of town, and the club was interested in dealing him. Enter Bud Furillo, who helped broker the trade by relaying the phone messages between the Rams' brain trust and Philadelphia Eagles owner Leonard Tose. When the deal was finally consummated, with Gabriel going to

Philadelphia for Tony Baker, Harold Jackson, the two first-round-ers, and a lower draft pick (instead of star defensive end Richard Harris), the Steamer didn't even ask for a reimbursement for the telephone calls.

•　　•　　•　　•　　•

In the Steam Room era, it was no problem for a writer to accept fabulous gifts and graft from the sports industry. He kiddingly referred to himself in later years as "the last crooked sports editor."

When the Steamer was a columnist and later a sports editor, it was a freebie frenzy. Promoters of every sport picked up his restaurant and bar tabs and paid for family vacations for him and his staffers. At Christmas time, booze arrived at his house by the case, special delivery, from Santa Anita, Hollywood Park, Caliente, the Olympic Auditorium, the Rams, the Dodgers, and the Angels. Dodgers general manager Buzzie Bavasi sent giant reed-woven laundry baskets stuffed with booze and candy and salamis and cheeses and crackers and other goodies. Season's greetings from Tony Hulman of the Indianapolis Motor Speedway meant a complete set of water glasses with the names of all the Indy 500 winners. Jack Kent Cooke, owner of the Kings and Lakers, sent pewter, with his name inscribed on every chalice, and ice buckets bejeweled with a likeness of his arena, the Fabulous Forum. They all showered the Steamer with tape recorders, miniature television sets, and transistor radios shaped like baseballs.

Race car promoters flew me and my brothers to the Indianapolis 500. The Angels took us on a road trip once. Las Vegas? My dad never spent a nickel on food or drink or hotel bills—although he lost a few at the craps tables. He worked out comps for friends, relatives, and his staff.

When he became sports editor in 1964, Furillo controlled about thirty tickets to the Rams games. He took care of his cronies, bartenders, and car dealers, and even Los Angeles County district attorney Evelle J. Younger. Sports tickets given to court clerks fixed traffic tickets and sometimes even more serious stuff, like a DUI or two.

One time, the Atlanta cops came to the paper and arrested the Steamer's night desk man for not paying his child support from a one-night stand in Georgia. The Steamer gained the valuable desk editor's freedom by working out a ticket deal for Falcons and Braves games. He also arranged for local fight promoters to take care of the desk man's child support arrearages.

●　　●　　●　　●　　●

The Steam Room fed its readers glimpses into major-league life—the habits and humors of the players, their insecurities, their

EVERYBODY WANTS TO SEE PELÉ
JANUARY 28, 1967

Having passed the critical stage, it appears the Steamer will survive the worst week in the history of intercollegiate, professional, and non-sectarian freeloading.

The Super Bowl and the World Series were kiddie events compared to the demands this week for soccer, L.A. Open, Santa Anita, and Riverside Raceway tickets. . . .

Usually, the Steamer can estimate the size of any crowd by the crab feelers for tickets. Judging by the requests for tomorrow's game at the Coliseum, professional soccer will succeed in Los Angeles.

As you may know, this is going to be a two-league town in professional soccer, where there has been none for 200 years. All of a sudden—two leagues. . . .

In the week of the Strub Stakes at Santa Anita, Palmer at Rancho, Foyt at Riverside, the heaviest requests were to see Pelé at the Coliseum.

Pelé is a little Brazilian who makes twice as much kicking a ball as Sandy Koufax ever did throwing it. . . .

. . . I'm wondering if he isn't the greatest athlete to ever perform in the Coliseum. . . .

. . . In his last ten years of soccer, Pelé, twenty-six, has never been shut out in a game. This involves about 300 games. . . .

It is said that the Milan team of Italy offered $1 million to Santos for Pelé. The offer was refused, of course.

Santos is waiting for Jack Kent Cooke, owner of the L.A. Zorros, to offer $2 million.

Jack has been pinching pennies long enough. It's time he went out and bought a star like Pelé if he expects soccer to go over here.

angers. They were authentically human portrayals of real people in a surreal world, gems of beauty mined from the mundane.

One time, while on the road with the Angels in Baltimore, the Steamer, as usual, got to the ballpark several hours before the game and hung around the clubhouse with a few of the players and the general manager, Fred Haney. It was early July in 1963, about a week before the All-Star game, and they all got a laugh about a story in the afternoon Baltimore paper in which Dick Stuart ripped Ralph Houk for not putting him on the American League squad as a reserve, even though the big first baseman had finished second behind Joe Pepitone in the players' balloting.

Stuart was on his way to career bests in home runs (forty-two) and RBIs (118), although the leather remained a problem. "Dr. Strangeglove" set a record that year for errors in a season for a first baseman, with twenty-nine. It still stands.

The story quoted Stuart saying, "It's tough to have a third-string catcher like Ralph Houk keep you off the All-Star team." It went on to report that the next time Stuart saw the Yankees manager, he was "going to tell Houk exactly what I think of him."

The threatening tone prompted an inquiry by the Steamer into the slugger's chances if Houk, who was very capable with his fists, responded to Stuart's upbraiding with an overhand right.

First to offer an opinion was a clubhouse visitor, Ryne Duren, the relief pitcher with the 100-mile-an-hour fastball, Coke-bottle glasses, and a lack of control that terrified opposing hitters. Duren had been on the Angels until they traded him during spring training to Philadelphia. He had driven down to Baltimore on a Phillies off day to pay the Steamer twenty dollars he owed him from a spring training bet that the pitcher couldn't stay on the wagon until the Fourth of July. Duren eventually did make it into long-term sobriety, but not this time. He'd been drunk a couple times by Memorial Day.

Duren had some experience with Houk. A former All-Star himself with the Yankees, Duren once drunkenly shoved a cigar

Houk was smoking all over his face. Houk, the team's bullpen catcher and coach, decked the pitcher. Duren said that "Stuart would be grossly overmatched" against Houk, recalling his own one-punch defeat.

Furillo took up Stuart's case. The Steamer had become pals with him years earlier, during the one season the player spent on the Hollywood Stars in the Pittsburgh organization.

"I happen to know Stuart isn't a cream puff," Furillo told his readers. He reminded them that Stuart, with the Stars, had won the House of Serfas arm wrestling championship, taking down a few football types for the title.

Haney wasn't buying it. "I don't believe Stuart has the technique of Houk," he said. "Houk picked up a few tricks in the war, you know."

"The Major," as they knew Houk, had won the Bronze Star, a Purple Heart, and the Silver Star with oak leaf clusters for his heroics at Bastogne and the Battle of the Bulge.

Furillo installed Houk as an eight-to-five morning line favorite. Then, from the Angels' clubhouse in Baltimore, he called Stuart in Cleveland, where the Red Sox were getting ready to play the Indians.

Reaching Stuart by phone in the visitors' locker room at Municipal Stadium, the Steamer wrote, "I advised him to think it over before making any crude assessments of Houk, in person."

Stuart assured Furillo, "I'm not out to fight the guy."

He just wanted to play in the All-Star Game.

"Ask Houk what I'm hitting against his club," Stuart told the Steamer. "I'm fourteen for thirty-six against the Yankees. Turn to page ten of your average book and you will find that amounts to .389."

In the end, The Steam Room sided with Stuart—not in tabbing him as the winner in a possible fight against Houk, but in agreeing that he got screwed in the All-Star deal.

"Most managers go along with the vote of the players," Furillo wrote, even for the backups. "The eccentrics seem to be the exceptions."

•   •   •   •   •

Characters abounded in The Steam Room, where the author sought to explain the sporting life from the perspective of his beloved eccentrics.

"I'm a strange guy," cantankerous running back Duane Thomas told the Steamer in August 1971, while working out in L.A. "I'm walking around wondering what the hell people are doing."

Thomas had just led the NFL in rushing and the Dallas Cowboys to the championship of Super Bowl VI. Then the team had tried to get rid of him in the off-season over his unfortunate characterization of Cowboys coach Tom Landry as "a plastic man." Dallas made a deal with the Patriots, but the New England club couldn't handle Duane and cut him loose. It appeared to the Steamer as if the league was trying to blackball the kid. He took a strong stance against it.

"Duane Thomas looks like a lot of young people who are experiencing euphoria from thinking," the Steamer wrote. "That's not a bad trip."

The Steamer disapproved of Thomas's poor word choice in regards to Landry, but was willing to overlook it if it meant getting Duane more touches in Dallas or anywhere else. He loved the kid's game.

"Let's get him on the field," Furillo said.

The Steam Room featured outfielder Jimmy Piersall so often, he should have paid rent. Piersall, author of *Fear Strikes Out*, which details his life as a talented and bipolar baseball star, phoned the Steamer in October of 1962 to tell Furillo he'd just beaten the rap on a Baltimore bust from earlier in the year, when they ran him in for going into the stands after a heckler.

"The judge was swell," Piersall said. "He told me, 'You're one of the finest examples I've ever seen of people who recovered from being mentally ill.'"

Millions of baseball fans got to know Art Fowler in the 1970s, when Billy Martin made him his pitching coach with the Yankees. The Steamer had known him a decade earlier with the Dodgers and Angels, where Fowler earned a reputation as a hard-drinking relief pitcher with a sense of humor.

During the Angels' brawl in Kansas City in 1962, Furillo reported that Fowler was the last reinforcement to arrive from the bullpen.

"I was smoking a cigarette," was how Fowler explained his tardiness. "I can't run good with a cigarette in my mouth."

A couple weeks later, Angels manager Bill Rigney gave Fowler a spot start in Washington, DC. With the Angels up a run in the top of the eighth, Rigney called Art back for a pinch hitter. Fowler ignored the manager, the Steamer reported, and went up to the plate and singled in two runs.

"Did you want me, Bill?" Fowler asked when he returned to the dugout.

As early as 1961, the Steamer got onto A's owner Charles O. Finley for being "slightly zany." He liked Finley, but he really loved his mule, Charlie O., a beast the owner had made into a mascot. The two of them toured the country with the team, and on a 1965 road trip to L.A., the Steamer, as sports editor, ran a front-page graphic on Charlie O.'s two-day Tinseltown itinerary.

"We love that mule," outfielder Ken Harrelson (who later became the voice of the White Sox) told Steamer in an interview. "He's an inspiration to us."

The column ran with a photo of Harrelson holding onto Charlie O.'s neck for dear life on a sprint around the Municipal Stadium track in Kansas City.

"I was riding him fine until [K.C. pitcher] Orlando Pena threw a bat at Charlie," Harrelson said. "Then the mule went nuts."

The Steamer favored Detroit Lions linebacker Wayne Walker, nicknamed "The King," and Walker's running buddy from the secondary, Rick LeBeau. In late '66, the two of them dropped by the paper to see the Steamer, who was out of the office, taking a walk. They left a note on his desk in which Walker identified LeBeau as a student of beat poet Allen Ginsberg and "the official guru of the NFL." Walker had just lost his job as the Detroit place kicker to Garo Yepremian, who, he said, spoke four languages fluently "but can't understand a word LeBeau says."

"How about this Garo?" Walker said in his note to the Steamer. "A month and a half ago, he had never seen a pro football game. Now he owns the NFL record of field goals in a game with six."

•   •   •   •   •

Portrayals of the sports world's banter, background, and history—such as that of the Angels clubhouse in Baltimore in July—were hallmarks of The Steam Room. Probably no sportswriter took the Stanley Woodward admonition to not "God up" the players more to heart than the Steamer. "God" them up? He did the exact opposite. He showed them as the human beings that they were.

His column on Bill Russell in the Celtic legend's first year as player-coach didn't put anybody on any pedestal. Instead, it showed Russell doing what coaches did in those days before the game—sitting around the locker room stuffing game tickets into envelopes, licking them shut, and handing them to the players.

"Where is 'Battling Nelson'?" Russell asked, looking around for backup forward and future NBA Hall of Fame coach Don Nelson. "I suppose he wants seventeen tickets."

Nelson, a former Los Angeles Laker, only needed seven.

Toby Kimball, the bald Boston backup forward, had already dressed for the game. Russell, however, told Kimball he needed him to go find starting guard K. C. Jones, who was strolling around the L.A. Sports Arena.

"You want me to go walking through the lobby like this?" the uniformed Kimball protested.

Russell said nothing. He only glared.

"I'll go," Kimball said.

"I thought you would," Russell replied.

Celtics announcer Johnny Most arrived. Informed that the team's other backcourt starter, Sam Jones, would not be playing due to injury, Most asked Russell what he should say about it to the Boston fans.

"He died," Russell said.

Even with some of the players his public hated most, Furillo showed them to be quirky goofballs. The Steamer flew up to San Francisco in 1966 to cover the despised Juan Marichal in the Giants pitcher's first start against the Dodgers since he hit Johnny Roseboro over the head with a baseball bat in the heat of a pennant race the year before. The Steamer had always liked the usually friendly Marichal, and it came through in his column on the high-kicking right-hander who had complained to reporters—after beating the Dodgers—about his sore ribs, a pinched nerve in a finger on his pitching hand, allergies, and a swollen ankle.

With Marichal wheezing, rubbing his side and gazing at his hurt finger, Furillo asked, "Is anything all right?"

WINNING TWENTY-SEVEN FOR PHILS EARNS CARLTON JEWELS
AUGUST 12, 1973

The reigning professional athlete of the year walked in for lunch looking like $10,000.

This accounted for the jewels just on the left hand and wrist of Steve Carlton. . . .

The last time I saw this many diamonds, Marilyn Monroe and Jane Russell were singing about them in a song in the movies. "Diamonds Are a Girl's Best Friend" was the name of it. Carlton is proving that man doesn't have to be alienated by them, either.

"Tell me about the rocks in your ring?" Carlton was asked.

"They're from the Hickok Belt," he said. . . .

For winning forty-eight percent of the Phillies' games last year—twenty-seven—Carlton won the Hickok up in Rochester, New York, as the Professional Athlete of the Year. . . .

The Steamer had a diamond identification bracelet given to him some time ago but won't wear it. Besides, I know my name. Who has to look at a bracelet to find out who you are? . . .

They paid Carlton $160,000 for the most incredible pitching season in baseball's history. It is one thing to win twenty-seven games for the Dodgers as Koufax did and it is something else to do it for the Phillies. . . .

"I want to do it again," he said. "I want to pitch with the Phillies until we can win the pennant. It shouldn't be long."

Marichal looked at the dapper Steamer for a second and answered, "I like your suit."

The Steamer's journalistic ease, combined with his access, enabled him to show his readers the how and why behind feats of athletic greatness.

Furillo went to Anaheim Stadium to interview Nolan Ryan the day after "The Express" threw his first no-hitter in 1973 against the Kansas City Royals. Ryan credited K.C. manager Jackie McKeon, whose protest to the umps in the third inning informed the pitcher of a mechanical flaw in his delivery: he was lifting his foot off the rubber during his windup.

"When I bring my foot off the rubber, it usually means I am rocking back too far and I get wild high," Ryan told Furillo. "[McKeon] settled me down. I cut my stride and everything turned out just fine."

It gave him scoops, like the time the Steamer got a call at home one night from Bob Cousy, the flashy Boston Celtics playmaker who was mad about the long and nearly meaningless NBA regular season schedule, at a time when only two of the eight teams in the league didn't make the playoffs.

"I'm fed up with playing basketball," Cousy told the Steamer in 1962. "For the first time, the thought of quitting is running through my mind. The idea of playing out the season gets tiresome when you know you've had the division title clinched for two weeks."

Furillo made a fine fly on the wall. Once, he sat in the dugout and listened in on a conversation between Jimmy Piersall and Dean Chance before an Angels spring training game in 1965, when the pitcher told the outfielder that Willie Mays and Ken Boyer had said they'd rather face Sandy Koufax than Jim Bunning. Piersall, who had famously done time in a mental institution, thought you had to be nuts to insinuate that Bunning was better than Koufax.

"Don't tell me anything about Koufax," Piersall said. "I never hit a foul ball off him in the short time I was in the National League. I hit Bunning into the upper deck in Detroit."

Furillo's affable standing in sports put him in position to

provide vivid descriptions of athletic greatness, even if he wasn't there to witness them. One night in 1964, he joined Chub Feeney in the Giants GM's box for a game in L.A. against the Dodgers. After a great catch by Willie Mays robbed Tommy Davis of extra bases, the Steamer asked Feeney to tell him about the best catch he'd ever seen Mays make.

Feeney bypassed Willie's most famous catch, the over-the-shoulder job he'd pulled on Vic Wertz in the 1954 World Series, a shot that any true baseball fan has seen a million times. Instead, Feeney told the Steamer about a catch Mays had made in 1951 in Brooklyn against the Dodgers. Carl Furillo sent a screamer on a low trajectory into right center, Feeney recalled. Mays sped in and over, snagged the ball ankle high, whirled 360 degrees counterclockwise off a dead run, and fired a strike to the plate to nail Billy Cox, who was tagging from third.

Even better than the catch, Feeney said, was Dodgers manager Charlie Dressen's remarks to the press afterward.

"Let's see him do it again," the officious Dressen told the writers.

•   •   •   •   •

Phil Silvers had already brought Bob Newhart onstage to do his stand-up comedy routine when the doors flew open in the back of the packed Hollywood Palladium. The occasion was the 1964 annual banquet for the Dodgers and Angels the weekend before the opening of the baseball season. It was put on every year by the Los Angeles chapter of the Baseball Writers Association of America.

Two months earlier, the outgoing chapter chairman, Bud Furillo, and his successor, John Hall of the *L.A. Times*, had put together the entertainment package. Furillo and Hall had asked Frank Sinatra if he could do a number. Sinatra had told them that he had a couple engagements on his schedule, but he'd see what he could do.

On the night of the dinner, they hadn't heard from Sinatra in over a month. Suddenly, there was a ruckus in the back of the room. The crowd turned around to see what the commotion was

about, and there was Sinatra, in a tux, followed by fellow Rat
Packers Dean Martin, Sammy Davis Jr., and Joey Bishop. Sinatra
took over for Sergeant Bilko, and the show was on.

At the end of the performance, Sinatra announced that his
lyricist, Sammy Cahn, had written a new song for the baseball
writers' dinner, "dedicated to my friend Bud Furillo." The finale
song went:

> *Who's always insisting we must do this show?*
> *Furillo, Furillo, Furillo.*
> *Who keeps on yelling print's better than dough?*
> *Furillo, Furillo, Furillo.*

For a short, fat newspaper guy out of Youngstown who lived
in Downey and drove a beat-up Impala, it was a fairly special
moment.

The Steamer had always been comfortable among celebrity
types and had been able to work them into sports-angled feature
stories almost from the time he first became a sportswriter. He
patrolled the Rancho Park and Riviera Country Club golf courses the week of the L.A. Open to find and interview comedians
like Bob Hope. He sought out Tallulah Bankhead in the wings
of the Biltmore Theater during her run with *Dear Charles*. When
Sinatra bought a piece of Cisco Andrade, forget about it—Furillo
was all over his favorite singer.

During the Angels' first spring training in 1961, Furillo spotted Groucho Marx in the box seats, taking in the desert sunshine at an exhibition game against the Giants. The Steamer
walked down for a chat and sparked a riff that could have been
lifted from *Horse Feathers*.

"I would never root for the Dodgers because I come from
New York," Groucho started off. "I was a Giant fan until they
built Candlestick. I'll be darned if I'm going to suffer a heart attack climbing that hill. No sir, I'll be at the Angel opener if I can
find a place to park. I may have to park at the Coliseum, which
could be dangerous. You know last year they caught a fellow trying to smuggle a bottle of beer into the Coliseum and they gave
him ten years? The whiskey people didn't like it."

Off the breakout success of his "2,000 Year Old Man" routine that made for a hit record, Mel Brooks came to Los Angeles to produce a television show that would be called *Get Smart*. Furillo saw him at Dodger Stadium and struck up a conversation that resulted in a column note.

"Can you write in my accent?" Brooks asked.

In 1969, Furillo interviewed sports nut Bill Cosby in his Beverly Hills office for a column. During their conversation, a friend of the comedian wearing an Afro and a dashiki slapped Coz some skin.

"Cosby gave it back," Furillo wrote. "Then they slapped each other with three fingers. Then they did the same in reverse. 'Cool it, man,' said Cosby. 'These militant handshakes are getting longer every day. I was working the other night and a cat gave me a militant handshake until I finally pleaded with him it was time to go. "This will only take another half hour," he told me.'"

The Steamer wrote that he witnessed a 1967 drinking contest between the fabled New York restaurateur, Toots Shor, and entertainment giant Jackie Gleason. Several hours into it, "Gleason struck up a conversation with a beautiful girl, as he's been known to do," Furillo reported. "The Great One held her hand. The lady looked to Shor for assistance. Toots replaced the girl's hand with his, as she left the establishment. Unable to note any change, Gleason held Shor's hand for several minutes before he got wise that the lady had left."

Jackie "admitted defeat," the Steamer said, and left the bar.

By the time of the baseball writers' dinner, Furillo had known Sinatra for eight years, since the Aragon-Andrade fight in '56. A huge sports fan, Sinatra cultivated the sporting press. In the pre-ESPN age, he called his writer friends for scores, if he wasn't pressuring them to spin positive for his pals like Leo Durocher.

The Steam Room's Sinatra connection thickened when the Angels were born and they did their spring training in Palm Springs, where the singer kept a house. One time, the Steamer dropped into a desert club called the Metropole and ran into Sinatra, who invited the writer and a bartender pal of his, Johnny

Ortiz, into the back room to meet some friends.

Ortiz was picking away at a buffet table when he heard a scuffle off to the side. He turned around and saw that Chicago mob boss Sam Giancana had the Steamer backed up into a wall and was jamming his finger in the writer's face. "Momo" didn't like it that Furillo had referred to himself as a "dago."

"It's 'Italiano.' No dago," Giancana told the Steamer, who did not debate the issue.

•   •   •   •   •

Bud Furillo's sports-centric worldview was occasionally disrupted by the social and political turbulence that surrounded the Steam Room era.

His observations of the roiling 1960s and beyond usually came with a sardonic twist, like the time he commented on football radical Dave Meggyesy's 1970 book, *Out of Their League.* At a press conference, the St. Louis Cardinals linebacker predicted that, upon the onset of the revolution, "football will be obsolete."

"What the Marxist in pads said is true, to some extent," Furillo wrote. "Football has grown obsolete in St. Louis. After years of winding up second to Cleveland, the Cardinals wound up in the mouth of the Mississippi last year, winning only four games."

His own politics were those of a Franklin D. Roosevelt/Harry S. Truman/John F. Kennedy Democrat. He voted for Eugene McCarthy in the 1968 Democratic primary, but he was proud as punch to support Hubert H. Humphrey in the general election race against Richard Nixon and George Wallace, and he never forgave the New Left radicals of the day for not supporting the Democratic nominee.

The *Herald Examiner* held strongly conservative views on just about everything, including rabid support for the Vietnam War. As a columnist, the Steamer occasionally slipped contrary views past the sports editor, who happened to be himself. For his forty-fourth birthday, the Steamer's staff got him a ticket to the rock musical *Hair*, which he found provocative as "a protest against the dumb things that are going on, such as war."

"Anybody who knocks war can't be all bad," he wrote in the 1969 column.

As the leader of what he called the toy department of the newspaper, the Steamer wrote columns that only parried the social and political upheaval of the era—probably because some serious stuff was playing out in the four corners of his own home. His second-oldest daughter, Jill, was arrested twice for antiwar activism, and she did a little time in Sybil Brand for blocking the entrance to the downtown L.A. draft induction center. His oldest, Gail, would have been hauled in, too, had she not outrun the cops during the Isla Vista bank-burning riots of 1970. These two always made for interesting conversation when the Steamer had the staff over for holiday drinks.

While the Steamer worked the stadiums of L.A. and the rest of the country, his daughters turned his house into something of a cell of the revolution. It began with Jill's 1969 arrest for handing out literature at Cerritos College opposing the Vietnam War. Somehow, campus officials never got word that the Free Speech Movement had been resolved several years earlier in favor of the First Amendment. The show trial of the "Norwalk Four" attracted a colorful vanguard to Downey Municipal Court. The Steamer rolled his eyes at his daughter's tie-dyed support committee, but he joined them in backing her, and ultimately she was exonerated.

On the heels of this people's victory, activists gathered in the Steamer's kitchen to plan strategy, write and edit underground newspapers, and listen to Bob Dylan. They met up at the Steamer's safe house to ride off in convoys to People's Park protests in Berkeley, or teach-ins at Cerritos College, or Angela Davis speeches in downtown L.A. The Steamer did not quite know what to make of the revolutionary generation, other than that he did not like its music. He did, however, give positive reviews to the Stanford band.

But the Steamer was also a staunch American traditionalist. He wrote a Father's Day column, also in 1969, in which he interviewed Dodgers backup catcher Jeff Torborg, who thought young people in the generationally torn country should show some love and respect to their elders.

"Hmmm," Furillo wrote. "I wonder what they think of that down at the commune."

He broke up the cell the day Jill left his car at a riot. The occasion was the Chicano Moratorium, the 1969 antiwar march in East Los Angeles that turned fatal when journalist Ruben Salazar was killed by a tear-gas projectile fired by a sheriff's deputy. Earlier in the day, Jill asked the Steamer if she could borrow his car to go to the beach—a revolutionary ruse. Instead, she used the vehicle to transport a carload of demonstrators to East L.A., where somehow the police lines got between her and the Steamer's wheels. When she came home without them, another riot broke out at 7335 Gainford Street in Downey, and it resulted in the Steamer throwing her out of the house. She went on to become a nurse and labor activist, and eventually became the executive director of the New York State Nurses Association.

The '60s were also known as a period of experimentation with mind-altering ingredients, some of which were unfamiliar to the Steamer. When he suspected his older sons of such dabbling, a straight right hand sometimes accompanied his lectures on the dangers of substance abuse. Bud Furillo also showed a softer side on the troubling issue; when the local police arrested one of his kids' neighborhood pals for mescaline, it was the Steamer who bailed him out.

On the matter of race relations, the Steamer had always been something of a progressive, having grown up in an integrated neighborhood in Youngstown where skin color didn't matter so much when everybody shared the common virtue of poverty. When the Watts Riots exploded in 1965 just a few miles down Imperial Highway from Downey, he implored his kids to stay cool. When Detroit caught the riot fire two years later, Furillo turned his column over to an interview with one of his all-time favorite athletes, Leon Wagner, the African American outfielder with the Giants, Angels, and Indians who grew up in the Motor City.

"There can never be mutual trust between the white and Negro races," Wagner told the Steamer, "until the white man gets some soul."

•   •   •   •   •

Furillo wrote The Steam Room in plain language that hearkened back to his journalistic upbringing in the old *Herald Express* newsroom, where one of the rewrite men gave him good advice for any writer.

"Write like you talk," Gene Coughlin, one of the best of the old bunch, told him. "When a reader has to drop your piece for a Webster, it's six-to-five you've lost him forever."

The Steamer followed Coughlin's advice for the rest of his career. His stuff at its best read like a conversation he carried on with an audience that was a lot like him—people who lived on the industrial southeast side like he did, or in the Valley flats of North Hollywood and Van Nuys, or in Burbank or Glendale or the West Covina hills all the way out to Pomona, or in middle-class Orange County towns like La Palma and Placentia.

They golfed on public courses, if at all. They worked construction or carpentry trades. They poured molten steel and assembled cars in Ford or GM or Chrysler plants, just like he used to do before he went into the newspaper business. They toiled on the assembly lines at Lockheed or North American Aviation. They hustled and sold and contracted—asphalt, roofing materials, electronics. They owned catering trucks. They drove eighteen-wheelers. They worked the docks.

But to his credit, Furillo's readership extended throughout Southern California, and was comprised of the white collars as well as the blues. His avid fans included the wealthy season ticket holders who lived on the Westside or south of the boulevard in the San Fernando Valley, as well as doctors and lawyers from Pasadena, Beverly Hills, the South Bay, and Newport Beach. They belonged to private country clubs and took steam baths at expensive athletic clubs. They dined at Chasen's and Dan Tana's and Musso & Frank Grill, as well as Dal Rae's in Pico Rivera, Trani's Majestic in San Pedro, and Little Joe's in Chinatown, a few of the Steamer's favorite places.

No matter their socioeconomic stripe, the Steamer's readers needed a sports fix every day, and they also got it from writers like Jim Murray and Jimmy Cannon and Mel Durslag. And of course they loved John Hall, a charter member of The Steam Room before it was even created.

When they turned on the radio, Steam Room fans listened to Jim Healy's fifteen-minute, rapid-fire sports show, in which the host intoned over the clickety-clack of a news ticker, "Dateline Miracle Mile"—followed by the bellowed query, "Is it true?" This led into a salacious tidbit, usually fed to the show by newspaper stiffs like Bud Furillo.

The Steamer lived like his audience, only more so. He was erratic, surrounded by chaos, a slave to sex, booze, and gambling.

"I never drank or smoked until I reached the age of eight," he once wrote.

He gambled to the edge of disaster, but somehow managed to pay the bills, feed his six kids, and keep the creditors at arm's length. When the House of Serfas shut down, he helped create a new scene out where he lived in Downey, at Johnny Ortiz's strip-mall joint on Firestone Boulevard called the Stardust. The proprietors poured free drinks to hot chicks, and that brought in the fellas. Once Furillo found out about the Dust, he convinced a good number of the athletes to give the place a look. The Rams came, and so did the Angels, as well as a few Dodgers. So did fighters and writers and even a few Hall of Famers, enticed by girls in miniskirts with hair ratted high who dug athletes and displayed casual attitudes toward sex.

In mid-'66, Furillo and a few partners opened up the Lancer Lounge. "The expansion club," he called it, with the other Downey joint providing after-hours dice and card game entertainment on the side, the Steamer wrote in his memoirs.

The Lancer served as a fine location for the Steamer to pursue the third prong of his trifecta of vice, which finished off his first marriage. His drinking led to the occasional alcohol-induced blackout, where Scotch whisky short-circuited the electrical synapses of his memory.

One of the writers on his sports staff, Steve Bisheff, remembered how Furillo, as sports editor, had once been missing in action for a few days. When the Steamer called in to report that he was still alive, Furillo asked Bisheff, "What day is this?" When

Bisheff told him it was Wednesday, the Steamer asked, "What happened to Monday and Tuesday?"

Even if he was sentient only five days a week, the Steamer still delivered for his hard-core following. They needed their fix on the Dodgers, the Angels, the Rams, the Lakers, the fights, the track, the colleges, even the Chargers. For the fifteen years of the Steam Room era, they got it from the voice closest to the city's sports pulse, at a time when it beat the strongest.

Chapter 4

BIRTH OF A NEW LEAGUE

If the National Football League owners had any class they would give back the $18 million they robbed from their American Football League counterparts in 1965 to effect a professional football merger. The NFL claimed the AFL was poaching on its territory. They held up the five-year-old league if it wished to achieve parity, a common collegiate draft and membership in the old, established party. It turns out that the NFL may have been the poachers.

—January 12, 1970

Bud Furillo hustled down from the press box after the Los Angeles Chargers beat the Denver Broncos, looking for Sid Gillman. The Steamer needed to interview the Chargers' head coach about his team's critical mid-season road victory that aimed the club toward its eventual American Football League Western Division championship.

As 19,141 disappointed Broncos fans filed out of the stadium, Furillo caught up with Gillman in the middle of Bears Field.

Gillman was not quite ready to take any questions. He was busy wrestling with Dean Griffing, the Broncos' general manager, for the game ball.

Normally, there should have been no discussion. You win a game like the Chargers just did, 23–19, and the trophy is yours—no need for any best two out of three falls.

Griffing, however, told Gillman that if he wanted any damn game ball for the Chargers' trophy case, he was going to have to pay for it. Cost of the ball was nine dollars and eighty cents, which Gillman refused to dig out of his pocket. Instead, he grabbed the memento out of Griffing's grasp.

Underneath a dry, mile-high sky on October 16, 1960, Furillo watched in amusement as the future Pro Football Hall of Fame coach and Denver's skinflint GM engaged in a tug-of-war right there in the middle of Bears Field.

In his Steam Room column in the next day's *Herald Express*, Furillo reported that Gillman eventually overpowered Griffing to set up one of the most exciting plays of the afternoon.

"Gillman, who knows a thing or two about ball handling, baffled Griffing with his sleight of hand," the Steamer wrote. "He faked one way, then handed off to Dick Chorovich, a 260-pound [Chargers] defensive tackle. Smelling glory which rarely comes to men of his position, Chorovich sprinted through the end zone with the ball and into the dressing room. Gillman trotted behind him and Griffing gave futile chase, threatening, 'I'm going to send you a bill for that ball.'"

More than half a century later, such a standoff would be unthinkable in the three-pieced corporate culture of American sports, where NFL general managers no longer fight over footballs, even though they now cost more than $100 each.

They've all become a $12-billion-a-year industry in which everyone is a financial winner before any game ball is ever snapped. Huge TV deals forged with four television networks have made professional football in America the most successful sports business in the history of the world. It wasn't always so big, and it wasn't always so rich that a general manager didn't have to worry about the coach from the other team getting out of town with a nine-dollar-and-eighty-cent football like it was nothing.

Pro football grew to dominate the American sports scene because a few men who had been frozen out of the existing monopoly rose up in 1960 to challenge it. Within fifteen years, the rebels would be hailed as heroes by their former oppressors. They would be incorporated into the establishment and memorialized with George Halas and Curly Lambeau and Tim Mara as legendary figures in the growth and development of the National Football League.

Men as rich and powerful as Lamar Hunt of the Dallas Texans/Kansas City Chiefs and Bud Adams of the Houston Oilers/ Tennessee Titans probably would have thrived under any circumstances. But one thing that sure helped make their American Football League respectable was the coverage they received from the smattering of sports journalists in the country who took their venture seriously.

They were writers who found drama and intrigue and humor in places like Bears Stadium in Denver when a cheap general manager and a genius coach fought it out in the middle of the field over a game ball. They saw the birth of the AFL as a great story rather than something to sniff at while enjoying cocktails with the old guard NFL owners.

In Los Angeles, in the nation's second-largest television market, nobody covered the AFL's underdog challenge to the NFL like the columnist at the *Herald Express* who called his space The Steam Room.

"Bud Furillo really made an effort to give fair coverage to the league," remembered Ron Mix, a Pro Football Hall of Fame offensive tackle for the Chargers. "Other writers would just take pot shots at us."

As a sportswriter, Furillo loved the underdog story. So when *Herald Express* sports editor George T. Davis offered him the Chargers beat, Furillo was very happy to accept it.

It took him onto different turf, for a sportswriter who mostly hung around locker rooms and sports arenas and bars. It took him into some very high reaches in American business. He got to know moguls such as Chargers owner Barron Hilton, the hotel chain heir and founder of the Carte Blanche credit card.

Furillo also met and drank and became friends with other giants of industry like Adams and Hunt. They all served as terrific sources of information and subjects of interest for the columnist in his first years of opinion writing. They remained contacts for him decades into the future of his newspaper career and later as a sports talk radio host.

The Steamer recognized right away that the Chargers and the AFL would endure as a sports enterprise, even if Los Angeles

would only serve as a one-year media way station in the launch-
ing of the new organization.

Ten months before they ever played a game, Furillo found
himself right in the middle of one of the biggest of the early AFL
stories. The Chargers didn't figure into it. Instead, it involved
the established football team in town, the Rams, and the best
college football player in America.

•   •   •   •   •

Furillo flew to New York in late November of 1959 to cover the
L.A. angles on the ceremonies honoring the nation's All-American football team. Mostly, he used the trip as an excuse to party
in the Big Apple with USC's representative on the All-American
teams, Marlin McKeever, later to become a longtime NFL tight
end.

A month earlier, on Halloween night, football fans had gone
nuts in front of their black-and-white TV screens at the sight of
one of the most incredible plays any of them had ever seen.
Ranked number one, LSU was playing number-three Mississippi, the Tigers' archrival. Ole Miss led late in the game when
the Rebels punted. LSU's Billy Cannon collected the ball on his
own eleven, then zigged and zagged and ran through Ole Miss
arm tackles and sped eighty-nine yards up the sideline for the
decisive touchdown. To top off the evening, Cannon tackled a
Mississippi ball carrier on the LSU three-yard line in the game's
final moments to clinch the win.

Cannon's big night won him the Heisman Trophy and made
him the most coveted player in the nation coming out of college. By virtue of their league's worst record, the Los Angeles
Rams had the number-one pick in the draft. The NFL's selection
process took place on November 30, the same weekend of the
All-American festivities that put Furillo and Cannon in the same
city at the same time.

Eight days earlier, Bud Adams's AFL Houston Oilers selected Cannon in the new league's "territorial" draft, where each of
the eight teams got first dibs on stars with local connections to
their regions, for purposes of marketability. Furillo had already

written a column warning the Rams that they'd be making a mistake if they went for Cannon.

"Best thing for the Rams to do is steer away from the first-round choices of Texas oil men," Bud Furillo wrote on November 26.

"[Cannon] will go for the dough," the Steamer wrote, surmising that whatever the Rams offered, the Oilers would top it.

The Rams ignored the advice and picked Cannon.

Between stops with McKeever at Toots Shor's and Birdland, Furillo spotted Cannon at one of the All-American bashes around Manhattan. Then he accomplished something the Ole Miss special teams could not—he cornered Cannon and asked him if he'd sign with the Rams.

"Ever since I was a boy, I've dreamed of playing for the Rams," Cannon told Furillo. "I'm going to play for the Rams and nobody else."

Cannon spoke before he listened to the Oilers, whose nickname didn't just bubble up out of nowhere. Their owner was an Oklahoma wildcatter by virtue of his birth who rose to the presidency of Phillips Petroleum.

Bud Adams also liked sports and wanted his own football team. He had made inquiries a year earlier about buying into the NFL's Chicago Cardinals. Rebuffed by the old league, Adams's interest in owning a football club captured the attention of Lamar Hunt, who had been contemplating the creation of a brand new league.

When Hunt asked him in, Adams became the first to join.

The Rams, knowing that Adams's oil money posed a grave danger to their signing the Heisman Trophy winner, moved quickly to help Cannon realize his boyhood dream. He still had a game of eligibility remaining, in a rematch against Ole Miss in the January 1 Sugar Bowl. Not a problem for Rams general manager Pete Rozelle, who presented Billy with a contract offer on the same November 30 date that the Rams drafted him.

The team offered Cannon a $10,000 bonus, a $10,000 salary for his rookie season and $15,000 for each of his second and third years. Unknown to the public at the time of the offer, but later to be revealed in U.S. District Court in Los Angeles, Cannon signed the contract.

In later years, such an impermissible benefit probably would have resulted in a Heisman winner having to return the trophy to the Downtown Athletic Club. The signing also would seem to amount to conduct unbecoming for a professional football executive, not to mention a soon-to-be NFL commissioner—making a boy sign a contract while he was still an amateur. But this was the beginning of the AFL-NFL draft war, and Rozelle knew he needed to act fast to squeeze out Adams.

Rozelle and the Rams should have listened to the Steamer.

They soon found out that a deal forged to the displeasure of a Texas oil oligarch is made to be undone.

Unimpressed by Cannon's pronouncement that the Rams were the team of his dreams, Adams initiated a conversation with Billy. On December 23—barely three weeks after he had signed with the Rams and nine days before his college eligibility would expire—Cannon did it again. He signed with the Oilers.

Cannon's Oiler deal didn't go public until New Year's Day, after the Sugar Bowl, a game that would feature no historic punt returns. The preoccupied Cannon, who was now the property of two professional football teams while still playing for one in college, carried six times for eight yards against the fired-up Rebels. Mississippi gained its revenge in a 21-0 pummeling of LSU in the game played in New Orleans.

The biggest story of the day, however, unfolded afterwards, when Cannon stood beneath the goal posts in Tulane Stadium and announced on national television that he was signing with Houston.

In Los Angeles, the response of Rozelle and the Rams set a tone to mark the state of legal relations between the AFL and the NFL for years to come. They sued.

"The Rams fulfilled their part of the bargain and expect him to fill his," Rozelle told reporters in L.A. the day Cannon changed his mind underneath the goal posts.

Billy and his legal team fired back.

The contract Cannon signed with the Rams? They said it was

backdated to January 2. In Billy Cannon's legal view, this made his switch to Houston okay.

He returned the $10,000 bonus check to the Rams, along with the $500 in expense money they gave him on draft day in Philadelphia, where the NFL conducted its annual selection of college talent, so as not to inconvenience then-commissioner Bert Bell, who lived on the banks of the Delaware River and didn't like to stray far from them.

At the *Los Angeles Herald Express*, the Steamer was busy breaking the story that the new AFL team in town, the Chargers, were about to sign Sid Gillman as their head coach. Furillo also worked his sources on the Cannon story. He wrote a column that questioned the Heisman winner's assertion of a backdated agreement.

"That's not the way I heard it, McGee," the Steamer wrote. "Billy better look again to see if that isn't a November date on his work sheet."

Four days after Cannon signed with Houston, The Steam Room reported the basic terms of the Oiler deal. In coming weeks, Furillo filled out the details in their entirety:

The Oilers would pay Cannon $33,000 per season for three years, or more than three times the NFL average salary and a third higher than anything the top stars of the day were making. Bud Adams would set up something called the Cannon Oil Company to pay Billy $25,000 a year in stock invested in five gas stations in Baton Rouge, Louisana, home of the LSU Tigers. Adams also wrote out a $10,000 bonus for Billy, and threw in a new Cadillac for the young man's dad.

Furillo first wrote that the deal was "supposedly negotiated on the Sugar Bowl turf, immediately after Mississippi had shown the twenty-two-year-old Cannon that you better get all you can in football because it's dangerous."

In April, The Steam Room reported that Adams—who had howled about the Rams signing Billy before he had completed his eligibility—actually cut his deal with Cannon nine days before the Sugar Bowl. Furillo's disclosure was accompanied by a photostat of the agreement that included the December 23 signing date.

If Adams played things funny, so did one of the Ram's minority owners. Fred Levy Jr.'s family made its money in Cleveland department stores. As a minority partner, Levy bought in with Dan Reeves in 1941 to acquire the Rams. After the Rams made their secret pact with Cannon—but before Houston's surreptitious deal was finalized—Levy bet Furillo a dinner that the Rams would sign Cannon first.

"Shame on Fred Levy," Furillo wrote in The Steam Room, when he found out he'd been rolled. "You just don't know who to trust anymore."

The Steam Room also poked Bud Adams for "spoiling Cannon's boyhood dream as he did," by luring Billy away from the Rams. "But such is life with Billy Cannon, the LSU All-American who thinks nothing of autographing legal documents for the National Football League, the American Football League, and all

AFL BRASS CONFIDENT UPSTART LEAGUE WILL MAKE IT

JUNE 29, 1962

NEW YORK—If you find the stock market baffling, try and figure out the American Football League.

It has been in operation three years. None of the eight members ever have made a quarter. Millions have been lost in operations.

Attorney fees trying to win a $10 million suit against the National Football League amounted to more than $300,000.

Now, the AFL wants to go down for double . . . It's appealing the suit, in which it didn't win a round in a recent decision by a federal court judge.

But, to see the happy faces around the Kenmore Hotel in Boston this week, you would think the AFL was in better shape than Brigitte Bardot. . . .

The other night I had dinner with [AFL commissioner Joe] Foss, Charger owner Barron Hilton, and coach Jack Faulkner. Foss, who even leads Walter O'Malley in cigar intake, predicted:

"We're going to make it." . . .

In spite of its previous staggering losses, I think the AFL is going to hang on long enough to make it.

Foss is a persuasive man.

the millionaires at sea," the Steamer concluded in his column.

•   •   •   •   •

Amid the Cannon controversy, conflagrations in the signing wars erupted elsewhere in L.A. The Chargers drafted Charlie Flowers, another All-American halfback, out of Mississippi, of course. Fifth in the Heisman balloting, Flowers finished tied for first with Cannon in multiple contract signings, with two. He agreed to play for both the New York Football Giants and L.A.'s AFL club.

Another suit was filed.

Charger owner Barron Hilton added to the fun. A Santa Monica resident, Hilton lived three doors down Ocean Front Walk from Los Angeles Rams running back Ron Waller. Putting the Charger roster together, Hilton invited his neighbor over for a drink.

"Barron offered Ron an hors d'oeuvre, a scotch and soda, and a two-year contract to play for his Los Angeles Chargers," Furillo reported in The Steam Room. "Waller accepted on all three counts."

Already warmed up with their Cannon filing, the Rams sued again to keep Waller out of the Chargers' attractive new uniforms, with the UCLA-blue shirts and lightning bolts on the helmets, pants, and shoulders.

With two suits pending against them, the Chargers went for the hat trick. They got it when they signed former Chicago Bears wide receiver Ralph Anderson and prompted a suit by the Bears' George Halas. Halas claimed that Anderson still belonged to him, even though the receiver hadn't caught a ball for the Bears in two years. Anderson spent the 1959 season in Canada, playing for the Winnipeg Blue Bombers.

You'd think the Ralph Anderson controversy would have been resolved when the receiver, the victim of a diabetic coma, collapsed and died the night after the Chargers' November 27 wipeout of the Oakland Raiders.

Wrong.

The Steamer ran into Halas the following spring in Arizona, and even Anderson's death wouldn't stop Papa Bear's pursuit of justice.

"Sid Gillman knew that boy had a contract to play for the Bears last season," Halas told Furillo. "I understand Barron Hilton is a nice fellow, but I can't let Gillman get away with what he did."

Elsewhere around the league, the AFL stung the NFL by signing much of the best college talent.

The Chargers got a win for the AFL when they outbid the Baltimore Colts for USC All-American tackle Ron Mix. It was a fairly simple decision for the lineman. According to The Steam Room, the Chargers offered Mix a $5,000 signing bonus plus a two-year guaranteed contract at $12,000 a season. The Colts countered with a $1,000 bonus and one year at $7,500.

Mix told Baltimore owner Carroll Rosenbloom he'd rather play for the Colts, but asked if they could come up a little on the offer.

"He said, 'Look, that league's going to fold anyway,'" Mix told me in an interview fifty-three years later. "'Take the $5,000, get the $12,000 contract and we'll see you next year.'"

Rosenbloom got that one wrong, but he wasn't the only NFL owner who lost out. The AFL was beating the old league in the signing game all over the country.

Lamar Hunt stuck it to the NFL and the Detroit Lions when he signed LSU defensive back Johnny Robinson, later to star for the Dallas Texans and then for the Chiefs on their Super Bowl championship team. Hunt beat out the Pittsburgh Steelers for TCU fullback Jack Spikes. Billy Sullivan and his Boston Patriots got the best of the Philadelphia Eagles in the fight for Northwestern fullback Jim Burton.

All the players were first-round NFL draft picks. Money made the difference in every case, especially with Cannon and his Rembrandtic deal with the Oilers.

Adams's masterpiece did hit one snag, however. In August, Cannon appeared in Los Angeles with the Oilers for an exhibition game against the Chargers. Cannon told the press that Adams shorted him on the filling stations.

"This led some reporters to believe Houston owner Bud

Adams was going back on some of the juicier clauses in Cannon's kingly pact," Furillo wrote a couple months later, when the Steamer was in Houston with the Chargers for their regular season game against the Oilers.

While in Houston, Furillo sat down for a drink with Adams. Their meeting was arranged by Jay Michaels, the MCA, Inc., talent agent and father of the great sports broadcaster Al Michaels. Jay Michaels helped arrange the first AFL television deal with ABC Sports and its legendary producer, Roone Arledge.

The Steamer asked Adams if it was true that he was pulling the plug on the gas stations. Furillo wrote: "'That wasn't the case at all,' Adams explained, over a tankard of high-octane and soda. 'We've purchased several properties and are going ahead with the program,' revealed Adams, who will be Cannon's partner in the deal."

Adams went on to tell the Steamer, "Billy gets confused sometimes by the advice he gets, all of which is not good. Somebody tried to talk him into putting up a cemetery, also a laundry, instead of going into gas stations."

The Oiler owner told Furillo that Cannon had since corrected his muddled view of affairs. "It will not be long now before you can drive your compact across country and have it serviced at a Billy Cannon Gas Station in Baton Rouge, Louisiana," Furillo was happy to report.

•　　•　　•　　•　　•

Bud Furillo's thirteen years on the sports beat at the *Herald Express* put him in a great position to cover the Chargers and their new league from the inside out. Hilton helped him from the start by hiring former Notre Dame coach Frank Leahy as the Chargers' first general manager. The Steamer idolized Leahy and maintained a close friendship with him even after others turned on the Notre Dame coaching legend. A Securities and Exchange Commission investigation into Leahy's oil stock dealings took the shine off his four-leaf clover.

Stressed out by financial controversy, Leahy suffered a nervous breakdown the summer before the Chargers' first season. He relinquished his position as general manager with the Chargers.

Hilton did another favor for Furillo on the sourcing front. He named Sid Gillman to replace Leahy and double as general manager. Furillo and Gillman went way back, to 1955, when the Steamer helped introduce Sid to the Los Angeles public in a three-part series. During Gillman's five-year tenure with the Rams, Furillo occasionally stayed up late at night and drank Scotch and listened to Art Tatum with the coach. Furillo listened some more when Gillman spun tales about his Ohio State days playing end under the Buckeyes' imaginative coach, Frances Schmidt, whose playbook contained so many shifts and formations that he couldn't keep track of them all.

"Son, I don't know for sure what you do on that play," Schmidt would tell a kid, "but you're doing it wrong."

Gillman has gained credit among football historians as the grandfather of sorts of the so-called West Coast offense, described by football scientists as a pass-first attack to set up the running game and the deep ball. Sid has also been credited with inventing the play-action fake off the Paul Brown draw. His influence ran through protégés such as Don Coryell and Bill Walsh and extended through the football eons through his "coaching tree" all the way to John Harbaugh, whose Baltimore Ravens won the 2012 Super Bowl championship nine years after Gillman died.

His Ram years started out strong with Gillman's appearance in the NFL title game his first year. They finished with a firing, due to the horrible 2–10 record in 1959.

When the end was near, The Steam Room reported that the Rams players had turned against Gillman for what Furillo described as the "sarcastic" attitude the coach displayed towards them. The day of Gillman's last game, Leon Clarke, an end on the '59 Rams, told the Steamer that the coach "degraded us to the extent we would go home and fight with our wives."

Everybody knew Gillman was done with the Rams. Co-captain Duane Putnam told the Steamer, "I am sorry only for his assistants."

DUTCHMAN GETS KICK OUT OF GILLMAN'S MISERY
SEPTEMBER 10, 1962

MINNEAPOLIS—On every visit to Minnehaha, I never fail to renew acquaintances with the old Los Angeles favorite, Norm Van Brocklin.

The beer in his refrigerator is always cold and clear as the land of sky blue waters.

The conversation is always foamy. Normally, Norman concentrates on the Rams—or his own Minnesota Vikings.

But this time, the Dutchman devoted his fiendish giggle to the disaster which befell his former L.A. mentor, Sid Gillman, in Denver over the weekend. . . .

The 30–21 victory by Denver and [coach Jack] Faulkner was a genuine delight to Van Brocklin, a founder of the Hate Gillman Society. Dutch was anxious to know if I had any details. . . .

I told him what I knew. That I was able to get Faulkner off Pike's Peak long enough for a telephone account of his slapping down of Sir Sidney. Faulkner related:

"Sid wasn't too happy with me before the game." . . .

Later, Gillman attacked Faulkner for sending him a game film with all the touchdowns removed. . . .

"I just forgot about all the scoring plays being taken out of the film," Faulkner testified. "You see, I have this television show and I used the touchdowns on the program."

After the Rams fired Gillman, Furillo was first to report that Leahy wanted to hire him for the Chargers. Once they made their deal, Gillman went to work putting together one of the great coaching and front-office staffs in pro football history. It included more key Steam Room sources.

As his principal offensive underling, Gillman picked Al Davis. Most recently employed as a USC assistant, Davis coached receivers under Gillman and coordinated the Chargers passing game. He left the team in 1963 to turn the Oakland Raiders into the winningest franchise in professional sports for the next twenty years.

For his secondary, Gillman hired one of his Rams assistants, Jack Faulkner, the future head coach of the Denver Broncos. Faulkner would later work as a key assistant when the Rams played for titles under Chuck Knox. He and Furillo had grown up together in Youngstown and played sandlot football with each other.

For player personnel director, Gillman retained Don Klosterman, the old Loyola quarterback Furillo covered on one of his first *Herald Express* beats. Klosterman later pieced up the great Kansas City Chiefs championship team of the late 1960s. He also GM-ed the Colts during their Super Bowl championship year in 1970 before heading over to the Rams, when Carroll Rosenbloom bought the team in the 1970s.

As Klosterman's player personnel assistant, Gillman listened to Al Davis's advice and brought in Al LoCasale, a northwest Philly kid. As a Penn undergrad, LoCasale bird-dogged talent for Davis, when the future NFL legend coached at the Citadel after the two met at a football clinic in Atlantic City. Davis liked LoCasale so much, he took him to USC and got him a job as Trojan head coach Don Clark's executive assistant. When Gillman asked Davis over to the Chargers, he agreed to hire LoCasale, too—another old USC source for Furillo.

Gillman rounded out his staff with a couple of new contacts for the Steamer. On the defensive side of the ball, he found a line coach who had just concluded his playing career with the Cleveland Browns. His name was Chuck Noll, and he would win more Super Bowls than anybody until Bill Belichick won six of them for the New England Patriots. It was Noll who built the "Steel Curtain" defense that brought four titles to Pittsburgh.

Gillman hired Joe Madro as his offensive line coach. Madro, who had worked the same job with the Rams, went to Oakland with Davis and scouted for him for seventeen years.

Furillo worked them all as sources and dominated his beat during the Chargers' one year in Los Angeles. He listened and learned from them. He held their information close and popped it at the right time, when stories were ready to be told.

•　　•　　•　　•　　•

Three weeks into the 1960 season, the Chargers lost on the road to the Dallas Texans and owner Barron Hilton fell into a serious funk. His team was 1–2. Even worse, the team's one home game drew only 17,724 fans. Hilton was on his way to losing $900,000 for the year.

"You can understand how a young man new to the ways of professional football might become disconsolate," the understanding Bud Furillo wrote in the next day's Steam Room.

At what he described as a post-game "wake," the Steamer wrote that Hilton, drinking with Furillo and some other writers and team executives, "sought balm," and that "there seemed to be no other way to ease his pain except to offer something ethereal."

Furillo consoled Hilton by predicting that the Chargers would win the AFL title.

They didn't show it in the loss to Dallas, but the Chargers did have championship talent—especially on offense, with quarterback Jack Kemp throwing the ball, halfback Paul Lowe running it, and all-league tackles Ron Mix and Ernie Wright creating space up front.

At the barroom wake, assistant coach Jack Faulkner jumped in to help Furillo cheer up Hilton. Sitting around with Hilton, Furillo, Chargers stockholder Joe Zoline, and *Sports Illustrated* pro football writer Tex Maule, Faulkner backed up Furillo's prediction of a Chargers championship.

"Hilton's spirits rose considerably," Maule wrote later in his own magazine piece. "'If we win,' he told the two cheer mongers, 'I'll buy you something nice. What would you like?' Furillo and Faulkner looked at each other. Both came out of the tough areas of Youngstown, Ohio—where street fights left them both with broken noses. 'If you win,' suggested Furillo, 'why don't you buy Faulkner and me new noses?'"

According to the Steamer's account, "Hilton surveyed the widespread breathing processes of the Chargers' secondary coach and the writer. You sensed he was thinking this might cost him more than bills run up by a transient coming across a misplaced Carte Blanche card."

Hilton assessed the messes spread across both faces. I don't know about Faulkner's nose, but the Steamer's was in pretty bad shape. It had been broken nine times. Still, Hilton agreed to the deal. He would pick up the tab on their nose jobs if the predictions came true.

Hilton's promise wasn't enough for Furillo and Faulkner. They demanded it be put in writing. Zoline, a Chicago-based corporate lawyer and chief executive with Carte Blanche, as well as the future developer of the Telluride Ski Resort in Colorado, drew up the documents.

"Know all men by these present," Zoline's draft stated. "For and in consideration of $1 and other good and valuable considerations it is hereby agreed as follows: If the Los Angeles Chargers win the 1960 American Football League title, the undersigned Barron Hilton will pay for new noses for Bud Furillo and Jack Faulkner."

The drive to the "Nose Bowl" was on.

•   •   •   •   •

The Hearst corporation and its *Herald Express* partnered up with the new team and the new league. The paper sponsored the Chargers' opening exhibition as a charity game, like the *Los Angeles Times* did every year with the Rams in their contest. Every year, the Times Charity Game nearly packed the Coliseum.

It didn't quite work out that way for Hearst and the Chargers. On the day of the first Chargers game ever, against the New York Titans, the team looked great in those fabulous new uniforms that also included the Bill Veeck innovation of names scripted on the back. Paul Lowe returned the opening kickoff 105 yards for a touchdown. But even with extensive pre-game building up in the Hearst press, only 27,778 fans showed up.

If that was an ominous development for the future of the American Football League in Los Angeles, the signs got a hell of a lot worse the next week, when Billy Cannon and the Houston Oilers came to town.

All that publicity over the lawsuit and the Rams and the Oilers and everything did nothing for the gate. The game drew 11,000.

The Steam Room advised patience. The Chargers would

catch on, Furillo wrote, if they just played "interesting football."

Starting with the Denver game in October, the team did its part. Paul Lowe was undrafted out of Oregon State and cut by the San Francisco 49ers before the 1959 season. When Gillman put the Chargers' roster together, he found Lowe working in the Carte Blanche mailroom. The team had such low hopes for Lowe that when they found out on picture day they were short on uniforms, he got left out of the shot.

Lowe may not have been in the team picture, but he ended up leading the club in rushing with 855 yards—second best in the league—with an AFL-best 6.3 yards per carry.

Dick Harris intercepted five passes. Paul Maguire played linebacker and punted. He would become better known later as the entertainingly eccentric NBC color man.

Sid Gillman was the face of the franchise, but the front man on the field and the most popular player on the team would one day become the Republican nominee for vice president of the United States.

A local kid from Fairfax High, Jack Kemp played college ball in town at Occidental. He finished second in passing yardage in the AFL's initial year. Handsome and articulate, Kemp would later represent Buffalo for eighteen years as a Republican congressman. President George H. W. Bush appointed him housing secretary. When Senator Bob Dole of Kansas won the GOP presidential nomination in 1996, he made Kemp his running mate. They lost to Bill Clinton and Al Gore. Who knows if Kemp would have gone anywhere in politics if it hadn't been for the name recognition the AFL gave him, because he sure didn't get much of it in the NFL.

In 1957, the Detroit Lions drafted Kemp on the seventeenth round but cut him before the regular season opener. Pittsburgh, San Francisco, and the New York Football Giants all gave him a look. He took a few snaps with the Steelers, but then didn't throw an NFL pass for three years before he got a job with Gillman.

Before anybody heard of supply side economics, or even Elbert Dubenion, who was Kemp's running mate as wide receiver on the Buffalo Bills' 1964 AFL champs, the L.A. Chargers quarterback made for good Steam Room copy.

About his NFL travails, Kemp told Furillo during the Chargers' pre-season camp, "It was the same story every place I went. I was the guy they kept on the roster for insurance. They should have dressed me in a policy instead of a uniform."

Kemp backed Bobby Layne in Detroit, Earl Morrall in Pittsburgh, and Y. A. Tittle and Charley Conerly, the latter two from his slot on the 49ers and Giants taxi squads. He said the first-stringers barely talked to him.

"Quarterbacks are a selfish breed," he told the Steamer. "They don't help each other. I learned more from the ends I worked with on the practice field."

Layne, one of the best NFL quarterbacks of the 1950s and one of the hardest drinkers in football history, did offer Kemp one piece of advice.

"Bobby noticed I never touched anything stronger than root beer," Jack said in The Steam Room. "One day he told me somewhat disgustedly, 'Kid, you're never going to make it in this league unless you drink.'"

Furillo noted, "Kemp remained a teetotaler, and Layne was right. Jack never made the NFL."

Late in November, Kemp's future team, the Buffalo Bills, came to Los Angeles and beat the Chargers, 32–3. As usual, the Coliseum was nearly empty, with only 16,000 in the house. Kemp stunk out the joint on a 13-for-30 day with five interceptions. It made him think back to Bobby Layne.

"Maybe I'll have to take up drinking and smoking," Kemp told the Steamer.

•   •   •   •   •

In early November, Furillo flew to New York with the Chargers to cover their game against the city's new AFL franchise, the Titans. While he was in town, he dropped in on his old neighbor from the Crenshaw District, Pete Rozelle. The first thing the Steamer noticed was that the draft wars and stress of his rookie year in the commissioner's chair appeared to be getting to Rozelle.

"It's been a face-wrinkling job [for Rozelle]," the Steamer wrote in his New York column. "Pete doesn't look thirty-four anymore."

The conflict between the AFL and the NFL created a conflict within Furillo, who was covering the Chargers and wanted the new league to succeed. But he also never missed a Rams home game in the preceding decade and had developed innumerable friendships with players and officials in the organization. He sat down with his friend from their days of editing rival JC sports sections and wondered if there was any hope for reconciliation.

"Into the fifteenth floor offices of the National Football League in Rockefeller Center flew the dove of peace, seeking harmony between the senior circuit and the new American Football League," the Steamer wrote of himself—a guy who wanted everybody to just get along.

Nobody smiled for the camera better than Pete Rozelle. His perfectly straight, white teeth, highlighted by the precise upwardly tilted crescent of his upper lip above the upper bridge, was just as much a Rozelle trademark as the TV deals he worked out with the networks.

But Rozelle didn't do much smiling when the dove of peace flew through his office window. He was looking down the barrel of a $10-million antitrust lawsuit filed against the NFL by the upstart league. AFL attorneys filed the action over some interesting NFL expansion decisions. For ten years, the league hadn't awarded any new franchises, even rejecting one expansion request submitted by Lamar Hunt in Dallas. It was this denial that motivated Hunt to create the AFL.

About the same time the NFL told Hunt no, it also turned down a group that wanted to establish a team in Minneapolis–St. Paul. Rudely rebuffed, the Twin Cities hopefuls, headed up by Max Winter, the former general manager of the Minneapolis Lakers, joined in with Hunt's forces.

During the AFL's incubation, the NFL suddenly changed its mind about expansion. It offered Hunt a franchise in Dallas. Now it was Hunt's turn to turn them down—he had already recruited ownership for the new AFL franchises and it would be very bad business form to abandon them.

The NFL responded with a chop block. The league laid out Hunt by awarding a new Dallas franchise to another Texas oil man, Clint Murchison, to compete with Hunt's new AFL enterprise in the Metroplex. NFL officials also re-contacted Max Winter in Minnesota and told him he could have a franchise up there after all.

Winter accepted the NFL opportunity, which prompted the AFL to ask the U.S. Department of Justice to please investigate the NFL for antitrust violations. The feds declined, so the AFL pursued its own antitrust action, filing a $10-million suit against the NFL in federal court in Baltimore.

During Furillo's afternoon in the commissioner's office, the dove of peace asked Rozelle about possible areas of agreement between the two leagues. Maybe they could get together on a common draft? How about inter-league exhibition games?

Many years before the Super Bowl would become the most popular vehicle to distribute televised commercial advertising in the history of American sports, the Steamer even suggested to Rozelle a post-season championship game between the winners of the two leagues.

Rozelle wasn't interested in any of it. In fact, on the issue of the common draft, he was scheming in the opposite direction. Three weeks after his meeting with the peace dove, the commissioner sent out notices to fifty of the country's top college football players asking them to hold off signing contracts with the AFL, which had already conducted its draft, until the NFL teams made their picks.

Furillo also asked Rozelle why the NFL wouldn't consider playing preseason games with AFL teams after the old league had already played exhibitions that year with clubs from the Canadian Football League.

"People don't play games," Rozelle told the Steamer, "with people suing them for ten million dollars."

•   •   •   •   •

After the disaster against the Bills, the Chargers won four

straight to win the AFL Western Division. The average score of 46–30 helped establish the AFL image in the early years as a league that had wide open offensive play but was a little short on the stop.

The Chargers didn't care. Neither did Furillo nor Faulkner. They made it to the Nose Bowl.

Los Angeles barely noticed. The Chargers crowds fell off to an average of a little more than 12,000 for the last three home games, including just 9,928 for Gillman's rematch with Griffing, which in effect amounted to a divisional playoff.

Vast emptiness floated across a sea of green bleachers and gray peristyle columns in the Los Angeles Memorial Coliseum, which then held about 103,000 fans. Talk about a terrible backdrop for TV. So AFL executives decided that, if the Chargers made the championship game against Houston, it would be played in Texas, no matter which team had the better record.

The Chargers crowds were so bad you could actually pull a hot dog out of a bun and throw it as far as you could without hitting anyone. I know this for a fact, because I did it as a six-year-old the Sunday afternoon the Chargers beat the Raiders in L.A., 52–28. I was sitting below the Coliseum press box with my older brother and sisters and a few of our friends from Downey. The Steamer, who doubled as the color man on the Chargers' radio broadcasts, was up in the KBIG booth with play-by-play man Tommy Harmon, the 1940 Heisman Trophy winner out of Michigan—"Old 98." The hot dog toss caught the Steamer's eye. I remember one of my sisters tapping me on the shoulder and pointing back toward the press box, and me turning around to see my father standing and screaming at me during a station break, his headphones still on. The hot dog stunt bought me a four-year ban from the Coliseum, imposed by the Steamer.

The week before the regular season ended at home against the New York Titans, Furillo wrote that Chargers owner Barron Hilton was "deeply disappointed" by the lousy crowds. Hilton told the Steamer that the Chargers would play their home games the next year on Friday and Saturday nights, because they were getting killed at the gate on Sunday afternoons. Too much competition from Rams road games on free TV, according to Hilton.

"People aren't going to come out for our games when they can get one for nothing at the same time," Hilton told the Steamer.

Maybe Hilton had a point, and maybe he didn't. Maybe there was another dynamic at work. Like, maybe the town preferred the Rams?

The established club was on its way to another lousy season: 4-7-1. But they still drew 75,000 to the Coliseum for the Colts on the Sunday after the Chargers failed to attract 10,000 on Saturday for the Broncos. No TV competition there for the Chargers.

A week later, the Rams played against the Green Bay Packers on Saturday, with 53,000 on hand. The next day, with no Rams on TV, the Chargers—already assured a spot in the Nose Bowl—pulled in just 11,000 for the Titans.

Right around then, Hilton's phone rang, San Diego calling. The Steamer broke the story about Hilton's conversation with Border City officials the day after the Titan game. No biggie, Hilton told Furillo. He planned on staying in L.A.

"I'm confident the Chargers will catch on here in a couple of years," Hilton said in The Steam Room.

Not that confident, it turned out. A week later, Hilton was quoted in an un-bylined *Herald Express* story saying, "I'd be remiss if I did not investigate the enthusiasm" of the San Diego proposal.

Hilton admitted to Furillo the next year that he knew the Chargers were done in L.A. the day of the horrible crowd for the Broncos.

"I knew this was a National Football League town and I had to move," he told the Steamer in September of 1961, when the Chargers were kicking off their new existence in San Diego.

•   •   •   •   •

Furillo built up the first AFL title game as one of the five biggest televised sporting events of the year—George Blanda and Billy Cannon and the Oilers against Jack Kemp and Paul Lowe and the Chargers.

The Steam Room had fun with the coaching matchup. It would be the Chargers' Gillman against one of his former Rams assistants, the Oilers' Lou Rymkus. Unlike Faulkner and Madro, Gillman did not tender Rymkus a job offer with the Chargers.

A year earlier, as the Rams limped to the end of a disastrous season, somebody in the organization had leaked stories about the players' discontent with Gillman. One of the reports really bugged Gillman. It blamed him for suspending team co-captain Duane Putnam for missing a team meeting in Philadelphia. Turned out, it was Pete Rozelle, not Gillman, who had sent Putnam home to L.A. while the Rams played the Eagles.

Gillman suspected Rymkus as the misinformed leaker. Sid "figured his old pal Lou had some ideas about succeeding him" as the Ram coach, Furillo wrote five days before the AFL championship. For the same column, the Steamer asked Gillman, "Aren't you proud of your pupil's success in his first head coaching venture?"

"Sid flashed a sinister smile to indicate how unfunny he regarded the question," Furillo wrote, "and replied, 'That goes to show you how much this business of coaching is overrated.'"

Houston beat the Chargers for the first AFL championship, 24–16, depriving Furillo and Faulkner of new, improved noses.

Billy Cannon broke the game open in the third quarter with an eighty-eight-yard catch-and-run for a touchdown. He was voted the game's most valuable player. How perfect can you get?

The Chargers' traveling press corps in Houston included three unfamiliar reporters. They wrote for the San Diego newspapers. The day after the game, Furillo wrote that the San Diego writers "were convinced their city would be the new home of the Chargers." On the plane ride home, Hilton maintained the façade that L.A. was still in play for the '61 season.

It lasted another nine days. That's when The Steam Room reported that the move to San Diego "appears certain." Team spokesman Don Richman told Furillo that the Chargers had already checked out Balboa Stadium. It would be no problem to expand its capacity to 30,000.

Furillo got Lamar Hunt on the phone.

"I think the Chargers will have a much better chance of success there," the father of the AFL told the Steamer. "Besides, I think they can cash in on the large Los Angeles television market."

It was something the Chargers continued to do as late as 2015—more than twenty years after the Rams and, later, the Raiders in 1994, abandoned L.A. and left it without an NFL team.

On February 10, 1961, the AFL approved the Chargers' move to San Diego from Los Angeles. Bud Furillo did not write the story—the paper ran a three-paragraph wire story. The Chargers had moved on.

So had the *Herald Express*, and so had The Steam Room. There was a new underdog team in town, this time playing American League baseball, and Furillo had been assigned to cover it.

•   •   •   •   •

L.A. may have lost the Chargers, but it won the honor of hosting the first Super Bowl ever played.

There wasn't much competition. No other city wanted the first AFL-NFL championship game. The contest had been arranged in only a matter of weeks. The Coliseum was barely two-thirds full, with 63,036 in the stands on the afternoon of January 15, 1967, before the NFL champion Green Bay Packers stopped fooling around and belted out the AFL's Kansas City Chiefs, 35-10, to begin America's most-watched sporting tradition.

It might have been a lousy crowd and a lousy result for the AFL, but the real winners were the men who fathered the new league—Lamar Hunt, Bud Adams, Al Davis, Barron Hilton, and the rest. Now they had a merger deal that would lead to an immersion between the two leagues over the next four years.

A fourteen-and-a-half-point favorite, Green Bay didn't put the game away until a couple minutes into the second half, when an interception by Willie Wood set up the TD that shot the Pack out to an 11-point lead.

There had been a little controversy before the game over which ball to use, because the AFL's weighed in a little slimmer

OIL MONEY BUILDING CHIEFS INTO A POWER

JANUARY 7, 1967

If National Football League draft standards are any gauge, the American Football League team in the Super Bowl is one of supreme quality.

The Kansas City Chiefs have done the best job in the AFL of out-bidding NFL teams in the stud market. This is because Lamar Hunt, the Kansas City president, has a heart of gold. Also, he is in oil.

When Lamar lost $1 million in the AFL's first year of existence, his father, H. L. Hunt, who is not believed to be a liberal, was asked how long his son could continue in football.

"Oh, about 150 more years," drawled the senior Hunt. . . .

Of course it is an open secret that the Chiefs paid Mike Garrett $450,000 to sign with them instead of the Rams. Cut that in half and you are close to the money spent in bonuses for Otis Taylor, Aaron Brown, Bobby Bell, Buck Buchanan, and E. J. Holub.

Pete Beathard, Jim Tyrer, Ed Budde, and Johnny Robinson came to play only a wee bit cheaper. . . .

[Gale] Sayers and Ronnie Bull are the only first round choices the Chiefs have lost since they set up operations beginning in Dallas.

In Dallas, they were known as the Texans, but the name never caught on in that state—so they moved. . . .

A Green Bay scout who watched the Chiefs play their final league game said that the only appreciable difference he could see between the two leagues was in the cornerbacks. . . .

You can be sure [in the first Super Bowl] it will be exploited by Vince Lombardi.

than the NFL's. They agreed to let the Chiefs use the AFL ball when they were on offense and vice versa for the Packers. The Steamer reported that size didn't matter to Wood, an old pal who quarterbacked USC during the Trojans' historically bad '57 season.

"Willie Wood caught and discovered there wasn't much difference intercepting an AFL ball, which the Chiefs used, and the NFL ball, which he's been intercepting since 1960," Furillo wrote.

Maybe it was the league's skinny pigskin that made Kansas City defensive back Fred "The Hammer" Williamson feel like he had to compensate by putting on a pre-game macho act. Williamson had made a nickname for himself that year by busting up opposing receivers with forearm smashes to the head, way before there were any rules to protect helpless receivers from traumatic brain injury. He told the writers he'd be looking to lay a hammer on the Pack.

Fred's remarks caught his opponents' attention.

"We will test the Hammer," Green Bay fullback Jim Taylor said to the Steamer between snifters at the Stardust in Downey, where the Packer great stopped in for some practice ahead of the big game.

In the fourth quarter, Lombardi gave Taylor the ball on the famous Packers sweep. The Hammer came up to make the tackle. Somehow, Taylor's knee found its way into the Hammer's head. The collision knocked out Williamson and left him unconscious on the Coliseum turf for eight minutes.

The rout did not come as a surprise to the AFL commissioner, who negotiated for his side during the mid-'66 merger agreement.

Al Davis placed the Raiders in trust for four months in 1966 while he ran away to run the league. He had argued, unsuccessfully, against agreeing to the championship game so soon, saying that the AFL wasn't ready to challenge the NFL at the top, especially against the dominating Packers.

"I said it when we merged and I'll say it again now, it was wrong to start off with the Super Bowl," Davis said in The Steam Room. "We should have built up with exhibitions and interleague play so that the public would have gotten a truer picture of the comparative strength of the two leagues."

Davis's Raiders gave a stronger account against Green Bay in the next Super Bowl game before losing, 33-14. Then Joe Namath and the Jets shocked the world, and the Baltimore Colts, and the NFL's old guard, in Super Bowl III, 16-7.

On January 11, 1970, Kansas City proved the AFL was the better league when the Chiefs beat the Minnesota Vikings in Super Bowl IV, 23-7. The only problem for the AFL owners was that they had to pay the NFL's guys $18 million to prove it, which prompted the Steamer's suggestion of a refund after K.C.'s snuffing of the Vikings.

Even with the Chiefs' stomping of Minnesota, the Steamer reminded his readers that Kansas City only finished second in its division, to the Raiders, before beating them in the playoffs.

"You shudder to think what would have happened had the AFL sent its number-one team to the Super Bowl," he wrote.

The Chiefs held their victory party at the Royal Sonesta Hotel on Bourbon Street. Lamar Hunt threw it open and picked up the tab—a dangerous play down in the city that care forgot. He even welcomed kids off the street to enjoy the free champagne.

"Anybody who wants to come to this party is welcome," Hunt told Furillo.

The Steamer felt vindicated with the Chiefs' victory. There weren't a whole lot of writers like him who took the AFL seriously from the start, especially in established NFL towns, where honks for the old league didn't give the new one a chance.

Too bad for L.A., the Steamer wrote. It could have been part of the better league, if it hadn't pulled a snob job on the Chargers.

"The Chargers were supposed to be bush," he said. "The NFL said so. That made it so."

Now, the Steamer said, with the physical beating the Chiefs laid on the favored Vikings, "The con is over."

Chapter 5

BELINSKY SPRING

Somehow you get the impression pitcher Bo Belinsky isn't the type of rookie who came to camp with hayseed in his hair and a straw suitcase. He reported for a press conference in a $200 imported mohair suit, diamond ring, gold watch, and brown suede shoes. The twenty-five-year-old Angel newcomer was nine days late for spring training yesterday and ten minutes tardy for his interview. . . . Spring planting didn't delay the anxiously awaited arrival of the obscure southpaw, who claims the screwball is his best pitch. (Of course.) Instead, there was a "nineball" poolroom championship in his hometown of Trenton, N.J., and: "The Angels had to make an adjustment on my salary. We compromised."

—March 2, 1962

The occasion was Bud Furillo's exclusive interview with the eccentric as well as fashionable rookie left-hander who, in a few weeks, would become the most talked-about athlete in the country. Under the shadows of the San Jacinto Mountains, the Steamer pulled Belinsky away from the other beat writers to a place where the two of them could be alone, by the clear blue waters of the swimming pool at the Desert Inn Hotel and Resort in Palm Springs, for a one-on-one interview with the baseball club's new pitching curiosity.

It was the Angels' second year of existence, and Furillo had been chronicling Belinsky's lack of whereabouts for days. A pool hustler who worked the rails up and down the East Coast, Belinsky had always ranked baseball on the lower rungs of his life's priority list, below the green felt tables and the women who gravitated toward his strikingly good looks. The Steamer said Belinsky could pass for Tony Curtis—"maybe, if Tony were taller and a bit more sure of himself."

The sport that paid the rent always seemed to come second to Belinsky. In his six-year tour of the bushes from Brunswick, Georgia, to Aberdeen, South Dakota, to Knoxville, Pensacola, Amarillo, Stockton, Vancouver, and Little Rock, Belinsky had gained a reputation for fun and frolic, not to mention his evil ways with women. He also struck out 183 batters in 174 innings the year before in Little Rock, and the overseas scouting reports told of an impressive screwball that had emerged in his Venezuelan winter-league campaign.

The Angels noticed, and who couldn't use a left-handed pitching prospect—then, or in any era? So they took a flyer and drafted Belinsky out of the Baltimore organization for $25,000.

At the Desert Inn press conference, Belinsky told the Steamer how he hustled pool for a living, how he once broke his hand slugging a guy who tried to steal his trench coat, how he taught Chuck Estrada to throw a curve, how he was really a better pitcher than Baltimore ace Milt Pappas. It was only the idiot managers who kept him out of the majors, he said.

"All they ever told me was, 'Go do your running,'" Belinsky told the writers.

The pitcher popped a beer—an audacious move for a rookie. Then he popped former Oriole manager Paul Richard for his hurtful and dismissive treatment of the pitcher at Baltimore's spring camp a few years earlier.

"Paul Richards said one thing to me—'Maybe I'll see you again sometime,'" Belinsky told the writers.

Yeah, Furillo liked this guy. He tabbed him as a sharpie who would enliven the spring sporting pages of the *Herald Examiner*. Belinsky sure enough did, making his media presence felt almost immediately. Before Belinsky ever threw a pitch, he held out.

Once signed, he twisted with the hotties in the Palm Canyon Drive nightclubs. He barely made the team coming out of camp, but then won his first five starts—including a no-hitter, as the Angels made a move on first place on July 4 and stayed in contention past Labor Day.

Bo's fast start and speedier lifestyle made him a national overnight sports sensation. He bought a candy-apple red Cadillac and became a boy toy to Hollywood glamour like Tina Louise, Ann-Margret, and Mamie Van Doren. Lesser lovelies looking for a way to Bo sometimes tried to gain access by way of the Steamer.

"Try the Cocoanut Grove," Furillo directed one late-night caller, referring her to the nightclub at the old Ambassador Hotel, where Belinsky often partied.

The prime promoter of the Belinsky phenomenon, Furillo's own career rode the wake of the pitcher's. National scandal columnist Walter Winchell plugged Furillo. The night of Belinsky's no-hitter, the Angels broadcasters put Furillo onstage with the pitcher. The Steamer made public appearances with Belinsky, drove him around town. They partied together and chased women on the road together.

The Belinsky Spring, unfortunately, didn't survive the long baseball summer. Belinsky's legs were shot by July, and the 5-0 start deteriorated to 10-11 by the end of the season. He insulted the fans, got in trouble late at night, and made himself into a distraction. The next year, the Angels farmed him out. The year after that, he bloodied up a sportswriter in a hotel room in Washington, DC, and then the Angels got rid of him for good.

It may have been *adios* to Belinsky, but there was way more to the Steamer's baseball coverage than a left-hander with no focus to his game.

Baseball played right into the writer's wheelhouse—his love of the whimsical and eccentric. It bombarded him with characters. Not just the flower of a single spring, like Belinsky, but genuine articles, like Jimmy Piersall. Once institutionalized for shortcomings in his mental health, Piersall told Furillo the story of how he once hid behind the monuments at Yankee Stadium when Bobby Richardson stepped into the batter's box. The umps came out to see if maybe Jimmy could use some more time in the sunroom, to which Piersall—famed for crazy antics throughout his career, like coming to the plate once in a Beatles wig and playing air guitar with his bat—responded to the men in blue: "We always play him this way."

There also was room for real serious sports stuff. A year before he'd ever heard of Belinsky, the Angels beat put Furillo right in the middle of one of the biggest stories in baseball history.

It was the Angels' first year of existence in 1961, and New York Yankees sluggers Roger Maris and Mickey Mantle battled each other in a season-long competition to conquer one of the game's most cherished records. As the Angels beat writer for the *Herald Express*, Furillo observed eighteen Yankees games in the season of '61 when M&M chased Babe Ruth's mark of sixty home runs in a single season. In his out-of-town capacity, Furillo developed a level of trust with the sluggers, who were mostly wary of sportswriters. By the end of the year, they welcomed his presence—especially Maris, who took the Steamer's calls amid some of the most pressure-packed moments of the home run derby for the ages.

Furillo had the whole American League to choose from for story material, and a good chunk of the National, too, during spring training and All-Star games. Around the batting cages, in the clubhouses, on the field, and in the bars, Furillo stumbled across characters and legends of the game.

The night before the 1963 All-Star Game, he lit up the Theatrical Lounge in Cleveland with Cincinnati Reds manager Fred Hutchinson, former skipper of the Seattle Rainiers and a contact from Furillo's days of covering the Pacific Coast League. The two of them were joined by Ed Bailey, the San Francisco Giants' catcher slated to start the next day's game for the National League.

Bailey was having himself quite a night in the Theatrical, "pouring drinks down faster than Hutchinson and myself, combined," Furillo wrote in his memoirs. "I reminded Bailey that as the starting catcher, he had to play three innings for the Nationals. He drank like he didn't intend to play at all."

Another time, at the Boston Red Sox spring training camp in Arizona, Furillo encountered Ted Williams working with a left-handed hitting prospect who held the bat high as the moon. "Don't let anyone change your style," Williams told Carl Yastrzemski, one Hall of Famer to another, as reported in The Steam Room.

The next year, around the batting cage at the Polo Grounds in Palm Springs, Furillo listened and reported as Willie Mays screamed at Angels manager Bill Rigney for naming Ryne Duren as his starting pitcher.

SPLENDID SPLINTER "A STRANGE PERSONALITY"
AUGUST 4, 1961

BALTIMORE—With Ted Williams, it always pays to get a fresh introduction, even though you might have met him a dozen times previously.

I had one of Ted's best friends—mine, too—do the honors yesterday in Boston at a rally for the "Jimmy Fund," which supports children's cancer research.

Curt Gowdy, voice of the Red Sox, summoned The Splinter.

"Sportswriter?" Williams queried, gruffly. "Don't hold that against him, Ted," put in Gowdy. "He's a fine fella."

"Well, maybe there are a few good sportswriters," Williams estimated, with a hint of uncertainty. . . . "I know what you're going to ask. What do I think of Maris's and Mantle's chances to hit sixty homers. They have a heckuva chance, because of the pitching. . . . They should break Ruth's record and Ford should win thirty games,

because the good hitters are scarce, too." . . .

Dressed in his familiar, open-necked knit shirt and slacks, Williams seemed to be dying a thousand deaths as he sat in the glare of the television lights for the ceremonies conducted to boost his favorite charity. Two things in life relieve tension for the high-strung star. Swinging a bat at home plate or struggling with a game fish on his line.

When the speeches were over, he kidded Danny Kaye:

"You got those goofy sandals on, need a haircut—and they call me a lousy dresser. Wear a tie in this world and they forgive you for everything else."

Then, before you could say home run, he had rounded the press room and was headed back for the fishing boat.

A strange personality.

"Willie gonna be sick today," said Mays, who wanted no part of the vision-challenged right-hander who threw 100 mph, with little idea where the ball was going.

Mays had observed that Duren wasn't wearing his eyeglasses. No worries, Rig told Willie. Duren's switched to contacts.

"How do I know he got the right ones in the right eyes?" Mays responded, according to the Steamer's account.

Covering the Angels beat brought Furillo face-to-face with important figures of different sorts.

"Who are you rooting for?" the Steamer asked Marilyn Monroe, when she showed up at Chavez Ravine in 1962 for a charity event before an Angel-Yankee game.

"Both teams," Marilyn cooed.

She died of a drug overdose two months later. The Steamer's penetrating question was among the last she ever answered in this world.

Another morning in Palm Springs, the Steamer was munching a snow cone to cure a severe hangover as he made his way through the clubhouse and into the dugout. He looked up and saw former president Dwight D. Eisenhower, in only his second month out of office, sitting on the Angels bench, taking in an intra-squad game.

Stunned by the presence of one America's greatest living heroes, the Steamer fumbled his snow cone. It splattered at the feet of the general.

"Real poise, huh?" Furillo wrote in the next day's Steam Room.

•   •   •   •   •

From his beginnings on the Angels beat, it was the same deal for Furillo as it had always been for fifteen years in the newspaper business: work the old sources, develop new ones, gain and keep their trust, find the characters, uncover the great stories, and tell the hell out of them.

The Steamer knew Angels general manager Fred Haney from the PCL days. Chief among Furillo's new sources on the Angels was their balding, silver-haired field manager, Bill Rigney, a former infielder with the New York Giants who managed the team for four and a half seasons. For steering the Angels into a third-place finish in their second season, the *Sporting News* named Rigney its Manager of the Year.

"How does Rigney do it? Maybe with patience," the Steamer wrote about one of his favorite people ever in sports. "He believes in the twenty-five men who play for him more than their wives or mothers do. He may know in his heart that some of them can't play and never will be able to play and that he should ask for the truck to take them to El Paso. But he gives them the Irish con and eventually something happens."

CARD CHEATS NOT WELCOME IN RIGNEY'S CLUBHOUSE
FEBRUARY 26, 1961

PALM SPRINGS—Bill Rigney has nothing against the medical profession. But there are two types of "healers" he doesn't want in his Los Angeles Angel ranks. Those who know how to doctor a deck of cards, and chiropractors who can set the dice bones to their liking.

Rigney gathered his flock around him at the Polo Grounds to warn he doesn't want any crap-shooters or poker players hustling out of his clubhouse. . . .

It's likely some of the experiences he remembers when he skippered the [San Francisco] Giants are behind his crackdown on gambling.

A story was widely circulated a couple of years ago about how Willie Mays allegedly was taken for a bundle in a crap game. Not by his teammates, however.

"I know of a fellow who was hit so hard in a 'friendly' little poker game with his teammates that he had to sell a brand new car to bail out of his losses," Rigney recalled. "I don't think he ever did explain it at home." . . .

. . . The deep-throated growls are reserved for the player who gets sleepy after dragging in a big pot.

Insistence by the majority to "get even" keeps the pasteboards rustling on the blanket long after curfew.

"It's tough enough to win a ball game when your mind's on it, let along losing a night's sleep to jacks or better," Rigney philosophized.

This philosophy's so sound I pass.

Rigney served almost as a father figure to the writer.

"Somebody has to tell you about not wearing brown shoes with black suits," Furillo once wrote.

Rigney, in turn, spotted Furillo as somebody he could trust. They dined and drank together. Rig gave Furillo the heads-up on upcoming roster moves and gave him insights into his strategic thinking.

The Steamer praised and promoted Rigney. This being baseball, Furillo also had to second-guess the manager. Rigney understood that it was part of the game, and he was okay with it because Furillo was always up front with him.

Early in the 1963 season, the Angels rode a three-game losing streak into New York. Furillo and the depressed Angels manager made their requisite stop at Toots Shor's, where each ordered an "astronaut," a vodka-rum concoction sprinkled with soda water and apple juice. A man from Chicago named Stanley Brown took the stool next to Rigney at the circular bar. Brown mistook the skipper for the chewing gum magnate who owned the Cubs and asked "Mr. Wrigley" why the Cubs didn't play at night.

"Well, Stanley, I'll tell you," Rigney replied. "If we started playing night games in our park we might start drawing big crowds, and that's not our purpose at all."

Rigney, who had enough trouble handling his own club, turned to Furillo and remarked, "Now I have to explain the Chicago Cubs?"

Some forty players went to camp with the Angels in 1961, and Furillo went to work getting to know and write about as many as he could, including big first baseman Steve Bilko, who had set home run records for the old L.A. Angels minor-league team. It looked to Furillo that the hefty Bilko had dropped a few pounds from his minor-league days, and the first baseman confirmed that he was twenty pounds lighter after shoveling coal in the off-season near his hometown of Nanticoke, Pennsylvania.

It bugged Bilko, though, that everywhere he went, everybody asked him about his weight.

"It's like I was a freak or something," Bilko told Furillo.

It wasn't just the people from the coal regions of Pennsylvania who were concerned about Bilko's midsection. The day Furillo dropped his snow cone at Eisenhower's feet, Bilko dove headlong to stop a ground ball from going into right field. This prompted a comment from the special guest on the Angels bench.

"That'll take some pounds off the big boy," Eisenhower said, quoted in The Steam Room.

Probably the most meaningful story Furillo wrote all spring was the feature he did on Bob Cerv. It focused on how the outfielder hit thirty-eight homers, drove in 104, and batted .304 for the 1958 Kansas City A's, playing with a broken jaw that had to be wired shut.

"With some hard work, I got so good the umpires could understand me when I cussed them," Cerv told Furillo.

A month into the 1961 regular season, the Yankees traded for Cerv, because their emerging star in right field, Roger Maris, needed a pal. Cerv and Maris had played and roomed together in K.C. They lived only a mile apart and liked to go hunting and fishing together in the off-season.

Back in New York, Cerv would later vouch for Furillo and introduce him to his roomie, right when Maris and Mantle began hitting so many home runs.

•   •   •   •   •

Four games into the '61 season, Furillo got his first taste of the chase to break Ruth's record.

It was the first game of a doubleheader in Yankee Stadium, with barely 7,000 people in the big ballpark. First inning, one on, Mantle up. Batting left, against ex-teammate Eli Grba, a rightie, Mickey launched a rocket to right that soared into the upper deck—"a terrifying wallop," Furillo reported to his Los Angeles audience.

Four innings later, the Mick did it to Grba again. They were his second and third homers of the season.

Mantle was on a clip to double the Babe's mark of sixty, and it wouldn't be long until the words "record pace" became the most often-used phrase in the national sporting lexicon.

For his next-day's column, Furillo sought perspective from a fellow Hearst sportswriter, Til Ferdenzi, the longtime Yankees beat man for the *New York Journal-American*. The Steamer didn't have much choice but to get his stuff from another writer, because Mantle had become something of a crank with the press.

Ferdenzi had a fairly decent take on Mantle's quick start.

"This is the first time since 1956 he has started a season in perfect physical condition," Ferdenzi told the Steamer. "He hurt his left shoulder in the 1957 World Series when Red Schoendienst fell on him with his knee at second base. It's bothered him every year since then, even though he wouldn't admit it to anyone."

Ferdenzi told Furillo that Mantle cut down on his swing when batting left-handed, to ease the pain in his shoulder. He placed a whole new emphasis on wrist action.

"Mantle didn't seem to be in any pain when he swatted his two homers from the left side of Grba," Furillo wrote.

It bothered Furillo when he left the ballpark with nothing from the mouth of Mickey himself.

"Maybe he'll loosen up when we convince him in L.A. it's not our intent to chop him up the way New York writers have in the past," the Steamer reported.

Mantle's trip to L.A. in early May left him in no mood to talk. He came to town with nine home runs and left with just as many, despite the friendly confines of Wrigley Field, the little park in South-Central where the Angels played their first season. Its power alleys measured only 345 feet, yet Mantle failed to clear either of them in the series. Mantle went 0-for-13 over the three games, two of which the Angels won.

"Our little park had their sluggers swinging a little harder, and it killed them," Rigney chortled in The Steam Room.

Not so much for Maris. He slugged two homers in the series, to give himself three on the season.

By the time the Angels returned to New York for a June series, Maris and Mantle had begun to get serious. They each had eighteen homers. With the Angels in town, Roger took the lead over Mickey, with two pops to Mantle's one.

Furillo still couldn't get Mantle on the record. But with Bob

Cerv's help, he broke through with Maris, getting a few moments in the dugout during batting practice the last day of the series.

"It's nice to have my old roomie with me again," said Maris, who had hit thirteen home runs in the twenty days since the Cerv trade. "He keeps me loose with his chatter."

Maris held the lead, 27–22, when the Yankees returned to Los Angeles in late June. This time, Mantle solved the complexity of little Wrigley. One of the two he parked over the three games landed at the base of the light tower beyond the center field wall. It had to be at least a 430-footer, according to my own calculation as measured from the Living Room A.C.

Furillo didn't write about the M's during this three-game set. He focused instead on Whitey Ford, who would win the Cy Young Award for the Yankees. Ford won his thirteenth in L.A. on his way to a 25–4 record, thanks to manager Ralph Houk, who pitched him every fourth day. He pitched barely once a week under Casey Stengel, who "didn't waste Whitey on the tail enders," Furillo noted in The Steam Room.

In early August, going into the far turn of the season during the Angels' last trip to New York, it was Mantle setting the pace with forty-three home runs—nineteen games ahead of Ruth's schedule. Maris's forty-one kept him well ahead of where Ruth was running thirty-four years earlier.

Furillo decided to make his move on Mantle. He broke away from the pack to have a chat before BP.

"Mickey's jaw tightened as I approached him in the batting cage," The Steam Room read on August 8. "He braced for a remark about the record."

The Steamer threw Mickey a changeup.

"'So what's new?' I asked him."

The question in the cauldron of Yankee Stadium tension loosened Mantle up a bit. He didn't say much, just mumbled some stuff about how the Triple Crown and how winning it in 1956 was more important to him than breaking Ruth's record. At least it was something.

Maris joined the conversation, and Furillo found himself in a one-on-two with the most sought-after pair of interviews in

American sports. The two acknowledged that they were pushing each other for the record.

"If Mickey hits eighty home runs, I hope I hit eighty-one," Maris told Furillo.

"Competition helps," Mantle added.

The Yankees swept the series, although neither M scaled the Yankee Stadium walls. Maris, however, drove in a run with a surprise bunt. With two outs in the third inning of the first game, with Bobby Richardson on third for the Yankees and the Angels leading 1-0, Angels third baseman Eddie Yost stationed himself deep behind the bag and well off the line. Richardson had no idea the safety squeeze was coming, but he made it home easily as the muscular Maris pushed the record out of his mind and the ball into the empty infield space vacated by Yost. The run tied the game and got the Yankees rolling toward the series sweep.

"The kid from Kansas City showed he's a team man first," Furillo wrote about Maris's well-placed bunt. Maris told him further, "I'm not feeding you a line that both Mantle and I want to help win a pennant for Ralph Houk more than anything else. That's our principle aim, not any records."

No doubt the Steamer believed Maris, especially Roger's remarks about the affection they shared for "The Major," the new Yankees manager. Furillo checked with Cerv, who confirmed that Maris didn't show much obsession with the record, at least on the outside.

"He never brings it up, even when we're alone," Cerv assured Furillo. "The extent of our conversation is what late movie to watch on television."

•   •   •   •   •

In between the Yankees games and the home run race, the Steamer found himself both entertained and tortured by the Angels' sometimes bizarre inaugural season.

Jimmy Cannon bet John Hall that the Angels wouldn't win fifty, but they surprised the baseball world by winning seventy-one in '61, and they did have five players who hit twenty or more home runs each, and they did help set a major-league record for the 248 balls batted over the outfield walls of their home park of Wrigley Field. The record for homers for a season in one stadium stood for thirty-five years until the major leagues moved into the thin air of Denver.

On their first road trip of the season, rain, snow, and cold forced postponement after postponement. The cancellations forced the Angels to play a twenty-seven-game, seven-city road trip that lasted from May 30 to June 18. It featured seven doubleheaders in one eleven-day period. On a June 8 doubleheader in Boston, the teams played to a 4–4 tie in the second game before it got rained out at 1:18 AM. It would be replayed in its entirety the same day, in another doubleheader.

"If you can pitch," Furillo wrote in his game story, "fly into Boston and you might get a start tonight."

If the Hall of Fame is interested in a depiction of baseball at its worst, the Cooperstown archivists might want to retrieve film of the July 21, 1961, game between the Angels and the Washington Senators at Wrigley Field. That's the night the two clubs sent a combined 105 batters to the plate, a new major-league record. The Angels pitchers walked twelve, the Senators eight, and they hit two. Six batters reached base via error.

The crowd of 6,914 began to leave in the fourth inning "in search of a pastime other than the national one," the Steamer wrote.

Tucked into a working-class residential neighborhood, the action on the streets of South-Central sometimes made its way into Wrigley, like the time a football flew in from Forty-First Place, over the left field fence. No problem for Kansas City A's center fielder Bobby Del Greco. He retrieved the ball and punted it back where it came from, "moving him within seven games of Red Grange's pace," the Steamer reported.

Now, the '61 Angels could score (744 runs, fourth in the league), hit home runs (189, second), and strike out (1,068, first). They also could give up home runs (180, first) and a hell of a lot of walks (713, first). They also led the American League in kicking the ball around, committing 192 errors (first) and compiling a fielding percentage of .969 (last).

Perhaps the defensive lowlight of the Angels season occurred on August 16, in the nation's capital. With the Angels
leading 2–1 going into the bottom of the ninth, Senators outfielder Marty Keough pleased the Griffith Stadium crowd of 3,497
when he clipped L.A. ace Ken McBride for a one-out single.
First baseman Bud Zipfel, a .200 hitter on the year, followed with
a walk. Out comes Rigney. Out goes McBride. In comes relief
pitcher Jim Donahue, who does his job. He popped up one guy
and got pinch hitter Jim King to roll a grounder to third, where
Eddie Yost had just come in for defensive purposes. Easy toss to
second, and the game's over.

But . . .

"Instead of hitting Rocky Bridges's glove to force Zipfel,"
Furillo wrote, "Yost aimed for right fielder Albie Pearson and hit
him on one bounce. Keough scored the tying run. But the cause
wasn't loss. Pearson is going to throw out the daring Zipfel at
third with ease, if he throws to third base. What did Albie do?
He heaved the ball into the Angel dugout."

Pearson's throw went directly to McBride, who had remained
on hand to watch the finish. Having left with the lead, McBride
fielded his tenth loss of the season, as Zipfel was awarded home
with the winning run.

The dispassionate McBride "stuffed it in his pocket and
headed for the clubhouse," the Steamer wrote.

•   •   •   •   •

Maris had regained the home run lead from Mantle, 49–46,
when the pair returned to Los Angeles on August 22 for a three-
game series—the last of the season between the Yankees and
Angels.

The first night in town, Maris made it fifty with a 420-foot
drive to straightaway center.

For the next day's *Herald Express*, the Steamer recounted
his conversation with Roger.

"Only eight other players in history have hit fifty or more
homers in a season," the Steamer reminded Maris.

"I thought it was seven," Maris responded. "It really doesn't make any difference."

The Steamer called Roger on his false modesty, saying, "Come on now, you know it does matter."

"He grinned, without saying anything," the Steam Room reported. "He felt better when he saw that Mickey Mantle seated close by was grinning, too."

The next day around the batting cage, Casey Stengel—who had been fired the year before because the Yankees had only won the American League pennant and not the World Series—came down from his Glendale mansion to say hello to the boys. Mantle cracked one in BP that made Stengel gulp. "Look out for that one," he said, within earshot of the Steamer. "It's across the street."

Cleveland Browns owner Art Modell, whose football team was in town for an exhibition against the Rams, also took in the pregame show around the cage. Modell told Furillo that Maris and Mantle could put $50,000 in their pockets right away if they signed a candy deal with M&Ms. Modell sighed at how much Joe DiMaggio had left on the table when his hitting streak stopped at fifty-six. "If he had made it to fifty-seven, the Heinz Company would have made him president," Modell told the Steamer.

Falling behind in the assault on Ruth with the season nearing its final month, Mantle showed signs of strain.

"Mantle was so upset about not hitting any home runs in the last stand here that he gave his hat a frightful toss after smashing a clean single," the Steamer wrote. "Mantle and Maris may not want to talk about Ruth's record, but they're thinking about it."

Mantle fell off as September wore on, and the competition became Maris vs. Ruth vs. 154 games. Baseball commissioner Ford C. Frick said that if Maris tied or broke the record in the expanded season of 162 games, he'd put an asterisk next to the mark in the record books.

It almost became a moot point on September 20. Maris went into the 154th game with fifty-eight home runs, and in the third inning, he hit his fifty-ninth. In the seventh, he ripped one down the line to right.

Bud Furillo watched on television from the press box in

Detroit, where the Angels were playing the Tigers.

"There it goes!" screamed former Tigers great Hank Green-berg, as the L.A. and Detroit writers jumped.

"Go it did," Furillo wrote, "but it hooked ten feet foul."

Maris then struck out, setting the stage for the asterisk.

From Detroit, the Steamer called the Baltimore hotel where the Yankees were staying. He paged Bob Cerv, his trusty Maris go-between. Maris picked up the page.

"Would you rather talk to Cerv or me?" he asked Furillo.

They chatted some, and Furillo told Roger it looked to him like the outfielder had dabbed moisture off his face when he returned to right field after the strikeout. Was he crying?

"I was just wiping off pressure that has built up for the past few months," Maris said.

Furillo's column noted that, coming into the 154th game, one of Maris's home runs had been taken off the board earlier in the year due to a rainout.

As Maris caught and passed Ruth over the eight extra games, The Steam Room came out in opposition to the asterisk.

"If Ruth had to play under the same conditions, he would appreciate what Maris has done," Furillo wrote. "Do you think he had sixty or seventy writers bugging him every day about how many homers he was going to hit? Did Ruth ever have to go from night game to day game and from doubleheader to doublehead-er the way Maris did in the expansion season?"

There will never be another Bambino, Furillo wrote, "but don't underestimate the crew-cut blond who worked against tre-mendous pressure to surpass him."

•   •   •   •   •

Even with his mohair suit and brown suede shoes, the Angels damn near ran Bo Belinsky out of Palm Springs in the time it took him to schmooze up the writers around the swimming pool.

Soon after the press conference, Belinsky met with Angels GM Haney and refused to sign his contract, then took his com-plaint to The Steam Room, which was first with the story on the rookie's holdout.

The Angels had offered him the major-league minimum—$6,000, Furillo reported—with a promise to bump it to $7,000 if he lasted a month. Belinsky, however, decided he needed a few dollars more.

He told the club the sweetener needed to be increased to $8,500.

"Bo came to camp talking as if he had given Warren Spahn lessons," the Steamer wrote. "Now he was the persecuted player caught up in the slavery system of baseball."

Angels traveling secretary Tommy Ferguson gave Belinsky the team management's view on baseball labor relations, handing him a one-way ticket out of town on the 5:10 Greyhound.

"I told Ferguson, 'Are you serious or delirious?'" Belinsky said to Furillo.

The answer would be the former.

"They told me I couldn't work out with the boys anymore because I wasn't signed," Belinsky said. "Some guy came up to me in the clubhouse and practically tore the uniform off my back. I don't know what they did with the number thirty-six. I don't think they retired it. I think they burned it."

All he wanted, Belinsky told the Steamer, was "to make enough money so I don't pitch myself into a bag of bones playing winter ball to make ends meet. I never would have flown out here if Mr. Haney hadn't told me I'd get the extra dough."

Haney, in his Milwaukee days, had been around greats like Spahn, Henry Aaron, and Eddie Matthews. And an unheard-of rookie was trying to hold him up?

"I didn't make him any promise of a bonus," Haney said. "A deal's a deal."

The Steamer worked the middle. Look, he told the Angels in his column. There's a market for his arm. The Mets want him, and maybe the Reds, too.

Furillo also advised the young pitcher to be patient. The money would be there if he produced.

Belinsky calmed down. He would not be on the 5:10 to nowhere. All he had to do now was prove himself.

On the mound, he flashed the new screwball he'd learned

in Venezuela and showed a good fastball. Control was an issue, but it was clear he had a major-league arm.

He could also handle himself on the dance floors of the Coachella Valley, The Steam Room noted, as the pitcher did a fine job emulating Chubby Checker on the Palm Canyon Drive club crawl.

More running and less late-night twisting and maybe Bo could have kept his spring ERA below 10.00. Maybe he would have struck out more batters than he walked.

With his numbers so bad, there was a real question of whether Belinsky would make the team.

According to Bob Rodgers, the Angels catcher, it was Bud Furillo who talked Rigney into giving the last chair in the bullpen to Belinsky.

"Bud said, 'You're not going to win anything anyway, so you might as well have somebody on the team who is a character, who can get you some publicity,'" Rodgers said.

Whatever the reason, Belinsky made the trip west through San Gorgonio Pass as the Angels broke camp.

Six games into the season, lefty Ted Bowsfield came up sore, so Rigney gave the start to Belinsky. Bo turned in six solid at Chavez Ravine to beat Kansas City—his first major-league victory and the Angels' first in their new rental, the landlord being Dodgers owner Walter O'Malley.

Furillo and Belinsky celebrated at the Thistle Inn, a nightclub in nearby Silver Lake. Proprietor Andy Spagnola, the Steamer's favorite bartender, popped the cork on a bottle of champagne.

"You'll always be the first guy who won for the Angels in Chavez Ravine," Spagnola told Bo.

Belinsky called his father, Ed, a TV repairman back in Trenton. The Steamer eavesdropped.

"Don't worry, I'm staying clean," The Steam Room reported from Bo's end of the conversation. "I'll give it a good shot this year . . . What do you mean I'll get in trouble with the girls? I told you not to worry . . . Go over to Jake's and have one on me."

Inspired by his victory, Belinsky bought a Cadillac, on time. He named it "Kitty Kat."

Next time out in the Ravine, he won again, going all the way with a four-hitter and eight strikeouts to beat the Indians.

In the Cleveland rematch, the Indians banged Belinsky around a bit, but Leon Wagner bailed out Bo with two home runs that covered a combined 880 feet. Ryne Duren struck out four in relief and Belinsky was 3-0.

The May 5 no-hitter against Baltimore came on a calm, clear, and cool spring night in front of 15,886 fans in Los Angeles. It was the first no-hitter in the American League since 1958. It made Belinsky the king of Los Angeles, and the Steamer was his prince.

Writing on a tight Saturday night deadline, Furillo couldn't do much more than report the basic facts. Belinsky struck out nine, walked four, only allowed four balls out of the infield, and popped up the Orioles' Dave Nicholson to end the game.

"I wonder how Paul Richards liked that," Furillo quoted Bo in his game story. The former Orioles manager had since moved on to Houston.

On the post-game show, Angels radio man Buddy Blattner screamed, "Get Bud Furillo in here!" to share the stage.

The next week, the Los Angeles City Council passed a resolution to commemorate Belinsky's accomplishment. He arrived fifteen minutes late for the ceremony, blaming his chauffeur—a Mr. Bud Furillo—for the delay. They'd first stopped to get the Caddy lubed and to renegotiate Belinsky's deal on the car. He traded in his no-hit ball for ten free payments—a $1,060 value, according to The Steam Room.

From City Hall, they were off to Scandia, a popular restaurant on the Sunset Strip. On the way, Belinsky told Furillo, "I need a business advisor." The Steamer would later introduce him to L.A.'s leading celebrity lawyer, Paul Caruso.

Belinsky ran his streak to five the next Friday night. He pitched into the eighth and struck out eleven to beat the White Sox.

A twist party followed at the Thistle Inn. The celebrants included Mr. and Mrs. Bud Furillo, actor Macdonald Carey, actress Jane Greer, and columnist Walter Winchell, who had

NO-HIT BALL HELPS PAY FOR BELINSKY'S CADDY
MAY 10, 1962

The zany monster telephoned at 7:30 yesterday morn. . . .

. . . In dictatorial fashion, Belinsky requested, "I would like it very much if you would drive me to City Hall this morning. Be here in a half hour." . . .

An obedient slave to pitchers of no-hitters and just about anyone wishing a ride to City Hall, I was on time. The southpaw explained why he needed a chauffer:

"I'm taking the 'Kitty-Kat' back where I bought it for a lube job."

"Kitty-Kat" is Belinsky-ese for Cadillac. Big Mack Kozak, owner of Crenshaw Cadillac at Crenshaw and Jefferson, personally greeted Bo. A former lineman at Wayne University, Kozak rushed the pitcher with:

"What will it take for the ball you got after the final out in your no-hitter last Saturday?"

"Well, you're not going to get it for a lube," assured business-minded Bo. . . .

"Would you consider $1,060 for it?"

Belinsky swallowed his gum, causing his words to stick together.

"Con-consider it? I'd throw in my glove."

"Your payments on the convertible are $106 a month," Mack reminded Bo. "I'll give you a check for the next ten on the ball."

Counting months on both hands, Belinsky grinned:

"No payments until February? It's a deal." . . .

"Pitch another no-hitter Friday night and I'll make ten more payments for you." . . .

"At this rate, I'll be out of the woods with just two more no-hitters."

For his first one, politicians tickled his ego for three-quarters of an hour, after he showed up fifteen minutes late at City Hall. Bo blamed the driver.

been on hand a week earlier for the no-hitter. The same night, Belinsky met Ann-Margret, his first prominent dating interest. From the Thistle Inn, it was over to Caruso's for some later-night entertainment.

The Steamer's chauffer service ran again that night. When Caruso's shut down with the rising of the sun, the driver must have decided it was too far out of the way to run Belinsky to his motel pad on the hill behind the House of Serfas, where he was living for five dollars a night. Instead, the Steamer drove him home to Downey.

My older brother and I had a 9:00 AM Little League game the next morning, a Saturday, and we had to be at the park by 8:15. When I got up to make myself a bowl of cereal, I saw my dad and my mom passed out on the living room couch. Neither moved when I nudged them, but I was not alarmed. We'd seen this sort of thing before as part of our early childhood education.

We found out about our overnight guest when we peeked in my parents' bedroom and saw Belinsky asleep on the bed. He woke up to the half-dozen Furillo squirts staring at him. He waved politely and shielded his eyes from the morning light.

This was something the neighborhood had to see—the sports celebrity of the week asleep in our parents' bed. The parade formed at the front door, and my sisters charged a dime each.

•   •   •   •   •

Belinsky and the Steamer didn't know it at the time, but as they fought through their Saturday morning hangovers, their relationship—not to mention Belinsky's pitching career—had reached highest water.

By current journalistic standards, some might sniff that this relationship challenged the bounds of appropriateness, with the Steamer committing the crime of trolling for chicks with Belinsky in the bars of Washington, DC, and bringing their catch back to the hotel lobby like fish on a string. Neither was exactly into Jack LaLanne, but once in a while the two ran outfield laps together when the team was on the road—another indictment of Furillo's inability to maintain his journalistic neutrality.

As a result of these ethical breaches, Furillo remained Belinsky's go-to beat writer to whom he fed his lines, like the time when a Boston paper called him "Bright Lights Belinsky."

"They don't have to worry about any in this town," Belinsky told The Steam Room, about blue-lawed Boston. "The last bright light they had here was the lantern in the Old North Church."

Soon enough, Belinsky traded in The Steam Room for the column space of Walter Winchell, who stepped in as Belinsky's

social director. He also served as Bo's unofficial procurer, turning over to the pitcher his telephone book filled with the numbers of hot young starlets.

The syndicated Winchell was in the latter years of a career
that made him one of the nation's leading radio and print commentators. Millions also knew Winchell as the narrator of the hit
TV show *The Untouchables*.

In mid-June, Walter took Belinsky and another far-more-tal-
ented Angels pitcher, rookie right-hander Dean Chance, to a
party at the Cocoanut Grove. Afterward, they detoured to singer Eddie Fischer's agent's house. When they left that affair at
five o'clock in the morning, Belinsky, the swinging bachelor,
and Chance, whose wife was eight months pregnant, provided
friendly transportation to a couple of women they met at the
party. Authorities identified one of them as Bridgette Whittaker,
whom Winchell described as a one-time New York showgirl who
was the estranged wife of a wealthy Denver socialite. Winchell
named the other as Gloria Eves, the cashier at a Hollywood Boulevard steakhouse who had the further distinction of being the
former daughter-in-law of British Petroleum board director Sir
Hubert Heath Eves.

Furillo's page-one news story in the *Herald Examiner* on
June 14, 1962, reported that on the ride home, Belinsky and
Eves fell into a dispute.

"Bo," the Steamer wrote, "decided it was time for [the] lady
. . . in the back seat to take a cab. When Bo 'helped' the woman
from his car, she suffered the wretched accident of a cut eye."

A Beverly Hills policeman who saw the battle did not make
an arrest.

"The whole affair was an accident," Eves told Furillo, only
to change her story later, when she sued Belinsky for $150,000.

The Angels fined Belinsky and Chance $250 each for a cur-
few violation.

Going into the Eves bout, Belinsky had been the winner of
six out of eight decisions on the year. After the unfortunate encounter, Belinsky went 4–9 the rest of the way.

The Angels, though, heated up.

•   •   •   •   •

Toward the end of June, the Angels beat the Yankees for the first time ever in New York. They rode that success into Washington, DC, and a doubleheader win over the Senators on July 4 that sent them home on the airplane to L.A. in first place.

More than 2,000 fans and the house band from the Long Beach Elks Lodge No. 888 greeted the team at the airport.

Even Camelot took notice. They had a new team in DC, too, that wasn't doing so well.

"It would only be fair to give this team a saliva test before you vacate the capital," Pierre Salinger, President John F. Kennedy's press secretary and an old USF buddy of Pete Rozelle, told the Steamer. "After all, you started out the same time as the Senators. You're first and we're last."

Pitching, power, and defense put the Angels on top.

Their main man was Leon Wagner, the former San Francisco Giant and St. Louis Cardinal who hit thirty-seven home runs on the season and drove in 107 to finish fourth in the American League's MVP vote. Wagner shook his hips on every swing to generate energy straight from the seat of his pants to the barrel of his bat. The move accounted for the nickname Furillo laid on Wagner—"Daddy Wags." Leon put the tag to use when he opened up a clothing store in the Crenshaw District. It advertised, "Get Your Rags From Daddy Wags."

Pitcher Ken McBride won ten in a row at one point. Second baseman Billy Moran played fifty-eight straight without an error and started in the All-Star game over Bobby Richardson. First baseman Lee Thomas, later to become GM of the Philadelphia Phillies, hit .290 with twenty-six home runs and 104 runs batted in. Little Albie Pearson, who crouched his five-foot-six frame into an eighteen-inch strike zone, led the league in runs scored with 115. Catcher Bob Rodgers threw out forty-six percent of the runners who tried to steal on him and finished second to Tom Tresh of the Yankees in Rookie of the Year balloting. Bo's late-night understudy, Dean Chance, won fourteen with an ERA of 2.96.

The Steam Room called the Angels' move on first "the most fantastic sports story of the last decade, at least."

Their reign atop the American League lasted two days. In their first game home, against the Red Sox, Belinsky walked four of the first five batters he faced and didn't last an inning. The crowd booed Belinsky off the field, and Bo gave them the old up-yours.

The Steamer wrote, "I was sickened by the demonstration."

Suffering from a pulled hamstring, Belinsky had a 4:30 PM appointment the next week to meet Angels trainer Freddie Federico to get some treatment on the hamstring.

Belinsky showed up at 5:45, and Fred Haney went nuts. The GM pulled the Steamer aside.

"You've been pretty good to this kid ever since spring training," Haney told Furillo. "If you have any influence on him, tell him this is the last mistake I'll tolerate. One more and he's gone, understand? He has to decide between being Winchell's boy or a member of this ball club."

Belinsky did manage to keep his name out of the papers for a while. On August 29, The Steam Room even reported, "Belinsky went through the current home stand without a single reprimand by management."

The Angels continued to apply the shock to the rest of the baseball world, going into New York for a four-game Labor Day Weekend series against the Yankees in second place, only three and a half games out.

They split in New York and were still in it. By September 11, they elevated to eighteen games over .500. Then they lost twelve of their last sixteen to finish in third place, ten back of the Yankees, who would beat the San Francisco Giants for their second straight World Series title.

•   •   •   •   •

The next year's spring, Bo narrowed his playing field down to a special someone.

Mamie Van Doren had racked up an impressive list of B-movie credits. She sang at nightclubs and did legitimate theater. An attractive blonde with a nice figure and some talent, she gained some separation from the rest of the Belinsky pack.

Bud Furillo first noticed Mamie while she was sunning herself behind home plate at the Polo Grounds in Palm Springs, taking in the game while Houston nicked Bo for eight hits and three earned runs in six exhibition innings.

That evening, Belinsky stayed out past midnight to play in a charity pool tournament, "with Mamie chalking his cue," the Steamer reported. When Bo and Dean Chance showed up to the park three hours late the next day, manager Bill Rigney fined them $500 each.

Belinsky blamed the hotel operator for blowing his wake-up call.

"Despite her negligence," Furillo wrote, "the telephone operator wasn't fined by Rigney."

Word got out that Van Doren wasn't just another floozy. The Steamer made some inquiries and learned that Belinsky had proposed marriage. Belinsky confirmed the wonderful news to Furillo. But it didn't work out between the kids, and The Steam Room reported later that the engagement was off.

The failure of the romance affected Belinsky's concentration. On May 19, the Yankees knocked him out in two innings. Belinsky's record fell to 1-7 and his ERA rose to 6.39. Not even Furillo could keep those numbers in the majors.

The Steamer's scoop the next day reported that the Angels had optioned "the most celebrated losing pitcher in the history of the game," as Furillo termed Belinsky, to their Triple A club in Hawaii.

The 1963 Angels went on to prove that 1962 was a fluke. Wagner continued to hit, and Little Albie topped .300. But Moran and Thomas fell off badly. The Angels finished ninth.

Probably the season's low point came in the second game of a doubleheader loss in Cleveland, when the Indians hit four home runs in a row off relief pitcher Paul Foytack. Furillo reported that it got so bad, the exploding scoreboard in Municipal Stadium ran out of ammunition.

Late in the year, the Angels brought Belinsky back up to see if he'd been chastened by his two months in the Hawaiian paradise.

The answer was no. At least, he was not very cooperative when the club requested that he start one of the last home games of the season.

"Why should the Angels cash in after wrecking me financially for two months?" Belinsky told the Steamer. Bo was angry because the team refused to release, waive, or trade him when it exercised its option to send him to Hawaii.

Belinsky said he would only pitch out of the bullpen. He relented, though, a couple weeks later, agreeing to start against the Orioles despite the club's obvious intent to exploit his name for commercial purposes.

Bo pitched well in the 7–2 win over Baltimore. He went all the way for his second win of the year, a five-hitter in which he struck out six. Paid attendance was 476.

The next January, Furillo took Belinsky to lunch at the Brown Derby. He asked if Bo was embarrassed by the turnout.

"Not at all," Belinsky replied. "Four hundred of those people came to see me get beat. Otherwise, the crowd would have only been seventy-six."

•   •   •   •   •

The Steamer's days on the baseball beat ended in the spring of 1964, when George T. Davis died and Furillo was promoted to executive sports editor of the *Herald Examiner*.

His elevation deprived the Steamer from the daily observation of what remains as arguably the greatest season any pitcher ever had in the history of the Angels franchise. In 1964 on a mediocre team, Dean Chance accounted for twenty of the Angels' eighty-two wins, with an earned run average of 1.65. He threw eleven shutouts, including four against the league-champion Yankees. He won the Cy Young Award at a time when only one such trophy was distributed between the two major leagues.

Early on, Furillo spotted Chance as a nasty and dangerous man. Standing six foot three and weighing 200 pounds, Chance turned his back on batters and swooped in with a three-quarter delivery that terrorized right-handed hitters. Right, left, it didn't matter—he'd knock anybody down, even his own teammates in batting practice.

"If anyone dug in, Chance played spin the cap," Furillo wrote in a 1963 spring training column, about the pitcher's approach in the pre-season.

Chance angered Lee Thomas with his slow curve, and scared Leon Wagner with a fastball under the chin.

"They're big leaguers," Chance told Furillo. "I want to get them in shape for the real thing."

In August of Chance's Cy Young season, the Steamer wrote, "I've never heard anyone in the American League say he can't wait to grab a stick and rush up to bat against Chance. The hitters feel their blood run cold as Dean goes into the windup."

Chance protested to Furillo, telling him, "You've got me wrong. I've hardly knocked anybody down since the All-Star game."

Dean was on the mound the next year when the Angels and Red Sox locked up in what The Steam Room headline characterized as the "L.A. Worst Beanball Brawl."

"The umpires say Chance started the mess when he sent a pitch under Felix Mantilla's chin," the Steamer wrote. "You suspect Felix went back to the dugout asking [Boston pitcher Dave] Morehead what he was going to do about it."

Next inning, Morehead "cracked Jose Cardenal on the wrist," the column said. Chance retaliated by hitting Morehead, who made Jim Fregosi answer with a fastball to the ass.

Red Sox manager Billy Herman told The Steam Room that he absolutely instructed Morehead to uphold the dignity of the game, that it was a matter of mutually assured destruction when it came to Dean Chance.

"I've seen that guy knock down twenty-four of our guys over the last two years," Herman told Furillo. "He has to be stopped."

•   •   •   •   •

For the rest of The Steam Room era, the Angels struggled in the Southern California sports market. In 1966, they moved to Anaheim, and Furillo gave them some identity when he nicknamed their new ballpark "The Big A." They became the kings of Orange County.

Whitey Ford checked out the crowd in the Angels' first year of suburban operation "and noticed a stunning change," the Steamer wrote, from the movie star set that filled the box seats for Yankees games at Chavez Ravine.

"You don't get the same clientele here," Ford told the Steamer.

Jim Fregosi, the Angels' best everyday player in their first decade, also had a nice rip for the Orange County fans.

"The people of Anaheim never come out to see the Angels play," the six-time All-Star told Furillo in 1972, after he'd been traded to the New York Mets for Nolan Ryan (and Lee Stanton). "They come out to see the other team, or to look at each other. They don't identify with the players."

The same column noted that Fregosi still kept his house in Anaheim, even as he bad-mouthed it.

On the '72 trip to L.A. with the Mets, Fregosi invited his new manager, Yogi Berra, over to his place for dinner. Berra declined.

"I've seen Anaheim," Yogi told Fregosi, according to The Steam Room.

The Angels had a couple more winning seasons, in 1967 and 1970, challenging for first place into mid-August before fading.

Furillo turned hard against the franchise in 1969 when the Angels fired manager Bill Rigney, whom the Steamer described as "the best friend I ever had in baseball."

The Steamer liked Angels owner Gene Autry just fine. "The Cowboy," famed as a country-western singer and TV and movie actor, always made for a good drinking partner.

"It was high noon in the desert," Furillo wrote in a March 1967 column. "Two old timers, Gene Autry and the Steamer, plodded along in search of an oasis. 'There's one up ahead,' said Autry, pointing out the Cabellero Room at Melody Ranch." Autry owned Melody Ranch, a Palm Springs hotel where his team was then staying.

"They waddled through the double doors," the Steamer

continued, "to work out on some tomato juice seasoned with vodka. 'It sure beats sarsaparilla, eh, Gene?' I said. The Cowboy grinned his acknowledgment and grimaced from memories of 100 movies and thousands of shots of sarsaparilla."

Yeah, he liked Autry, but the Steamer also held the distracted Angels owner accountable for failing to improve the team. As early as 1962, when the second-place Angels flew east for the crucial late-season visit to New York, he blasted Autry and other high-powered team executives and stockholders for not making the trip. Autry, whose interests included hotels and radio and television as well as baseball, claimed business conflicts.

"Any business seems more important than the baseball business" to Autry and the others, Furillo wrote.

In 1966, The Steam Room poked the Angels organization for failure to adequately invest in its farm system. He knocked Autry directly in 1968 for not giving his front office any direction.

"Autry wields the power and everybody else is afraid to make a decision until he shows up," the Steamer wrote. "There is no telling when that will be because he wears so many hats. By the time he rides into Anaheim, things are usually in a state of complete chaos, as they are now."

When the Angels fired Rigney in May of 1969, Furillo reported the Angels had only had twenty-four men on a roster authorized for twenty-five. Inept upper management had gone twenty-seven days without filling the spot. He characterized the Angels farm system as "Tobacco Road."

"Absentee ownership," he wrote, "has victimized this club."

The Steamer, as sports editor, never wrote about the Alex Johnson love fest in Anaheim, leaving it to *Herald Examiner* beat writer Dick Miller to quote the 1970 American League batting champion as saying, "going to hell would be an improvement" over playing for the Angels.

Johnson made the comment a week after Miller reported that utility infielder Chico Ruiz had pulled a gun on Alex in the Angels clubhouse.

•   •   •   •   •

Bo Belinsky? His end with the Angels came in August 1964 at the Shoreham Hotel in Washington, DC, when he got a late-night call from *L.A. Times* beat writer Braven Dyer, who was in his cups. Dyer wanted to discuss an Associated Press story that said Bo was thinking about quitting baseball. An argument ensued, and Dyer headed to Belinsky's room to press the issue.

It wasn't long before Dyer, in his sixties, was on the floor and bleeding, either from a punch or a shove or a slap, possibly in response to an aggressive action by the writer. Next thing Belinsky knew, he was on a plane back to Los Angeles, suspended, and never to play for the Angels again. He spent the next six years going up and down with the Phillies, the Astros, the Cardinals, the Pirates, and the Reds before his major-league career ended in 1970.

The Steamer checked in with him on occasion, and vice versa. In 1967, with Belinsky in spring training with the Astros in Cocoa Beach, Florida, Furillo saw in the paper that Bo had tossed a few scoreless innings. Furillo called Belinsky's hotel room to congratulate him. A sweet Southern accent greeted him.

"Pardon me," the Steamer said. "I must have the right number."

In late summer of 1972, two years after Belinsky was out of baseball, Furillo reported that the pitcher, along with his old road dog, Dean Chance, was promoting a fight in Canton, Ohio, featuring heavyweight contenders Earnie Shavers and Vicente Rondon. At the time, Belinsky was going through a divorce with former Playmate of the Year Jo Collins.

"It's like an unconditional release," Belinsky told the Steamer.

Furillo's last column on Belinsky came in June of 1973, when he covered a press conference on the release of the Maury Allen book about the pitcher, entitled, *Bo: Pitching and Wooing*.

Belinsky showed he was twice as bad as he was at the press conference around the pool in Palm Springs eleven years earlier.

This time, he was twenty minutes late.

Chapter 6

CASSIUS CLAY CALLING

It's always a nervous situation to get a long distance telephone call from home in a foreign press box. This was the case at Metropolitan Stadium in Minnesota yesterday. You suspect the worst. Either the kids set fire to the neighbor's house, or the boss has put a torch to your name on the payroll. The caller identified himself: 'This is Cassius Marcellus Clay, the Great. Will you be here in time to witness the annihilation?"... The chat with CMC made it clear he's a distinct threat for Archie Moore's title as the world's heavyweight con man, but I've always been a sucker for brass chaps.

—April 16, 1962

The temperature hovered just above freezing and more than an inch of snow covered the ground outside the baseball park in Bloomington, Minnesota, where the Angels were beating the Twins, 6–3, in the Sunday afternoon finale of their 1962 season-opening road trip.

Suddenly, the press box phone rang. On the other end of the line was Cassius Clay, a young kid from Louisville who had ridden the rails into L.A. a few days earlier. He had achieved some recent success in his field and wanted to check in with Furillo to maybe get a mention in The Steam Room.

In his time, the fighter who would change his name to Muhammad Ali would see his name in the paper as much as any athlete ever. He'd generate love and hate and marvel like no man in the history of American sport. A born showman, his face sat right there at the top of the list of the most recognizable in his century—Ghandi, Churchill, Hitler, you name 'em. Kings and cripples would stand in his awe. He would be known, as he said, from the beaches of Miami, to the jungles of the Congo, to the sidewalks of New York, to the deserts of Arabia. He would challenge the most powerful government on earth and face its wrath—and in the end, earn its highest civilian honor, the Presidential Medal of Freedom.

But in early 1962, when he was still Cassius Clay, the future heavyweight champ still needed to work the street corners of L.A. to sell tickets to his upcoming fight with journeyman George Logan. The light-heavyweight champion of the Rome Olympics in 1960, Clay had won his first twelve fights as a professional, and his series of fights in Los Angeles in 1962 would further burnish his brand, get him some experience and help prepare him for his push toward the title.

Of course, Furillo would be there to see Clay knock out Logan in the fourth round at the Sports Arena the night of April 23, 1962, in front of 7,500 fans. The Angels kept the Steamer away from the Sports Arena the July 20 night Clay KO'd Alejandro Lavorante in the fifth in front of 11,500. But after the baseball game, Furillo hustled down from Chavez Ravine to the post-fight party at the Alexandria Hotel to get some one-on-one face time with boxing's star on the rise. The Steamer was back ringside the evening of November 15 when Clay flattened Archie Moore, the legendary light-heavyweight champ, inside four rounds, this time before a packed house of 16,200 in the same Sports Arena.

Post-L.A., the Steamer's personal contact with Clay cooled as the fighter beat Sonny Liston for the heavyweight championship, changed his name to Muhammad Ali, and refused induction into the United States Armed Forces. Still, the intergalactic celebrity put in a call every so often to Furillo to get a little space in The Steam Room, say, if the closed-circuit TV gate in Los Angeles needed a little stimulation.

Over the next eleven years, Furillo covered two of Ali's three fights with Joe Frazier, two more with Jerry Quarry, and two of the three with Ken Norton. On occasion, the champ saved a special greeting for the Steamer when he saw him. "Bud Furillo! Bud Furillo!" Ali screamed, as the Steamer and an entourage consisting of three of his kids entered a jam-packed hotel ball-room on the Las Vegas strip, where Muhammad was training for his 1972 fight against Jerry Quarry. Ali, between rounds in a sparring session, bolted toward my pop as if he was going to tear his head off. "No, champ, no," said assistant trainer Drew Bundini Brown as he held Ali back, with help from some other handlers. A tough-looking security force that covered the doors eyed us suspiciously.

I looked at my dad. He was cracking up with laughter. I guess he'd seen this sort of thing before.

Bud Furillo's coverage of Ali captured a great convergence of boxing history, with the Ali story patching into the tales of other champs of the era such as Floyd Patterson, Joe Frazier, George Foreman, and the fabulous Archie Moore, whom the Steamer loved, admired, and bathed in ink.

Like it did everybody in American society, the Muhammad Ali story challenged The Steam Room. It raised lightning-rod issues such as race, politics, religion, and war, the sharp-edged dividers of 1960s America. In his weaker journalistic moments, Furillo played to the jingoes. At his best, he made his readers aware of the shortcomings of stereotype. Always, he captured the sense of fun, and with Ali, you didn't need the Freedom of Information Act to find it.

•   •   •   •   •

George Logan once ranked as high as fifth in the world among all living heavyweights. Fighting out of Boise, Idaho, Logan put himself on the boxing map in 1959 when he knocked out the washed-up former champ Ezzard Charles. But Logan had lost three of his previous six coming into the Los Angeles fight with Clay. He never had a chance against the superstar on the rise, in a fight where everybody would have been better off if Logan had just taken a plea bargain. Clay chopped up Logan, but he never put him down, and the fans booed them both out of the ring.

With the fight not being much of one, the next day's Steam Room pretty much ignored it. Instead, Furillo focused on the vanity of the fighter who was about to emerge as the top sports figure of his generation.

"Using strokes more delicate than those with which he razored George Logan into fourth round submission, Cassius
Confidence Clay powdered his handsome features in a Sports
Arena dressing room," The Steam Room began. "He explained
between dabs of the puff: 'There are seven or eight pretty girls
waiting for me.'"

The day of the fight, Furillo reported in his column that
"the millionaires behind Cassius Marcellus Clay are delighted
with his teetotaling habits, but can't do much about the fighter's
strong attraction to the ladies." In later years, Ali's managers
had to carve libido time into his training schedule. *New York
Times* columnist Robert Lipsyte wrote in his 2011 memoirs about
how Ali, in the middle of a 1975 charity boxing tour in Florida,
emptied his entourage out of a motor home he used as a dressing room. Emptied it, that is, of everybody "except three foxes
he picked out of the crowd," Lipsyte wrote. When Ali made his
pick for an afternoon roll and ducked back into the van with his
selected fox, trainer Angelo Dundee asked Lipsyte not to write
about the encounter, and an unnamed press agent told the writer he'd never get another word with the champ again if he did.
Lipsyte ignored the admonition in a freelance piece he wrote
for the *New York Times Magazine*. Sure enough, he said in his
book, he never got another interview with Ali.

Lipsyte's reporting on Ali's sexual promiscuity came two
years after Furillo highlighted it in The Steam Room on June 13,
1973.

"There are three things that catch up with a fighter—wine,
women, and song," The Steam Room reported in its coverage of
Ali's signing for his second fight with Ken Norton in Los Angeles. "Muhammad doesn't drink and he can't sing."

Two years ahead of Lipsyte's magazine piece, the Steamer
used Ali's terminology of "the foxes" to describe the gorgeous
women who pestered the fighter. Ali "carries on, uh, conversations with them when he should be preparing for his combat ex-
aminations," Furillo wrote. "They exert a pressure on him that no
man could withstand, even the phenomenon who is Muhammad

Ali."

The night of the Logan fight, the Steamer stood with Clay and a small gaggle of writers while Cassius, after winning his fight, peeked through the stands on the ground floor of the Sports Arena to watch the crowd chaser. The number-two-ranked heavyweight in the world, Eddie Machen, was in the ring with Bert Whitehurst. Clay summarily dismissed Machen as "not good enough to fight me," Furillo reported. Cassius then returned to his dressing room for another workout with his mirror.

"I got to keep my good looks," Clay said to himself, examining a tiny scar above his right eyebrow while the Steamer watched and took notes.

Pretty as Clay was, his performance against Logan drew a sniff from Archie Moore, the sport's intellectual driving force as well as its light-heavyweight champion. Moore drove up from his ranch outside San Diego to observe the young fistic sensation. When it was over, Archie told the Steamer that boxing historians should put an asterisk next to Clay's prediction that he would knock out Logan in the fourth round.

"When you talk of knocking a man out," Archie said in The Steam Room, "you must at least knock him down."

Moore, of course, was the target of Clay's whole expedition to Los Angeles, the reason he came to town in the first place. At age forty-five (or forty-eight, depending on which reference source you prefer), Moore had already fought 217 times, knocked out 131 men, and boxed 1,467 rounds. Twice he battled for the heavyweight championship, losing in a classic to Rocky Marciano and a stinker to Floyd Patterson that was covered by the Steamer. He held the light-heavy title for ten years. You could argue that there were times over the previous decade when Archie was the best pound-for-pound fighter in the world. One more big purse—against Clay—and he could make the comfortable transition into his retirement years.

The night Clay bloodied Logan, Archie played it coy.

"In time," Moore said to the Steamer, regarding a fight against Clay. "He needs the proper buildup. Alejandro Lavorante is about his speed."

•   •   •   •   •

Apparently drunk in the euphoria of the Belinsky Spring, The
Steam Room was way off its fight-prediction game going into
Cassius Clay's bashing of Lavorante, a very large Argentine who
had once worked as a chauffeur for his strongman president,
Juan Peron.

Keep in mind that Furillo had correctly predicted a few
years earlier that Ingemar Johansson would knock out Floyd
Patterson in their first heavyweight championship fight. It was a
major upset. Then, in the rematch, the Steamer had flip-flopped.
He'd picked Patterson to regain the title, even though the smart
money was now on the Swedish slugger and his famed "toonder-
bolt" of a right hand, which had put Patterson on the deck seven
times in the third round of their first fight.

Furillo, who covered both New York fights, spent enough
time at Patterson's training camp in Newtown, Connecticut, before their second engagement to come away with the impression
that Floyd had become something of a fanatic about regaining
the championship. He predicted Patterson by a KO in the June
20, 1960, rematch at the Polo Grounds. The Steamer's selection
prompted Jimmy Cannon to chide him the day before the fight,
"What are you trying to do, embarrass your paper?"

Patterson, hurt in the second round, avoided the early knockout and then battered Ingo into unconsciousness with a leaping
left hook to win it in the fifth. So Furillo kind of knew what he was
talking about when it came to heavyweight fights—which made
his prediction of a Lavorante knockout of Clay inexplicable.

Lavorante had KO'd Zora Folley the year before at the Olympic Auditorium. It was an impressive outing for the Argentinian
hero. But c'mon, Steamer. Just four months earlier, they had tak-
en Lavo out of the Sports Arena ring on a stretcher after Archie
Moore got through with him. Lavorante had even lost to George
Logan three months before that.

The day of the fight, Furillo wrote that Clay was "the deserving favorite." The Steam Room noted that Clay had predicted a
fifth-round knockout, and that most of his forecasts turned out
just as he said.

"But you might be wrong tonight, handsome," Furillo said in his column. In its analysis of the Greatest's early professional career, The Steam Room detected that the brilliant young fighter seemed "easily stunned by a solid punch." Reason being, the Steamer said of the most talkative boxer ever, "His mouth flies open."

"If Lavo lands his lethal right, it could be a good night," Furillo wrote.

Covering the Angels game in Chavez Ravine against Cleveland the night of the fight, the Steamer hoped his pal, starting pitcher Ted Bowsfield, would live up to his reputation as a quick worker. Bowsie told the Steamer he'd do his best to get him out in time for the ten o'clock bell for round one.

"I don't want you to miss that fight," Bowsfield said in The Steam Room. "Get me a ticket. If things go right, I'll shower, shave, and join you before the fifth round, if it goes that far."

You can imagine how the Indians appreciated those remarks. Clay's fifth-round prediction held true, but the Indians bettered it by scoring a TKO over Bowsfield in the third. The Steamer worked all nine innings in what turned to be a two-hour-and-fifty-three-minute game. It wrapped up well after Clay had put Lavorante to bed.

With the fight over, Furillo rushed down the hill to the Alexandria Hotel on Fifth and Spring to personally apologize to Clay for the insane prediction published in the paper that day. Cassius "graciously" accepted, The Steam Room reported. Even though he was a bit tired after his night's work, Clay sat down with Furillo to map out an itinerary toward the title.

"If you insist, the plan is this," Clay told the Steamer. "I should like Archie Moore to be the next rolling stone to gather canvas moss."

Problematically, Clay informed Furillo, Archie was demanding $1 million, which was only a little less crazy than The Steam Room's prediction of a Lavorante victory. There would have to be some negotiation on the issue of Moore's pay. Looking even further into the future, Clay nestled a coffee cup into the hands that had just defeated the hope of l'Argentina. He massaged the cup as if it were a crystal ball.

"Here's how I rate my possible opponents and their longevity," the soothsaying Clay told the Steamer. "Moore will fall in three rounds. Johansson's turn will come in the seventh round. Cleveland Williams could go in five and Machen, six. For the moment, I wish to rest. Visit with my fans and see lots of people who have never met me and want to meet me. They will see the other side of Cassius Clay. When I'm not fighting, I'm an ordinary guy like anybody else. I'm a nice, friendly boy and very playful. I'm crazy about children. Every time I see any of them, I want to pick them up and hug them."

The guest list at the Clay victory party at the Alexandria included a Mr. Archie Moore. Furillo sought out the Ol' Mongoose for comment.

"I must fight this boy because he demands it," Moore told the Steamer. "I believe in live and let live. But if he wants to die, who am I to delay the execution?"

Archie grabbed the Steamer by the arm and gripped it tightly, Furillo wrote, as if "to divulge a secret."

"Seriously," Moore said. "I am working on a new punch. You're the first to learn this. It is called . . ." Archie paused for effect before finishing: "The lip buttoner."

•   •   •   •   •

Back in the '50s, when Sugar Ray Robinson's manager, Ernie Braca, had young Bud Furillo under his New York wing, the bookie of Broadway introduced the L.A. writer to a cool cat of a light-heavyweight named Ernest "Tony" Anthony. The Steamer took a liking to the good-looking prospect who, besides fighting, also played trumpet well enough to gig some decent clubs in the world's greatest jazz town.

Furillo, in his pre-Steam Room days, built up Anthony the same way he would five years later with Bo Belinsky. Fighting out of New York, Anthony knew his way around the ring some, too, pushing his record to a respectable 31–4–1 against good competition. Braca talked and Furillo wrote about blowing Tony up into a heavyweight and putting him in the ring with Patterson, who beat Archie Moore for the title Rocky Marciano vacated.

First, they thought it would be a good idea for Anthony to win the light-heavy title, so Braca signed him for a September 20, 1957, championship fight against Moore in the Olympic Auditorium. It turned out that Archie had more trouble with the scales than Anthony. He needed to visit them six times to make the 175-pound weight limit. Then he took Tony out in the seventh.

Furillo didn't get to see the fight because his Trojan football beat took him up to Multnomah Stadium in Portland, where the Beavers shut out USC's worst team ever, 20-0.

In the pre-fight hype, Furillo gained his introduction to the erudition of Archie Moore. A month before the bout, Moore invited the press to a barbecue at his training camp in the mountains forty miles east of San Diego. It was here that Furillo gained a first-hand observation of Moore's potentially problematic issue with weight, which the fighter insisted he controlled with a secret diet.

"Fat men of America, rejoice," the pre-Steamer wrote in an August 25, 1957, story for the *Herald Express.* "This diet is unbelievable. I watched Archie sit down to put away two pounds of barbecued ribs, a half a loaf of French bread, a half a pint of potato salad, and a quart of ice tea. Moore polished off the feast in seven minutes. 'That's about as much time as I'll need to chew up Anthony,' Arch smiled."

A great reporter ready in any circumstance to fire a tough question at anybody, Furillo asked Moore how much he weighed.

"I didn't throw this party to be ridiculed," the champ replied.

After the barbecue, Furillo wrote, "Arch poured himself into his custom-made $28,000 Jaguar, sped home, and jumped rope to the accompaniment of Ben Webster's incomparable tenor sax. Some routine, eh?"

Once situated in The Steam Room, Furillo found it to his advantage to stay in close touch with Moore, and Archie found the column to be a fine outlet to strike back at the injustices propounded by boxing's sanctioning bodies, especially when they sought to strip him of his title. Anthony Maceroni, a Providence, Rhode Island, mortician who had once served as president of the National Boxing Association, threatened to lift Moore's light-heavy crown in early 1960 for not defending it frequently enough.

"What's that undertaker trying to do, kill me?" Moore said to the Steamer.

The champ thought about it a second, then saw how his death might register as a conflict of interest for Maceroni, a man who put bodies into the ground for a living. Archie told the Steamer how he would foil the obvious plot.

"Before he gets my business," Moore said, "I'll have myself cremated."

Maceroni's group did eventually take away Archie's championship, but nobody really noticed. The New York State Athletic Commission and *Ring* magazine, both of which surpassed the NBA in sanctioning prominence, continued to recognize Moore—and continued to recognize him even after Archie, in his travels through Europe, dropped a non-title ten-rounder in Rome to Giulio Rinaldi.

Furillo caught a nice break when Rinaldi and Moore met again in New York for Archie's belt on June 10, 1961. On the road with the Angels the weekend they played the back-to-back doubleheaders in Boston, he didn't have to cover the second one, because it took place on a Saturday and the *Herald Express* didn't publish on Sunday. So while the baseball team labored through another eighteen innings in Boston, he skipped town and flew ahead to New York to see the Moore-Rinaldi rematch. Archie won a unanimous decision to retain his title, with the judges scoring it 9–5, 11–4, and 11–3.

The Steamer's card weighted more in Archie's favor. According to the Monday Steam Room, Moore "baked Giulio Rinaldi's face in an oven of gloves for forty-five minutes to convert it into pizza, heavy on the sauce."

He watched the fight ringside with Toots Shor, Rocky Marciano, and Don Ameche, the actor whom the Steamer knew as the owner of the old Los Angeles Dons professional football team that the humble Ameche had named after himself. After the seventh round, Marciano thought he saw a decisive turn of events in Signor Rinaldi's favor. Rocky pronounced to the foursome,

"Moore's all through."

Having once knocked Archie out, you'd think Rocky's observation would have caused heads to nod in studied agreement. Instead, it elicited scorn from the renowned bartender in the group. No sooner had Marciano offered his insight than Shor, according to The Steam Room, turned to Ameche and said, "Double our bet. I never saw a fighter who knew anything about fights."

Furillo attended the post-fight press conference when Moore told boxing writers, "I was determined to give this young man a lesson because of what happened in Italy last [October]."

It wasn't so much that he had lost a non-heavyweight championship fight for the first time in nine years, Archie said. It was the racket the Rinaldi fans made when they celebrated his victory.

"When he went home to Anzio, they rang church bells all night long," Moore said. "They kept me awake."

Having been to Italy, the Steamer pointed out to Archie that Anzio is actually 125 miles from Rome, where the fight was held.

"That's right," Moore responded. "Rome is quite a distance from Anzio. But there is a valley that runs between the cities through which sound traverses. And I sleep with my windows open."

•   •   •   •   •

For Bud Furillo, the highlight of the Clay-Moore fight was Archie's workout the Sunday afternoon four days before the bout.

America had just forced Castro and Khrushchev to back down in the Cuban Missile Crisis, and USC had beat Stanford the day before to improve its record to 7–0 on the way to the national championship. The country was feeling good, and so was the Steamer. What better way to spend a weekend than watching an Archie Moore workout at Jake Shugrue's gym at Seventy-Eighth and Hoover in South-Central Los Angeles?

A steel-drum band was beating out a calypso rhythm in the street when the Steamer drove up in his blue-gray '59 Chevy Impala. For Archie, the sounds of the soul psyched him up for his violent mission.

"Music is important to war," Moore told the Steamer as he prepared for his sparring session. "Almost since time began, men have marched off to battle with it."

Archie gave Furillo a brief history lesson on the fife and the drum, the origination of the Sousa marches, and the role of rhythm in the tribal wars of Africa.

"You know I'm a jazz purist," Moore said to the Steamer. "But for my work, I prefer a semi-native beat."

Told by Furillo that young Cassius Clay had worked out in this very same gym a few days earlier to the popular new Latin rhythms that had begun to punctuate the air waves, Moore said, "This doesn't ruffle me any more than his insolent remarks. I have a right hand that is going to knock that boy fighter right on his bossa nova."

With that, a collection of some of the top jazz artists in Los Angeles arrived at the gym and set up for a jam session to accompany Archie's sparring work. It was Buddy Collette on sax, Gerald Wilson on trumpet, and Chico Hamilton on drums. Legendary R & B and rock 'n' roll producer Bumps Blackwell came along for the ride with his vibes. Archie stepped into the ring, the band ripped into "Stompin' at the Savoy," and you could just forget about it from there.

Unfortunately for Furillo, this brief period of ecstasy would be marred in the Sports Arena by the actual fight itself. Moore entered the ring to what The Steam Room described as "the greatest ovation ever given any fighter in Los Angeles. It started from the time he left his dressing room and didn't stop until long after he climbed through the ropes."

But neither the capacity crowd nor the drums of war could stir Archie's warrior heart. Maybe it was the sight of Cassius Clay—just twenty years old, beautiful, sculpted as if by Michelangelo, soaring into his prime. At the opening bell, Clay bounced up on his toes and danced a circle around the ring. Cassius rose what must have been a foot above the crouching, balding, graying, and aging Moore. It was over before anybody threw a punch, and Archie knew it. He put up little defense as Clay launched into early flurries of lefts and rights. Cassius bounced

dozens of blows off the top of Archie's head in the first three minutes and returned to his corner at the end of the round with his
arms raised in victory. Archie came out of his crouch once in the
second to direct an authoritative right at Clay's jaw, and it may
have caught the young man backing up. Clay responded with
an unending barrage that finally staggered Moore in the third
and caused him to fall three times in the fourth before referee
Tommy Hart called off the jam.

The Steam Room was both highly impressed and deeply
disappointed.

"The great Clay may someday succeed in proving to the
world that he is more important to Louisville than the Kentucky
Derby," Furillo wrote. "The kid talks big and packs a truncheon
wallop in either hand to back up his boasts. Nobody is ques-
tioning his skill. The town merely wants to know where Archie
displaced his Thursday night at the Sports Arena."

Maybe the Steamer was being unfair to the grand elder of
his sport who would only fight one more time, against wrestler
Mike DiBiase in Phoenix. It's easy to say now, especially after
looking at the tape, that Archie never had a chance. It was one
of those transitional moments in boxing where the old give way
to the young. Muhammad Ali himself would later play Archie's
old-and-in-the-way role to Larry Holmes and Trevor Berbick.

Still, Furillo, as a watchdog journalist looking out for the
interests of the sports consumer, had to call out Archie. Once
he stopped the fight, Referee Hart "left Archie on the floor with
nothing more than a backward look of disgust," the Steamer reported, savaging a fighter he deeply respected, only because he
had to. "Apparently, Hart had no reason to believe Moore was in
any pain. The huge crowd was too embarrassed to boo."

Furillo wrote that Moore left the ring in "eerie silence."

"I didn't know whether to feel sorry for the old warrior—
or those who paid thirty dollars apiece to sit uncomfortably
through the spectacle. There was this comment from [L.A. Rams
halfback] Jon Arnett, who now must explain it to his wife: 'The
only good thing I can say about the fight was, it got me out of
the house.'"

CASSIUS A POET AND HE KNOWS IT
JANUARY 27, 1963

The first question was Clay's, when I reached Cassius at a Pittsburgh hotel after his latest predicted conquest.

"How am I being treated in the newspapers out there?"

"In the *Herald Examiner*, your fight with Charlie Powell rated an eight-column headline, two pictures, and as many stories," I informed.

"That is very nice. Send me three tear-sheets and tell the people of Los Angeles I love them. They respect the word of Cassius."

It's not easy to dispute the handsome talking machine from Louisville. He may stand up a few hundred young ladies from coast to coast, but never an opponent. . . .

"It's a good feeling to walk into a town three weeks before a fight and say a man must fall in three. You tell it on TV and radio. You shout it from the rooftops and the street corners. You tell it everywhere.

"You get to the arena to face a record-breaking crowd and you hear the announcer say:

"'*In this corner, Cassius Clay!*' *The people answer: 'Boo . . . Boo.'*

"Then you get a funny feeling listening to all those people booing.

"The first round goes by and nothing happens. So does the second. It's difficult to even think about the fight when you hear the audience yell:

"'It's the third. What you gonna do, big mouth?'

"Half the round is over and there is Powell, still standing. It frightened me. I jumped in, threw a few haymakers, and he falls. The boos stop. The cats are silent for a moment. Then they begin to scream: 'It's a fix.'

"Sure it was fixed. Moore was fixed. Lavorante was fixed. It will be a fix when Doug Jones falls in six."

For Clay to use verse to sum the fate of his March opponent came as no surprise. Cassius is a poet and he knows it.

•   •   •   •   •

A couple years after his L.A. fights, Cassius Clay changed his name, announced his conversion to Islam, and suffered a federal indictment because he had nothing against those Vietcong and sure wasn't going to let his government draft him into combat for the purpose of killing them.

He also beat Sonny Liston twice and successfully defended

against Floyd Patterson, Ernie Terrell, and everybody else before world boxing's sanctioning bodies—aligning themselves with the foreign policy predilections of U.S. military—stripped him of the title.

Bud Furillo wrote columns off press conferences and telephone interviews with the champ, but after the '62 L.A. fights, he didn't cover Muhammad Ali in action again until the state of Georgia licensed him to fight Jerry Quarry, the heavyweight champion of Los Angeles.

The Steamer had chronicled Quarry from the days of his national Golden Gloves victory, through his rise as a main-eventer at the Olympic Auditorium, to his title-shot losses to Joe Frazier and Jimmy Ellis. The night of the October 26, 1970, fight at the City Auditorium in Atlanta, Quarry barely played a supporting role to Ali's remarkable return. Jerry threw a couple of hooks and bulled Ali into a corner once. Otherwise, his face played catch with Ali's jab. His left eye blew open late in the third round, and that was it.

It was the Steamer's opinion that, if anything, the forced three-and-a-half-year layoff left Ali looking bigger in his grown-man body, fresher, and better than ever. A week before the fight, Ali told the Steamer in a phone interview that he hadn't really missed the isolation, the physical pounding, or the violence of the fight game.

"But I did miss the idea of earning a living," he said.

Ali played it cool going into the fight, refusing to react to the protests of the American Legion or the blatherings of Georgia's segregationist governor, Lester Maddox. He gave respect to Quarry, called him the best fighter in the world besides himself and Joe Frazier, even though Jimmy Ellis had beaten Jerry fairly easily.

When the bell rang for the first round, it was easy to see that these two men didn't belong in the same ring together at the same time. Ali outweighed Quarry by twenty pounds and enjoyed a ten-inch advantage in reach. He circled the ring like a shark in search of blood and found it in the third, when he gashed Quarry for the TKO win.

Furillo came away from the bloody night in Georgia with two distinct impressions of Ali.

"First, he is stronger," the Steamer wrote. "Second, he is faster."

Before the fight, Angelo Dundee told Furillo, "If the jab is cookin', Ali should have an easy time."

In The Steam Room, Furillo wrote: "It turned out that the jab was broiling. Quarry's nose went splat the second time Muhammad mashed it. Then he leaned down and said something to the twenty-five-year-old Californian. It seemed like he said, 'How did you like that?'"

•   •   •   •   •

Probably nobody assisted Ali more in becoming "The Greatest" than his trainer, Angelo Dundee, a source and contact Bud Furillo had first met about five years before the 1962 phone call to the Bloomington press box.

"Unfortunately," the Steamer wrote regarding his introduction to maybe most famous corner man in the fight game ever, "it was at the poker table."

Dundee was closing gashes over the eyes of Carmen Basilio when he first fleeced Furillo in the late 1950s over five-card stud. The Miami-based trainer may have lightened the Steamer's wallet, but he gave back to the writer in his bestowal of priceless fight-game understanding. Besides Ali and Basilio, Angelo had also worked the corners of champs such as Sugar Ramos, Luis Rodriguez, and Willie Pastrano by then. He would later hook up with Sugar Ray Leonard.

In an April 1960 column, when Dundee was in L.A. for a Luis Rodriguez fight against Alvaro Gutierrez, the Steamer reported that Dundee had learned the corner arts from practitioners such Charlie Goldman, Chickie Ferrera, and Ray Arcel. Goldman, best known as Rocky Marciano's trainer, showed Dundee how to wrap a fighter's hands. Ferrera, who had Dick Tiger and Nino Benvenuti and more than a dozen other big names, "taught him the tricks for stopping cuts," according to The Steam Room. Arcel, the instructor of fighters from Tony Zale to Larry Holmes, schooled Dundee on how to keep them going even when they didn't want to.

"He was the master psychologist," the Steamer said of Arcel. "Ray had to be. It was a wonder the way he could coax heavyweights into coming out to soak up punishment from Joe Louis round after round until they were KO'd. Invariably, Arcel was in the other corner when Louis fought."

Dundee knew, though, when to pull the plug. Eight months earlier, it was Dundee who stopped the fight, when Basilio stood up to a beating being administered by Gene Fullmer in a middleweight title fight at San Francisco's Cow Palace, covered by the Steamer.

"I felt bad because I knew he wouldn't like it," Dundee told Furillo, of his stopping the Basilio fight. "But there was no point in Carmen proving his bravery. He has done enough of that."

Dundee showed up in Caracas fourteen years later as an observer the night George Foreman knocked out Ken Norton. It was Foreman's last fight before the Rumble in the Jungle with Ali outside Kinshasa.

"If the fight goes six rounds, I believe Foreman will blow sky high and get knocked out," Dundee said in a 1974 Steam Room dispatch from the Venezuelan capital.

Foreman blew Norton out in the second, it turned out, but you could see Dundee's game plan at work seven months later in Zaire, when Ali rope-a-doped Foreman for six rounds, and then a seventh, before knocking him out in the eighth.

•   •   •   •   •

In Ali's three-year absence from heavyweight prizefighting, Bud Furillo covered the finals of the World Boxing Association tournament, arranged to create a placeholder champ until the real one returned. Jimmy Ellis, a former sparring partner of Ali's, won the WBA tourney with a decision over Quarry in Oakland.

Unfortunately for Ellis, winning the WBA crowd meant he had to fight Joe Frazier, a terrifying mixture of muscle and energy who had come out of the Philadelphia slaughterhouses to butcher every heavyweight placed in front of him.

Furillo had become acquainted with Frazier in 1966, when Smokin' Joe visited Los Angeles for a while and exhaled Chuck Leslie, Al Jones, and Eddie Machen in the Olympic Auditorium ring. Two years later, Frazier won the vacated heavyweight championship, as recognized by the New York State Athletic Commission—as good a sanctioning agency as any. Ali's financially preordained return to boxing lay ahead for Frazier. But the fighter, who sang in a soul band and rode choppers for kicks, first had to deal with Jimmy Ellis in Madison Square Garden the night of February 16, 1970.

In the week before the fight, Furillo ate dinner one night at Toots Shor's with Angelo Dundee, who trained Ellis. As Furillo and Dundee dined, Frazier's trainer, Yancey Durham, walked up to Dundee and gave him another full plate of food.

"Keep this for your fighter," Durham told Dundee, according to The Steam Room, in reference to Ellis rather than Ali. "He won't know where his next meal is coming from after the fight."

"This shouldn't be the case," Furillo wrote. The Steamer noted that both fighters were guaranteed $150,000 against thirty percent of the gate, including TV revenues. Nobody would be going hungry.

On fight night, Ellis boxed to a first-round advantage, but in the second round, Furillo reported, "Frazier fired out at Jimmy in the manner of an offensive lineman making his block." Dundee told the Steamer beforehand that Ellis's plan had been to jab, hook, and sharpshoot with the right, but Frazier's charge from the second-round bell, Furillo said, "plowed it under." During the referee's instructions, Ellis had sought to intimidate Frazier with a cold stare and monologue. As the third round got underway, the Steamer reported, "Joe told Jimmy his time had come. Ellis ran out of rebuttal from his mouth and with his fists."

Ellis endured an early onslaught in the round. He rallied late and threw everything he had at Frazier, who laughed at him when the bell sounded.

"Is that all?" Frazier asked Ellis before walking back to his corner, according to The Steam Room.

In the fourth, "Frazier went to the body with gloves that

slammed into Ellis as if they were weighted with sand," the Steamer reported. "The resistance ran out of Ellis like water from a levee until he pitched on his face from a left hook." Ellis got up, but went down again late in the round, and Dundee would not let him come out for the fifth.

"Happily, nobody was killed," Furillo wrote. "Because of a gravedigger's disagreement, the dead haven't been buried in this town for thirty-six days. Frazier should be prevented from fighting again until things are back to normal."

•   •   •   •   •

Sometimes, the hype is real. Hyperbole can be understatement, and it can be true, on occasion, that expectation delivers beyond what you might hope. Every once in a while in the world of American sports, where over-promotion mostly tends to annoy, there will be a game or a race or a fight that turns into something so spectacular, it locks into the muscle memory of your brain. Then it lasts forever.

On the night of March 8, 1971, Muhammad Ali and Joe Frazier stepped into the ring at Madison Square Garden to achieve this mark of history. They would meet two more times over the next three years, and their third fight on the Western Pacific isle of Luzon would be remembered by boxing writers as the most exciting of their series and one of the greatest in the history of the sport. Ali's later knockout in the heart of Africa over George Foreman, the seemingly indestructible one-time Olympic hero, also would be analyzed as the one that truly established him as "The Greatest."

Despite their epic stature, neither "The Thrilla in Manila" nor "The Rumble in the Jungle"—nor any other heavyweight championship fight before or since—featured two men who came into it so close to their athletic peaks, with undefeated records and legitimate claims on the title.

For Bud Furillo, it would be his eighth heavyweight championship fight, and his only one in which Muhammad Ali was a participant. He would cover three more, but none of them would have made for a decent prelim the night Ali and Frazier lit the

Garden marquee.

Furillo termed Frazier "the most destructive force" in boxing. He predicted that Smokin' Joe's relentless pressure would
deprive Ali of rest and wear him out by the twelfth round. A
week before the fight, the Steamer paid a visit to Frazier's training camp in New York for a first-hand look at the contestant's
preparation. He saw Frazier as an angry man who basically hated to train, but doubled the work "to compound the misery."
Then he'd take his displeasure out on "the striking parts" of any
fighter who stepped in the ring with him.

"When it's over, then he's free again . . . to sing . . . to ride
motorcycles and enjoy all of the things his ferocity has brought
him," the Steamer wrote.

As for Ali, Furillo's pre-fight analysis noted that Muhammad
maintained his edge of greatness despite the forced layoff. He
gained motivation, Furillo wrote, by "believing that all the sick,
hungry black people of the planet can better themselves only if
he wins."

A close fight through eight rounds, the match escalated in
intensity in the ninth, when Ali stopped clowning and smashed
Frazier with his best punch of the night, a right hand "that put
a shimmy in Joe's right wheel," Furillo wrote. Ali maintained his
momentum into the tenth, counterpunching effectively enough
to gain a slight edge on the scorecards of two of the three judges.

Frazier, however, turned the fight decisively in his favor in
the eleventh round with a left that knocked Ali into the bottom
strand of the ropes and nearly to the canvas.

"Ali staggered around the ring and they would have pinched
him for sure if he had been walking in that manner around the
Bowery," Furillo reported in The Steam Room. "He held on as if
Allah depended on it and perhaps it was prayer that saved him.
Nothing else seemed to be working."

Frazier went for the kill in the first minute of the twelfth,
a sixty-second span Furillo characterized as "sheer agony for
Muhammad."

"Frazier kicked the living hell out of [Ali] in that round, and
the crowd of 20,455 couldn't understand what was holding him

up," the Steamer wrote. "His legs buckled several times and he would fall into the ring ropes."

That was the moment when Furillo recognized there was more than shuffle to Muhammad Ali. Along with the magnificent physique, the "truncheon wallop" in either hand, the good looks, the way with women, the constant stream of braggadocio, and the conviction to confront the military-industrial complex—on the night of the first Frazier fight, Muhammad Ali showed the Steamer that he was one of the most courageous fighters to ever step in the ring.

Buzzed by a stream of Frazier fastballs to the body and head, Ali somehow rediscovered his jab and managed to create some space between himself and the mound of fury in front of him. He tossed in a few overhand rights, which began the closure of both of Frazier's eyes. Maybe because of his vision issues, Frazier returned to the body and hooked at Ali's midsection, as he "used to go after sides of beef in a Philadelphia slaughterhouse," Furillo wrote.

The battle continued into the fourteenth, with Ali—nearly fully recovered from Frazier's onslaught a few rounds earlier—taking note of the massive welt rising from Frazier's brow. He "was inspired to trade with Joe," the Steamer reported. But Frazier had some guts of his own. He laughed, Furillo said, "and poured back the punishment."

Going into the fifteenth and final round, the scorecards later showed that Frazier only needed to avoid a knockout to win the fight. He did better than that. He clinched the victory forty seconds into the round with a classic left hook, pretty as a Ted Williams swing, brilliant as a starry night by Van Gogh. The blow came from the leg strength built up in those double-time workouts Furillo had described in his advance columns. It landed on the right side of Ali's jaw. It lifted him off his feet, and dropped him flat on his back for a count of four. If the knockdown ensured Ali's defeat, the fighter's ability to get up from it truly established Muhammad's impeccability in the estimation of Bud Furillo's Steam Room.

"The fact that Ali finished the round and the fight dispelled for all time the notion that he couldn't take a punch," Furillo wrote. "He took a few hundred."

Throughout the fight, the Madison Square Garden crowd had mostly favored Ali. With the knockdown, they turned thumbs down on the fallen Muslim as if he were a Christian in the times of Rome. They roared for the lion of Philly to finish the job, but Muhammad made it to the wire, still on his feet.

"A clever fellow [who] has eluded the government for three and a half years, [Ali] was able to keep away from Frazier for the last two minutes," Furillo wrote. "This he did with great courage. He was through. He couldn't fight anymore because Frazier's early body shots had brought the hands down to make the jaw a lantern that was lit and ready to be shot out."

Nobody disputed the judges' decision, but Frazier looked more beaten up after the fight than Ali, and Muhammad's ability to finish it on his feet made a rematch inevitable.

"Some will say that Ali will take Frazier now that he has this tough fight under his draft-skipping belt," The Steam Room concluded. "The way he stood up to Frazier's smoke and pressure makes it plain he has the heart for anything. Maybe even soldiering."

•   •   •   •   •

It's hard to say when the transformation began—when Muhammad Ali, in the mind of the American public, went from a national figure much of the country hated as an aider and abettor of "those Vietcong," to one who became mightily beloved by most, somebody who won his title back twice, lit the Olympic torch in Atlanta, and endured Parkinson's disease with dignity on a public stage.

Public opinion later caught up with his opposition to the war in Vietnam, and who's to say Ali's stance didn't help change the country's collective view of it? No matter—the swing in the polls against the war corresponded with the upward trend in Ali's approval ratings. His image changing on the fly, Ali stopped into Los Angeles in March 1972 on his way to Tokyo. He had won three fights since the loss to Frazier, and Mac Foster in Japan would be his fourth victory.

Bud Furillo caught up with Ali during the SoCal stopover, over lunch at Benihana's in Beverly Hills. Pursued by two presidential administrations and denied the opportunity to work his trade, Ali said that any disappointment he felt toward the government had dissipated with the U.S. Supreme Court's 8–0 vote that overturned his draft evasion conviction. Chief Justice Warren E. Burger's crew did its thing three months after the Frazier fight.

In fact, Ali was now ready to offer his ambassadorial services to his country's leaders. He told the Steamer that he'd been invited to visit China, where cracks had begun to form in the Cultural Revolution. The fractures had become so pronounced, Chairman Mao's government had even invited a team of American ping pong players to come on over, where they had their asses handed to them by the locals in a diplomatic series of test matches. President Richard M. Nixon, following the ping pong path, had made his own visit to the Chinese mainland and returned to the United States just a couple weeks before Ali's stopover in L.A.

Muhammad said that, once he finished his summit with Mac Foster in Japan, he'd like to make the short jump to China and take up where Nixon left off.

"I'm going to meet the same people Nixon did," Ambassador Ali said. "Nixon opened the way. Now I'm going to give the president a hand."

Ali had just turned thirty, and the Steamer noted that the sharply suited champ tucked his thumbs into his suspenders as he spoke. Despite the banker's look, Ali insisted that he was still the same guy Furillo had spoken to a decade earlier at the Alexandria Hotel, after the Lavorante fight.

"Only I have more sense," he told the Steamer.

In the ten years since his three-game series in Los Angeles, Ali had dined with presidents and kings and had become internationally famous.

"I've been to Arabia, Genoa, Rome, Milan, Buenos Aires, Caracas, Lima, Trinidad, Syria, and Mali," Ali told the Steamer.

Recently, Soviet premier Alexei Kosygin had invited Ali to visit Russia. Everywhere he went, Ali said, people wanted to know what had happened in the Frazier fight.

"They had a day of mourning in Kuwait when I lost," he said. "The stores closed the next day."

It being March of 1972, Frazier was still ten months away from his unsuccessful encounter with George Foreman in Jamaica, the one where he got knocked down six times in two rounds. Before the debacle in Kingston, worldwide observers wanted nothing more than another Ali-Frazier fight.

"The rematch is going to draw five million people from all over the world, from the deserts of Arabia to the saloons of Alabama," The Steam Room quoted Ali from Benihana's.

Muhammad added, though, that "Frazier and I must be paid."

About $5 million each would cover it.

"The slave days are over," Ali said.

On his brief stop in Los Angeles, Ali was scheduled to make an appearance at a Friar's Roast for Sammy Davis Jr. During the luncheon at Benihana, Ali turned to his trainer, Angelo Dundee, to reveal the real reason he had lost the Fight of the Century.

"I had several secret workouts for the fight," Ali told Dundee, according to Furillo. "As you know, Sammy is the best imitator in the world. He played like he was Joe Frazier. Why, he was so good I thought Frazier was five-feet-four, weighed 120 pounds, and went around singing 'What Kind of Fool Am I?'"

•   •   •   •   •

Ali beat Foster in Japan, then came back to the United States for six more wins in his 1972 comeback tour. Bud Furillo covered the stop in Las Vegas where Ali, in a seventh-round TKO win, flicked the jab and Jerry Quarry "caught them all," the Steamer wrote.

The Ali-Frazier series would resume, but not without a couple of snags. Foreman was responsible for the first, in January 1973, when he disrupted the timetable for the rematch by depositing Frazier on the Jamaican canvas a half-dozen times. Ken

Norton, a Marine who fought out of San Diego, screwed it up even more two months after Foreman's demolition of Frazier, when he broke Ali's jaw on his way to a twelve-round decision.

The Steamer, as sports editor, assigned himself to cover the March 31, 1973, fight at the San Diego Sports Arena. The night before, he enjoyed a few cocktails at a party in Downey. He and some pals made a pre-dawn run for the border. Furillo passed out on the drive to San Diego—"too much to eat," as Bob Lee might have said. When he regained consciousness, Furillo apparently lost his enthusiasm for attending the fight.

"We're going home," the Steamer announced gruffly.

Back in L.A., the Steamer watched the fight on television, the first commercial broadcast of an Ali fight since the Zora Folley knockout in 1967. Furillo snagged a few quotes from the post-fight interviews on TV and got some more observations from Angelo Dundee, courtesy of former *Herald Examiner* sportswriter Steve Bisheff, who had since moved to one of the San Diego papers to write a column and who drove Dundee to the hospital after the fight. Furillo put a San Diego dateline on his story and ran it as if he were in the house. Sportswriters would get fired for that sort of stunt these days.

I know for a fact he was ringside when Ali and Norton met in the rematch at the Forum in Inglewood later that year, because he took me with him. And I know he got his own quotes afterward because I waited for him in the human gaggle outside Ali's dressing room.

You've got to think he made it to Madison Square Garden, too, when Ali and Frazier, as non-champions, met for the second time. At least, his name was on the story in the *Herald Examiner* the day after the fight on January 28, 1974. It said that Ali "wound up the fight with a display of all his boxing beauty and grace that turned the crowd on like this was Woodstock instead of the Garden."

With the crowd of 20,748 on its feet at the finish, Ali "threw machine gun combinations, bolos, straight rights, and upper-cuts, and when he broke into the Ali shuffle, the reaction bordered on hysteria," Furillo wrote.

With the Frazier loss avenged, the fight mob now wanted Ali and Foreman. It would happen, eventually, in the middle of a Kinshasa night. First, Foreman needed to make a little extra money. He picked Ken Norton for his easy payday.

"I've got bills," Foreman told Furillo in a telephone interview a couple weeks before the March 28, 1974, slaughter in Caracas. "I boxed four rounds with the electric bill, shadowboxed two rounds with a lawsuit, and finished up with two more on alimony."

Foreman's championship defense against Norton helped balance his books. He earned $700,000 for the two rounds.

Four days before the fight, a little-known promoter by the name of Don King announced in Caracas that he had accumulated $10 million in Swiss, English, and U.S. currency. It was his intention, Don King said, to stage an Ali-Foreman fight in the jungles of Zaire.

Norton expressed mild irritation with King's presumptuousness. When it came time to do something about it, the challenger froze.

During the referee's instructions, Archie Moore, attending ringside in a colorful Jamaican getup, whispered to the Steamer that Norton refused to look up from his shoes.

"What's Kenny looking for on the floor?" Archie asked.

"A soft spot to land," the Steamer answered.

Furillo wrote that Norton "never got out of his trance" in the ring with Foreman.

"The challenger stiffened like one of Pat Collins's subjects once Foreman began to hypnotize him with his stare and then his punches," the Steamer observed.

The champion hurt his knee the day before the fight and required a shot to hold down the swelling—not that he needed it.

"Foreman could have fought Norton on crutches and won," Furillo wrote in his column the next day.

Don King formally announced in May that Foreman and Ali, with the blessing of Mobutu Sese Seko, the president of Zaire, would fight in October in the country formerly and currently known as the Republic of Congo.

"Pardon me while I pack," the Steamer wrote.

It wouldn't be necessary. In a month, Bud Furillo would be out of the newspaper business. Radio stations paid more money, but they didn't send the talent overseas to cover fights. The Steamer would never see another performance by the fighter he called "Ali Blah-Blah." But he'd seen enough of them and studied the best of the rest—Henry Armstrong, Joe Louis, Sugar Ray Robinson.

When he dashed off his memoirs in the months before he died, there was no question in the mind of Bud Furillo who was, in fact, "The Greatest."

"Ali," the Steamer said, "just as he claimed."

Chapter 7

A LOVELY DAY AT DODGER STADIUM

Some of you were there the night Sandy was taken out in the fifth inning of his seventh loss last year. It was August 17 against the Reds, and 43,778 people gave him an ovation when the announcement was made that Koufax had to leave the game because of an injury. Sandy's arthritic elbow had never been known to flare up during a game as it did that night. You didn't need field glasses to see the face fire with pain when he tried to throw curves. Dodger vice president Buzzie Bavasi and team physician Dr. Robert Kerlan hurried to the clubhouse when Sandy was taken out. . . . Dr. Robert Woods, another team physician, loaded up the hypodermic with cortisone. Dr. Woods plunged it into the inflamed elbow. Koufax groaned as Maury Wills and I, who were watching, cringed.

—November 19, 1966

In the final days of the scalding 1965 National League pennant race, Bud Furillo sat down in the Los Angeles Dodgers dugout next to the greatest pitcher of the era.

It was the day of one of Sandy Koufax's greatest achievements, before his arthritic elbow forced his premature retirement the next year. Koufax had just fanned twelve batters on the St. Louis Cardinals to break Bob Feller's single-season strikeout record, and the timing of the 2–0 shutout was pretty good. It kept the Dodgers one game behind the league-leading San Francisco Giants, with just eight games left on the schedule.

Inside the clubhouse, baseball writers from across the country waited to ambush Koufax. The Steamer, however, slipped away from the pack. One of his favorite tricks was to sneak into the dugout and listen in and take notes while the star of the day did the exclusive post-game interview with Dodgers backup play-by-play man Jerry Doggett.

When Koufax finished his interview with Doggett, the Steamer got up to head back into the clubhouse—and that's when Sandy called him back.

"Let's sit here awhile," Koufax said.

The Steamer settled back on the bench in the seat next to Koufax. The two of them enjoyed the view from the dugout, looking out over the field and the blue sky of a late-September Saturday in L.A., while the pitcher called a timeout for a brief moment of reflection.

"It's a pleasant afternoon at the ball game, huh?" Sandy inquired of the Steamer.

A month earlier, thirty-four people had been killed in the Watts Riots. Five days after the riots ended, another one had broken out in San Francisco when Giants pitcher Juan Marichal smashed Dodger catcher Johnny Roseboro over the head with a baseball bat.

Soon afterwards, the Giants got hotter than 103rd Street the night they turned it into Charcoal Alley. They won fourteen straight and seventeen of eighteen. By September 16, they looked to be in control of the National League race, having moved out to a four-and-a-half game lead.

Then the Dodgers took their turn. They won thirteen straight over the last two weeks and fourteen of their final fifteen—eight by shutout, three by Koufax, including this one on the September 25 day he broke Feller's record of 348 strikeouts that had lasted for nineteen years.

L.A. caught the Giants two days later and passed them the day after that. On the second-to-last day of the season, the Dodgers—behind Koufax—beat the Milwaukee Braves to clinch the pennant.

In this pennant race marked by streaks, Furillo put together one of his own. For nine straight days, he wrote columns on the Dodgers that chronicled their run-up to running up the NL flag.

The Steamer spotlighted the biggest hit of Rookie of the Year Jim Lefebvre's life, marveled at Al Ferrara's timely dropping of a foul pop, and paid tribute to career minor-leaguer Lou Johnson's clutch hitting and fielding. He showed how Willie Davis, the self-described "man of a thousand stances," finally settled on one that worked and how Davis used it to pop two home runs to win a game in the final week.

Furillo wondered about the sanity of fans driven so crazy by the pennant race that they abandoned their cars in traffic so as not to miss a single pitch by the brilliant Koufax. He implored Dodgers management to pay more money to Koufax and his running mate in the Dodgers rotation, Don Drysdale—an issue of labor relations that would grow more prominent the following year.

On Koufax's record-breaking day, the Steamer was afforded a few minutes of quiet time with the athlete who ranks as perhaps the most cherished in the Los Angeles sports memory. Only Magic Johnson compares.

Sixteen days earlier, Koufax had thrown a perfect game against the Chicago Cubs, right after it seemed like the Giants had put the Dodgers away in a two-game Chavez Ravine sweep, the first meeting between the clubs since Marichal's ADW on Roseboro. With his smokestack-lightning fastball and a violent curve that broke sharp as broken glass, Koufax struck out fourteen Cubs, including the last six in a row, on his way to setting them down twenty-seven straight.

Two starts later, Koufax shut out the Cardinals in St. Louis on four hits. He shut them out again the next time out, when he broke Feller's record. Then he pitched his third straight shutout against the Cincinnati Reds on September 29. It was his fourth in five games going back to the perfect game, and he still had enough to come back on two days rest to beat the Braves in the clincher. He would finish the season with twenty-six wins, 382 strikeouts, and the second of his three Cy Young Awards.

About to turn thirty, the veteran of the broiling pennant races in 1959, 1962, and 1963 knew to appreciate these precious moments. His arthritic elbow had already become a problem, and his prime time in the finger-snap of history would soon give way to the crush of the eons.

In one of the most hallowed moments of one of his most spectacular years, during one of his team's most intense competitions, Koufax turned down the volume of his world and invited Bud Furillo to share the calm, to enjoy a sense of timelessness as they looked out at the purple majesty of the San Gabriel Mountains beyond the pale-blue outfield walls.

Timelessness didn't last very long for the Steamer. He was on deadline.

In his piece for the next day's paper, Furillo focused on Feller's mark and Sandy's admission in the dugout that he "was determined to break the strikeout record in this game." Furillo noted, "All twelve of the Cardinals who went down Saturday struck out swinging . . . refusing to give in to the world's greatest pitcher."

He followed Koufax as the pitcher made his entrance down the ramp from the dugout into the clubhouse, and wrote about how Sandy's waiting teammates gave him a standing ovation. He saw Sandy's "warm-up jacket drenched in perspiration" and how it was "crudely stitched in the back to hide a rip." He wrote about how the players, after cheering their star, quickly cracked wise. With the Giants playing a tight one on TV up at Candlestick Park, John Kennedy, the late-inning defensive replacement for Jim Gilliam at third base, suggested that Koufax fly to San Francisco to close out the game for the Braves.

Cameras whirred and questions flew, and the writers took notes as fast as they could to get it all down for the next day's paper, just a short while after Koufax and Furillo had sat alone in the corner of the Dodger dugout.

What a pleasant afternoon at the ballpark it was.

●   ●   ●   ●   ●

As a rookie columnist, Bud Furillo lucked into an eight-year unfolding of what is still the best baseball story in L.A. history. From the spring of 1959, when the Steamer first began to clear his throat in The Steam Room, until the fall of 1966, when he became a seasoned voice in the local sports pages, the Los Angeles Dodgers won four National League pennants and three

World Series championships. In a fifth season, they tied for first place but lost a three-game playoff for the NL flag. A half-century later, it was still the best run they've ever had, in Los Angeles or Brooklyn.

Vin Scully's voice rang familiar and comfortable in backyards, at the beach, at the kitchen table, and mostly at the ballpark, where transistor radios carried his disembodied description of the games in stereo, from foul pole to foul pole. Farmer John, a butcher in Vernon, used the Dodger airwaves to sell whole-fed, Eastern live pork that was brought out fresh and "dressed" right there in the West.

Singer and comedian Danny Kaye recorded a hit with "The D-O-D-G-E-R-S Song (Oh Really? No, O'Malley!)," an ode to a mythical L.A. victory over the "Jints." It continued to get airplay decades later, in esteemed Southern California disc jockey Dr. Demento's popular radio broadcasts of musical novelties and oddities.

During the Dodgers' first years in the Coliseum, fans brought trumpets and exhorted the team in a cavalry call to "charge." A few years later, when the team moved into the new stadium built into the side of a low-rise hill overlooking downtown, there was no need for the bugles. Whenever Maury Wills reached first base, the fans clapped and screamed and shook the five decks that soared skyward behind home plate. The scoreboard flashed "Go! Go! Go!" and off Wills went against the nerve-damaged opposing pitcher. Then Jim Gilliam got him over to third and Ron Fairly or Wes Parker or Sweet Lou Johnson got him in, and Koufax or Don Drysdale or Johnny Podres or Claude Osteen or Don Sutton, with help from Larry Sherry or Stan Williams or Ron Perranoski or Phil "The Vulture" Regan, would shut the other guys down. Next thing you knew, you had to sweat out another pennant race where only one team survived. Nobody had ever heard of a "wild card."

Furillo spent a couple nights a week, or more, at the Los Angeles Memorial Coliseum in the team's first Southern California championship year of 1959. He was chained to the Angels beat from 1961 to 1963, but even in those seasons, he broke free on

his off days to pour some stiff Steam Room takes on the Dodgers, catching up with Koufax or Drysdale or general manager
Buzzie Bavasi to find his own angles on the team and its players
and executives. He played big roles in the *Herald Examiner*'s
post-season coverage of the Dodgers when they lost the playoff
to the Giants in '62, and again when they swept the Yankees
in the 1963 World Series—maybe the greatest sports moment in
Los Angeles history. Then came his season-ending, nine-column
streak in 1965, followed by his reporting on Sandy Koufax's

PENGUIN PERCHED ON THIRD FOR DODGERS
JUNE 21, 1973

Forty-two persons were auditioned
at third base by the Dodgers in Los
Angeles until the club gave the job
to The Penguin.

It appears at last that the team
has found the right bird for the
position.

Penguins are cool. You don't
see penguins getting rattled like
the people who played third base
for the Dodgers. Penguins can play
any base.

For instance, Ron Jaworski,
of the Youngstown State Penguins,
played catcher until he left home
plate to sign with the Rams as a
pitcher.

The Penguin, who signs in as
Ron Cey, is unconcerned with the
problems that have beset Dodger
third basemen of the past. . . .

He doesn't know that Jim Bax-
es, while playing third base for the
Dodgers, once threw a black cat out
of his path—and hurt his arm. . . .

What about it Mr. Cey. Are
you living dangerously out there?

"I don't believe in jinxes,"
he said. "You make your own
jinxes." . . .

. . . [Cey] is hitting over .300,
doubling to all fields when needed,
and doing it with a waddle that's
exciting.

The Penguin's waddle gives
me goose pimples. It's like listen-
ing to "Aquarius/Let the Sunshine
In," or Sinatra singing "Lady Is
a Tramp" to Hayworth. It's the
Michigan marching band or Eddie
Jackson cakewalking in front of
Durante.

They say Dodger coach Tom
Lasorda named Cey The Penguin.

"He wasn't the originator,
Chuck Brayton, my coach at Washington State, was," said Cey. . . .
"Everybody runs differently. It
doesn't matter of you run funny or
not so long as you get there."

final year in 1966. His dispatches from the trainer's room, where the pitcher spent hours after the game with his elbow in an ice bucket or getting a cortisone shot plunged directly into the joint, were as vivid as any in town.

Besides capturing the agony of Koufax enduring another cortisone shot to help the Dodgers win the pennant, Furillo documented the growth of Drysdale from temperamental complainer into Hall of Famer. He wrote about the emergence of Wills from loner to team leader. He brought out color and humor in characters like Al Ferrara. He worked the bloodlines to tell the story of a cousin, Carl Furillo, who won some big games for the Dodgers in L.A. before angrily turning on the organization at the end of his career. He gave field manager Walter Alston a forum to explain his decisions, and prodded president and owner Walter O'Malley for inside information. He liked them all and praised them for the team's successes, and, when circumstances demanded, held them accountable.

Bud Furillo wrote about the youthful coming together of Steve Garvey, Davey Lopes, Bill Russell, and Ron Cey, a group that would constitute the longest-lasting infield in baseball history. They would grow together and win league championships and eventually their own World Series under the Steamer's pal, Tommy Lasorda.

•   •   •   •   •

Assigned to Vero Beach to help cover Dodgers spring training in 1959, Bud Furillo got an early feeling that the club was in for something big.

The year before, in their first season in Los Angeles, the Dodgers fell flat, with mostly an old team left over from the East Coast. They had some prospects, but the kids needed seasoning, and maybe a few more teaspoons of ability. The '58 Dodgers broke last and finished seventh. Baseball pundits predicted more floundering in '59 for a club that just wasn't on the same talent plane as Milwaukee or San Francisco.

True, nobody like Aaron or Mathews or Mays or Cepeda peopled the Dodgers roster. But in his first dispatch from Florida,

Furillo picked up on intangibles such as energy and a sense of urgency. Players came to camp in shape. Manager Walter Alston played no favorites. He made it clear that incumbency wouldn't buy advantage anywhere on the field.

"Competition breeds greatness," the Steamer wrote, "and never have I seen more in evidence than here in this teeming baseball factory known as Dodgertown."

Furillo told Dodger fans to keep an eye on three players. In an off-season deal with the Cardinals, the Dodgers acquired Wally Moon, a twenty-nine-year-old former Rookie of the Year who had four solid seasons in St. Louis before an elbow injury in 1958 hurt his numbers.

"We're going on the hunch that last year was a fluke," Dodger general manager Buzzie Bavasi told the Steamer.

Furillo bought in on Moon, saying his acquisition, in exchange for Gino Cimoli, "may be the best move the Dodgers have made since they traded in Brooklyn for Los Angeles."

Nobody figured Wally would win games with his brain as well as his bat. A left-handed hitter, Moon, who had earned a master's degree in administrative education from Texas A&M, taught himself an inside-out swing to take advantage of the short left field situation in the Coliseum, where the Dodgers played for four years before they moved into their new stadium. If you could get the ball into the air in left, you had a good chance for extra bases, in a field where it was only 251 feet down the line. To compensate for the short dimension, the designers who drew a ballpark into the football stadium added in a forty-two-foot-high screen. The analytical Moon then learned to lift the ball into and over the netting. He finished the 1959 season with nineteen home runs, eleven triples, twenty-six doubles, and seventy-four runs batted in. Moon hit .302, started in the All-Star game alongside Willie Mays and Henry Aaron, and ranked fourth in the year's Most Valuable Player voting.

Back from his fact-finding trip to Florida, the Steamer also predicted success for one of the organization's most valued assets. Don Drysdale was a six-foot-five kid from the San Fernando Valley who looked great in 1957, the Dodgers' last year in

DRYSDALE TABBED AS DODGER TO WATCH IN '59

MARCH 27, 1959

Steam Room clients are hereby informed that [Don] Drysdale is likely to be the most valuable player owned by the Los Angeles Dodgers.

It's like this. The tall bat-tamer from Van Nuys has conquered the problem of growing up.

Passing into adulthood as a twenty-one-year-old last season, Drysdale encountered every obstacle but the finance company. His handsome salary blocked that possibility. . . .

Let's examine the misery which confronted Don.

(A) Army duty interrupted his spring training.

(B) He worried about the left-field screen at the Coliseum, which used to scrape his knuckles when he reared back to fire.

(C) Pitching instructions given him to combat the screen didn't suit his delivery.

(D) His temper ran wild, without Roy Campanella around to harness it.

(E) He fell in love.

Well sir, before anybody could figure out what was bothering the kid, he was 1–7 instead of 7–1. Things looked so bad that many felt a brilliant career had been ruined.

Something Drysdale wouldn't do, however, was give up on himself.

One by one, he conquered his problems.

Once again his sidewinding stuff became poisonous to National League batters. . . .

The steadied Drysdale won eight of his last eleven games, six of them in a row. Overall, it was a 12–13 season.

This was far from the twenty wins expected of him at season's outset, but extremely encouraging after that brutal beginning. . . .

The six-foot-six-inch Drysdale practically opened the Dodger camp at Vero Beach, Florida, being one of the first arrivals. Nobody worked any harder. . . .

Everything points to a big year for Don Drysdale, perhaps even bigger than his 17–8 season in 1957.

Brooklyn. His first season in L.A., he started out 1–7. Don's problem was, he'd been psyched out by the same thing that made Wally Moon a star: that short left-field screen in the Coliseum.

In his travels to Vero Beach in the spring of '59, Furillo picked up on some changes in Drysdale's mental approach—not just to the screen, but to life in general. During the off-season, Drysdale married a Rose Parade princess, and the Steamer predicted that marriage would settle Don down and make him grow up.

"Everything points to a big year for Don Drysdale," Furillo wrote.

The pitcher delivered on The Steam Room's prediction, leading the league with 242 strikeouts, winning seventeen, and throwing four shutouts. One of the best-hitting pitchers of all time, he also slugged four home runs. He started in one of the All-Star games and pitched three hitless innings, striking out four.

Furillo identified catcher Johnny Roseboro as the third player on the verge of a breakthrough. The year before, Roseboro was hurried into the catcher's position left vacant by the car crash that paralyzed the Hall of Famer from the Brooklyn days, Roy Campanella. Roseboro hit well enough, but the Dodgers were forced to play his bat in the outfield much of the time because he wasn't getting the hang of the game behind the plate.

From the squat, Roseboro "reached for a low pitch like a lady warding off a mouse," Furillo observed in 1958. To help the new guy out, the Dodgers brought Campanella, in his wheel-chair, to Florida in the spring of '59 to give Roseboro a few tips. Inspired by Campy, "Johnny is now scrambling in the manner of a dog, burying a bone," Furillo wrote. In 1959, Roseboro threw out sixty percent of all the runners who tried to steal on him—the best in the National League.

With those three leading the way, the Dodgers started fast and stayed near the top of the tightly packed National League standings through the first half of the season. On July 4, only five and a half games separated the top five teams.

A few other pieces fell into place in the second half, when the Dodgers reached into the minors to bring up pitcher Roger Craig, who won eleven games in three months, and shortstop Maury Wills, a twenty-six-year-old rookie who overcame a shaky start to raise his batting average 117 points from July 3 to September 29.

On the Sandy Koufax front, flashes of brilliance began

to show. The night of August 31, with 82,000 in the Coliseum (60,194 paid) and the second-place Dodgers trailing San Francisco by two games, Koufax struck out eighteen Giants in a 5–2 win. He got Willie Mays, Willie McCovey, and Orlando Cepeda twice each. He struck out seven in a row in the middle innings, and he struck out the side in the ninth on ten pitches.

Even though he had thrown 147 pitches, Walter Alston sent Koufax up to the plate to lead off the bottom of the ninth in a 2–2 game. Damn if Koufax didn't get a hit. Jim Gilliam followed with another, and up came Wally Moon.

"[Wally] strides to the plate with the confidence of a marshal pacing his way toward a gunslinger at sundown," Furillo wrote.

Before he took his purposeful walk, Wally, according to the Steamer, turned around and told on-deck hitter Norm Larker, "You can take a seat, man. I'm going to hit one out of here."

Moon then stepped into the box, eyed San Francisco right-hander Jack Sanford, took a peek at the screen 251 feet away in left—and then lifted one over it.

Puffing on a cigarette after the homer, Wally told the Steamer, "You know, I'm going to miss this park when we move."

An appreciative Sandy Koufax rewarded Moon with a kiss.

•   •   •   •   •

Duke Snider, a Hall of Famer, hit .308, with twenty-three home runs and eighty-eight runs batted in. Gil Hodges went .276 on the season with twenty-five and eighty. It was their last productive year for the Dodgers.

Jackie Robinson had been retired for a couple years. Campy was in a wheelchair, Don Newcombe was in Cincinnati, and the shortstop, Pee Wee Reese, was coaching third base. Carl Erskine pitched ten innings and retired. Besides reliever Clem Labine, that left only one other holdover still on the L.A. roster who had contributed to the glory of Ebbets Field.

Carl Furillo, the Steamer's first cousin once removed, was a charter member of the Boys of Summer, his story immortalized along with Robinson and Reese and the rest in Roger Kahn's great book. Nicknamed "The Reading Rifle" after his hometown in Pennsylvania and for his strong throwing arm in right field, he had been one of baseball's best players for a decade. Twice, he led the league in outfield assists, and ten times he finished in the top ten, throwing out runners on the base paths. He hit over .300 four times, won the 1953 National League batting championship with an average of .344, and compiled a lifetime mark of .299. He drove in 1,058 career runs. He was named to two All-Star teams. He finished sixth in the 1949 MVP voting and ninth in 1953.

He had a solid 1958 when he hit .290 and drove in eighty-three runs to lead the club, but Carl sat on the bench for most of 1959. He only went to the plate 103 times, and only got into twenty-five games in the field. In the Roy Campanella benefit game against the Yankees, Ryne Duren hit him in the ribs with a fastball, and the Dodgers used that as an excuse to put him on the disabled list, even though Carl said he was okay. He did suffer real ailments to his legs, but mainly it was Wally Moon and Don Demeter who cut down on his playing time. The Dodgers needed to get younger, and Carl Furillo, at thirty-seven, was going in the wrong direction.

Even in his best playing days, Carl was never exactly a ray of sunshine in the clubhouse. Roger Kahn said he was always kind of self-conscious about his eighth-grade education. Jimmy Cannon described Furillo as "a bitter man" who considered the Dodgers "a cheap outfit" that had misled him about money from the start.

"He despised the people he worked for," Cannon wrote in 1960.

Carl's antipathy stewed thicker on the bench. By April 22, less than two weeks into the '59 season, an un-bylined story in the *Herald Express* reported that he wanted a trade.

It gained him little sympathy from the GM.

"He's getting paid, isn't he?" Buzzie Bavasi told the paper.

When the grumbling got worse, Bud Furillo put his name on the copy.

"Cousin Carl," as he called him in print, was the Steamer's grandfather's brother's son. The Steamer knew Carl a little bit from his visits back East as a young writer, introduced to the player by his own father who had moved from Youngstown, Ohio, to Norristown, Pennsylvania, and who made it over to Brooklyn to watch his cousin play baseball.

While Carl sat idle in '59, Bud wrote on June 17 how his blood resented the "test tubing" of rookies like Ron Fairly and Frank Howard.

"Don't you think it's time we asked Walt Alston and Bavasi how long Los Angeles fans have to be tormented watching rookies strike out while a .326 hitter is eating his heart out on the bench?" Bud wrote.

Carl got his chances in the post season, and came through with some contributions with the bat. The Dodgers finished the season tied for first with the Braves, setting up a three-game playoff. L.A. won the first game in Milwaukee, 3–2, on seven and two-thirds scoreless innings of relief pitching by Larry Sherry and a tie-breaking, sixth-inning home run by Johnny Roseboro. Back in L.A., in Game Two, the Braves led 5–2 going into the bottom of the ninth. L.A. made it 5–4 on consecutive singles by Moon, Snider, Hodges, and Larker. The Braves brought in their ace— the great lefty, Warren Spahn—in relief, and the Dodgers countered with pinch hitter Carl Furillo's right-handed bat in place of the left-handed hitting Roseboro. Furillo drove a ball deep to right that scored Hodges with the tying run. Carl stayed in the game in right field and came up again in the twelfth inning, with Hodges on second and two out. The Reading Rifle bounced one behind second that Milwaukee shortstop Felix Mantilla gloved but threw away trying to get Furillo at first. The hit-and-error allowed Hodges to score and the Dodgers to win the pennant.

"Pardon the personal touch," Bud Furillo wrote in The Steam Room the next day. "But I'm awfully proud of a second cousin named Carl today."

The Steamer called Carl "the forgotten man" and the "nerveless old pro" on the L.A. roster. He played press agent for his cousin, but Carl flared terse answers when the writers came around for interviews.

"It's good to win one of these playoffs for a change," is all the Steamer could pull out of him.

In the World Series against the White Sox in Comiskey Park, Chicago bombed L.A. in Game One, 11–0, with thirty-nine-year-old Early Wynn overcoming the gout to pitch seven scoreless innings. Bare-armed muscle man Ted Kluszewski hit two home runs and drove in five.

After the game, the Steamer cabbed thirteen miles to Big Klu's hometown of Summit, Illinois, a southwest inner-tier industrial suburb. Steamer stopped into a joint on Archer Avenue called Chester's Tavern, where bartender John Strazelczk poured whiskey with a beer back. In celebration of the hometown hero, Strazelczk joyously announced, "The drinks are on the house!"

"I had a lot of fun at Chester's," Furillo wrote, "until Chester came in and stopped the giveaway."

Next day, the Dodgers trailed 2–1 with two outs in the top of the seventh, when pinch-hitter Chuck Essegian, a Stanford grad who is one of only two athletes to ever play in both the Rose Bowl and the World Series (Jackie Jensen of Cal and the Yankees was the other), hit a home run to tie it. Then Jim Gilliam walked, which brought up Charlie Neal, who blasted one 425 feet to left center, his second home run of the day.

A batting tip from the fellow in the wheelchair helped the Dodgers second baseman at the plate.

"Charlie came to see me a lot this summer in New York," Roy Campanella, in Chicago for the Series, told the Steamer after the game. "We talked about his style and decided he should stand up a little straighter instead of crouching so much. It worked out all right, didn't it?"

Relief pitcher Larry Sherry finished it off for the 4–3 win.

Carl Furillo enjoyed his second big moment of the fall in Game Three, in front of a Coliseum crowd of 92,394, which stood as a World Series record for exactly one day when it was surpassed by the 92,650 at Game Four, which itself was shattered by the 92,706 in the house for Game Five. That record has lasted every day of the fifty-seven years since.

Furillo's hit came in the bottom of the seventh of a scoreless tie. Pinch hitting for Demeter, one of those young players he resented, Furillo bounced a pitch from Gerry Staley up the middle and to the left of Sox shortstop Luis Aparicio and over his outreached glove. Aparicio said he lost the ground ball, curiously, in the white shirts of the crowd. Two runs scored, Sherry closed for Don Drysdale for his second save of the Series, and the Dodgers won, 3-1.

This time, the Pennsylvania cousin had more to say.

He told the Steamer that the pinch single "gave me a bigger thrill than a home run I hit against the Yankees in the 1953 Series." Bud wondered why Carl wasn't starting, but the pinch-hitting hero told him to forget about it.

"Everything is working all right this way," Carl said. "Why change it?"

Carl batted only two more times in the Series, popping to third and striking out, while the Dodgers went on to win the Series in six. Gil Hodges hit a tie-breaking, eighth-inning homer in Game Four, setting off a crowd roar that *Herald Express* sports editor George T. Davis said may have been the loudest he'd heard at the Coliseum in more than thirty years.

Koufax pitched a five-hitter as the Dodgers tried to end it at home, but the Sox scratched for a run on a double-play ball for the only run in a 1-0 Chicago victory in Game Five.

Back in Comiskey Park, Larry Sherry, who pitched 7.2 innings of shutout relief to win Game Four, added 5.2 more scoreless frames in Game Six for another victory. His two wins plus two saves added up to the Series MVP trophy for the L.A. kid.

"He's so good," Bud Furillo wrote after Sherry's Game Four win, "I may switch from Chianti."

•   •   •   •   •

The next May, that was it for Carl Furillo and the Dodgers. When he tore a calf muscle in opening week, it made it easy again for the Dodgers not to play him. A month into the season, he'd been to the plate only ten times.

Then it got ugly. The Dodgers announced on May 15 that they were releasing Furillo for the purpose of sending him to Spokane, where they offered him a job working with their young prospects. It would have kept him on the payroll at his major-league salary of $33,000.

Hard-headed Carl refused the assignment, so the Dodgers withdrew the offer and stopped paying him. He sued and eventually won the $21,000 balance on his 1960 deal, but he never got any more work with the Dodgers, or with any other major-league club. He complained to his grave that he'd been blackballed.

For years, Carl also ripped the Dodgers for screwing him out of thirty-five dollars a month on the pension differential he would have received, had he finished the season and gained credit for a full fifteen years in the majors. His cousin in the L.A. press corps took up the cause the day after Carl's release. With the defending champs bumbling around at 12–16, the Steamer wrote, "It's unfortunate that Carl had to be the victim when Buzzie Bavasi pressed the panic button."

In his second-day story, Bud quoted Carl as saying: "I think this is one of the lowest things they could have done. Maybe they didn't want me to hook up with some other ball club and come back for revenge."

Bavasi spun things differently. Buzzie told Bud he'd put Carl on waivers the week before, but that no other club claimed him. Then Carl "knifed us" by refusing the Spokane assignment, Bavasi said.

"I don't know why writers are feeling so sorry for him. Ballplayers have been getting released since time began," Bavasi said in The Steam Room.

The next spring, Carl drove to Palm Springs to see if the expansion Angels could use a thirty-nine-year-old outfielder. They said no, and he said it was part of an international baseball conspiracy to deprive him of his right to make a living. Bud did a story quoting Angels general manager Fred Haney as saying, no, there was no blackball, the guy was just too old and they already had too many old guys around.

Contact between Bud and Carl fell off to nearly nothing once the player's days with the Dodgers were done. Carl moved back East and worked for an elevator contractor during construction of the World Trade Center when Roger Kahn contacted him for his chapter in *The Boys of Summer*.

The two Furillos saw each other a few times when the Steamer went into radio and spent his springs with the Dodgers in Vero Beach through most of the '80s. Carl's anger had dissipated some, and he accepted the Dodgers' offers to appear at their fantasy camps and the like.

At an old-timers' game at Dodger Stadium in 1985, the Steamer took me down to the clubhouse to introduce me to my first cousin, twice removed. Carl's grip felt strong and he still had a hulk of a body for a sixty-three-year-old man, but he barely looked at me when we shook hands. Then he looked at my dad, glanced back at me for maybe a second, and turned back to my dad and pronounced, "He doesn't look a fucking thing like you."

•　　•　　•　　•　　•

Before he motored down to Palm Springs to begin his coverage of the expansion Angels, the Steamer swung by the Dodgers' offices on January 19, 1961, to say goodbye to his goombah.

This was at the old Statler-Hilton on Wilshire, while the Dodgers' park up on the hill was under construction. The hotel layout wasn't too shabby, from Furillo's perspective. Bavasi's office, looking out over the pool, was right next to the hotel beauty salon, "which explains why Buzzie always looks so pretty," Furillo wrote, although Carl Furillo might disagree.

The Reading Rifle was gone, but Bavasi still had twenty-five other major-league pains in his ass to deal with. One was named Johnny Podres, who barged in on Bavasi while the GM and the Steamer were hanging out.

"Hi, Buzz," greeted the smiling Podres, famed as the Game 7 winner of the 1955 World Series and one of the great Dodger clutch pitchers of all time. "Guess what I want?"

As if Podres had to ask.

"Money," frowned Bavasi.

An off-season resident of Witherbee, New York, where the average high temperature on January 19 is twenty-eight degrees, Podres had flown out to sunny Southern California, at the Dodgers' expense, to get some treatment on his bad back.

"Podres is the only pitcher in the world who develops a chronic back ailment every January 8th," Bavasi told Furillo. "He calls me long distance and moans, 'My back's killing me, Buzz. Send me some transportation money so I can get some treatment from Doc Kerlan.'"

Bavasi found it curious that Kerlan and Podres put more time in at Santa Anita, the gorgeous racetrack at the base of the San Gabriel Mountains, than in any therapy room.

"That's where they spend the afternoons together," Bavasi explained.

Now you had Furillo and Podres and Bavasi yukking it up around the GM's desk, when in walks Norm Larker, who was coming off a .323 season.

"Hi, Dumbo," Bavasi greeted the outfielder/first baseman with the large ears that earned him a nickname he didn't like.

"Can the Dumbo," Larker said. "I don't want anybody calling me that anymore. I didn't mind it when the guys on the ball club did it, but now I get it from everybody on the street. It ain't nice."

Tommy and Willie Davis were next to enter. Brothers only in the sense that they were both African American males, Willie D. actually did have a brother, in the biological use of the term, by the name of Tommy. This ruffled Buzzie when he saw that Willie's brother Tommy had recently gotten his name in the papers for starring in a basketball game.

Bavasi read the story and was horrified at the prospect of a rising young baseball star debilitating himself by playing basketball with a crippling injury. He picked up the phone and meant to call the Dodgers' Tommy, but mistakenly dialed Willie's number. Who should answer the ring but Tommy, Willie's brother, who got an earful from Buzzie.

"We've got too much invested in you to have you get hurt in that silly game," Bavasi told basketball Tommy, according to The Steam Room. "Stop it, do you understand?"

The call miffed Willie's brother.

"What right has that man tellin' me not to play basketball?" he asked Willie, according to The Steam Room.

They all thought it was pretty funny when Willie and Buzzie

BIG NEWK PAYS PRICE TO LISTEN TO THE COUNT
JUNE 15, 1962

CHICAGO—Before yesterday's finale at the Ravine, I sat in the Angel dugout with a pitcher who, in his heyday, could have given Belinsky and Chance lessons on keeping late hours.

To Don Newcombe I said:

"Remember the time Bavasi fined you $300 on the road because the Basie tunes you were playing on your tape recorder woke him up at 4:30 in the morning?"

Big Newk shook his head in assent.

"Snider called the tape recorder my sin box. When you heard it late at night, you knew Newk was up to no good."

When Bavasi socked Newcombe with the fine in 1958, Ed Roebuck cooed to Don:

"Geez, Newk, for $300 you could have hired the whole orchestra."

shared the story, but the real Tommy D. had business on his mind in the GM's crowded office. He told the Steamer he'd tried off-season work as a car salesman and a haberdasher, but neither occupation had worked out.

"Then he put the bite on Bavasi," The Steam Room reported.

Bavasi, amused by Tommy D.'s request for more money, laughed some more when he picked up a letter he had just received from Maury Wills.

He read it to the room:

"Dear Buzzie . . . Just got back from a fishing trip and caught two dozen steelheads. I'm freezing a dozen and sending them along to you. I'm also returning the contract you sent me and hope you can improve on it."

•   •   •   •   •

By 1962, Bavasi had pieced together a new club ready for a big run.

The Dodgers were brash and dashing, dynamic and fresh-faced, and gaining in experience with Wills, Willie, Tommy, and the college bonus babies—Ron Fairly out of USC and Frank Howard of Ohio State. Roseboro behind the plate and Gilliam at second had become solid veterans. Third base would be a problem for more than another decade, but Koufax, Drysdale, and Podres had to be the best 1-2-3 in the game, and the bullpen led by Ron Perranoski was good enough.

Bud Furillo lauded the GM for changing over of the roster.

"You must have a man behind the scenes who will guarantee you the guys you need for a pennant winner," The Steam Room read. "The Dodgers have that man in their general manager, Mr. E. J. [Buzzie] Bavasi."

Bavasi's genius showed most prominently in the promotion of Wills.

"It was a Bavasi move to bring Wills up," Furillo wrote. "Maury is only the best shortstop in baseball today."

On the mound, the Koufax-Drysdale combination edged closer to lethality. Sandy won eighteen in 1961, led the league in strikeouts with 269, and cut down on his walks. Don's thirteen wins gave him seventy-two over five years. He also hit twenty batters with pitched balls, making it the fourth straight season he'd led the league in this violent category.

The Steamer had occasion during the spring of '61 to chat with former Dodgers pitcher Sal Maglie, who was the pitching coach for the Boston Red Sox at the time. Revered in baseball lore for his propensity to spin batters out of the box with inside fastballs, Maglie, nicknamed "The Barber," took credit for teaching Drysdale the importance of the close shave.

As a youngster, Drysdale spent too much time arguing with opposing batters. Maglie told him to just shut up and knock them down.

"They'll get the message," Maglie assured the young pitcher.

In 1962, the Dodgers moved into their new stadium and won 102 games. Wills stole 104 bases and was voted Most Valuable Player in the league. Drysdale, in the new ballpark with 390-foot power alleys and heavy night air that slowed down the flight of the ball, won twenty-five games and the Cy Young Award. Tommy Davis led the league in batting at .346 and in RBIs with 153. Frank Howard slugged thirty-one homers and drove in 119.

Going into the All-Star break on July 8, the Dodgers cruised

"THEFT-O-METER" NEEDED TO CLOCK MAURY'S PROGRESS
JUNE 11, 1962

What this country needs more than a good five-cent cigar is a Cobb-Wills Theft-O-Meter.

Who can deny that Dodger shortstop Maury Wills has a shot at the base-stealing record of ninety-six established by the immortal Ty Cobb with Detroit in 1915?

The idea of keeping a day-to-day chart on Wills's efforts to overhaul Cobb would have as much appeal in Los Angeles as did the Maris-Mantle-Meter with Ruth last year.

The suggestion to start a Theft-O-Meter went out by telephone yesterday from me, watching the Angels in Chavez Ravine, to Dodger publicist Arthur Patterson, listening to Scully in Houston.

"Pardon me," interrupted Patterson. "While you were talking, Wills just stole his thirty-fourth base."

into first place ahead of the Giants with a 2–0 win behind Koufax. With Sandy carrying a three-hitter into the ninth, Alston came out to the mound to take Koufax out of the game, a rarity. The Dodgers skipper had his reasons. First, he wanted to stay in first place for the All-Star break, and he had Drysdale going in the bullpen. For another thing, the index finger on Koufax's left hand was killing him. According to Jane Leavy's book on Koufax, his finger had gone completely numb, the result of an injury he had incurred three months earlier when he got jammed at the plate and the knob of his bat crushed an artery in his hand, cutting off the blood flow to his finger.

Sandy got another start the first game after the break. Koufax again pitched a shutout through seven innings, but Alston again had to take him out when Sandy's finger went numb. The win was Koufax's fourteenth and last of the season.

Bud Furillo, deep in the excitement of the Angels' summer of '62, pulled off the beat to spend an off-day with Koufax, who was back in L.A. on the disabled list with the bad finger. They met at the pitcher's side business, Sandy Koufax's Tropicana Motor Hotel on Santa Monica Boulevard in West Hollywood. The place would later become home to singers such as Jim Morrison and Tom Waits and many of their colorful friends with odd habits.

Koufax showed Furillo his finger.

"It was loyally discolored in Dodger royal blue and white," the Steamer reported. "Sandy wiggled it and said, 'Doc [Robert] Woods feels I'll be ready to go in two weeks."

Two months was more like it. Neither Koufax nor the Steamer nor, apparently, Dr. Woods, realized the extent of the danger. None of them knew there was a real possibility they'd have to amputate the finger if they couldn't fix the circulation problem.

•   •   •   •   •

Even without Koufax, the Dodgers kept winning. By August 10, they had built their lead to five and a half games. Then they went to San Francisco and drowned in the Candlestick Park infield.

To slow down the Dodgers, the Giants' ground crew irrigated the dirt around first base. They also mucked up the shortstop position to cut down on Wills's range. The Dodgers didn't even try to steal in the first game and got pounded, 11-2. In Game Two, the muddy grounds fouled their heads. Wills popped out his first time up and complained about the field when he came to bat again in the third. When he wouldn't let it go, home plate umpire Al Forman threw him out of the game. The Dodgers lost, 5-4.

The series finale "almost was the first game ever to be called on a sunny day because of wet grounds," Hall of Fame baseball writer Bob Hunter wrote in the *Herald Examiner*. The umps ordered sand to be hauled in and spread around the slog pits at first base and shortstop. Wills still went 0-4 and the Dodgers lost, 5-1.

Down in L.A., where the Angels were playing the Red Sox, the teams had a visitor in the park in the person of Ford C. Frick, commissioner of baseball. Bud Furillo, keenly tuned to the happenings 400 nautical miles north, cornered Frick for a comment on the travesty that was altering the dynamics of the National League pennant race.

Frick played it obtuse.

"I just came from there," Frick told the Steamer. "I saw the game Friday night. If playing conditions were poor, this wasn't observable from the stands."

In the bogs of Candlestick, the Dodgers lost their groove. Then they lost the last four games of the season. At the end of regulation, they were 101–61, or forty games over .500, but only tied with the Giants for first place.

By the time the playoff with the Giants got underway, the vital signs had returned to Koufax's finger. With its blood flowing normally again, on September 21, Sandy pitched for the first time since July 17. He walked four in the first inning and Alston got him out of there in a loss to the Cardinals. He tried it again at home against Houston on September 27, and gave up only three hits and struck out four in five innings. He left with the lead in a game the Dodgers lost.

It was nothing but misery in his one inning-plus in the play-off at Candlestick. Felipe Alou lined a double to left and Willie Mays hit one over the chain-link fence in right center. Jim Davenport homered to lead off the second. Ed Bailey, far removed from the Theatrical Lounge in Cleveland, singled sharply to left.

Sandy was done for the day.

"I felt just like I do the third week of the season," he told reporters afterward. "Nothing hurt, there was nothing wrong, and I had nothing on my fastball."

The 8–0 defeat was the Dodgers' third straight shutout loss. The teams headed south for Game Two a day after U.S. Marshals, half a country away, escorted James Meredith onto the Ole Miss campus as the school's first-ever black student. The Steam Room observed, "Walter Alston may have to enlist Federal aid to get some of his players admitted to home plate."

Their scoreless string hit thirty-five innings before pinch-hitter Lee Walls's three-run double keyed a seven-run sixth. Ron Fairly's sacrifice fly scored Wills in the bottom of the ninth to win it for the Dodgers, 8–7, and the series was tied, 1–1.

The third-game series decider turned into one of the most painful losses in Los Angeles sports history. The Dodgers took a 4–2 lead into the ninth inning. Then relief pitcher Ed Roebuck, who got Podres out of a bases-loaded jam in the sixth, allowed four of the five runners he faced in the ninth to get on base. They all scored and the Giants won, 6–4.

Furillo described the losing clubhouse as "the saddest thing I've ever seen in sports"—drunken, naked players crying, staring at the floor.

"The scene had all the gaiety of the county morgue," The Steam Room reported. "Only the corpses were still gurgling—beer and tears."

Some of the writers badgered Alston about leaving Roebuck in too long when Drysdale, who only pitched five innings in Game Two, was available.

Yes, he could have switched things up, but Alston told the press the main reason why the Dodgers fell short.

"We didn't lose the pennant today," Alston said, as reported in The Steam Room. "We lost it on July 17th when we lost Sandy Koufax."

Furillo concurred.

"You sort of get the idea," Furillo wrote, "a healthy Sandy Koufax might have won one more game for the Dodgers."

•   •   •   •   •

With the Angels in seventh place, out of the race by fourteen and a half games, and getting killed by Detroit on a Sunday afternoon in July of 1963, Bud Furillo slipped out from behind his typewriter in the Chavez Ravine press box to search for the general manager of the landlord Dodgers.

He found Buzzie Bavasi in the Stadium Club, watching Jack Nicklaus win the PGA on television.

"What do you want?" Bavasi snapped. He was irritated because the Dodgers were losing a doubleheader to the Braves.

The Steamer wanted to write about anything other than the Angels, so he asked Bavasi to give him some insight into his ball club. Despite their difficulties in Milwaukee that day, the Dodgers had taken a six-game lead in the National League pennant race.

"Tell me something so I can write a column about your club," Furillo said.

"Write about the Angels," Bavasi responded.

Furillo rejected the suggestion. He insisted that Buzzie provide him with an analysis of the Dodgers' success.

"Pitching," Bavasi answered.

It was a word that had come to be defined by the name Koufax, who, in 1963, would go 255 innings with an earned-run average of 1.88. He'd strike out 306 and walk a career low 1.7 per nine innings. He won his first Cy Young Award and was voted the league's Most Valuable Player.

Another word Bavasi might have applied would be "managing." Walter Alston's defining moment in a Hall of Fame career came on May 6, a day when the Dodgers blew a lead in Pittsburgh for their seventh loss in nine games.

On the ride to the airport afterward, the players complained about an assortment of issues, chief among them their bus, which had cramped seats and no air conditioning. You can imagine the commentary when a sleek new air-conditioned ride carrying Roberto Clemente and the Pirates passed them on their way to airport. According to Bob Hunter's account, the heightened grumbling set off the temper of the usually mild-mannered Ohioan who wore jersey number twenty-four.

Alston ordered the driver to pull over. Then he "rose from his seat, his face white," according to Hunter, and asked, "Is there any player who wants to check the buses now?"

When nobody responded, Alston told the Dodgers that, as of that moment, he was the team's new bus coordinator.

"If any one of you doesn't like it, then come to me," he informed his players, according to Hunter, "and we'll step outside and discuss it. Then the next man can come out and I'll discuss it with him."

Nobody pressed the issue with the six-two, 195-pound manager.

When they got to St. Louis, the Dodgers beat the Cardinals two out of three. Home for the Giants, they swept three over the defending National League champs, one of which was a no-hitter by Koufax. By June 7, they were in first place, and after July 2, they were never out of it.

Tommy Davis hit .326 to lead the league, again. Frank Howard slugged twenty-eight home runs, including one that went *out* of the Polo Grounds in New York. Drysdale won nineteen, Perranoski sixteen out of the bullpen, and Koufax finished with eleven shutouts.

The Cardinals made a September run at the Dodgers, but L.A. swept them three straight in St. Louis, and that was the end of that.

Next stop was the Bronx.

•   •   •   •   •

Bud Furillo came into the 1963 World Series knowing the Yankees better than his hometown club. He'd covered fifty-four of their games the previous three years and had forged good relationships with their stars. He once picked Mickey Mantle up at the airport. Whitey Ford always gave him great stuff, and he snagged one of Yogi Berra's most memorable quotes.

It was the eighth column note in The Steam Room dated September 6, 1963, when the Yankees were cruising to the American League pennant and the Dodgers appeared solid in the National. The Yankees were home and the Steamer was in L.A. when he called up Yogi to talk about the World Series. Furillo wrote that Berra told him to pass along some advice to Tommy Davis about the lengthy left-field, late-afternoon shadows in Yankee Stadium.

The Steamer wrote that the master of tangled meaning told him to tell Tommy D.: "It gets late early out there."

Fifty years later, the Yogi Berra Museum and Learning

IT GETS LATE EARLY IN LEFT FIELD
SEPTEMBER 6, 1963

Yogi Berra says to pass this Yankee Stadium leftfield information along to my man Tommy Davis for the World Series. Shadows make it tough to see in leftfield. Yogi said to tell Tommy D.: "It gets late early out there."

Center, on the campus of Montclair State University in Montclair, New Jersey, authenticated it on Twitter as the "first reporting" of the quote.

Coming off back-to-back World Series championships, the 1963 Yankees looked deeper and better-armed than the '61 and '62 clubs. Rookie pitchers Jim Bouton and Al Downing were so impressive during the regular season, they convinced manager Ralph Houk in the post-season to consign to the bullpen the previous season's twenty-three-game winner and World Series hero, Ralph Terry. The Yankees defense played eighty errorless games, with shortstop Tony Kubek and second baseman Bobby Richardson making up one of the game's best double-play combinations. Injuries to Mantle and Maris forced Houk to play John Blanchard and Hector Lopez for long stretches, thereby strengthening his bench. The team got younger at first base with Joe Pepitone and in the outfield with Tom Tresh, both of whom made the All-Star team. The Yankees catcher, Elston Howard, hit twenty-eight home runs and won the AL MVP award.

"This is the best team I've ever played for," Whitey Ford, who had only played on six World Series champions, told Furillo on July 24.

"We have twenty-five players who contribute to winning," Ford said.

As a kid who grew up sixty miles from Cleveland, Furillo saw the great Yankees teams of the DiMaggio years. On the eve of the '63 Series, he looked up the Clipper to compare and contrast. DiMaggio told the Steamer he was partial to the '38 and '39 teams that had swept the Cubs and Reds, and the '37 team that had beat the Giants in five.

"Three different National League champions won only one game from us," DiMaggio said.

For more perspective, Furillo consulted with third base coach Frankie Crosetti, who had played or coached on twenty-two pennant winners and seventeen World Series champions going back to the Babe Ruth days of 1932. Crosetti liked the '36 champs the best, but the one he enjoyed the most was in '32 against the Cubs, under the Yankees' second-year manager, Joe

McCarthy, who had been fired by the Wrigleys two years earlier.

On the bus ride through the streets of Chicago after the four-game sweep, "Somebody started to sing 'The Sidewalks of New York,'" Crosetti told Furillo. "Pretty soon, everybody was singing. Every time we finished a chorus, McCarthy shouted from the back of the bus, 'One more time!'"

•　　•　　•　　•　　•

The canvas had been placed on the easel, and now it was up to the artists in Dodger blue and Yankee pinstripes to leave their impressions.

This was a big one, this 1963 World Series. The two teams had met in the baseball finals seven times in the previous twenty-two years, and one or the other or both had been in every one since 1955. Now they played on different coasts, so it wasn't just for the city championship anymore. Now it was East vs. West, Atlantic vs. Pacific, Old vs. New. Hollywood was taking on Wall Street, the Sunset Strip was matched against Broadway. It had the backdrop of the Dodgers' abandonment of Brooklyn, and the matchup of an iconic superstar on aging and sore legs against a pitcher just beginning to be recognized as the best of his era.

Oddsmakers established the Yankees as 8–5 favorites, the dreaded East Coast media bias at work. Jimmy Cannon compared the Yankees to Mount Everest.

"They're the champions, just as the mountain is," the great columnist wrote. "Only the men who try to scale it are the adventurers."

Not even a Sherpa could help the Dodgers, according to Cannon, who said that not a single member of the L.A. club could crack the Yanks' starting eight. He was mostly right, although he was nuts if he would have taken Tresh over Tommy Davis. Wills also probably deserved an edge over Kubek.

Furillo, who hung out too much at Toots Shor's, found himself blinded by the eastern pundits. The restaurateur, himself an observer of more than three decades of Yankeedom, told The Steam Room, "This is the one the Yankees want the most."

The Steamer found the pre-Series remarks of Elston Howard

to be persuasive. Howard, Furillo wrote, is "fired up for this series and speaks with open contempt of Dodger pitching." The
catcher who threw out forty-four percent of base stealers over his
career expressed no fear of the Dodgers' speed.

"Luis Aparicio knows some tricks about running bases, too,
but he doesn't bother me," Howard said.

The Steamer picked the Yankees in six.

The teams opened the series on a brilliant, eighty-degree
Indian summer day in the Bronx, with Yankee Stadium's middle
deck and its dugouts laced in the traditional red, white, and
blue bunting. First thing Furillo noticed when he worked the
cage before Game One was the increased bulk of Joe Pepitone.
The Yankees' first baseman told the Steamer that he put on three
sweatshirts to pump up his physique, to try and intimidate Koufax in the pregame warm-ups.

It was a nice try.

Wearing only his Dodger grays and a long-sleeved under-
shirt, Koufax struck out the first five batters he faced. Frank
Howard showed some real muscle in the second inning when
he hit a ball 460 feet, to the base of the wall in center field. He
stretched it into a double. Two batters later, Johnny Roseboro
lofted one about 150 feet short of Howard's distance, but he put
it in a better spot—down the line in right, and over the 296-foot
mark that left-handed Yankees batters so enjoyed over the years.
The three-run homer made the score 4-0. Koufax struck out fifteen—including Pepitone, once—to set a World Series record,
and the Dodgers won, 5-2.

Assigned to cover the Series from the Yankees' perspective, Furillo wrote that the pinstripers "chose to be guess-hitters
against the game's greatest," and "They guessed wrong fifteen
times."

Yankees bat boy Tony Floria "enjoyed the day off," The
Steam Room said, "with fifteen of the fellas bringing back their
own bats after strike three to slam them into the racks."

Dominated by Koufax, "The only thing the Yankees could
hit was their fists against the dugout wall," the Steamer said.
"Their helmets took a vicious beating, too, especially the one

Mickey Mantle slammed when he was called out on strikes in the second inning."

When Koufax struck out the side in the fourth, Yankees fans swung over to support the Brooklyn-born southpaw, giving him standing ovations after each strikeout. Exactly 69,000 fans had filled the big park, and pretty much all of them were on their feet when pinch hitter Harry Bright stood in against Sandy with two outs in the bottom of the ninth and his strikeout total even with Carl Erskine's 1953 World Series record of fourteen.

The Steamer knew Harry from the Pacific Coast League days, when Bright played for the Sacramento Solons. The well-traveled first baseman—who also caught and played third base and the outfield—was in his seventeenth year of professional baseball. The Yankees picked him up early in 1963 from Cincinnati for his right-handed pinch-hitting bat, and it did contribute seven home runs to the club's American League conquest.

"Once in awhile this year, Harry Bright hit a home run for the Yankees in this situation," Furillo wrote. "When he stepped in to bat for the pitcher, Harry was looking to do something like that. Only the odds were 69,000-1 against him. The crowd and Koufax."

With the count 2-2, Koufax "threw me a fastball," Bright told Furillo. "I knew it was coming. It was no surprise. But what the hell could I do? There were 69,000 yelling for me. They were yelling for me to strike out."

"Harry Bright didn't disappoint them," the Steamer wrote.

L.A. got all the runs it needed in Game Two's 4-1 win when Roger Maris stumbled in right trying to track a first-inning liner by Willie Davis. Two runners scored. Dodgers first baseman Moose Skowron, a former Yankee, knew how to take advantage of the shallow fence in right and put one over it for a run in the eighth.

Harry Bright struck out again, pinch-hitting in the fifth inning against Johnny Podres, whose back wasn't feeling so bad.

"At this point," The Steam Room said, "it would appear Harry Bright will strike out only two more times as he zeroes in on the record for pinch whiffs."

The series shifted to the Dodgers' beautiful new ballpark for the third game, with Drysdale carrying the ball for the home team on a brilliantly sunny day. He shut out the Yankees on three hits, striking out nine in L.A.'s 1-0 win, to keep the sweep in order. The Dodgers scored their only run in the first off Jim Bouton, who would later write the entertaining and groundbreaking book *Ball Four*, which revealed some naughty secrets about the baseball life. On this day, Bouton walked Jim Gilliam in the first inning and then authored a wild pitch that put Junior in position to score the game's only run when Tommy Davis smashed a ball off Bobby Richardson's leg.

Pepitone, his muscles not quite big enough, hit a fly to right with two out in the ninth that would have reached the twentieth row in Yankee Stadium. In L.A.'s park, Fairly caught it on the warning track.

The Yankees now had thirteen hits and three runs in three games.

It left their general manager talking to himself—and to Bud Furillo.

"I was afraid this might happen," Roy Hamey told the Steamer, about a Yankees club that peaked too soon. "We didn't hit the last three weeks of the season. We didn't hit the way I know we can."

Averaging a run a game through the first three, the Yankees maintained that pace in Game Four. In the seventh inning, Mantle drove a solo shot off Koufax over the 380 mark into the left field pavilion for the Yankees' scoring allotment. It tied the score, 1-1, two innings after Frank Howard's blast off Ford deep into the second deck.

The Dodgers broke the tie in the bottom of the seventh, thanks to an error by Pepitone at first. Yankees third baseman Clete Boyer had jumped high to make a terrific play on a high chopper by Gilliam. On his return to earth, Boyer delivered a strong and accurate throw to first.

Like Luis Aparicio of the White Sox four years earlier, Pepitone blamed the cruel Southern California weather conditions and the outrageous fashion preferences of Angeleno baseball fans for what happened next.

"I didn't see the ball," Pepitone told Furillo. "It was a good throw by Boyer, belt high. But it was coming out of those white shirts and the sun behind third base. I put up my bare hand to protect, hoping it would hit one of them. But the ball hit me on the right wrist, the forearm, and my chest."

Once it skidded past Pepitone, the ball continued merrily up the right field line. After a wrestling match with Pepitone trying to round first, Gilliam cornered second on the fly and slid into third, carrying the go-ahead run. Willie Davis got him home on a fly to center.

Koufax made the lead hold. One of his ninth inning outs came at the expense of Mantle, who watched helplessly on a slow curve at the knees. With two on and two out, Hector Lopez rolled a grounder to short. Wills rushed in to field it at the cut of the grass. Maury threw easily to Skowron at first, and L.A. swept New York.

The Dodgers mobbed Koufax, and thousands in the crowd of 55,912 engaged in the Chavez Ravine post-game ritual of throwing their blue seat cushions into the air and raining them down on the field.

Jimmy Cannon memorialized the sight in his column the next day.

"The mats drift down like immense snowflakes falling from a Warner Brothers sky," Cannon wrote. "The Yankees wouldn't doubt that the snow falls blue in this suburb of Disneyland because they lost although their pitchers only threw two hits yesterday to the scurrying elves who represent this village . . . in the National League."

If some New York writers had a hard time dealing with the Yankees' loss, people like Ford and Berra fashioned less biting points of view.

"They didn't exactly kick the hell out of us," The Steam Room quoted Ford, after the sweep. "They just got four good pitched games."

Between them, Koufax, Podres, and Drysdale gave the Dodger bullpen the Series off. They threw three complete games and worked thirty-five and a third of the thirty-six total innings. The three Dodger starters gave up only twenty-one hits, Perranoski in the bullpen one more. They struck out thirty-six and walked five. Thanks to those three, the Dodgers never trailed in the Series.

Berra, in perfectly clear syntax, told Bud Furillo that in his fourteen years of post-season play, "That's the best pitching I've seen."

•   •   •   •   •

Dodger fans in the Steam Room era freely exercised their First Amendment right to second-guess Dodgers manager Walter Alston, which at times motivated Furillo to frequently come to the defense of "The Quiet Man."

Early in 1959, with the Dodgers in second place and playing fairly well, Furillo said he had never received a single letter from a fan that ever said anything positive about Alston, the forceful but low-key skipper.

"He doesn't wave his arms," Furillo wrote of Alston, and "he doesn't shovel dirt with his spikes." All Alston did, the Steamer said, was look about five moves ahead to put the pieces in place for a checkmate.

Furillo described a Coliseum situation one night in 1959, when the Dodgers and Phillies each scored in double digits and Philadelphia ran out of left-handed relief pitchers going into the bottom of the ninth. Alston's bench still had a left-handed pinch hitter, Norm Larker, and the manager planned the inning around when and how to use him. The call came in a nice spot— bases loaded and one out. Then, when the Phillies shifted into double-play position, Alston made them pay.

"He flashed the squeeze," the Steamer said.

Larker got the bunt down, and the runner on third, Don Demeter, made it home easily.

The Steam Room chronicled a fine example of Alston's strength and silence in 1966, when lefty reliever Ron Perranoski threw a couple shutout innings and got the first out in the ninth in a one-run game against the Braves in Chavez Ravine.

Up came Hank Aaron for the Braves. Out came Walter Alston for the Dodgers.

"Yet the appearance of Alston was appealed by Perry," Furillo wrote. "He made his case to the manager's back as Smokey suddenly found something extremely interesting to watch out in center field, while Perry pleaded his case. Alston paid him no mind. When Perry wasn't looking, Alston summoned Phil Regan, who grounded Aaron out."

The Steamer gave Alston a little shot now and then, like in the early '70s, over the manager's handling of some of his up-and-coming talent. One member of the youth brigade, Bobby Valentine, eventually got shipped out to Anaheim, where he sounded off in The Steam Room about his former manager's disdain for players who cheered in the dugout.

"We don't do that up here," Alston told Valentine. "That's not the Dodgers' major-league image."

No matter.

Alston's reserved approach over his twenty-three-year managerial career helped the Dodgers win six National League pennants and four World Series championships, and himself six Manager of the Years awards from *Sporting News* and the Associated Press.

•   •   •   •   •

In 1964, the Dodgers lost two of their first three, and they were out of the race.

Koufax put up more incredible numbers: a 19–5 record, an ERA of 1.74, seven shutouts, his third no-hitter.

He also came up with one incredibly sore elbow. It started hurting in spring training, and in mid-August, with the seventh-place Dodgers twelve and a half out of first, they shut him down.

Team physician Dr. Robert F. Kerlan diagnosed Koufax with a traumatically arthritic elbow.

"His muscles are his worst enemy," the legendary L.A. sports doc told Furillo. "They're just too big, and they put too much strain on his elbow."

It would never get better.

Neither did the Dodgers in 1964. They finished tied for sixth.

In spring training the next year, Koufax's elbow hemorrhaged after a game in Vero Beach, and he flew back to L.A. for treatment. The Steamer met with the pitcher and the doctor in Kerlan's office on April 2 and saw the damage up close.

"I haven't been able to straighten my arm out for the past year," Koufax told the Steamer. He said the six months of rest helped, but "the elbow was swollen when I woke up Wednesday morning. I couldn't raise my arm to a forty-five-degree angle. I didn't have any natural movement at all."

"You've heard of water on the knee," Kerlan said to the writer. "Well, this is water on the elbow."

•   •   •   •   •

Coming off their disappointing finish in 1964, the Dodgers traded hitting for pitching in the off-season—Frank Howard to the Senators for Claude Osteen, who gave L.A. 287 quality innings and fifteen wins with an ERA of 2.79, but whose acquisition cost the club its only legitimate power hitter. Then Tommy Davis broke his ankle in early May, and the writers said there was no way this team of banjo hitters could win anything, not with a team batting average at the end of the year of only .245.

But there they were, in first place for all but twenty-three days of the season, including the only one that mattered, which was the last.

"There is no way you can call this a good ball club," Furillo wrote midway through the season. "They have three super players and a handful of professionals, some of whom aren't major-leaguers. But they battle like hell to stay where they are—on top of a league which includes five teams with more overall talent."

Wills, Drysdale, and Koufax—the three supers—finished third, fifth, and second in the NL MVP balloting.

Early in the year, Furillo called it "a master stroke by the Alston-Bavasi brain trust" when they named Wills team captain. Maury had always been "a moody loner," according to The

Steam Room, but the appointment "won genuine approval from the squad" and brought it closer together than any time since Pee Wee Reese wore the figurative "C" on his jersey.

In one of his best seasons, Wills led the league in stolen bases for the sixth straight year with ninety-four, turning that many of his 167 singles and forty walks into doubles and sometimes triples. A two-time Gold Glover at shortstop, he led the league in assists in 1965 with 535.

The Steamer said Wills was as exciting as any player in the league, including Mays.

"I'd rather watch Wills play one inning than most players ten years," Furillo wrote.

Don Drysdale won twenty-three and hit seven home runs, one of which traveled 450 feet. He drove in nineteen runs in 130 official at bats. His slugging percentage of .508 was 117 points higher than anybody else on the team.

"The Big Warrior," as they called him when the Vietnam War began to heat up, "pitches every game as if it were for possession of Dong Xoia," Furillo wrote. Drysdale told The Steam Room that the club's diminished firepower forced the staff to pitch like every game was 0-0, "knowing we can't afford to give up runs."

As for Koufax, the night he struck out fourteen Mets to win his twentieth game on August 10, Furillo began the campaign for the Dodgers to up Sandy's wages to $100,000. Only Mantle and Mays were getting that kind of money then—no pitchers.

Furillo counted thirty journalists at the post-twentieth press conference. Koufax answered every question and "didn't raise an eyebrow" about it. When the interviews ended at 10:45 PM, "the world's most famous arthritic elbow went into the ice," the column said. "He walked out of Dodger Stadium at 12:30 this morning. There's a lot of hell connected to being the best pitcher in baseball."

•   •   •   •   •

The Steamer, who was now the sports editor, made it out to the ballpark almost every Sunday in '65 for both the Dodgers and Angels, giving his beat writers the day off. He also made the short hop from the paper to the Ravine at least one night a week, looking for legend and lore in a sport that was steeped in it.

He got a dose of history at the Dodgers' home opener, when the visiting Mets came to town under manager Casey Stengel, a baseball storybook unto himself. Over the previous fifty-five years, Stengel played in the first game ever at Ebbets Field, batted against Babe Ruth in a World Series, studied at the feet of John McGraw, and managed as many World Series championship clubs—along with Joe McCarthy—as anybody in baseball history. Casey and Joe each won seven for the Yankees.

On the mound that night for the Mets was Warren Spahn, the high-kicking winner of 363 games—more than any lefty ever. Cut loose in the off-season by the Milwaukee Braves, Spahn hooked on with Stengel, who gave him double duty as a member of the starting rotation as well as pitching coach.

In the dugout next to Stengel was Yogi Berra. The three-time American League MVP with 2,150 career hits had been fired after one year of managing the Yankees, even though his team had won the American League pennant. Berra found work under his old skipper on the other side of town as a player-coach on the losing, amusing, but still amazing Mets.

Three days short of his forty-fourth birthday, Spahn got the April 20 start against the Dodgers, and he kept L.A. off balance all night with curve balls that broke into the edges of the strike zone and screwballs that spun away from right-handed hitters. With the teams scoreless, the Mets scrounged up a few late runs to take a 3–0 lead into the bottom of the ninth. Spahn came out to finish the job, but Wes Parker, the Dodgers' switch-hitting first baseman, opened the inning with a single to right. Willie Davis then grounded what looked like a double-play ball to first baseman Ed Kranepool, who had just entered the game as a defensive replacement.

"Kranepool accepted the ball, and then, in the manner of a quarterback trying to run out the clock, held on to it," Bud Furillo wrote.

Singles by Tommy Davis and Johnny Roseboro scored two runs for the Dodgers, and put runners on first and third and nobody out in what was now a 3–2 game. Stengel called time and strolled out of the first-base dugout to talk to Spahn.

"Casey wobbled to the mound," Furillo wrote, "crossed in front of it, and said in a voice best suited to calling trains, 'I got McGraw and Ribant down in the bullpen. Which one of those fellas should I bring in?'"

Mulling his obvious conflict of interest, "Spahn kicked the dirt," Furillo wrote.

"'How do you feel?' Stengel inquired.

"'I feel good,' Spahn assured. 'Let me pitch to the next kid.'

"'You may feel good,' said Stengel, 'but a few of those balls they've hit off you have been pretty lively, although I guess the first baseman helped out.'"

The pitching coach advised the manager to leave in the starter. Stengel agreed with the advice and stuck with Spahn.

Next up was Dodgers rookie Jim Lefebvre, and Spahn struck him out on screwballs. Then, the key play of the game: Fairly bounced a comebacker to Spahn, who fielded it and saw that Tommy Davis was halfway to home plate. Spahn stared at Tommy and Tommy stared back, time suspended in the forty-five feet of air that separated them. Spahn finally threw to third and Tommy broke for home, but Charley Smith's peg to back up Mets catcher Hawk Taylor nailed Davis at the plate.

Now all Spahn had to do was take care of the weak-hitting John Kennedy, which he did, for the 2,500th strikeout of his career. At the time, it was the fourth best in baseball history, behind Walter Johnson, Cy Young, and Bob Feller.

"I never had any bigger one in my life than that last one," Spahn told Furillo in the Mets' clubhouse after the game, possibly forgetting the two times he fanned Mickey Mantle in the World Series.

Spahn also told the Steamer, "It's my first win for Casey after twenty-three years."

The lefty pitched for Stengel for one year, in 1942, when Casey managed the Boston Braves. Spahn went into the service the next year, and the Braves "discharged" Stengel, in Casey's words, the year after that. The Steam Room picked up the chatter from there.

"Yogi Berra, a younger man, in the locker next to him, said to Spahn: 'If you pitched to everyone like you did the last three batters we wouldn't be here this late.' Spahn smiled. So did Yogi, who has learned a new cheer. 'Let's Go Mets,' he shouted, in a Yankee accent."

•   •   •   •   •

Furillo watched from his living room the sunny Sunday afternoon in August when the Dodgers played the Giants up in Candlestick and Juan Marichal clubbed Johnny Roseboro.

The Steamer couldn't believe it. He knew Marichal pretty well, liked him a lot, and had gotten some great stuff out of him earlier that season in Chavez Ravine when Drysdale hit a wicked shot off Juan's ass.

"This place is dangerous," Marichal told the Steamer, after the June game in which he won a classic over Drysdale, 2–1. Earlier in the year, Jim Lefebvre had smashed one off Juan's forearm. "Don't they like me here?" he asked the Steamer.

Marichal showed little mirth the lovely day he walloped Roseboro. Watching on television, Furillo observed that Marichal—one of the best control pitchers ever—appeared to be off his game early, when he knocked down Wills and Fairly with head-high fastballs. Furillo suggested that Giants manager Herman Franks might have ordered the dustings, although nobody would ever really know because of the rule of omertà.

"They never cop out on each other in baseball," Furillo wrote. "But we know that swinging his bat at Roseboro's head had to be Juan's idea, and he must be punished severely."

As sports editor, Furillo topped his section the next day with a seventy-two-point headline: "Juan Disgraces Baseball."

National League enforcers did suspend Marichal for two starts.

Like the Dodgers, the Giants moved on from Bloody Sunday shaken by the violence. They lost eight of their next twelve and slipped into third place, two back of the Dodgers and one behind the Reds. Then Mays, the '65 National League MVP, hit eight home runs in two weeks while San Francisco won fourteen in a row to build up its nice mid-September advantage.

•   •   •   •   •

The night of the perfect game, the Steamer was home watching TV when the phone rang. The call was for me, from a sixth-grade pal.

"Turn on the radio," he told me.

We gathered around Vinny, just like the 1930s. Cubs pitcher Bob Hendley took a no-hitter into the seventh himself, but Lou Johnson ruined his with a double, and then it was all Koufax as Sandy led 1–0 going into the ninth.

"There are 29,000 in the ballpark and a million butterflies," Vin Scully intoned.

Koufax overcame his flutters to go for the kill. He struck out Chris Krug and Joey Amalfitano, his fourth and fifth whiffs in a row. Now Sandy was one short of twenty-seven straight outs.

"It is 9:46 PM," the great announcer spoke into our living room and thousands of others from the desert to the sea. "Two and two to Harvey Kuenn, one strike away, Sandy into his wind-up, here's the pitch—swung on and missed, a perfect game!"

As he liked to do in big moments, Vinny let the crowd tell the story. Cheers filled the airwaves for thirty seconds.

The next day, Bud Furillo gained an exclusive interview with Koufax at Sandy's house in Studio City. They talked about Koufax's difficult early years, when his teammates would get mad at him for not getting the ball over the plate in batting practice. Sandy discussed his emotions, how he needed to control them when he pitched, to not get so mad at himself when he made a mistake. They talked about Bob Feller, about no-hitters, and how the Steamer's mother thought Sandy should be nominated for sainthood.

Koufax said he had been too tired the night before to do much celebrating. He'd gone to dinner with Cubs pitcher Larry Jackson, then it was home to bed.

"That was one ball game," he told the Steamer. "I've still got to go back out there four days from now and try to win again."

•   •   •   •   •

When the Dodgers returned home on September 24 with a six-game winning streak, Furillo climbed aboard for the nine games leading up to the clinch job.

Banging out a column a day, the Steamer led off with a focus on Jim Lefebvre, the Rookie of the Year second baseman who had homered in three straight games going into the first of three against Bob Gibson and the St. Louis Cardinals. Gibson kept Jimmy in the park, but Lefebvre's bases-loaded, ground-ball single off reliever Hal Woodeshick scored two in the eighth and gave the Dodgers a 4–3 win. They were Lefebvre's fifteenth and sixteenth RBIs in the last nineteen games.

"It is certainly a shame Jimmy Lefebvre had to stumble into a slump at this stage of the race," the Steamer wrote. "Still, his eighth inning single with the bases loaded scored a couple of runs, which gave the Dodgers one more than St. Louis. Grown people grew hysterical at the sight of the ball cutting outfield grass up the middle. News of the Dodger win reportedly increased the smell of gas fumes in San Francisco, where the Giants say they ain't worried, despite the odor, with a one-game lead and only nine to play."

Lefebvre's no-homer slump continued the next day, when a measly single staked Koufax to a 1-0 lead on Sandy's way to breaking Feller's record with the 2-0 shutout.

With eight games to go, the media crush pressed harder. Koufax, in the dugout, knew what was waiting for him in the clubhouse, where, Furillo wrote, "the television cameras and writers from all over the country tensed for his arrival."

"I can't run away from it, can I?" Koufax said to Furillo with resignation, during their moment of peace in the dugout.

It was Drysdale's turn on September 26 to shut out the Cardinals, 1-0, on five hits, striking out five with no walks. Al Ferrara's clutch error saved the day for Don and the Dodgers.

L.A. had pieced together a run in the first in its customary fashion. Wills got a bunt single, stole second after being picked off first, went to third on Cardinals first baseman Bill White's error, and Gilliam drove him home with a single.

Ferrara's heroics occurred in the second inning, after Ken Boyer put himself in scoring position for the Cardinals with a single and a steal of second.

St. Louis shortstop Dick Groat then lifted a foul fly to right. Ferrara raced over to catch it.

"Fortunately," Furillo wrote, "the ball took a Dodger bounce out of Ferrara's basket."

Boyer, on second, would have made third easily had Ferrara held onto the ball. No catch, no tag, so Boyer stayed on second. Groat then grounded sharply to Drysdale, who wheeled toward Clete's brother and erased him in a rundown. Tim McCarver's ensuing fly to left surely would have scored Boyer, if Ferrara's flub hadn't kept the runner on second.

"It's easily the most important fly ball I've dropped in my career," Ferrara told Furillo.

The Steamer wrote, "The Sunday salutations went to Don Drysdale, Maury Wills, and Jim Gilliam for their prominent roles in arranging a new start of the National League. The cheers were richly deserved, but please, let us not forget Al Ferrara, baseball's unsung hero."

The win put the Dodgers in a first-place tie with the Giants, with seven to go. They stayed there the next day with a 6-1 win over Cincinnati, when Willie Davis overcame a season-long slump to hit two home runs.

"It just took me five months to get comfortable at the plate," he told Furillo.

Up in San Francisco, the pennant race news included a report that Willie Mays wanted to be properly compensated for his MVP season.

"On a day when the Willie in San Francisco was reported to be asking for $150,000, our Willie settled for a couple of hits," the Steamer wrote. "They were big hits, the kind their Willie hits—four base hits. Mays with fifty is only forty ahead of our Willie, but remember, there are still six games to go."

With the glove, "Davis was scraped off the fence in center field after catching a Pete Rose smash in the fifth inning," Furillo reported. It was the second straight time that baseball's

WILLIE D. ON THE ART OF SLAP-HITTING
AUGUST 10, 1969

Willie Davis is getting into this pennant race with a little different approach than the one he used in those of the past. Willie wants to hit and run instead of hit and watch.

Everyone in the Dodger organization has taken a shot at telling Willie how to hit. The current general manager and the slap hitter from Pittsburgh, Matty Alou, have finally gotten through.

"Al Campanis told me there won't be enough money in the world to pay me if I hit .325," said Davis. "That's impressive. I look at the little guy from Pittsburgh and I say to myself, how can he outhit me every year?" . . .

The man of a thousand stances, Willie has added lumber. . . .

He bought a new shipment of bats last weekend in St. Louis. . . . They weigh thirty-nine ounces apiece and stretch out thirty-six inches. . . .

Davis is changing his swing as well. He's done that before about as many times as Clark Kent has changed costumes. But Willie explains that this one tops them all.

"It used to take me a minute to get out of the batter's box after going for the long ball," he said. "I'd wrap that bat around my neck and I would take forever to get unwound. This didn't give me the opportunity to take advantage of my greatest asset in this game, my speed." . . .

Only twenty-nine, Willie D. may even hit upon the idea of bunting himself on base someday.

all-time hit leader had been robbed in the game. Two innings earlier, Lou Johnson, the twenty-nine-year-old rookie, "left his imprint on the boards in left," the Steamer said.

"I want to tell you that is some fence out there," Johnson said in The Steam Room. "It is a pleasure to run into that fence. Last year I hit a brick one in Salt Lake City and it didn't feel as good."

In the Dodgers' tenth straight win on September 28, Johnson put one over the boards to put L.A. in first place, a lead they would never give up.

Sweet Lou had played for fifteen minor-league clubs before the Dodgers brought him up in May after Tommy Davis broke his ankle. His biggest hit of the regular season came in the twelfth inning to break a 1–1 tie and beat the Reds.

"He walked to first base, jogged to second, danced to third, which he pounded with both feet after a high leap," The Steam Room reported. "He jumped on home plate and into the clutches of his back-slapping teammates who mobbed him."

Since his call-up from Spokane, Johnson, along with slamming into the baby-blue boards in left field to catch fly balls, stood in at the plate and refused to yield to sixteen pitches off his arms, ribs, hips, and head. He hit twelve homers and finished twenty-fourth in the league's MVP voting.

On his $11,500 big-league salary, Johnson did whatever it took to make sure the Dodgers cashed post-season checks.

"He wants that World Series money more than the Pakistanis want Kashmir," Furillo wrote after Johnson's homer beat Cincy.

Koufax's third straight shutout, on September 29, increased the Dodgers' lead to two games with four to play. Earlier in the day, the Dodgers announced that they would begin selling World Series tickets. Then the Cardinals beat the Giants in the afternoon to drop L.A.'s magic number to two.

"When the Cardinals held on to beat the Giants shortly after four o'clock, the customers swarmed the park like locusts," the Steamer said. "Only some of the 52,312 locusts drove cars which they chose to abandon in the middle of the surface roads inside the stadium parking lots. After fighting the freeway crush outside for an hour, some of 'em grew panicky in their haste to see Sandy. When you combine a traffic jam, heat, and pennant fever, man becomes deranged."

Koufax saved plenty of his thirteen strikeouts for the traffic-delayed Dodgers fans. He had at least one in every inning in his two-hit, 5–0 defeat of the Reds.

Maury Wills's bases-loaded triple in the seventh cushioned Koufax, who had worked Jim Maloney for a walk himself to reach first base ahead of the three-bagger. Sandy then scored on a ninety-yard run.

Up two with four to play, thoughts of 1962 lingered in the Dodgers' minds.

"We don't want that to happen again," Drysdale told Furillo, recalling the team's loss of six of its last seven games three years earlier.

The Steamer said, "Best advice is to hold all tickets until the result is official."

With Milwaukee in town for the season's final four, Drysdale struck out eight, didn't walk anybody, allowed only three hits, and threw only eighty-nine pitches. The 4-0 Dodgers victory on September 30 was their thirteenth straight. They needed it to stay two up on the Giants, who also won that day.

Looking ahead to the next year's holdout, Furillo wrote that Drysdale, like Koufax, also merited a pay increase into $100,000 territory.

"You can't spend all our money in one week!" Bavasi yelled at Furillo, for bringing up the topic of Drysdale's pay barely a month after the columnist had advocated a six-figure sum for Koufax. "What is it with you? Are you getting a commission from our pitchers?"

"It was a thought," the Steamer wrote, "inasmuch as Mays promised Jimmy Cannon some new suits if he gets his salary to $150,000."

More than 50,000 fans filled the park on October 1, a Friday night, hoping for the clincher. It didn't happen. Claude Osteen, the tough-luck pitcher, pitched in tough luck again. He lost to the Braves, 2-0, dropping his record to 15-15 despite his nice earned run average. The winning streak was over, but the Giants lost, too, so the Dodgers still led by two with two to go.

Pitching on two days' rest, Koufax returned to the mound October 2 with yet another spectacular performance. He struck out thirteen Braves to make it thirty-seven in his last three starts. He also drew a walk from Tony Cloninger to force in a r un in the Dodgers' 3-1 victory that got them into the World Series. The Steamer called it "the proudest team ever to win a major-league pennant."

"They are kind enough not to laugh at you and me and everyone else who said they couldn't win in a league loaded with balanced talent," Furillo wrote.

The Steamer had to search in the trainer's room to pull a

quote from an emotional Maury Wills, who was sitting all by himself, in one of his best seasons—and on his birthday, no less.

"His eyes were moist and the streak of silver down the middle of his brown hair seemed to have widened an inch," Furillo wrote. "The silver fox touch made him look older than his years, which reached thirty-three on Flag Day."

Maury told the Steamer, "This justifies everything I believe in. We didn't have the talent, but we had the right mental approach and attitude for this game."

In a rare departure from the Koufax cool, Sandy, in a clubhouse interview, "exploded," Furillo wrote, when a TV reporter stupidly asserted that it would have been a backed-in title for the Dodgers if the Giants had lost that day.

"Backed in? We won fifteen out of sixteen and you say we backed in?" Koufax said to the guy.

Furillo said Koufax had a right to be "angrier than I've ever seen him."

"Anybody who calls them cheese champs should be arrested," The Steam Room asserted.

●   ●   ●   ●   ●

The Dodgers' seven-game World Series victory over the Minnesota Twins felt anticlimactic, after the warfare of winning the National League.

Furillo, as sports editor, stayed home to put out the paper for Games One and Two in Bloomington, when Koufax's observance of Yom Kippur for the Series opener was a bigger story than the Twins' two victories.

Stuck in the office for the Minnesota games, the Steamer made an interesting point about the Twins when they came to L.A. up two games to none.

"They don't play very well in Dodger Stadium," he wrote.

Minnesota, in fact, lost five of nine to the seventh-place Angels that year in Chavez Ravine. Zoilo Versalles, the Twins' AL MVP shortstop, made five errors in the nine games. Their big-bopping lineup with sluggers like Harmon Killebrew and Bob Allison hit only one homer all year in the Ravine. They played to crowds as small as 4,989. They averaged less than seven hits a game against Marcelino Lopez, Rudy May, and Fred Newman. How many could they expect against Osteen, Drysdale, and Koufax?

The answer was hardly any.

The Dodgers swept the Twins in the three games in Los Angeles by a combined score of 18-2. Osteen pitched a shutout in Game Three, Koufax another in Game 5. In the Dodgers' 7-0 rout that sent them back to Minnesota up one in the series, Frank Quilici joined Joe Pepitone and Luis Aparicio to maintain an American League tradition of blaming an error on the white-shirted background.

"Charles O. Finley might have something," Furillo wrote after the Dodgers fifth-game win. "Charlie says they should use orange balls. They would blend in nicely with the lemons in the American League."

Mudcat Grant hit a three-run homer and pitched a six-hit complete game as the Twins won the sixth game to tie the Series back in Minnesota. That just set up Koufax for his second shutout, 2-0, and another World Series MVP award. Lou Johnson helped him out with a home run off the foul pole in left, the second of the series for the career minor-leaguer.

"The Dodgers," Furillo wrote when it was all over, "have now completed their practical joke on baseball."

•   •   •   •   •

Having advocated the financial cause of Koufax and Drysdale during the heat of the championship season, Furillo, during the Hot Stove League competition, broke a story that added some tension to the labor relations problem brewing in the Dodgers empire.

He received a tip from a still-unknown source that the team's owner, Walter O'Malley, had been deposed in an antitrust lawsuit that the state of Wisconsin had filed against the National League and the Milwaukee Braves over the baseball club's proposed move to Atlanta.

In his testimony, O'Malley estimated his team's 1965 profits to be $2 million. It may not sound like much compared to the

$44.9 billion Exxon Mobil reported in 2012, but it was still more than two and a half times the Dodger payroll of $750,000.

"Apparently Mr. O'Malley, you made money last year," one of the lawyers said to the owner during the deposition.

"I've never shown much interest in losing money," O'Malley replied, in an exchange reported exclusively in Furillo's column.

Contacted by The Steam Room, O'Malley said, "I testified in round figures without expenses being deducted. We're not a public corporation. We never have given any figures out."

The Steamer's February 3 story reported that the team grossed a little more than $6 million, for an impressive margin of thirty-three percent.

"Like O'Malley, we can only deal in round figures in estimating Dodger profits for 1965," Furillo wrote. "But it's safe to say we're as close as Mariner got to Mars in the same summer—and it only missed by 10,000 miles or so."

Tellingly, The Steam Room reported on the possibility of a

SUPERSTARS TAKING NOTE OF DODGER PROFITS?
FEBRUARY 6, 1966

The *Herald Examiner* disclosure the other day that the Dodgers banked $2 million for the 1965 season didn't exactly come under the heading of news to Buzzie Bavasi. After all, Walter O'Malley gets first count, and Buzzie gets second count.

But it made Mr. B uneasy to see the club's profits become a matter of public information. . . .

A graduate of Actors' Studio, Bavasi is marvelous at moaning at signing time. For instance, when the Cubs announced a deficit of more than $300,000, Bavasi summoned Don Drysdale and Sandy Koufax and called Maury Wills off a banjo job at which he was making better than scale.

Mr. B. held up the Chicago report.

"Now you can see what we're up against in baseball," he whined. "And the Cubs don't even have a light bill to pay."

The Dodger superstars walked out without signing, and now you wonder if they'll hold out for one-fifth of the $2 million before they get on the plane to Vero Beach.

player revolt.

"The payroll may go up," Furillo said, "like Wilt Chamberlain after a rebound when this information is discussed by the players, their wives, and other advisers."

Twenty-five days later, the Dodgers' team plane departed Los Angeles for Vero Beach, minus Sandy Koufax and Don Drysdale. The holdout was on.

•   •   •   •   •

All the boys wanted was $500,000 each, spread over three years, a sum that would have made them the highest-paid players in the game. With the two of them, and Wills, leading the Dodgers to three world championships in seven years, they knew it would be hard for the Dodgers to say they didn't deserve it—harder still, after Bud Furillo's revelation about O'Malley's pleasant year.

The Steamer swung by Sandy's house on March 15, just as the great pitcher was returning home from playing eighteen holes at La Costa. Or was it 234? He'd been down there instead of Vero Beach for two weeks.

Koufax sounded relaxed.

"None of us are mad at Buzzie and I don't believe Buzzie's mad at us," Koufax told Furillo. "This is a business deal. I hope it all works out. If it doesn't and I need a couple tickets to a Dodger game this summer, I might even call Buzzie and ask for them."

The Dodgers offered Koufax $100,000, and Drysdale $85,000.

Furillo reported that public sentiment appeared to be swinging toward management—no surprise in a Southern California region then historically troubled by labor agitation. Bavasi and O'Malley, pushing buttons in the mainstream media, tried to make out Drysdale and Koufax to look like Wobblies.

Koufax sought to explain their position in simple terms that people might understand more easily in entertainment-conscious Southern California.

"You don't go into a movie knowing how much everybody in the picture is making," he told The Steam Room. "You don't come out of a movie theater saying that one of the actors got too much for his part. You just say it was a good or a bad movie."

It irritated the hell out of Koufax and Drysdale that some elements in the public perceived them as petty, jealous rivals.

Sandy moved to scotch that notion in The Steam Room.

"People have been playing Don and me against one another for years, comparing us and what have you," Koufax told Furillo. "We are not competing. We're on the same team."

Furillo wrote a column on one valuable endorsement the pitchers received. The news was provided exclusively to The Steam Room by one of its most reliable and trusted sources, linebacker Wayne Walker of the Detroit Football Lions.

Walker wrote a letter to Furillo saying he had been wandering around the outback of Michigan when what should visit him but a spaceship from Zaleechee, a galaxy previously undetected by reputable astronomy. An orange-and-green man had gotten off the spaceship, Walker said, and told him, "We've been studying your planet for a long time, and it will turn into a ball of fire if the Dodgers don't sign Koufax and Drysdale."

Furillo followed up on the communiqué with a column saying the Dodgers "should have come forward long ago and offered these boys what they deserve."

He suggested $150,000 for Koufax and $100,000 for Drysdale. The Dodgers' offers to the players "make the team look cheap," Furillo wrote.

Looking for backup work, the pitchers passed their screen tests and were given parts in the Hollywood epic *Warning Shot*, starring David Janssen.

Soon afterward, O'Malley and Bavasi saved the world from having hell rained down on it from Zaleechee. They paid Koufax $125,000, and Drysdale $110,000. The holdout was over.

"It's a long way from a million dollars," Furillo wrote of the pitchers' deal with the club, "but at least the boys are in a good neighborhood."

•   •   •   •   •

In his final year of pitching, Koufax led the league in wins (27), ERA (1.73), shutouts (5), innings pitched (323), and strikeouts

(317). He won his third Cy Young Award, finished second in the MVP balloting to Roberto Clemente, and once again was the player most responsible for the Dodgers winning a National League championship.

Koufax had already told another reporter, Phil Collier of the *San Diego Union*, that 1966 would probably be his last year.

There wasn't a Dodger fan in town who didn't know about Koufax's post-game routine of putting his left elbow in a rubber tube and soaking it in ice after every start. On a cold June evening in Candlestick, Bud Furillo again sat late into the night with Koufax at the ice bucket, long after the other thirty or so reporters had departed the Dodgers clubhouse. Sandy had just struck out eleven Giants and beat them with a four-hitter. The press held him up so long, he only had a pot of cold canned spaghetti waiting for him from the post-game team meal.

Before Koufax dumped his elbow in the ice, "he compared his arms," Furillo wrote. "The right one hung straight down his side. The left one was as bowed as Frank Malzone's legs. 'Will you believe this used to be a matched set?' Sandy said, gazing at the left arm which can be straightened out no longer."

A couple months later, Koufax's elbow erupted in pain during the game against the Reds. Alston had to come get him in the fifth inning, before Dr. Woods gave the pitcher the cortisone shot that made the Steamer and Maury Wills turn their heads.

Kerlan told Furillo afterwards, "He doesn't sleep for a couple nights after one of those shots."

The doctor said to the writer, "One of these nights the same thing is going to happen and that will be it."

Furillo talked to Koufax a couple days later and asked him how he felt.

"It's never been this bad," Sandy told the Steamer.

A day later, the cortisone kicked in, enabling Sandy to take care of the Cardinals on six hits, striking out ten. The August 21 win was Koufax's twentieth of the year. He shut out the Astros on September 11 to put the Dodgers in first, where they stayed the rest of the way.

Drysdale, meanwhile, tumbled to 13–16 and an ERA of 3.42,

WILL ELBOW ALLOW SANDY ONE MORE PENNANT?
AUGUST 21, 1966

Being as how he left his last game with his elbow hurting, the season to speculate on how long Sandy Koufax can continue as a pitcher is now underway.

A columnist in San Jose who claimed to have sources as close as anyone to Koufax contends that Sandy will walk away from the game when the current chase for the National League flag has ended.

Perhaps San Jose is right. With a condition such as Sandy's his next game could be his last, or, his last game was.

The question was put to Koufax, thirty, going on thirty-one this December 30.

Baseball's greatest pitcher, ever, was asked how long he planned to go on throwing the ball.

"I have no idea," he said. "As long as it will let me."

Koufax paused on the telephone to think a little more about it.

"I've been in the game twelve years now," he said. "That's a lot more than many players would like to get in the major leagues. . . .

"A long time ago, I used to think that fifteen years in baseball would be great. But that was a long time ago."

What he meant by that, I don't know. Sandy obviously doesn't think in his heart he'll be pitching in 1969.

He is an arthritic. He understands the facts of life with arthritics. His doctor is one.

It is one thing to have arthritis and almost inexplicable to demand of a limb to pitch with it. . . .

"It has never been this bad," he said. "At the moment, I just can't throw. . . . But I'd like to be on one more pennant winner."

---

his highest since the Coliseum days. In mid-August, he was only 8–13, but he got himself together down the stretch, winning his last four decisions, including two by shutout.

Then there was Phil Regan—"The Vulture," Koufax nicknamed him, because of the relief pitcher's propensity to fly in from the bullpen in close games and pick over the carcass until it wound up in his win column. Phil won fourteen and saved twenty-one. He made the All-Star team and finished seventh in the MVP balloting.

Regan, acquired in the off-season from Detroit, once played semipro football for a team in Michigan, the Grand Rapids

Sullivans. The club also featured a linebacker soon to be a heavyweight contender, Buster Mathis. This was information you would only get in The Steam Room.

"Now Regan is 12-1 and Mathis is 250 pounds and undefeated," Furillo wrote on September 6. "Young men looking for a spring board to success should apply to the Grand Rapids Sullivans."

When he was with the Tigers, the Vulture pitched more like a canary. Furillo wrote that he never got along with Tigers manager Charlie Dressen: "'Throw the curve,' Dressen would insist. Regan threw it reluctantly, and it would usually travel about 400 feet into the stands."

In L.A., Regan came up with a new pitch.

"A dignified gentleman of the grand old game, Roseboro refers to Regan's fantastic new pitch as the country sinker, or just plan sinker," Furillo wrote. "Nine other clubs call it a spitter."

Along with the holdouts, Osteen had another good year, and rookie Don Sutton began his Hall of Fame career by winning twelve, posting an ERA under three, pitching more than 200 innings, and allowing only 1.081 walks and hits per nine innings. It's a category in which he would lead the league four times.

The Dodgers hit a little better than in '65 and held off the Giants for the flag, in a race that went down to the last-day doubleheader, in which Koufax beat Jim Bunning in the nightcap in Philadelphia to clinch the pennant in the 162nd game.

Advancing to the World Series against the Orioles, L.A. was done after the fifth inning of Game Two when Willie Davis dropped two fly balls and threw one away for three errors in the same chukker. The rest of the team committed three more errors in the other eight innings for a game total of six.

"Willie was two for four with one assist," Furillo wrote. "Willie caught two, dropped two, and helped Ron Fairly watch another one fall in."

It turned out that the six errors in one game added up to three times as many runs as the Dodgers scored in the four-game sweep they suffered to the Orioles. L.A. scored a couple runs early in Game One, then no more over the final twenty-seven innings. In Baltimore, the Dodgers were shut out twice, 1-0.

In assessing the swift Series extermination, the Steamer fore-saw an extended period of doom for the Dodgers, based on the sport's past performance charts.

"What happens to teams that lose four straight in the World Series?" Furillo asked on October 10, looking back at the '63 Yankees and '54 Indians and overlooking the '50 Phillies. "The pattern suggests decay. Is it possible the Dodgers, who have been the dominant team in baseball—since the fall of 1959 until yesterday's fall in Baltimore—may be showing signs of wear?"

A month and a half later, the bad news the Dodgers knew was coming finally arrived.

•   •   •   •   •

"I guess it was the fifteen or eighteen cortisone shots that made up my mind," Koufax told reporters early in the afternoon of November 18, 1966, at a press conference he called at the Bev-erly-Wilshire Hotel.

Koufax had arranged the meeting to announce his retirement.

On top of the needles to the elbow, Sandy talked about dope. He fixed on codeine pretty much every day, even when he pitched. They shot him up with phenylbutazone—"bute," they called it around the track. Two years later, Dancer's Image would be disqualified from winning the Kentucky Derby for having the same stuff in his system that Koufax had in his.

So the Dodgers' strongest horse gave out.

"Koufax was our super star, also a super gentleman, who handled fame much better than most," the Steamer wrote. "He was kind to his fans, even though they almost barreled him over sometimes in search of his autograph and pieces of his clothing. Now he leaves the stadium. We will miss him very much."

Thirteen days after Koufax's retirement, the Dodgers traded Maury Wills to Pittsburgh. The deal came after Maury left the O'Malleys in the middle of a post-season goodwill tour of Japan.

Walter told The Steam Room that he was "damned annoyed" about Wills's stunt, but that "no personal animosity" was at-tached to the decision to get rid of him. It was just business, the godfather/owner told Furillo.

It was a decision "hastened," O'Malley told the Steamer, by Koufax's retirement.

It was time to tear up the squad.

• • • • •

The Dodgers lost more than they won in '67 and '68, and only Don Drysdale's streak of fifty-eight and two-thirds consecutive scoreless innings made anything about those two seasons memorable.

He broke the record the night of Bobby Kennedy's funeral. Drysdale told the Steamer afterward that he was so shaken up by the senator's assassination and the country's outpouring of grief, he was barely able to work himself up for the game.

"The crowd of 55,000 did this for Big D with the reception it gave him when he appeared on the sideline to warm up," Furillo wrote. "When he pitched for the seventh out in the third inning [to break the record], the standing ovation was the loudest and longest I've ever heard at Dodger Stadium."

A week later, Buzzie Bavasi announced his departure from the organization. He was off to San Diego to become president of the expansion Padres. Furillo hailed Bavasi's rise "from office boy to the best general manager in baseball."

Despite the two down years, Walter Alston remained firmly in control of the on-field product, but his successor began to gain prominence through the pages of The Steam Room.

By the summer of '68, Furillo had known Tommy Lasorda for fifteen years, from when the Steamer's father told him to take care of the kid from Norristown training in San Bernardino with the St. Louis Browns. Furillo fulfilled his obligation, introducing Lasorda to the L.A. scene and getting him tickets to the best sporting events in town.

By 1968, it had become pretty clear that Lasorda, a scout and minor-league manager in the organization, was a comer. Tommy, who in those days was still capitalizing the "S" in Lasorda, had just taken a job to manage the Dodgers' Rookie League club in Ogden. The question was whether the organization could hang

ALSTON WIELDING QUICK HOOK WITH THE KIDS
JUNE 20, 1973

To hear some of them tell it, the Dodgers fielded a cross-eyed team last year.

They kept one eye on the game and the other on the manager in the third base dugout.

"One mistake and you're out of there," the player said. "It doesn't do much for your confidence."

But this wasn't the case with the man [Walter] Alston selected to succeed Maury Wills. He stuck with William E. Russell, of Pittsburg, Kansas, a town so small there wasn't room for the final letter of the name of it, the H. . . .

Alston stayed with Russell, and Bill proceeded to lead the league, in errors. He made thirty-four, more than any other shortstop in both of the National divisions. He also made more hits than most of them. Only Don Kessinger batted higher than Russell's .272. . . .

As this was written, Russell had an eleven-game hitting streak going. And I am still picturing in my mind some of the magnificent plays he made on television Sunday in Montreal. . . .

Wills is gone. Long live Russell. . . .

"Russell is a likeable kid," Alston said. "He likes to agitate a little bit. But he worked hard. And he's easy to coach. I get a kick out of managing this team. . . . We have a lot of youth out there."

on to him. Bavasi wanted him in San Diego. The Steamer reported that the expansion club in Montreal liked him as a possible manager. A couple other clubs were interested in him as a pitching coach.

Furillo advised that the garrulous Lasorda would make a very good replacement for Alston when the time came.

"LaSorda is better around kids than Hans Christian Andersen," the Steamer wrote. "And he knows just as many stories."

As a scout, Tommy gained legendary status for the tactics he employed to sign the talent he identified. In closing the deal with Fremont High star Willie Crawford, Tommy unexpectedly showed up at the funeral for the young man's grandfather. Then he eulogized the gentleman for twenty minutes, even though he had never met the deceased in his life.

"It was quite an honor to eulogize a man who had been a

deacon in the church," Lasorda told Furillo.

"How did you know that?" the Steamer asked.

"I heard the minister say he was," replied Tommy, who, by the time of this 1973 Steam Room column, had elevated to the big club to take over coaching duties at third base.

Crawford, of course, signed with the Dodgers, and he eventually made it to the major leagues, as did forty-one other players whom Lasorda either signed into the pros or coached on their way up.

With Lasorda constructing the pipeline, the Dodgers developed some new kids who contended for divisional championships in '69, '70, and '71. Ted Sizemore, Billy Grabarkewitz, and Bobby Valentine were pretty good, but management got rid of them in favor of a new crew consisting of Steve Garvey, Ron Cey, Davey Lopes, and others. They came together in the closing days of The Steam Room era and won a World Series in 1981.

Chapter 8

THE REEVES AND ALLEN MESS

Yesterday, Reeves and Allen appeared in public together, brief-
ly, to announce the latter's return as coach. But the cold war
goes on between them. Their relations remain chilly. They had
to turn the heat on in the Palisades Room of the Century Plaza
Hotel, as Allen read a prepared statement and sought to hurry
away before Reeves got in his licks. . . . As the new coach of the
Rams, bearing a striking resemblance to the old one, left the
podium, Reeves said: "Thank you, George. Can we do this?"
Reeves extended his hand. Allen hesitated, then accepted, then
accepted again for more pictures. The handshakes appeared to
be insincere.

—January 7, 1969

On a gloomy fall day in San Francisco, Bud Furillo listened
while George Allen whined.

The Los Angeles Rams head coach was upset because his
8-1 team needed to score twice in the last three minutes and
eighteen seconds just to gain a tie with the 4-5 49ers. Looking
to explain how the Rams failed to subdue an inferior opponent,
Allen blamed Kezar Stadium. He called the field a "disgrace"
to the National Football League.

Furillo saw Allen's point. Tucked into the southeast corner
of Golden Gate Park, Kezar Stadium was falling apart. Flocks
of seagulls strafed the fans, the locker rooms were the smallest
in the league, and the drainage system was so bad, the field
remained cuppy two days after a Northern California rainstorm
that preceded the Rams-49ers game.

"Everything about Kezar is so depressing that even the

hippies in nearby Haight Ashbury are moving out," Furillo wrote.

In a couple of years, the 49ers would abandon the stadium, too, but that didn't do Allen any good on the Sunday afternoon of November 17, 1968, when his Rams could only tie the 49ers, 20–20.

Allen, in his post-game remarks to reporters, spun back to a third-down play in the second quarter, when L.A. wide receiver Jack Snow appeared to have caught an eight-yard pass in the end zone from quarterback Roman Gabriel. To Allen's dismay, the referees said Snow failed to get his feet down in the field of play, and they waved off the touchdown.

It was the coach's position that the officials were confused by the festive decoration of the Kezar end zones, to the point that they couldn't perceive in bounds from out. Replays did suggest that the officials missed the call, that Snow did get his feet in for the touchdown. In those days, however, there was no such thing as holding up a game for twenty minutes so the black-and-white shirts could review the tape over and over again to make sure the destiny of the republic was not set off course by an incorrect call.

So instead of the Jack Snow touchdown, L.A. had to settle for a Bruce Gossett field goal, which in the end reduced the final score to the 20–20 tie, instead of a 24–20 Rams victory.

Controversial though it may have been, the call played only a small role in the misfortune that beset the Rams that day in Kezar. Overall, their performance was marked by a game-long repetition of blunders, none of which had anything to do with the field. Furillo's game story noted that the great defensive end, Deacon Jones, for instance, jumped offsides to keep a 49ers touchdown drive alive on their first possession, an infraction that would have occurred under laboratory conditions as well as in the bogs of Kezar. Gabriel also threw an interception that San Francisco converted into a second-quarter field goal, a goof that had nothing to do with any end zone paint job.

Allen, a stickler for special teams play, must have gone completely nuts in the third quarter, when the Rams lined up offsides on a 49ers field goal try that missed; the penalty gave

San Francisco a second chance at the three-pointer, and the hometown 41,815 chortled in delight when kicker Tommy Davis directed the bonus boot through the goal posts. L.A. center Ken Iman screwed up a snap on a Rams field goal attempt in the same quarter—yet another special-teams mistake that cost Allen points, and for which the Kezar Stadium turf was utterly blameless. Then, in the fourth quarter, with the Rams on their own five-yard line, even Allen had to hold the end zone color scheme harmless when running back Dick Bass knocked the ball out of Gabriel's grasp on a play-action fake. The 49ers recovered the fumble and advanced the football into the end zone, despite its garish red-and-gold markings.

Oh, and the Rams dropped five of Gabriel's passes, including one in the end zone that Willie Ellison boxed, according to Furillo's story.

The mistakes added up to a twenty-point swing against L.A.

Rather than discuss his team's own periodic imperfections, Allen laid the harsh criticism on the field, and it was true that Kezar's notoriously wretched drainage system left portions of the field looking as if they had been set aside for migrating waterfowl.

"The Louisiana bayou is coming in nicely at Kezar," Furillo wrote.

While Kezar's environmental conditions seemed to defy the engineering imagination of mankind, it was human error itself that drove Allen to the point of madness. Overlaid atop the swamp was that end zone paint job containing psychedelic properties that in Allen's estimation confused the referees on Roman Gabriel's pass to Jack Snow in the second quarter.

"The officials are color-blind from all the colors they paint in the end zone," Allen told the press. "Let's go back to grass with a chalk stripe so the officials can keep track of what's happening in the end zone. What's all the paint in the end zone for—television? That end zone was a disgrace."

Allen's diatribe, widely reported in the media, gained the attention of the man who had hired the coach almost three years earlier.

Dan Reeves, who bought the club in 1941, had already won himself a couple of NFL championships. Apparently those early successes had satisfied his appetite when it came to winning, because in the years afterward, there were long stretches where it never seemed to be a priority. Reeves preferred to spend long evenings on the town with his friends and in the clubby atmosphere of a select few in the business of owning professional football teams.

It's not that Reeves was against winning. It just had to be done in a fashion he would enjoy. And even though George Allen quickly turned the Rams from losers into NFL title contenders, Reeves wasn't having a whole lot of fun with it. Allen's obsession with winning came at the expense of important things like social time with the owner. Reeves loved to unwind on game days—and the other six in the week—with a toddy or two. Allen drank milk.

Besides his stick-in-the-mud coach, something else had sapped Reeves's joie de vivre: he had been diagnosed two years earlier with Hodgkin's Disease. By late 1968, he was spending most of his time in New York City, getting treatment.

But Reeves still read the papers, and he didn't like it that his coach was popping off about the field. So he called Mal Florence, who covered the Rams for the *Los Angeles Times*, and told him, "We don't alibi. It's not in the Ram tradition."

Reeves may as well have ordered Allen placed into stocks in front of the peristyle end of the Coliseum. A sensitive kind, Allen felt publicly humiliated.

The next week, with the Rams still driving toward a late-season showdown with the Baltimore Colts for the NFL Coastal Division championship, L.A. scored an exciting 24–21 victory over the New York Football Giants.

In town for a rare visit to Los Angeles, Reeves went to the game and appeared to have spent a good part of it enjoying cocktails with friends. After the game, he paid his first visit of the year to the Rams' locker room. Spotting Allen, Reeves approached his head coach with an extended hand.

"George, how was the field today?" Reeves asked, according

to *Herald Examiner* columnist Mel Durslag, who had been speaking to Allen.

Allen apparently was less than thrilled to see his boss in the locker room. In fact, Durslag wrote, "The coach snapped."

"Dan, you had no right to criticize me in the paper," Allen told Reeves, according to Durslag. "You embarrassed me and my family. Here I am, working sixteen to eighteen hours a day, trying to build our team into a winner, and you make a fool of me."

Allen rejected the owner's hand. He walked away, leaving Reeves suspended in midair, while Durslag and Furillo, who had just joined the party, watched.

Reeves did not appreciate the petulance.

"George, you come back here," he demanded.

The coach refused.

It was the Sunday before Thanksgiving, and the two did not speak again until the day after Christmas when, at eight o'clock in the morning, Reeves phoned Allen.

The coach would say later that it sounded like owner was drunk again.

Allen could have used a pop himself when Reeves quickly got to the point in their brief conversation.

"Merry Christmas, George," Reeves said. "You're fired."

•   •   •   •   •

It was the best Rams story since the firing of Joe Stydahar in 1952, maybe better. It certainly was more of a spectacle. Instead of the defending champ of a coach sitting home alone in his Crenshaw District apartment with twenty-seven-year-old Bud Furillo, drinking whiskey and keeping quiet at his kitchen table while waiting for the phone call from the executioner, the blubbering Allen played it out on live local television, crying to the cameras to get his job back, with six of his best players standing behind him.

Going public worked out for George Allen, who was reinstated when the team doctor intervened on his behalf and convinced Dan Reeves to change his mind. Reeves relented and brought Allen back, but the owner got his way in the end. Five months before he died, in December 1970, Reeves fired Allen again. With the Rams on the precipice of decline, the coach didn't fight the second firing. He wound up going to Washington, where he took the Redskins to a Super Bowl before he got fired there, too.

Bud Furillo again worked his contacts from both the Reeves and Allen camps to dominate the story, with major help from *Herald Examiner* columnist Melvin Durslag, a close friend of the coach who shared a birthday with George that the two celebrated together every year. For the two years the story lasted, Furillo and Durslag broke news and explained why stuff went down the way it did, sometimes before it even happened.

The story of Reeves and Allen was built along two lines that followed the career paths of the two men who ultimately gained entry in the Pro Football Hall of Fame. Furillo was something of a participant in the Reeves chronology, having begun his newspaper career around the time the Rams moved to Los Angeles from Cleveland, and having held Stydahar's hand during his 1952 firing by the owner. The Steamer went back a ways with Allen, too, writing about him ten years before he took the Rams job, when Allen was the head coach at Richard Nixon's alma mater, Whittier College.

Reeves's path intersected with Furillo's when, in the words of The Steam Room, the owner "shrunk the size of the country one day" in 1946 by moving the first professional sports team in the nation west of St. Louis. In between winning the NFL titles in '45 and '51, Reeves really made history when his team became the first in major-league professional American sports to break the color barrier. Of course, the L.A. Coliseum Commission wouldn't let Reeves play in the big stadium unless he integrated the team. Good for the commissioners. But the fact remains: Reeves still signed Kenny Washington and the UCLA All-American's fellow Bruins alumnus, Woody Strode, to Rams contracts a full year before the Brooklyn Dodgers made Jackie Robinson baseball's first African American player. If Reeves wanted to be a jerk about it, he could have moved to Orange County, like his successor, Carroll Rosenbloom, or shaken down the city of

Irwindale to build himself a stadium in a gravel pit, like Al Davis tried to do with the Raiders forty years later. He did neither.

"Pioneered Professional Sports in the West," reads Reeves's plaque in the Coliseum's Court of Honor, in the marbled peristyle of the stadium's eastern end. "Loyalty, Integrity And Humanity Came With Him."

You can't argue with any of it.

The thing about Reeves, though, was his thing about firing coaches.

Before George Allen, Reeves fired eight of them in nineteen years. Bud Furillo wrote about seven of the terminations. Clark Shaughnessy, the offensive innovator and perfector of the T-formation—canned. Joe Stydahar, the champ, but still the recipient of the early morning phone call from Reeves—ousted. Hampton Pool, picked for his more exciting offensive game plans—dumped. Sid Gillman, Pro Football Hall of Famer, offensive genius, perfectionist of the deep passing game, inventor of the play-action fake, for Christ's sake—beheaded. Bob Waterfield, local hero, husband of Jane Russell, QB on both Rams title teams—assigned to the ash heap of history. Harland Svare, starting right-side linebacker on the New York Football Giants' 1956 NFL champs, defensive stalwart—fired, two days before Christmas in 1965 instead of one day after it in 1968.

When he wasn't firing coaches, Reeves, a successful stockbroker, lost money on the Rams in the early years of the L.A. operation. He sought to spread the misery around by selling chunks of the team to four partners for one dollar apiece, in exchange for their agreement to incur a share of the financial misfortune. The owners' group came to include comedian Bob Hope, but nobody laughed when they turned on Reeves and he held his line against them.

The squabbling lasted for years, and the disagreement at the top hurt the product on the field. It also cost them a chance to hire maybe the greatest coach in football history.

"I would have been out there years ago if there hadn't been so much fighting among the Rams owners," Vince Lombardi told The Steam Room years later, during the Reeves-Allen confrontation.

Reeves resolved the Rams ownership problem when he paid the other guys $4.8 million to regain a controlling interest in his team. It made for a pretty good deal for the fellows who bought cheap. Reeves enjoyed the last laugh, though, when his boy, the one-time Rams PR man and general manager, Pete Rozelle, became NFL commissioner. Rozelle then swung the TV deals that made all the NFL owners richer than rich and set the NFL on course toward becoming the $12-billion-a-year enterprise it is today.

Despite the TV windfall, the Rams continued to lose on the field.

It was never worse than 1962, when they went 1-12-1. In a late October showdown between two 0-5 teams, the Minnesota Vikings mauled the Rams in the first half, taking a 31-0 lead on their way to a 38-14 victory. When Rams quarterback Zeke Bratkowski got hurt and had to be assisted off the field, the crowd cheered. When bandleader Johnny Boudreau tried to stir the crowd with what had become the town's traditional "charge" bugle call, the crowd booed.

The public demanded coach Bob Waterfield's firing, as if Reeves needed anything to prompt him. Furillo blamed the players.

"Fire them, too," he wrote after the Vikings' fiasco.

Furillo attributed the ongoing failure to years of horrific player personnel decisions. Most prominent, of course, was the disastrous trade Rozelle had orchestrated in 1959 to send nine players to the Chicago Cardinals for washed-up fullback Ollie Matson. The Steam Room liked to remind readers that, over the years, the team had traded away big names like Norm Van Brocklin, Andy Robustelli, Gene "Big Daddy" Lipscomb, Dick "Night Train" Lane, Jimmy Orr, and Harland Svare. They all starred with their new clubs, as did Bill Wade, who, like Van Brocklin, quarterbacked another team in another city to an NFL championship.

The Steamer gave up in 1961, when the Rams traded their best wide receiver, Del Shofner, to the Giants.

"If 20th Century Fox got rid of stars as often as the Rams, the corporation would be 19th Century Fox," Furillo wrote after the Rams sent Shofner out.

In running down the diaspora, the Steamer caustically told L.A. fans, "Be patient. The Rams eventually will succeed in trading away complete sets of offensive and defensive All-Pro teams."

The Rams, with the league's worst record in 1962, got the first pick in the NFL draft in 1963. They wasted it on Terry Baker, a fine human being and Heisman Trophy winner out of Oregon State. Problem was, Baker "couldn't throw the ball far enough to make it at quarterback, go deep enough to catch it at end, or run fast enough with it at halfback," Furillo wrote.

Shoots of grass, however, began to spring up in the desert of the Rams' depth chart. In 1957, they drafted Jack Pardee out of Texas A&M, and he would become a two-time All-Pro linebacker. The same year, they picked Purdue defensive lineman Lamar Lundy, and followed up that selection four years later with a fourteenth-round offensive tackle out of South Carolina State named David "Deacon" Jones. The Rams immediately switched Jones to defense, where he became one of football's all-time greatest pass rushers.

The next year, they drafted Merlin Olsen out of Utah State on the first round, a defensive tackle who lined up next to Jones and turned the left side of the Rams line into a hellish circumstance for opposing blockers. In 1963, the Rams traded for Rosey Grier, who became the final member of the "Fearsome Foursome" defensive front that still ranks with the best in pro football history.

The Shofner trade? It gave the Rams the second pick in the same 1962 draft in which they had landed Olsen. They spent it on Roman Gabriel, who stood six foot four and whom Furillo frequently referred to as "the world's tallest Filipino quarterback." Gabe threw for 29,444 yards in sixteen NFL seasons, which ranks him forty-six in league history—better than Pro Football Hall of Famers such as Terry Bradshaw, Joe Namath, Bobby Layne, Norm Van Brocklin, George Blanda, Lenny Dawson, Roger Staubach, and Bob Waterfield.

L.A. drafted a very solid offensive line along the way in tackles Joe Carollo and Charlie Cowan and guards Joe Scibelli and Tom Mack, topped off in a trade with the Green Bay Packers for center Ken Iman.

They scored a good running back in the '59 draft in Dick Bass from Pacific and a great safety in Eddie Meador out of Arkansas Tech. They acquired Minnesota's first-round 1965 draft pick, Jack Snow, for wide receiver Red Phillips and defensive tackle Gary Larsen. They obtained Billy Truax, a very capable tight end with an extremely long neck, in a 1964 trade with Cleveland, and in 1965, they drafted defensive back Clancy Williams, out of Washington State, who intercepted twenty-eight passes from 1966 through 1970.

Now it was time for Reeves to find a coach to match his team.

• • • • •

By 1966, Vince Lombardi, who was winning championships in Green Bay, was no longer available. So Reeves went after the next-best pick in the coaching draft. His selection was the flourishing assistant under George Halas in Chicago, the architect of the defense that had won the Bears the NFL title in 1963, the players' favorite, the former Whittier College head coach, and the one-time Rams assistant and car wash owner in the San Fernando Valley: George Allen.

Halas, a friend of Reeves but committed to rivalry with the Rams owner, wasn't about to let anybody just pluck Allen away like nothing. The Papa Bear knew Allen was one of the top defensive theorists and motivators in the sport. He'd been mentoring him for nearly a decade. After winning the NFL championship two years earlier, Halas had promised Allen his job. Only it looked like Papa Bear would never quit.

"Allen watched his thirties turn into his forties in Chicago," The Steam Room reported, fearing that the seventy-year-old Halas "might be the first 100-year-old coach."

After firing Harland Svare, Reeves offered the job to the antsy Allen, and on January 10, 1966, "George caught the first thing smokin' for Los Angeles to straighten out the Rams," the

Steamer wrote.

Halas sued, accusing Allen of violating his contract to stay with the Bears for two more years. In a trial in the Cook County Circuit Court, Allen testified that he'd never read the terms of his deal. The judge agreed with Halas that a valid contract did exist, which was enough for Halas to announce from the witness stand that he had proven his point.

Under oath, Papa Bear dropped the suit.

So Allen moved west, where the Steamer resumed what had been a friendly and professional relationship with the coach, going back to when he wrote a feature on Whittier College before the Poets played the undefeated Air Force in 1956.

"We are going to be fired up like the neighbor's incinerator on wash day," Allen told Furillo the week of Whittier's 14–14 tie with the Falcons, referencing the popular backyard trash burners suburban Angelenos formerly used to eliminate their refuse, before air pollution control officials banned them as dangerous to public health.

As a head coach and a writer, Allen and Furillo were friendly as could be for a scotch drinker like the Steamer and a coach whose idea of a good time was a bowl of ice cream. Allen still told Furillo funny stories, like the one about the ball-retrieving team of 1964. Allen's football-centric view of the world also amused Furillo. Over his eighteen years in the coaching business, Allen published his journals under the 565-page title, *Winning Football Drills*, a book "soon to be made into a major motion picture," Furillo wrote.

While Furillo found the coach's obsession a worthy target for the occasional barb, the Steamer also saw soon enough that Allen knew what he was doing. One of Allen's first moves was to talk former Chicago Bears middle linebacker Bill George out of retirement. Allen then put a call into Jack Pardee, who quit football in 1965 to battle cancer. But saving his life only partially accounted for Pardee giving up the game.

"I got tired of losing," he told Furillo. "Football wasn't fun anymore."

To fill the third linebacker spot, Allen swung a deal with the

Philadelphia Eagles for Maxie Baughan, whom the Rams coach considered "the best right-side linebacker in the game," according to The Steam Room.

Furillo wrote that Allen brow-beat Eagles' coach and general manager Joe Kuharich on the phone for thirty-one straight days before Philadelphia agreed to send Baughan to the Rams.

"Allen got into the habit of calling Kuharich at ten o'clock at night, which is 1:00 AM Philly time," The Steam Room reported. "Weary from lack of sleep, Kuharich finally agreed to trade Baughan to the Rams."

"Trader George," as the writers began to call Allen, also pried receiver Bernie Casey away from San Francisco, middle linebacker Myron Pottios from Pittsburgh, and cornerback Irv Cross from Philadelphia. The deals reversed Dan Reeves's past practice of trading experienced players for draft choices.

Sometimes Allen traded draft choices he didn't have, but that was another matter. The idea was to build a team that could win right away.

"I don't know what fuzzy-cheeked kids can do," Allen told Furillo. "I like bald-headed men."

The new-aged Rams mixed nicely with the maturing draft talent Reeves had accumulated through the years. All it took for the elements to come together was the belief Allen instilled that they could win right away.

"The future is now," Allen told them, in a slogan that branded his twelve-year career as a head coach in the NFL.

•   •   •   •   •

It took Allen exactly one game as head coach to establish himself throughout the league as something of an oddball.

The Rams opened the 1966 season on the road in Atlanta, against the expansion Falcons. The new club had sixteen rookies on its roster, but Allen felt he needed an edge. The week before the game, Atlanta had released a placekicker and end named Bob Jencks, a former Chicago Bear who had played two years for the team while Allen was an assistant there. The week of the Falcons game, Allen called Jencks and said he'd heard that the

"Buddy" Furillo's prowess on the accordion once paid his family's heating bill, 1930.

A young Merchant Marine, 1940s.

On the prowl for a story in the Olympic Auditorium ring, mid-1950s.

Who had a cooler hat in this 1957 photo: the Steamer or USC-Green Bay Packers star Willie Wood?

The Steamer with his cousin, Dodgers right fielder Carl Furillo, 1958.

The Steamer with his all-time hero, Rocky Marciano (*center*), late 1950s.

The Steamer, caddying for Eddie Arcaro (*left*) and Bill Shoemaker, probably needed
the tip money to pay off his losses at the track, 1960.

The Steamer forged a good relationship with Mickey Mantle, 1961.

The Steamer with Maris—who hit 61 in '61—and John Hall, 1961.

Just a few months removed from his presidency, Dwight D. Eisenhower answers a couple of interview questions from the Steamer in the Angels dugout, 1961.

The Steamer with nature-loving sports nut Gypsy Boots on his left, and Mamie Van Doren with loverboy Bo Belinsky on her left, 1962.

The Steamer with (*seated, left to right*) *L.A. Times* sportswriter Dan Hafner, Angels manager Bill Rigney, and Ross Newhan of the *Long Beach Press-Telegram*, along with (*standing, left to right*) John Hall, Angels PR man George Goodale, and Braven Dyer of the *L.A. Times*, early 1960s.

The Steamer idolized Frank Sinatra, early 1960s.

The Steamer with the kings of the Rat Pack, Dean Martin and Frank Sinatra, at a baseball writers' dinner, mid-1960s.

Even the Goose Girl couldn't help the Steamer pick winners at Hollywood Park, 1965.

The Steamer has a word with Kansas City Athletics mascot Charlie O, while Charles O. Finley, owner of the team and the mule, listens in, 1965.

And the winner of the Cy Young Award goes to . . . Sandy Koufax, 1966.

Angels manager Bill Rigney (*far right*) with *Herald Examiner* stalwarts (*left to right*) Allan Malamud, the Steamer, Bob Hunter, Jack Disney, and Mitch Chortkoff, 1966.

Getting into the St. Paddy's spirit with lightweight champ Rodolfo Gonzalez, 1972.

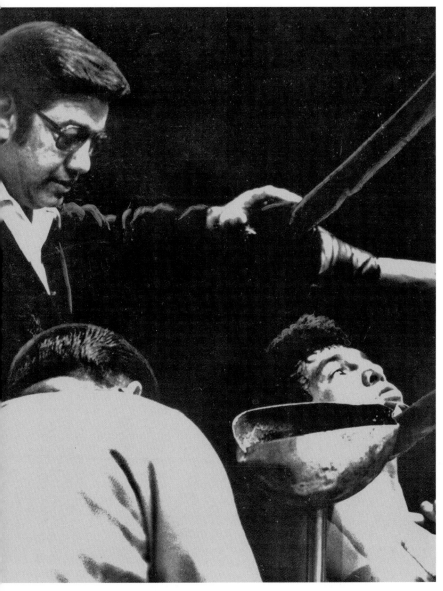

The Steamer working Mando Ramos's corner in a title bout, early 1970s.

There was no finer sportswriter in L.A. than Melvin Durslag, early 1970s.

Having a chat with Willie Mays on the Steamer's short-lived TV show, mid-1970s.

The Steamer loved the antics of San Diego's Famous Chicken, the mascot that toured the country and performed in front of millions.

To Bud —
Thanks for being with us.
It was a great honor for our
squad and a most enjoyable day
for me.
Sincerely,
Terry Donahue

At practice with Terry Donahue and the UCLA Bruins, 1976.

Cigar-chomping USC coach John McKay celebrated often with writer pals like the
Steamer and Bud Tucker, 1970s.

Rams coach Chuck Knox wasn't laughing when he got locked in overnight at the
Steamer's bar, mid-to-late 1970s.

With O. J. Simpson, late 1970s.

The Steamer thought Pelé may have been the greatest athlete to ever play the Coliseum, late 1970s.

Wilt Chamberlain would have won the tip from the Steamer, early 1980s.

The Steamer had a way of putting athletes like Steve Garvey at ease, early 1980s.

All smiles with sportscaster Jim Hill and Dodger great Dusty Baker, early 1980s.

Mark Spitz dropping into the studio minus his seven golds, early 1980s.

Smiling for a KABC promotional shot, early 1980s.

Steve Carlton didn't like to do interviews, but he didn't mind talking to the Steamer every once in a while, early 1980s.

The Steamer gives the author a boxing lesson during Raider-Redskin Super Bowl week in Tampa, 1984.

Howie Long was a big Raiders favorite, 1985.

The Mick and the Steamer sometimes had a few sips together when Mantle visited L.A., 1980s.

"Back off, Yogi, I've got this," mid-1980s.

City of Hope honored the Steamer for his charity work, 1985.

player was looking for work. He never did offer Jencks a job, but he did speak to him for two and a half hours on the phone, to gain some insight into Atlanta's strategy for the season opener.

Armed with the inside information provided by Jencks, the Rams built a 16-0 second-quarter lead, thanks to three field goals by Bruce Gossett and a fifty-one-yard touchdown pass from Gabriel to Snow. Then, Furillo reported, the Rams "forgot everything Jencks told them." Randy Johnson threw two touchdown passes to make it scary before the Rams got out of town with a 19-14 win.

After the game, Atlanta coach Norb Hecker said that Allen's contact with Jencks amounted to "dirty pool," Furillo reported. A former Green Bay Packers assistant, Hecker said, "Lombardi never did that."

Falcons assistant Tom Fears, the former Rams split end who caught the winning pass in the 1951 title game, chased Furillo down to make sure there was no mistaking what he thought of the new L.A. coach.

"You tell Allen for me, he's a fruitcake," Fears told Furillo.

The next day's Steam Room included Fears's unflattering characterization, as well as Hecker's remark. Allen laughed them both off.

"Those goofy guys," he told The Steam Room. "If we knew everything they were going to do, we should have won by a lot more than we did."

The Rams coach liked it, though, that the Jencks contact bothered the Atlanta staff. He promised more antics for the next week's game with Chicago.

"I'm lining up the Pinkertons to spy on the Bears," he winked at Furillo.

Even if he was a fruitcake and not Lombardi, Allen improved the Rams to 2-0 the next week with a 31-17 win in Los Angeles over Halas and the Bears. The Coliseum opener attracted more than 58,000 fans, a bigger crowd than any that came out to see the Rams in 1965. After the game, the Bears' Dick Butkus, Richie Petitbon, and Bennie McRae walked over to the Rams' locker room to say hello to their former defensive coordinator.

"I've never seen a losing club go so far out of their way to congratulate the winning coach," Furillo wrote.

When the Rams improved to 4-1, Furillo, in hyperbole not altogether inaccurate, asserted that the new coach was the best the team ever had.

"He's given the team a desire it hasn't had in a decade," the Steamer wrote.

As coach, Allen doubled as cheerleader. TV cameras constantly showed him on the sidelines clapping for his players, exhorting them to give him not just everything they had, but then some—110 percent, Allen demanded.

Every play was the most important ever. Every game was bigger than the last.

Allen once told Furillo how it bothered him to see a head coach wearing headphones. Leave them for the coordinators, Allen said. A head coach's job is to coach.

"Good grief," Allen said in The Steam Room. "Do you need headphones to find out if you're getting beat by two touchdowns? You've got to get in the middle of those players when they come off the field and fire them up, keep them going."

A four-game losing streak in the middle of the season held up Allen's induction into the Hall of Fame. And Green Bay's continuing dynasty kept the Rams from thinking about winning anything as foolish as the Super Bowl, the new championship match for the newly merged professional football monopoly.

In those days, the second-place teams in the NFL's Eastern and Western conferences met in Miami in something called the Playoff Bowl. Going into their second-to-the-last game of the season, at home against Detroit, the Rams were right in the middle of the Playoff Bowl picture. They desperately needed to beat the Lions to keep that chance alive, and Allen thought a large and enthusiastic Coliseum crowd would inspire his team to win this crucial game.

Allen invited Furillo to lunch the week of the Lions game. The Steamer inspired him when he ordered a daiquiri.

"By gosh," Allen said. "I'll have a blackberry brandy. On the rocks."

SAYERS HIDES OUT, KILLS RAMS
OCTOBER 24, 1966

CHICAGO—Gale Sayers ran out of the "I-Formation" with the impact of the Chicago wind to knock the hats off the Rams yesterday, 17–10.

What's unusual about that? . . . The Bears attack out of the "I" only on kickoff returns.

They hide Sayers behind Dick Gordon on the goal line. Then, at the last second, Sayers swings out to catch the ball. He usually runs ninety-three yards with it to touchdowns, as he did to beat the Rams. . . .

"[Assistant coach] Abe Gibron . . . came up with the idea," Sayers said. "I tell Gordon which way to go just before the ball is kicked. On the runback that went all the way, I told him to take the ball if it was kicked to our left. I would take it if it came right."

Ram placekicker Bruce Gossett set the ball up on the left hash mark after the Rams had scored to tie Chicago at 7–7 in the second quarter. . . .

Sayers didn't appear to be touched when he went ninety-three yards to score. . . .

"I was going three-quarter speed when I caught up to my wedge of blockers," Sayers said. "Then I made a couple of head and shoulder fakes. If I dip my head or shoulder in one direction, the players coming down to get me will go that way. This provides our wedge with better blocking angles. The blocks were perfect. When I got by the wedge . . . it was all over." . . .

Meanwhile, [Bears owner-coach George] Halas was sipping from a soft drink can that smelled suspiciously of something stronger.

Papa was asked by an outlander if the victory was sweet revenge for the loss of former aide George Allen to Los Angeles.

Papa set down his drink, sort of hard.

"To hell with revenge. It is always a pleasure to beat the Rams—no matter who is coaching them."

Over drinks, the coach informed the writer of the critical nature of the Lions game, and how important it was for the Rams, in their effort to qualify for the Playoff Bowl, to fill the Coliseum.

"Can I help in any way?" the Steamer asked. He offered to run a front-page picture in the sports section of the Fearsome Foursome.

"Couldn't you use the linebackers, too?" Allen asked. While

Furillo thought about it, George added, "And don't forget Clancy Williams." The cornerback already had eight interceptions.

"This could be the biggest week of our lives," Allen told Furillo. "Every play Sunday could be the biggest play of the game."

Despite Furillo's efforts in the sports pages of the *Herald Examiner*—he ended up going with a classy shot of Dick Bass making a cut—the L.A. public failed to respond. Unimpressed by the Playoff Bowl hype, only 40,039 turned out for the game. Still, in front of a two-thirds empty Coliseum, Bass ran for 107 yards, Bruce Gossett kicked three more field goals, and Chuck Lamson returned a Karl Sweetan interception forty-four yards for a touchdown as the Rams beat the Lions, 23–3.

The Rams and the Baltimore Colts carried 8–5 records into their season finales, tied for the Playoff Bowl berth. The Rams concluded their season at home against Lombardi and the Packers. This time, the town got interested, even if it was to see Jim Taylor and Paul Hornung and Bart Starr. More than 72,000 showed up—a bigger crowd than the one that would watch the Packers defeat the Kansas City Chiefs in Super Bowl I a few weeks later. L.A. fell behind 27–9 in the fourth quarter, and two late touchdowns still left them short of the Playoff Bowl, when the Colts beat the 49ers on the same day.

•   •   •   •   •

Allen faced a huge challenge in toughening up the Rams. They had an image around the league as a bunch of fast-living, Tinsel Town softies.

Quarterback Bob Waterfield's marriage to actress Jane Russell stamped the club as the "Hollywood Rams" almost from the start. In the early 1960s, middle linebacker Mike Henry replaced Johnny Weissmuller in the Tarzan movies. It seemed like everybody on the team had some kind of a bit role in a movie or TV series. Who can forget Roman Gabriel's American Indian character, Blue Boy, in the John Wayne movie *The Undefeated*?

"Yeah," said left tackle Joe Carollo, who had a side gig as a professional wrestler. "It was more fun than it was serious football."

The club had long enjoyed the relaxed atmosphere of Southern California, and with it developed a reputation for frolic. Some players opened night spots around town—ferocious linebacker Don Paul had the Rams Horn in Encino; Bob Waterfield opened the Pump Room nearby on Ventura Boulevard; and down in the 'hood, Ollie Matson offered the fine fare of the Entre Nous on West Jefferson Boulevard.

Vic Lindskog, who played on two NFL championship teams with the Philadelphia Eagles, coached the Rams' offensive line in the early 1960s. The surroundings disgusted him.

"In that Hollywood atmosphere, they'll never be nothing but a bunch of playboys," he told The Steam Room in 1960.

Lou Michaels drove the point home in a conversation with Furillo before the 1963 Pro Bowl. Traded from the Rams to the Pittsburgh Steelers, Michaels said his career path took a side route due to the distractions of living and playing so close to the Sunset Strip.

"I came from a small town," the Swoyersville, Pennsylvania, native told Furillo. "I wanted to see and do everything."

Management didn't seem much concerned with the players' lives off the field. In fact, when the Rams broke preseason training camp, they directed the young and single to the motel located behind the House of Serfas hangout on the hill, not too far from the Coliseum. The arrangement worked fine for players concerned about getting home safely after getting plowed after practice. Carollo lived there for a while, as did the running back Jon Arnett.

In the bar, the Rams ran into regulars like Eli Grba of the Angels, Hot Rod Hundley of the Lakers, Johnny Podres of the Dodgers, and many of their teammates. Sportswriters, of course, favored the place. John Hall of the *Hollywood Citizen News*, the *Mirror*, and then the *L.A. Times* lived there for a while. So did Jack Disney of the *Herald Examiner*.

Furillo never received his mail at the House of Serfas. He just drank there.

Allen, in one of his first moves as the Rams coach, found the team a new practice facility in Long Beach. The relocation from their previous practice site at a city park in the San Fernando Valley coincided with the sad passing of the House of Serfas as L.A.'s go-to sports bar. Ernie Serfas and his brother, Nick, shut it down when they opened a golf course in Corona.

With the team's daily operations moved to Long Beach, some of the players moved south, too, and those with a taste for booze and an eye for pretty girls with beehive hairdos and miniskirts changed their favored night spot to Downey, where the Steamer lived, and the Stardust Lounge, where Furillo drank.

"That's where the girls were," Carollo said.

By the time Allen became coach of the Rams, the Stardust had already become a little bit like the Lindell in Detroit. It had never been declared off-limits by Pete Rozelle, but it definitely was on the watch list.

It solidified its reputation as a house of sin the week before the January 1965 Pro Bowl, when Gino Marchetti, the great Baltimore Colts defensive end, put a blitz in there on Cleveland Browns quarterback Frank Ryan. Marchetti was still mad that the Browns had slaughtered the Colts in the previous month's NFL championship game, 27-0. A few nights before the NFL's All-Star game, Marchetti was getting lit in the Dust with Furillo when in walked Ryan. The Steamer notified Marchetti of the QB's entry, and the defensive end bolted for the quarterback. Several third parties intervened to keep Marchetti from registering the sack. Marchetti made up for it in the Pro Bowl, when he got to Ryan on the first play of the second half and knocked him "insensible," according to the *Herald Examiner*'s Bob Oates.

Allen knew about the Stardust and didn't like it that some of his players spent so much time there. About halfway through his first season as the Rams coach, Allen called Carollo in for a chat. The coach didn't care much for Carollo, even though the tackle started seventy-one straight games for the Rams before Allen traded him to Philadelphia in the 1969 deal for Pro Football Hall of Fame offensive tackle Bob Brown.

"He said, 'Why are you hanging out in the Stardust Lounge?'" Carollo said in an interview.

The girls, of course, Carollo told the coach. But the tackle's sensible answer was met with a rejoinder that astonished the 265-pound, fourth-year man out of Notre Dame.

"He said he was having me followed," Carollo said.

Surveillance was just one of many tactics Allen employed to impose discipline on his players who for years had been operating without much of it. During the off-season, he assigned each of them a weight to be maintained over the spring and summer, and he sent the team's trainer to personally visit each player twice during those months to make sure they were staying in shape. When training camp began, they would be subject to fines of twenty-five dollars for every pound over the limit. Once they reported for duty at camp, the players belonged to Allen. He installed an electronic alarm system to catch curfew cheats sneaking out.

On road trips, Allen sequestered his team in hotels far removed from nightlife. In San Francisco, for instance, the team used to stay at the Mark Hopkins Hotel, Furillo pointed out, because it was owned by Gene Autry, the singing cowboy who also had a piece of the Rams. The night before the Rams' 1966 game against the 49ers in San Francisco, Allen was horrified to see drunken L.A. fans mingling with his players.

"The game seems to be incidental to everybody," Allen told the Steamer. "There are too many distractions in this town."

In later years, the coach bedded his club in lodgings south of the San Francisco airport, in San Mateo.

"There isn't a beer sign within a five-dollar cab ride of them," Furillo wrote in 1969. "Peace and quiet have resulted in winning Sundays for the club."

After the Rams took care of the 49ers, 27–21, in their fourth game of 1969, some of the players asked Allen if it would be all right if they celebrated afterward at the Top of the Mark, the drinkery atop the Hopkins.

"Coach Allen blew up," The Steam Room reported. Furillo quoted him as saying, "Here I was, feeling like a million dollars, and somebody has to spoil it by wanting a party. This isn't a party team anymore. This is a business trip. We came up here together and we'll go home together."

The Steamer wrote, "Needless to say, what had been a team victory was transferred into a team flight home. Nobody missed it."

• • • • •

Although Allen returned the Rams to relevance, Furillo noticed as early as the 1967 preseason that something was not right between the coach and Dan Reeves.

With the Rams killing San Diego, 50-0, in an exhibition game, the Chargers had the ball late in the contest and were driving for a score. Allen, who had taken his first-teamers out of the game, rushed the Fearsome Foursome back onto the field to try and stop San Diego from putting any points on the board.

The substitution caught the owner's attention.

"He's a killer," Dan Reeves told Furillo.

Reeves once said that the peculiar Allen "takes all the pleasure out of winning."

It also embarrassed Reeves in the tight-knit NFL owners club when Dallas Cowboys president Tex Schramm, another former Rams PR man, accused Allen of spying on his team before a 1967 game.

Allen not only didn't deny it, he laughed it off in his comments to The Steam Room, after the Rams' blowout win on the road over the Cowboys.

"There was a guy up in a tree throughout our Friday morning practice in Long Beach taking notes," Allen told Furillo. "If we had been close enough, we would have thrown a rock at him. For all we know, he was working for the Cowboys. Maybe we'll protest that."

The '67 Rams turned out to be one of the best teams in franchise history. On the way to a regular season record of 11-1-2, Gabriel compiled his second-highest passing efficiency ranking ever, trailing only the mark from his MVP year in 1969. Olsen and Jones played to their peak abilities in anchoring the defensive line. Jack Snow averaged an NFL-best 26.3 yards on twenty-eight catches and embellished a reputation on his eight touchdown receptions as somebody you couldn't catch from behind if he got a step on you. Fourth-year running back Lester Josephson, in the best season of his career, ran for exactly 800 yards and caught thirty-seven passes for exactly 400 more and scored eight touchdowns. The veteran offensive line played like a unit that had been together for years—which it had been, with the weekly pregame introductions of Carollo, Scibelli, Iman, Mack, and Cowan sounding like the reading of a single name as they ran out of the Coliseum tunnel, one after the other. The Rams won eight games by two touchdowns or more. They led the league in most points scored and fewest allowed. They scored two of their greatest wins ever, one where they blocked a punt in the last minute to beat Lombardi's champion Packers, in a December game they needed to win to stay alive for the playoffs. A week later, Jones and Olsen smothered Johnny Unitas, and Gabriel completed eighteen of twenty-two for 257 yards and three TDs in an L.A. rout of the Baltimore Colts for the Coastal Division championship. Ten Rams made the Pro Bowl roster.

Even though the Rams finished the season with a record that was two and a half games better than Green Bay's, they still had to travel to Milwaukee for their playoff game against the Packers, where their season died. The Packers crushed them, 28–7, with Green Bay tackle Forrest Gregg running Deacon Jones out of the pocket play after play. Relaxed and comfortable under the protection of Gregg, Bart Starr completed seventeen of twenty-three passes. The loss relegated the Rams to the Playoff Bowl, where they beat Cleveland, 30–6.

The victory did not result in a parade down Broadway. Allen, though, had the Rams ready for a big year in 1968, despite a labor dispute in which the newly formed National Football League Players Association called a preseason strike. The owners countered with a lockout. When the union and management bosses finally reached an agreement, Allen sought to make up for the time lost to picketing by running his players through three-a-day drills.

"They're terrific," the coach told The Steam Room. "You can get so much more done practicing in the morning, afternoon, and at night. Of course we would have to change the meal hours."

"Presumably, breakfast would be served right after dinner, at midnight," Furillo commented.

In 1968, the Rams fielded almost the exact same team as they had in 1967, with one exception. Lester Josephson, the 6-1, 207-pound, fifth-year man out of Augustana, one of the Rams' Pro Bowlers from the previous year, lost his footing coming out of the tunnel during introductions for an exhibition game. The slip snapped the Achilles tendon in Les's left leg and knocked Josephson out for the year. He was never the same, although he did get a small part a few years later in the Warren Beatty production *Heaven Can Wait.*

"Fans in Los Angeles are growing impatient with Coach Allen for not devoting more time to drills on how to come out of the tunnel," Furillo wrote after the Josephson injury. "This is an important detail that shouldn't be overlooked."

The '68 season proceeded much like the one before it. The Rams looked impressive in winning their first six games, and even a 27-10 loss in Baltimore in the season's seventh week didn't throw them too much off track. Neither did the tie that Allen blamed on the same Kezar Stadium field where Dirty Harry would later drop Scorpio on the thirty-eight-yard line with a gunshot blast to the leg. The Rams looked like the best team in history the Sunday they beat the Vikings, 31-3, in a game where Joe Carollo and friends pitched a shutout against Alan Page and Carl Eller and the Purple People Eaters to keep Gabriel's uniform ambulance white on a muddy field in Minnesota.

The crash came the next week in the infamous "lost-down" game against the Bears in the Coliseum. Brian Piccolo, who would later die of cancer and have a TV movie made in his remembrance—starring Bud Furillo in a reporter's role—scored a touchdown and ran and caught passes worth eighty-two yards for the Bears in their 17-16 victory. Gabriel was knocked unconscious early in the game, but it was the refs who were woozy late when they forgot to give the Rams a down back on a holding call, when Gabe had the team moving in the final minute.

The loss eliminated the Rams from both Super and Playoff Bowl consideration.

•　　•　　•　　•　　•

Bud Furillo usually took a week or two off during the holidays, but Thanksgiving, Christmas, and New Year's always meant time in the office for a newspaperman—especially since the Steamer became sports editor, and especially since Dan Reeves chose the morning after the celebration of the birth of the baby Jesus to fire his coach.

Word spread fast, and Furillo had the story on the front page of the *Herald Examiner* that afternoon. It was all about a "personality conflict" between the owner and the coach, the story said, and Reeves took the blame, saying the problem probably was more his fault than Allen's.

Furillo recalled the blowup in the Rams locker room a month earlier, when the coach refused to shake the owner's hand and then upbraided him in front of the Steamer and Melvin Durslag. The story also said players such as Eddie Meador, Maxie Baughan, and Jack Pardee would retire if the coach stayed sacked.

The next day, the story elevated some more. Durslag's column contained the most in-depth account to date of the Allen-Reeves locker room face-off that had begun to leak out second hand. Mel wrote that after Allen refused Reeves's command to "Come back here, George," members of the Rams' front office staff "herded the owner out of the room to avoid a scene." The column reported that Reeves, a notorious lush, appeared to be bombed.

"For this writer, and for Bud Furillo, the *Herald Examiner* sports editor who now had walked in, the situation was sticky," Durslag wrote. "Here was a juicy scandal. It is, however, a point of ethics in this business that one doesn't take advantage of owners, coaches, or players who have been drinking, no more than a gentleman takes advantage of a lady who has passed out."

Armed with the backing of some of his players as well as the support of the public—outraged Rams fans lit up phone lines at the *Herald Examiner* and other sports desks around town, threatening to cancel their season tickets—Allen called a press conference at the Sheraton-West Hotel to more or less demand his job back.

Allen unsuccessfully fought back tears, Furillo wrote, when he told reporters, "I would bury my pride to come back to the Rams. My only interest is the Los Angeles Rams." Allen told them how he found the suggestion of a personality conflict with the owner baffling because he and Reeves hardly ever spoke to each other.

"I have seen Reeves once in the last seven months," Allen said. "I've had six conferences with him in the last two years. I have never been to his home, nor ever had dinner with him."

The floodgates to Allen's eyes broke loose when six of his best players—Meador and Pardee, along with Roman Gabriel, Deacon Jones, Charlie Cowan, and Lamar Lundy—took turns at the press conference to say they were done with the Rams if Reeves didn't reverse his decision.

"The Pro Bowl game will be the last time I represent the Rams," Deacon Jones said, "unless George Allen returns."

Reports had already emerged that Pittsburgh and Buffalo had contacted Allen about their vacant head coaching positions. Allen didn't want any of it.

"I know I can get a job somewhere else, but I don't want to leave Los Angeles," he told reporters, according to Furillo's story. "We accomplished some things here but there is still so much to be done here that I wanted to finish."

Allen had compiled a 29-10-2 record in his first three years as the Rams coach. He transformed the team from seven-year loser into one of the best in the league. He increased the average crowd from 40,333 in 1965, the year before he took over, to 65,127 in 1968. He knew the Rams had a great shot of making it to the Super Bowl the next year, and he also knew the Steelers and Bills faced massive rebuilding jobs.

Furillo wrote that a Rams spokesman "ruled out the possibility that Reeves would reverse his field . . . even though only thirty-three shopping days remain before the pro football draft."

The Steamer also reported that Reeves hoped to lure Vince

Lombardi out of Green Bay, where the fabled coach and general manager had turned field duties over to Phil Bengston. Furillo reported that Lombardi, at age fifty-five, "misses the fire" of game days and wanted to get back into coaching somewhere.

"Who will be the next daring man on the Rams trapeze?" Furillo asked.

The question lingered for five days, overshadowed for a while by the slightly less dramatic buildup to the Rose Bowl, where the two top-ranked college football teams in the country, Ohio State and USC, were about to play for the national championship.

Furillo wrote the game story on the Buckeyes' 27–16 victory, but the national championship game failed to rise to the top of the *Herald Examiner*'s sports page the morning of January 2. That's because Furillo scored a major scoop on the latest development in the Reeves-Allen soaper.

"Reeves Wants Allen Back," the big type said. The Steamer exclusive read, "Shifty Dan Reeves reversed his field and is willing to bring back George Herbert Allen as the Rams coach, the *Herald Examiner* learned today." Already, Furillo reported, Allen had been "invited to talk over his return to the club." The story said that "mounting pressure from many of the Rams players and thousands of fans is responsible for Reeves's decision to reconsider the action he took against Allen when their clash of personalities no longer became bearable at eight o'clock in the morning the day after Christmas."

Furillo listed "another factor" that went into Reeves's surrender to Allen: to get Lombardi, Reeves would have had to give up a piece of the club, a price too high for the fifty-one percent owner.

A new element to the story also emerged in the person of Allen's chain-smoking, tough-talking, football-understanding wife, Etty, who had taken a role in her husband's affairs. According to the Steamer, it was her inclination that George should tell Dan to keep his goddamned job, to use one of her favorite words. Furillo wrote that he'd been hearing reports "that Allen will bow to his wife's wishes and refuse to return." Furillo reported that Allen's new job offers now amounted to "several."

"All of a sudden George finds himself in the driver's seat instead of out in the cold without a job in the middle of winter," the Steamer's story read.

The coach, of course, heard Etty out. But, the Steamer wrote, "It behooves Allen to consider those players who supported him."

Furillo didn't know it yet—or at least he hadn't reported it—but Allen had met with Reeves as recently as New Year's morning. The conference was arranged by the Rams' team physician, Dr. Jules Rasinski, a close friend of both men. Furillo reported later that Rasinski spoke to Reeves the morning of December 31 and told the owner that for George Allen, "returning to the Rams was the thing uppermost in his life."

At first, Reeves said there was no way he'd take Allen back. But that with the Rasinski plea, "the chances of my taking him back had narrowed to 100–1."

The odds continued to recede when Reeves spoke to Rasinski again that night to say, "I would be glad to meet with George."

Rasinski served as mediator the morning of the Rose Bowl when Allen drove from his home in Palos Verdes to the Reeves's estate in Bel Air. When Allen arrived, Reeves greeted him by saying, "George, we've never had a drink together. What'll you have?"

Furillo reported that Allen ordered a scotch and soda, while the hard-drinking Reeves reversed field and poured himself a Coke, straight up. Allen's daughter, Jennifer, wrote in a book that her dad, who was inexperienced in the ways of drink, asked for a double blackberry brandy. Given the lifelong attention the Steamer paid to this important issue, I'm going with Furillo on this one, with all due respect to Ms. Allen. My guess is that Furillo's source on the scotch and soda was Reeves, a fellow who knew a man by what he drank. Jennifer Allen could have gotten her information from Rasinski, a close family friend, or maybe she got it from her pop, who probably paid as little attention to the detail of his drink order as he did in 1968 to the Rams' running-out-of-the-tunnel drills.

Three days after the New Year's Day meeting, Furillo reported that the "rapidly dissolving personality clash" between

Reeves and Allen was giving way to another face-to-face get-to-gether between the two.

Etty remained an obstacle to the deal.

"I want to stay but I have to convince my wife that this is the right thing," Allen told Furillo.

Maybe Mrs. Allen was a bit more astute than her husband in assessing one of the finer points of the coach's return: as Furillo reported in his January 4 story, while the Future was Now, there would only be two more years of it for Allen in Los Angeles.

"It is unlikely that Allen will receive an extension of the two years remaining on his contract if he does decide to stay with the Rams," the Steamer wrote.

Two days later, on January 6, Furillo popped a front-pager that Allen and Reeves had met that morning at the Rams' offices on West Pico Boulevard and had scheduled a press conference that afternoon to announce Allen's reinstatement. Furillo covered the event, but saw icicles in the air.

Reading from a prepared statement, Allen admitted to a certain level of culpability in his problematic relationship with Reeves. He committed to improving communication with the owner, "thereby enabling us to view our problems with clarity, and to resolve them with dignity," as opposed to having them worked out through drunken 8:00 AM telephone calls the day after Christmas.

The coach said he was "very happy to be returning as Dan's coach," and that "I want very much to return to my players and finish the task to which I dedicated myself."

George did not mention Etty or what she thought of his decision, but he made it clear that this matter was not so much about her.

"I owe this to the players, and to the fans who have been so loyal to me," he said.

The new Rams coach, after reading his statement, tried to scoot out of Century Plaza unnoticed, like Patterson from Comiskey Park after the first Liston fight, although Allen did not don a fake beard.

Reeves chased him down at stage right.

In a week's time, the owner had been transformed into the most hated man in Los Angeles. He needed the photo op with the popular coach.

In the next day's *Herald Examiner*, the picture showed the dark-eyed Reeves looking up at Allen while the coach peered off into the distance. It looked as if Allen couldn't wait to sprint past the owner and get back onto the practice field, which he did that day, as head coach of the NFL's Western Conference All-Stars in the Pro Bowl, which was thirteen days away.

Successful in blocking Allen's exit, Reeves, like he did in the Coliseum locker room the day of the Giants game, extended his hand. This time, Allen accepted it, while the photographers did their thing.

It was a picture worth a thousand words, minus a thousand and one.

Moving to the podium as Allen left the building, Reeves told the writers he was unmoved by the coach's televised tears or the threats of his players. If anything, they had made Reeves even more firm in his inebriated decision to fire his winning coach.

"Players can't run a franchise," he told the writers.

No, Reeves said, it was Dr. Rasinski and only Dr. Rasinski who had convinced Reeves to change his mind. Reeves admitted that he had spoken to two other coaches about the Rams job, that both were interested, but that both would remain nameless.

"One is believed to be Vincent T. Nameless Lombardi," Furillo wrote.

The Steamer speculated that the other could have been USC coach John McKay, who turned the Rams down in 1965 before Reeves disrupted the Chicago Bears' order of succession.

The Rams owner played it coy in how he had offered Lombardi the job but refused to put up a percentage of the team to bring Vince's frozen-tundra toughness to sunny L.A. He made one point very clear, though.

"There is no change in George's contract," Reeves told the press.

That meant Allen's salary would remain at $40,000, and that he would be gone when the contract expired in two years.

•   •   •   •   •

With Allen back in charge of field operations, the Rams won their first eleven regular season games in 1969, but lost their last three, and then a playoff game in Minnesota. They would return to Miami for their second Playoff Bowl appearance in three years.

They had hoped for something better, like maybe a berth in the Super Bowl, but the Vikings took care of that notion in Bloomington, 23–20.

A week before the game, Allen flew the team to Minnesota so the Rams could practice in the refrigerated conditions of the upper Midwest, to acclimate to the weather. Paul Caruso, the celebrity attorney, suggested that the players fight extradition, according to Furillo's reporting.

The Macalester College practices in St. Paul meant the Rams would not be home for Christmas, but Allen told Furillo, who put on his earmuffs and stocking cap to cover the preparation, "This is the best thing we've ever done. We'll be physically prepared for anything now."

On Christmas Eve day, the exuberant Allen clapped his hands amid the freezing snow and frosty breath and told cornerback Jim Nettles, "This is interception weather."

"Nettles," Furillo wrote, "looked at Allen as if he were some kind of nut."

Roman Gabriel won the NFL's 1969 Associated Press Most Valuable Player Award, but he was outplayed in the loss to the Vikings by Minnesota quarterback Joe Kapp, a Cal guy and Canadian Football League alumnus.

In beating the Rams, Kapp fluttered twelve passes into the breadbaskets of his receivers for 196 yards, forty-six more than the strong-armed Gabriel covered with his twenty-two completions. Kapp also bootlegged and barrel-rolled for forty-two yards on seven carries, including the winning points on two-yard run around end in the fourth quarter.

"Joe doesn't throw a pretty pass," Furillo wrote in his game story the next day. "All it does is bobble into the receiver's hand, which is essentially the idea of the passing game, I guess. As a runner, he is reminiscent of Frank Howard trying to beat out a bunt. But he makes first downs by catching the defense coming to the inside, leaving him outside to plod forward."

Furillo kindly pointed out for his friend, Joe Carollo, who had since been traded to Philadelphia, that his Hall of Fame replacement at left tackle, Bob Brown, enjoyed a terrible game. In the third quarter, with the Rams up 17–7 and driving, the referees called Brown for clipping. The fifteen-yard penalty killed the drive and forced the Rams to punt for the first time all day, and then Minnesota drove eighty-two yards for a touchdown. A game that would have been nearly over at 24–7 had been turned into a taut 17–14. After the Rams fell behind, 21–20, in the fourth quarter, they got stuck deep in their own end. Gabriel retreated into his end zone to pass. Then the Vikings' exceptional defensive end, Carl Eller, circled Brown and sacked Gabriel for a safety.

It just wasn't L.A.'s day against a Vikings team driven by its the motto, "Forty Men to Play Sixty Minutes."

"They lived up to it and were the best team," Furillo wrote.

In the Playoff Bowl, the Rams looked terrific.

Gabe was on fire, throwing for 224 yards and four touchdowns in the 31–0 crushing of the Dallas Cowboys—the defending Playoff Bowl champions. Deacon Jones, who got handled by Vikings offensive tackle Ron Yary in the slightly more meaningful playoff game in Minnesota, rallied in the warm weather of Miami to earn defensive player of the game honors.

Despite the historic victory—it was the last Playoff Bowl ever—for most Rams fans, the season felt like it ended in failure.

Five days before the 1970 NFL draft, Furillo raised some issues about the future of the team. The Rams still had their first-round pick, and they would use it to select a great one in middle linebacker Jack "Hacksaw" Reynolds out of Tennessee. They also had a second rounder, which they duffed, on wide receiver Donnie Williams.

Beyond the first two rounds, Furillo noticed that L.A. had traded away its picks for the third, fourth, fifth, and sixth rounds. Over lunch with Allen in Long Beach, the Steamer also pressed the coach about his dealing the previous year of wide receiver Harold Jackson and defensive end John Zook to the Eagles for running back Izzy Lang, who carried the ball one time in 1969 for as many yards—one. Jackson would go on to play sixteen years and catch 579 passes, for a career 17.9-yard average. Zook played eleven years in the league. Lang never played again, but he did go on to get arrested twenty-four times, including four times for impersonating NFL players such as Joe Morris, Lawrence Taylor, Leonard Marshall, and Doug Williams. He'd forge their names to cash checks.

Allen grew testy over the Steamer's challenges.

"Are you my friend or my enemy?" Allen, the future pal of Richard Nixon, who kept lists of his enemies, asked the Steamer.

"A newspaperman," Furillo shot back.

"I'd like to think you are my friend. Why don't you write about the Miami game and what a fine team we had?"

The glory of the Playoff Bowl was past, so the reporter continued to ask prickly questions about the Izzy Lang deal.

"You still don't understand," Allen said.

"Nobody does," Furillo wrote.

"It was all part of the deal for Jim Purnell, who did a great job at linebacker for us," the coach continued, regarding the second-stringer picked up in the off-season from Chicago (although records do not show that the Rams gave up anybody for the rights to the defensive stalwart from the Bears).

"If I didn't get Purnell, it would have been a terrible trade," Allen said. "Purnell is a heckuva kid. Have you ever met him?"

Allen said he was unconcerned about not having the mid-round picks.

"I don't pay any attention to those gasoline tank draft choices," he told Furillo.

Having not done his due diligence on some of the players who would have been available in those middle rounds, the coach failed to fill up on several players who proved over their careers to be pretty good. They included Hall of Fame defensive back Mel Blount, as well as two-time All-Pro DBs Charlie Waters and Ken Ellis. Another defensive back drafted late, Lemar

Parrish, went to the Pro Bowl six times. Tim Foley, Vic Washington, Jim Carter, Jim Otis, Mike Mosely, Dave Washington, and Tom Banks all also played in at least one NFL All-Star game each, as did Jake Scott, who came out of the gasoline tank to earn a Super Bowl MVP trophy—against a Washington Redskins team coached by George Allen. Super Bowl-winning kicker Jim O'Brien also eluded Allen's attention, along with several other mid-to-late rounders who played for years in the NFL.

"It's surprising how many people don't know how to win," Allen said.

Allen cited the Pittsburgh Steelers as an example of a franchise that was doing everything wrong. Not only did they keep a gasoline-tank draft pick and blow it on a Hall of Famer like Mel Blount, they also insisted on using their first-round pick—the overall number one of the draft—to take a quarterback out of Louisiana Tech named Terry Bradshaw.

"I'd take that first choice and a couple of others and go out and get some football players," Allen said in The Steam Room. "Gosh, there are so many guys around here who don't know what it takes to win."

The bumbling Steelers had proved their idiocy the year before, when they made no apparent effort to deal an unproven talent, such as defensive tackle "Mean" Joe Greene, to acquire a known commodity like Allen did, such as, say, Izzy Lang.

"How long do they want to make their fans wait?" Allen asked the Steamer.

The answer was four years. That's the time it took for the Steelers under coach Chuck Noll—the former L.A. Chargers assistant—to win the first of their four Super Bowls under the banner of the Steel Curtain. Continuing to torment their supporters, the next year Pittsburgh blundered into drafting Hall of Fame linebacker Jack Ham, guard Gerry Mullins, and free safety Mike Wagner, an eleventh-round gas tanker, all of whom were pillars in their Super Bowl movement. In 1972, the Steelers' foolish reliance on the draft netted them another Hall of Famer, Franco Harris, a graduate of Penn State and the University of Immaculate Reception. In 1973, they picked up a starting corner in J. T.

Thomas. It only got worse in 1974, when they drafted three Hall of Famers in wide receiver Lynn Swann, middle linebacker Jack Lambert, and center Mike Webster.

While Pittsburgh built for the future, the Rams' streak of double-digit-victory seasons ended at three, and so did Allen's time in L.A.

Furillo predicted that the Rams would go to the Super Bowl under Allen in 1970, in the fully merged league. He also bet Allen a bottle of blackberry brandy that he would not be fired.

Things started well enough for the '70 Rams as they scored impressive victories over St. Louis, Buffalo, and San Diego, the third of which Furillo was awarded a game ball because of his snarky prediction at the weekly George Allen Breakfast Club press conference that the Chargers would win. The Rams beat them, 37–10.

The fourth week saw a transition at the top in what was now the NFC West when San Francisco beat the Rams in L.A., even without any fancy artwork in the drab Coliseum end zones. The loss to the 49ers began a 2-3-1, six-week stretch for L.A. The Rams won three of their last four but couldn't overcome San Francisco, and they were out of the playoffs.

Before the '70 season began, it was clear that Reeves's health was failing him badly. The team's owner stopped into town in August on a rare escape from his cancer treatments in New York, and spent a few of his brief moments in Los Angeles with Furillo. Reeves had recently had throat surgery and could barely talk, but he had some things to say about Allen that made the Steamer's blackberry brandy bet with the coach a sure loser a month before he made it.

No, he was not going to fire Allen, Reeves said, unless the coach broke league rules he sometimes ignored, such as trading draft picks he didn't have. But when the coach's contract expired at the end of the season, the owner suggested it would be highly unlikely that he'd have Allen back.

According to the owner, the coach insisted at the time of his reinstatement that he come back only under the terms of their then-existing deal.

"George said at the time he was brought back he didn't want an increase or an extension of his contract," Reeves, who gave Allen neither, said to Furillo.

In the same column, the Steam Room told his readers why Allen only wanted to finish out his five-year contract. The coach "has an intense dislike for his employer," Furillo wrote.

According to his daughter's book, Allen, in the days after the 8:00 AM "Merry Christmas, you're fired" phone call, characterized Reeves as "a loser." He ripped the terminally ill Reeves for his prolific boozing in the face of death.

"He's drinking to forget he's alive!" Jennifer Allen quoted her father as saying, during his holiday season spent in firing limbo.

During a Monday Night Football game in late October of 1970, Howard Cosell reported that Allen would be gone at the end of the season, even if they won the Super Bowl.

Furillo followed up on Cosell's report to add, "Virtually all communication between Allen and Reeves has ended. The gulf between them hasn't closed because of their intense pride."

The Rams finished their 1970 season with a 31–3 victory in New York over the Football Giants. As soon as the team walked off the Yankee Stadium field after the December 20 game, the hourglass flipped, and the sands drained out George Allen's time as "the best coach the Rams have ever had," in Furillo's estimation.

A day before Reeves announced that Allen was through, Furillo's column, under the headline "Steamer's Hotel Full of Rumors," reported not only that was Allen gone, but where he was going—to the Washington Redskins.

One of the Steamer's better sources around town, Jack Kent Cooke, owned the Lakers and the Kings and had recently opened the Forum as the fabulous new home for his NBA and NHL franchises. Cooke also owned a piece of the Redskins and would later become their majority stockholder.

Somehow, word got to Furillo that Cooke and Allen were flirting.

"A Forum employee told a *Herald Examiner* employee that

Allen will go to work for Jack Kent Cooke on Friday," the December 29 Steam Room reported. "George's contract with Rams president Daniel F. Reeves runs out Thursday."

You'd be right if you called Cooke a Forum employee, and Bud Furillo most certainly worked for the *Herald Examiner*.

Furillo had the second firing of George Allen in the afternoon paper when it happened the next day.

"There have been strong reports," Furillo wrote in the same story, "that Allen will be named coach and general manager of the Washington Redskins." The story reported that Allen was unavailable for comment, but the Steamer did manage to track down George's wife, Etty, at what he called "their pretentious Mediterranean style home in Palos Verdes."

He quoted her as saying, "This is not bad news for my husband but bad news for the players and the fans of Los Angeles."

• • • • •

A week later, Allen did sign with the Redskins, for eye-popping terms that Melvin Durslag reported exclusively in the *Herald Examiner*.

Washington opened with $125,000 a year for seven years, then increased the pot with a car and driver. Allen drew to a $25,000 signing bonus, $150,000 toward buying a house, a $250,000 life insurance policy, an unlimited expense account that team president Edward Bennett Williams famously said he exceeded, hotel and travel expenses, six weeks' vacation, permission to cut his own endorsement deals, and a five percent stock option on the team. Allen then raked in the complete and utter control over all football-related operations that he most coveted.

Furillo's news story said Allen, in charge in Washington, "may try to deal with the Rams for some of the veterans he brought to the club such as safetyman Richie Petitbon and linebackers Jack Pardee and Myron Pottios."

The "Ramskins" deal in fact was consummated on January 28, 1971. Allen acquired Pardee and Pottios from L.A. (and Petitbon in a later transaction), along with Maxie Baughan, defensive tackle Diron Talbert, guard John Wilbur, and special teams specialist Jeff Jordan. They helped Allen make it to the Super Bowl, where the '73 Redskins lost to the undefeated Miami Dolphins, 14–7.

In return, Allen relinquished a first-round draft pick that the Rams used to pick Isiah Robertson, the so-called "Black Butkus," who was pretty good, but c'mon—he was no Butkus in any shade of skin. The Rams also got linebacker Marlin McKeever and a few gasoline tank draft picks the next year. One of them turned into Dave Elmendorf, who intercepted twenty-seven passes in his career, made second-team All-NFC in 1974 and second-team All-Pro in 1975, and started for the Rams' 1979 Super Bowl team. The trade also freed up the middle linebacker position for Hacksaw Reynolds, who played it as well as anybody for the next decade.

DIALING UP A GABRIEL DEAL
JUNE 8, 1973

Given permission by the Rams to make a deal with Philadelphia for Roman Gabriel your reporter failed miserably last night.

The end result was that the Eagles drew back a player the Rams said they never offered in the first place, defensive end Richard Harris, and tossed in a journeyman back, Tony Baker.

"You tell the Rams we'll give them Baker, Harold Jackson, and two first round draft choices," Eagle owner Leonard Tose said from his pretentious Philadelphia home to mine on the outskirts of Bell Gardens.

So I telephoned Don Klosterman at Doc Kerlan's house in Brentwood and he said Baker was unacceptable.

"Call Tose back and see if he has anything else to give," he said.

Why not, I thought, it's only eighty-five cents for three minutes and I am dialing direct to Philadelphia and even to Brentwood.

"They don't want Baker, eh," said Tose. "Okay, now it's just Jackson and two firsts."

"That's what it was all of the time," Klosterman said. "They weren't telling you the truth when they said Harris was in the Tuesday deal." . . .

Back to area code 215 and the Tose residence.

"What you reported about

One player who didn't switch sides was Roman Gabriel, who became the world's angriest Filipino quarterback when Allen stiffed him on a promise to take him back East, too. Gabe blew a fuse when Allen suggested that the QB's marital problems hurt the Rams in 1970.

Furillo's May 6, 1971, Steam Room column, written off a press conference the day before, when the Rams signed the QB to a long-team deal, contained the most visually descriptive quotes to ever come out of Gabriel.

"When Washington comes here, Mr. Allen is liable to leave the Coliseum with a football in his mouth," Gabe told Furillo and other reporters.

It was Allen and the Ramskins, however, who prevailed in the December 13 game, 38–24, in front of 80,402 in the Coliseum. Furillo reported that "Slender George," as he called him,

---

Harris, Jackson, and two firsts on Tuesday was accurate," said Tose. "But there is no way we'll offer that now. Mike McCormack (Eagles coach) told Klosterman that at five o'clock this afternoon. We feel as if we're being jerked around—and so is Roman."

Returning to the Brentwood number, Dr. Robert Kerlan, who is recovering from surgery, answered the phone.

"Grand Central Station," he shouted. Klosterman took the instrument from him.

"I'm telling you they never had Harris in the package on Tuesday," the Ram general manager said. "That's a lie. We would have taken that in a New York minute."

The mention of New York brings to mind an earlier conversation with Ram owner Carroll Rosenbloom who checked in from Florida in the bizarre telephone orgy.

"I still love you Buddy boy, but the Eagles lied to you," said Rosenbloom. "If they were telling the truth, they'll make the same deal now."

"No we won't," said Tose, another eight-five cents away. "We're not going to give up Harris now because of the way the Rams have handled this whole thing. . . . You call any five owners you want to pick and ask them if Jackson and two firsts isn't a fair deal for Gabriel."

"I can't, Mr. Tose," I said. "My dialing finger is sore."

"left with the game ball under his arm," instead of halfway down his gullet. Allen called it "the biggest win in my coaching career to date."

Dan Reeves died four months after he uncoupled Allen, and his survivors sold the Rams to Robert Irsay, who traded the team to Carroll Rosenbloom for the Baltimore Colts.

L.A. replaced Allen by stealing UCLA's Tommy Prothro, who washed out after two years. The Rams concluded The Steam Room era under the leadership of head coach Chuck Knox. In time, Reeves probably would have fired Knox, but he no doubt would have raised a cup when the forces of "Ground Chuck" defeated Allen's Redskins in the 1974 playoffs, 19-10.

Chapter 9

HORSEPLAYER'S ADVOCATE

While Saturday's hero, a fullback named Quicken Tree, paraded in the end zone with a horseshoe of flowers around his neck, the villain, Nodouble, sneaked away, leaving $274,484 in uncashed tickets behind him. Those who backed him were kindly folks who had come to Santa Anita looking to double their money on the 6-5 favorite in the glamour race of the West, the $100,000 Guaranteed Santa Anita Handicap. Aptly named, Nodouble didn't run back to his victory in the Big 'Cap of 1969. Instead, he finished eighth, carrying 130 pounds and $274,484. Nodouble should have been made to answer. But being a horse, he put on his plaid jacket, strolled home, took a shave, got a date, and went out to dinner. It proved once again you can't trust a horse.

—March 9, 1970

In his coverage of the Southern California horse racing circuit, Bud Furillo may have crossed one of the reddest lines in journalism.

Rather than maintaining a safe distance from the action, the Steamer interjected himself into the story. His frequent appearances at the betting windows clearly tainted his objectivity. His heart lay with the horseplayer, and it was their interest that shaped his writing, because their point of view was indistinguishable from his own.

He spent a lifetime trying to beat the odds, and like the thousands who aided him in the assault on the pari-mutuels, the good days trailed the bad by several lengths. Yet he never showed his bitterness in print, and he papered over the upward distribution of his wealth into the pockets of the monarchy with an absurdist's sense of humor.

Consumed by football, assigned to baseball, and later to take charge as editor of the *Herald Examiner* sports section, Furillo still found time to write a few columns every year on the winter meeting at Santa Anita. Then he followed the herd across town to Hollywood Park. Summer meant a trip down the coast to Del Mar—"the most delightful place in the world to lose your money," the Steamer called the track north of San Diego, where the turf met the surf. He also loved to scurry across the border to drop off some more cash at Agua Caliente and its famed Future Book.

The Steamer hung out some with track owners like Mervyn Leroy and Marjorie Everett. He once pulled a quote from owner-breeder Ogden Phipps of Claiborne Farm in Kentucky. He colored his stuff with takes on jockeys like Bill Shoemaker and Eddie Arcaro and trainers on the order of Bobby Frankel. He worked the backstretch to attain the wisdom of the hot walkers and even got stories out of people like Santa Anita Turf Club maitre d' Nat Golde, who told him about the time movie-studio brother Harry Warner walked in and asked, "What's good today?"

"Prime rib," Golde replied.

"What race is he in?" Harry inquired.

When it came to his audience, though, Furillo's copy was aimed at folks like himself—the players who fueled the entire operation. He knew who they were because they were everybody he had ever known, like his cronies at the Lancer Lounge, the bar in Downey he partially owned.

A few days after the Cowboys knocked the Rams out of the 1973 NFL playoffs, the Steamer was brooding. He'd tabbed L.A. to win the Super Bowl in the first year of his friend Chuck Knox's tenure as head coach. Now the Rams were out of it, just like he was out the few hundred bucks he put on their nose.

The Steamer's pals tried to pick him up. They figured a good way to improve his mood would be to get him out into the fresh air.

"Let's go down to the track," Sal the Chalk Player suggested.

"What for?" Furillo asked, his thinking clouded by depression.

"Because it's open!"

Sal and the Steamer were joined by a few other Lancer regulars, including one who doubled as the neighborhood loan shark—a handy guy to have along at the track, if you could handle the juice. One time, when they got shut out over the first five races, Furillo's dim-witted bartender at the Lancer looked over the entries for the sixth race.

"This next race is tough," the bartender pronounced.

"You think the last five were easy?" shrieked the Chalk Player.

When he first broke into the newspaper business, one of Furillo's most important duties was to drive sports editor George T. Davis to the track and to get him home safely when things got out of hand at the clubhouse refreshment stand, which was often. Seeing the young writer's affection for losing money at the track, Davis made him a tout. They named the column "Señor Sombrero," and its ethnic stereotyping would make the sensitive reader of today shudder in discomfort. Words like "little," for instance, were pronounced "leetle," and it went downhill from there.

Sombrero was born at the 1954 Del Mar meet, conceptualized as one *Mexicano*'s effort to get rich off the races so he could go home and buy his own hacienda. Invariably, Sombrero lost all his money and had to take on loans. Yet he stuck around for a decade, extolling the fighting spirit of the hapless horseplayer.

"Amigos, never has the hour looked so dark for us," Sombrero said in a Churchillian accent during a '55 cold snap, when he went thirty-tree of thirty-five races without cashing a ticket. "But we must not give up on the *caballos*. We will bet them at the win windows, at the place windows, at the show windows."

It took him a few decades, but Furillo eventually figured out that the only way to play the track was for laughs. When Lucky Debonair won the 1965 Santa Anita Derby a few weeks ahead of his victory in a bigger derby in Kentucky, Furillo reported that the 61,245 fans at the track became the first group in California history to load more than $5 million into the tote board.

"The machines performed flawlessly," the Steamer reported.

"However, the bettors made a few mistakes."

Cougar II, the great Chilean thoroughbred trained by Charlie Whittingham, won $1,162,725 over his career for owner Mary Florsheim Jones.

"In return," Furillo wrote of the footwear heiress, "Mary has made sure that Cougar is kept in the best of shoes."

The afternoon of February 26, 1967, more than 51,000 turned out at the base of the San Gabriel Mountains for the thirtieth running of the Santa Anita Handicap, the biggest race in Southern California. A very capable Pretense, with Bill Shoemaker up, defeated long-time local champion Native Diver, probably the most popular horse in town during the Steam Room era.

Furillo described Native Diver, winner of thirty-five stakes and handicap races at the L.A. and Bay Area tracks between 1961 and 1967, as "the Archie Moore of racing." Like the light-heavy champ who held his crown long after he turned forty, Native Diver excelled in his sport well beyond retirement age. At age eight, the Diver was "now eligible for Social Security," The Steam Room pointed out.

Pretense's victory in the Big 'Cap shifted $100,000 from the players' wallets into the bank account of his owner, Liz Tippett, "who doesn't appear to need it," according to The Steam Room. "One of her divorce settlements brought her $3 million."

Tippet, Furillo noted, "is the wife of Colonel Cloyce Tippett of Ocala, Florida, who owns an aircraft company and a few mines in Peru." The couple lived in a manor on Llangollen Farm, the 1,100-acre estate she owned in the rolling foothills of the Blue Ridge Mountains in Virginia Hunt Country, where the gentry had been killing foxes since the days of Jefferson. She acquired the property as a gift from her first husband, New York Herald Tribune publisher John Hay Whitney, and kept it after they divorced in 1940. Tippet, formerly Mary Elizabeth Altemus of Philadelphia, then went through a couple more marriages, according to The Steam Room, before she hooked up with Colonel Tippett.

"There is nothing to indicate that Liz comes from great wealth," Furillo wrote, "except that she wears full length mink coats and carries a poodle named Killer in her purse. Killer is one year older than Pretense but he can't run as fast."

•   •   •   •   •

Earlier in his life, there were times when it was 4-5 the Steamer would ever get out of the danger zone the track can pose to every player.

"Every teenager goes through it," Furillo wrote. "Before surrendering to work, the track is tried out for a living."

For a good couple decades after succumbing to this realization, the track still had a nasty hold on him. He spent way too much time and lost way too much money for way too long. The resulting losses forced improvisation in other details of responsible parenthood, such as feeding his family.

"I could work miracles with eighty cents after a losing day at the track," the Steamer wrote in another column. "A pound of neck bones, one and a half pounds of spaghetti, a can of tomatoes, a can of tomato paste—that was dinner. I gave the recipe to other horseplayers. They were grateful."

I don't remember ever going hungry, but I do remember many a neck-bone spaghetti dinner, and I remember my mom sweating out a Hollywood Park race one Saturday in July, telling me the outcome was important only because the next week's grocery money was riding on it.

As we watched on the black-and-white, the bending sunlight cast long shadows from the horses in the post parade and lit up my mom's hands that shook in our living room as she dragged on a string of unfiltered Camels. They shook less when the old man's horse came in first. I think it was Native Diver, in one of his three Hollywood Gold Cup victories. There would be no neck-bone spaghetti that night.

•   •   •   •   •

He bet money and won on champions such as Citation, Damascus, Round Table, and Swaps, but the best horse the Steamer ever wrote about was Buckpasser. It was the day before the first Super Bowl, between Green Bay and Kansas City, to be played in Los Angeles. Furillo noted that Buckpasser's $34,050

DAMASCUS CLEARS HEAD, WINS PREAKNESS
May 21, 1967

That Bill Shoemaker is a keen judge of horseflesh. It was confirmed again in the running of the Preakness Saturday.

The Shoe refused to write off Damascus for his disappointing third in the Kentucky Derby two weeks ago.

"The horse was nervous Derby Day," said Shoemaker.

It has not yet been determined what upset Damascus other than Proud Clarion in Kentucky. Who knows what problems lurk in the heads of horses?

Maybe Damascus was apprehensive about the escalation in Vietnam, or he might have been concerned about problems that bigger than king-sized cigarettes pose for their smokers. Maybe somebody stole his Right Guard.

At any rate, he raced with a clear head to make a farce of the Preakness at the country's oldest race track, Pimlico. George Washington once raced horses there. It is believed that Johnny Longden was the contract rider for the Washington stable.

paycheck for winning the 1967 San Fernando Stakes at Santa Anita "is twice as much as the Packers can make apiece if they run away from the Chiefs today."

Buckpasser shipped to Southern California as the reigning Horse of the Year and the winner of thirteen consecutive stakes races at tracks all over the country—Hialeah, Aqueduct, Del Mar, Arlington Park, Saratoga, and Santa Anita. The victory in the San Fernando increased his career earnings at the time to fourth-most among any horse that had ever raced.

None of it was ever easy on Buck's backers, the Steamer pointed out.

"He doesn't run off and hide from the opposition," Furillo said. "A friendly sort, Buckpasser cruises alongside to chat with his four-legged friends. Baseball would never tolerate this kind of fraternizing."

It took him a while to get serious in the San Fernando, but Buckpasser, in front of 51,840 people, won by a length and a half.

As exciting as the race was, the Steamer, as always, kept

watch over the horseplayers' cash movements. The column reported that "men carrying satchels full of money" unloaded it in the show pool. "Ten percenters," Furillo called them, for their minimally guaranteed twenty-cent return on every two dollars wagered on Buckpasser to finish third. On this day of the 1966 San Fernando Stakes, "They stuck up management for $58,618.62, the minus pool that set a Santa Anita record."

• • • • •

In assessing Nodouble's failure in the 1970 Big 'Cap, the Steamer's main problem, of course, was that he had tabbed the horse in his column the day before the race to repeat as winner of the Big 'Cap.

Furillo had done his homework. He reported that, since winning the race the year before, Nodouble had won the Brooklyn Handicap in New York, the Hawthorne Gold Cup in Chicago, the Michigan Mile in Detroit, and the Arkansas Derby in the state where he had established his residence. He came into the race with career earnings of $754,229.

"Approaching middle age, Nodouble seems destined to become another of America's millionaires," the Steamer wrote in his Big 'Cap selection preview. "When he retires, he'll be in position to invite President Nixon to watch Arkansas play Texas at Fayetteville from his private box."

Nodouble failed to crack seven figures, his career pretty much gelded after his poor showing in the Santa Anita Handicap. The Steamer reported that, six furlongs into the race, the horse "had found his groove back there in eighth place and stayed there."

"Quicken Tree watched it all from last place," he wrote. "Being twelfth man provided him with a horse laugh which he gave to the chalk players when he went by the grandstand the second time with his position improved to first."

• • • • •

The Steamer always loved a jockey fight, and he got a good one once in 1968, when Alvaro Pineda and Miguel Yanez whipped

each other coming down the hill on the Santa Anita turf course
that seemed to drop from the sky.

Pineda, atop Young Pro, got bumped into Hed's Cadet, with
Miguel Yanez in the stirrups. Even though he initiated the contact, Pineda had the audacity to call Yanez a son of a bitch. The
affronted Yanez then smashed Pineda across the back with his
whip. Pineda struck back with a lash across Yanez' right arm.

"Then he said to hell with it, went back to riding, and won
the race with Young Pro," Furillo recounted.

Hed's Cadet finished last, but Yanez sought a rematch in the
jockey's room. Taking up the challenge, Pineda belted Yanez
over the head with his helmet.

"Both boys slugged it out in the center of the room," the
Steamer reported, "until the bell sounded for the sixth race."

•   •   •   •   •

One January morning in 1960, Furillo got an early morning
wakeup call from Santa Anita's PR guy to witness a couple other
jocks duke it out.

Eddie Arcaro and Bill Shoemaker were a bit more legendary
than Pineda and Yanez. They had won more than 13,500 races
between them over the course of their careers, including nine
Kentucky Derbies and the two Triple Crowns that Arcaro scored
with Whirlaway in 1941 and Citation in 1948.

Friendlier rivals than Yanez and Pineda, Arcaro and Shoemaker were playing against each other in a charity golf tournament. They needed a caddy, and they gave Furillo the nod to
carry their bags.

On the first tee, Shoemaker got all ninety-seven of his pounds
into a drive that rocketed ahead 210 yards. The suspicious Arcaro asked that the stewards run a saliva test on his opponent.

"You look like you might be hopped up," Arcaro told Shoemaker, according to The Steam Room.

The jockeys saddled up Furillo, but he broke down on the
first fairway, dragging their bags across the early-morning dew
at Santa Anita Golf Course. They brought in professionals for
the next seventeen. Shoemaker shot a seventy-nine, a nose better

than Arcaro's eighty—which was saying something. Eddie had a schnoz to match Durante, and was kind of sensitive about it.

"How can anybody call me Banana Nose," Arcaro told Shoemaker, within earshot of Furillo, whose multi-fractured nose had been spread over most of his face, "when that fellow has one that looks like a bunch?"

Shoemaker, a seven handicapper, later built a tennis court in his Beverly Hills backyard, where the jockey had some of his fairly athletic neighbors over to play. When the Steamer dropped in for a visit in 1973, the Shoe told him he could hang with Elgin Baylor but that the running back out of USC who was about to become the NFL's first 2,000-yard man was just too much for him.

"[O. J.] Simpson is too fast," the jockey told Furillo. "It's tough to get the ball past him."

•   •   •   •   •

Furillo admired the Shoemakers and Arcaros, but he truly connected with track figures like Bobby Frankel, a five-time Eclipse Award winner as the best trainer in the country, whose horses earned more than $220 million in purses. At the time of Frankel's death in 2009, it was second best in world history, behind D. Wayne Lukas.

It was Frankel's abject lack of sentimentality that drew the Steamer close to him.

"There isn't a horse I would trust," Frankel told Furillo in a 1973 column.

Astounded by the trainer's frank disclosure, the Steamer wrote, "Frankel was asked why you can't trust a horse like a dog or a killer whale."

Bobby had an easy and obvious answer.

"If a fly is bothering a horse, he's going to kick at it," Frankel said. "He isn't going to look first to see if you are there. You get behind them, they let go with a kick, and it's Boom!"

Like the Youngstown product who wrote The Steam Room, the Brooklyn-born Frankel came from an urban background where horses were put to their best use on racetracks for the livelihood and entertainment of city boys like themselves. Neither much cared for cowboy boots or hats.

"I get tired of looking at a horse pretty quick in my barn if it doesn't win," Frankel told Furillo.

Renowned for buying and selling horses at the bottom rungs of the game, Frankel didn't wait around to drop them in class even further if they didn't produce. It was all about the purse money to Frankel, and Furillo seemed to understand the trainer's priority.

"I don't run them to kill them," Frankel said. But he conceded that it didn't bother his conscience to run a sore horse if it had been claimed out of his barn and it was his last opportunity to ring some cash out of the beast. "That's business," he said. Thoroughbreds, Frankel explained to the Steamer, lived to run. Most everything else about them was myth, the trainer thought, especially the notion they were any more sentimental than him. Frankel wasn't sure a thoroughbred knew one two-legged creature from the next.

"I've heard those stories about how the owner comes to the barn with sugar," he said in The Steam Room. "The horse lets out a whoop and the owner is thrilled because the horse recognizes him. I don't carry sugar."

Horses, Frankel said in the column, are "not that friendly," or even that smart with words or numbers.

"You can't teach them to say hello," he said. "They can't count like Trigger."

•   •   •   •   •

The Steam Room offered its readers a history lesson on the sad day in August of 1971, when Agua Caliente burned down.

Sportsmen had raced and bet on horses at the Tijuana track for decades, even before its 1929 opening. One aficionado was Pancho Villa.

"He usually won," the Steamer said.

California boxing promoter "Sunny" Jim Coffroth had acquired the 308-acre property in 1916, opened the track in its then-modern form in 1929, and made it the site of the first "hundred grander" in the western continent. The fast lane in

Prohibition-shackled Southern California led straight to Caliente, "towards the longest bar in the world," Furillo wrote, "which measured about seven furlongs." Coffroth and Company also opened the fabulous Gold Room casino, a popular attraction for high rollers in the years before Las Vegas was Las Vegas—and at a place and time when the table games played safer than the races.

"You couldn't be sure what a horse would pay at Caliente," the Steamer wrote. "A horse could be 8-1 when the bet was placed, 5-1 at the clubhouse turn, and 9-5 in the stretch."

John Alessio, a one-time San Diego shoeshine boy whose fine work on the footwear of local financier C. Arnholt Smith got him into the banking business, fixed up the credibility problem. It was Alessio who introduced the totalizator board to Mexican horse racing.

Alessio acquired the track in 1947 and made it one of the most successful gambling establishments in the world. It had its famous "future book," of course, where you could get big odds before the masses bet them down. Caliente took bets on every track in the world. Its "5-10" became one of the most famous wagers in sports, and one of the richest, too, for anybody who could pick the winner of those six races in a row.

Other complicated financial maneuvers by Alessio north of the border attracted federal attention, and he was indicted, convicted, and imprisoned for tax evasion a few months ahead of the fire.

"Those who knew and liked the man were saddened by his fate," wrote Furillo, who knew and liked Alessio because the man took care of the Steamer in the Caliente Turf Club and on south-of-the-border family vacations to Rosarito Beach and elsewhere.

As the embers cooled, Furillo prepared for the future.

"Caliente has survived many crises," he wrote. "Already, ways have been found to recover from the fire."

The plan was to turn the plant over to the greyhounds, where the dogs run into the present day.

"As for the horses," Furillo wrote, "there is always the bull ring."

•   •   •   •   •

Conflict of interest has always darkened an ethical corner of sports journalism on the matter of covering horse racing. I'm sure many a writer wrote, "with blood in his shoes," as the Steamer liked to phrase his squishy feeling on the many occasions he lost important bets.

But a reading of his horse racing columns does not show them to have been affected much by the outcome of his action. He always maintained a good cheer, using his misfortune at the track as column fodder. He fully disclosed his plays, usually days before the running.

Furillo's readers knew or should have known the grave risks entailed in taking his advice at the track. In my reading of his columns during the Steam Room era, he did not pick a single Kentucky Derby winner, though he tried year after year. The week of the race, he doctored up his column picture with a long white mustache, an elegant Van Dyke beard, a black-string bow tie, and a white Stetson befitting a member of the Honorable Order of the Kentucky Colonels.

When he was a semi-professional tout, under the Señor Sombrero pseudonym, his alter ego was always broke. On the rare occasions he got one right, he never let you forget it. He hit the jackpot in the 1961 Santa Anita Handicap with Prove It. The horse went off as a 6–5 favorite, but the Steamer had him at 10–1 at the Caliente Future Book.

"It's like money in the bank," the horse's jockey, Bill Shoemaker, told Furillo the week of the race. "Only two things could go wrong. The horse might fall down, or I might louse it up."

Prove It stayed afloat and the Shoe stayed out of his way, and Furillo gloated all the way to Tijuana to collect his fortune on a ten-dollar bet, reminding readers in five separate columns that he not only picked the winner, but more importantly, he beat the price.

Bravely, he never ran or hid from his losing predictions. He owned up to them, recounted them, and glorified them, although his admissions sometimes came in the guise of a forehand smash to the idiot jockeys who ran his picks out of the

SHOE ALL BUT GUARANTEES FUTURE BOOK PICK IN BIG 'CAP

FEBRUARY 10, 1961

Before Prove It ever got to the races at Santa Anita, the sneaky Steam Roomer pitched a sawbuck on his nose in Johnny Alessio's Future Book for the Santa Anita Handicap.

The odds were 10–1. Now they're 6–5.

The totalisator will blink out a 3–5 quotation for bettors on February 25, day of the race.

Prove It appears to be such a lock that Duffy Cornell, public relations representative for the Caliente track, offered to pay me off on the ticket. At 8–1. Duff was lookin' to save the boss some loot.

You can't blame him for trying. If Prove It wins, Alessio is likely to take the biggest trimming in Future Book annals since Samson was sheared.

The other night at "Murph" and "Slugger" Sturniolo's Derby restaurant, I drew aside my favorite horsebacker, Bill Shoemaker.

"Shoe" handles the reins for Prove It. When I told him about my ticket, he assured:

"It's like money in the bank."

. . .

Only two things could go wrong. The horse might fall down. Or I could louse it up."

. . . I couldn't throw out the chance of human error. . . .

. . . I remembered that the "Shoe" has pulled a boo-boo or two. There was the time he misjudged the finish line aboard Gallant Man in the Kentucky Derby. And there was the time he took a siesta aboard Swaps in the Californian at Hollywood.

So my problem is to make sure Shoemaker remains alert in the "Big 'Cap." Here's my proposal, "Shoe."

Suppose I bisect the Future Book and staple half of it to your right leg. It will be specially treated in a solution of insomnia.

I'm willing to cut you in on half the action to make sure you don't, er, louse it up. Fifty bucks is better than nothing.

In return, I don't expect you to cut me in on the $10,000, which will be your end of the winner's purse. Fair enough?

money. For instance, he never got over Ron Turcotte's botchery of the 1968 Strub Stakes at Santa Anita, when the jockey famous for being the human attachment to Secretariat couldn't get Damascus into the end zone at 1–5. Six years after the flub in the

Strub (pronounced "Stroob"), Turcotte flew west to ride Prince Dantan in the 1974 Big 'Cap.

"The rider of the Triple Crown king acted like he was Arcaro with Secretariat going for him," Furillo said. "Let's see what he can do with Prince Dantan."

Furillo's selection in the race was Quack. "Probably the best older horse in the country when he's right, which is about once every six months," he wrote, "and the Steamer will back him to the hilt in his relentless struggle against the bookies. The five-year-old carries a lot of weight other than the 126 on his back in the Big 'Cap. He goes about 1,150 pounds. If he belonged to the Washington Redskins, George Allen would fine him unmercifully."

Looking at the rest of the field, the Steamer feared Ancient Title. Earlier in the meeting, the horse had won the Malibu Stakes at seven furlongs, the San Fernando at a mile and an eighth, and the Strub at one and a quarter.

The last horse to do that at Santa Anita was Hillsdale in 1959, who then finished second in the Big 'Cap "when the Steamer had him at 8-1 in the Future Book," his pre-race prognostication said. The problem in '59, the Steamer said, was that jockey Tommy Barrow "rode Hillsdale the way Turcotte handled Damascus."

The Steamer saw more trouble in Tri-Jet, another instigator of bad memory.

"I could have killed him," Furillo wrote, "when he beat me out of the win mutual with Forage in the San Pasqual. Susan's Girl suckered Forage on the pace."

Big Spruce was a Big 'Cap entry "looking for mud," the Steamer said. "Sprucie Baby moves way up in the slop. So do pigs."

Furillo could not resist one more crack at Turcotte. "He would do better" in the Big 'Cap, he wrote, "if he brought Secretariat with him."

The Steamer passed on covering the Big 'Cap for a faster race run the same day. Trading in the smog of Arcadia for the even dirtier air of Ontario, he chose to write on the fifth

California 500. Bobby Unser won the Indy-style open-wheel auto race with an average speed of 137 miles per hour, which was quite a bit faster than Quack, who finished fifth in the Big 'Cap.

The Steamer's pick got out okay, but couldn't handle the slow track softened by rain earlier in the week. Quack, racing in front of the 52,797 who made him the 2–1 favorite, was still in it heading for home "but lost his punch in mid-stretch and tired late," according to the chart published the next day in the *Herald Examiner*. Big Spruce, as predicted, liked the slower, if not muddy footing and "rallied in somewhat close quarters nearing the furlong pole and finished with good speed," to snag the show money.

Ancient Title merited the concern Furillo had expressed a couple days before the race. He went to the front between calls "with little need of coaxing" and "bravely kept to his task in a good try," to finish second.

The winner, under the expert handling of Ron Turcotte, was Prince Dantan. He paid twenty-eight dollars.

•   •   •   •   •

The Steamer may have lost a few paychecks at the track, but he found a groom working the barns at Hollywood Park who showed how the disciplined horseplayer could make a buck.

John Serio had exercised horses from the days of Man O' War. He broke Man's most successful son, 1937 Triple Crown winner War Admiral. He'd worked at tracks across the country for more than forty years by the time Furillo caught up with him.

A story followed Serio as he made his rounds across the country, that he had stashed upwards of $200,000 in winnings.

"I got money, but I'm not telling you how much," Serio said, heating up some canned soup in the tack room where he lived on the Hollywood Park backstretch. "You can get knocked in the head on the racetrack if some of these drifters find out you have money. It happened twice in the men's room to the same guy here last year."

Serio said he hadn't placed a bet in ten years, but that he had made enough in his playing days to more than cover his rent, which was free.

"I would bet only to show—a couple hundred a race," he told Furillo. "My system was to look for small fields, under ten horses in good allowance races. I would bet horses that were consistently in the money. I didn't lose a bet in a month."

For the undisciplined, Serio had another piece of advice. He quoted for Steam Room readers the wisdom of legendary jockey Isaac Burns Murphy, three-time winner of the Kentucky Derby.

"The only way to beat horses," Murphy said, before his untimely death from pneumonia in 1896, "is with a whip."

Chapter 10

FIGHT TOWN

A tall skinny kid knocked me out once on the fan-tail of the motor ship Chester Sun, a lady who didn't make it as big as, say, the Enterprise, during World War II. When the Steamer got up, he rubbed his jaw and smiled. Most guys smile after they get knocked out. Maybe it's just a silly grin. Then I made a profound statement to this Greek kid who did it. His name was George Something. "Beware of tall skinny kids," I said. "They have a wallop behind those spindly arms."

—October16, 1966

A bout an hour before the fight, Mando Ramos's handlers sent word from their dressing room at the Palacio de los Deportes that they needed Bud Furillo immediately.

The world was in the waning days of Spanish fascism, and Ramos, a tall, skinny Chicano kid from Long Beach, was in Madrid to try and win back the vacant World Boxing Council lightweight championship.

Representatives of Mando's entourage found the Steamer ringside, where the columnist had settled into the press row to cover Ramos's fight against Pedro Carrasco, the hope of Spain.

Andrew Ramos, the fighter's younger brother, carried the message of urgency to Furillo.

"Jackie McCoy wants you right away," the brother told the writer.

The Steamer hustled down to Mando's dressing room, where McCoy, the trainer of five world champions over his forty-six-year career, said he'd run into some trouble with the regime of Generalissimo Francisco Franco.

"The Army just came in here and took my Spanish second away," McCoy informed the columnist. "They said he wouldn't be back."

There'd been a lot of that sort of activity over the years in Franco's Spain. Jackie didn't know if they dropped his guy out of helicopter or what. All he knew was he needed a cut man, fast.

He asked the Steamer for help.

"How about working our corner?" McCoy inquired.

As a columnist, the burdens of objectivity never bothered Furillo much, or even at all. Of course he would work the corner—there was no question about it. So he tossed the folded towel over his shoulder and tucked the swabs behind his ears. He hauled the stool up the steps, but the Steamer didn't know yet to bring it into the ring under the ropes rather than swing it over the top strand, and the result was an inadvertent smashing into the back of McCoy's head. There was another unfortunate moment when he removed the spit funnel before Ramos had completed his expectoration, and a gentleman seated in the front row was treated to an unexpected shower.

In covering the fights, the seat in Mando's corner put the Steamer in an even better position to lend perspective, which, after all, was his job as a columnist. And there was no problem at all playing a favorite—it had always been part of his deal. Fighters were always in his top rung of favorites, and he liked them even more if they were from L.A.

During the fifteen years of his column's run, the Steamer caught the trailing edge of Sugar Ray Robinson's career and a smidgeon of Muhammad Ali's beginning. He saw Archie Moore at his best and covered a little bit of Carmen Basilio when the great welterweight champ cashed in on a couple of West Coast swings toward the end of his career.

He admired Cuban welterweight expatriate Jose Napoles when he was in his championship prime, and Mexico City's hard-hitting bantamweight champ, Ruben Olivares, who also fought regularly in L.A. Those two had to be ranked the best pound-for-pound fighters to play the town during the Steam

Room era. But Napoles and Olivares were out-of-towners, mercenaries flown in mostly to fight other out-of-towners, collect their money, and head home to their haciendas.

Mando Ramos, on the other hand, was one of three homegrown fighters who ignited the spectacular L.A. boxing scene of the period. The spindly-legged boxer-puncher with the fabulous footwork had grown up in Long Beach, and the other two who made L.A. the best fight town in the country for a while also came from close by. Raul Rojas grew up tough in Firestone Park, in South L.A., before becoming the king of San Pedro and then of all the featherweights in the world. Jerry Quarry, born of Dust Bowl folk in Bakersfield, reached heavyweight maturity in the southeast suburbs and incorporated his new home town into his nickname—"The Bellflower Bomber"—when he won the national Golden Gloves title in 1965 with five straight knockouts.

Whenever they fought at the Olympic or the Sports Arena or the Coliseum, or Madison Square Garden, or Madrid, against the best in the world, Ramos, Rojas, and Quarry represented L.A. and all of Southern California, whether they liked it or—in Quarry's case—not.

The three of them made it to the top of the world rankings, with Rojas and Ramos winning titles after first coming to prominence at the Olympic Auditorium, the hallowed downtown boxing hall hard against the eastbound lanes of the Santa Monica Freeway. During The Steam Room years, the Olympic stamped authenticity on the Los Angeles boxing brand and became one of the most electric stopping points on the L.A. sports scene.

On big nights—like when Rojas chopped up Pajarito Moreno in their first fight ("nine minutes of blood-letting," Bud Furillo called it), or when Quarry was working his way up against George "Scrap Iron" Johnson, or during Mando's first fight with Frankie Crawford, or when Danny "Little Red" Lopez went to war with Tury Pineda—L.A.'s fight mob oiled up early. They went to nearby bars like Georgino's on Sunset Boulevard or the Gala Cellar on Figueroa or joints a few miles farther out like the Steamer's joint, the Lancer Lounge in Downey, where the proprietor who edited one of the local sports sections arranged buses for the customers headed downtown.

They poured in through the turnstiles under the Olympic marquee at Eighteenth and Grand and into narrow, dimly lit passageways, past oil paintings of the great fighters from the building's past, through the cigarette and cigar smoke that billowed from ringside into the rafters. Bookies took action in the front rows while drinkers threw back shots from half-pints they chased with Schlitz poured from the tap at either end of the building. The place buzzed at a low roar that erupted into three-figure decibel levels when the action got hot. Good-looking women swung their hips down the aisles and drew wolf whistles from the howling legions, from the first row to the top of the balcony. Fans showered the ring with cash and coin to reward prelim fighters who left nothing behind, and ringsiders needed an umbrella to protect themselves from beer showers that rained down when the folks from the upper precincts took issue with the judges' decision.

In the early years of the Steam Room era, the L.A. fight game had been in critical condition. Boxing suffered everywhere in the country, thanks to racketeering-influenced corruption, nationally televised ring killings, and funny outcomes at the top of the ticket in the Patterson-Liston-Ali circle of heavyweight championship fiascoes. Los Angeles had been a town that used to showcase two weekly boxing cards. All of a sudden, it was down to less than one. The Hollywood Legion Stadium shut down in 1959, and the Olympic staged only eighteen boxing shows in all of 1964.

Then along came Rojas, Quarry, and Ramos, their careers aided by the first of many TV contracts in 1965 that would shoot the Olympic into L.A. living rooms for the next twenty years. Gyms sprang up all over town and filled the Olympic cards with kids who dreamed about fighting on TV and winning world championships.

It helped that Bud Furillo covered the hell out of it. The Steamer got on board early with Rojas and watched him become the featherweight champion of the world. He boosted the young Jerry Quarry and attended to his career as it progressed upwardly, if unevenly, to join the top contenders of the heavyweight division.

Ramos was probably the best of the L.A.-based fighters of the era, winning main events before he turned eighteen and becoming the lightweight champion of the world before he was old enough to drink—legally. Furillo saw Mando win and shared his pain when he lost, although they didn't have to sew up the Steamer's eyes after the Ismael Laguna fight like they did Mando's. The Steamer was there when Mando arrived as the town's new golden boy, and he was there at the end when he was beaten down in a corner "like a wounded animal," as Furillo described Ramos's last L.A. fight.

Now it was midnight on November 5, 1971—happy hour on the schedule of Madrid Standard Time, where *la gente* liked to stay up late. The Ramos camp needed somebody to help out in the corner, and figured they would call on Bud Furillo. When it came to the L.A. fight game in the Steam Room era, he'd been there the whole time.

• • • • •

Furillo was only a few months into being a columnist when he found himself sitting through another State Athletic Commission investigation into boxing-industry misbehavior.

This time, it was a prominent fight promoter testifying in May 1959 that a couple of mobsters had threatened to kill him. Jackie Leonard put on fights at the Hollywood Legion Stadium, and he also had a piece of welterweight champion Don Jordan. Leonard told the commission that the underworld boxing czar, Frankie Carbo of New York, and his henchman, Frank "Blinky" Palermo, were mad at him because he had rebuffed their effort to extort Jordan's purse money.

"Nobody ever does this to us," Carbo told Leonard, according to Jackie's testimony to the commission. "We'll meet you at the crossroads, and you're going to get hurt."

Two weeks later, somebody cracked Leonard over the head in as convenient a crossroads as any—the alley behind his house in the Valley. The attack landed Jackie in the hospital. As the investigation unfolded, "All the subway passages led to Carbo," Furillo wrote. Indeed, Carbo, a former triggerman for Murder

Inc. known as "Mr. Gray," and Palermo, a fight fixer out of Philadelphia, were eventually convicted and imprisoned on federal charges in the extortion and assault conspiracy.

The day of their conviction, the Steamer was covering the Angels in Washington, DC, but he swung over to Capitol Hill to check in on Senator Estes Kefauver's committee that was investigating corruption in the boxing game. After the hearing, he scored himself an interview with John G. Bonomi, the assistant

LAW OF JUNGLE IS THE ONLY ONE BLINKY, "MR. GRAY" UNDERSTAND
May 21, 1959

The testimony ranged from the comic to the macabre at the boxing probe yesterday. But more important, what did it prove and what will come out of it?

Well, it pointed up the fact once again that characters like Frankie Carbo and Blinky Palermo are allowed to flourish in a sport which looks the other way at their tactics of intimidation.

Chief of Police Bill Parker is hopeful this inquiry will lead to criminal action against the pair, who threatened the lives of Hollywood promoter Jack Leonard and manager Don Nesseth, manager of world welter champ Don Jordan. All that the Blink and Carbo wanted was to be cut in for fifteen percent of the fighter. . . .

At the moment, Carbo is a fugitive from justice, flitting around Florida, enjoying the freedom of the state's pink flamingoes. He is under indictment in New York. Yet "Mr. Gray" operates casually, inviting boxing folk from all over the country to visit with him, such as Leonard did in Miami.

Palermo is due to return here next month from Philadelphia, to answer a charge of stealing eighty cents worth of magazines. If Blinky doesn't jump his bail, he will have to answer the more important accusation of threatening Leonard and Nesseth. . . .

According to the testimony of Leonard and Nesseth, Carbo and Palermo flaunted the fact that they had "taken care" of people who crossed them in the past.

Because they have been uncanny in evading the law, perhaps it would be best if Carbo and Palermo were herded into an alley, with Jordan left to handle them. The law of the jungle seems to be the only one they understand.

district attorney from New York and scourge of organized crime who was on loan to Kefauver. It was Bonomi whose investigation into labor racketeering in New York took a sideways turn into the fight game.

Now that Carbo was done, Bonomi and Kefauver were pushing for a national boxing commission to clean the mob thugs out of the game.

"Bonomi believes that boxing is worth saving," Furillo wrote. "He feels confident a national commission regulating major events will keep it healthy, even spur competition and new talent."

Kefauver and Bonomi never got their national boxing commission, but the knee-drop they laid on the throat of the underworld pretty much eliminated the Mafia's influence inside the ring. At least in Southern California, it would never threaten the sport again.

A death, however, would.

It came on one of the biggest fight nights in the city's history, March 23, 1963, a doubleheader staged in Dodger Stadium, in a ring set up on the pitcher's mound.

Emile Griffith, who had killed Benny "Kid" Paret in the Madison Square Garden ring a year earlier, lost the opener in a welterweight title fight with Luis Rodriguez—setting up the featured featherweight championship bout between the champion, Davey Moore, and the Cuban challenger, Sugar Ramos.

In front of 26,142 fans, Ramos belted Moore to the canvas in the tenth round. On his way down, the back of Davey's head hit the bottom strand of the ropes. Moore got up, but couldn't weather a punishing attack by Ramos. The round ended with Davey strung over the ropes. Referee George Latka checked Davey out and stopped the fight.

The weird thing was that, even though he was about to die, Moore did an interview in the ring and told the national TV audience, "It just wasn't my night."

Down in his dressing room, he answered a few more reporters' questions. Then he complained of a terrible headache. He fell into a coma and never came out of it. He died seventy-five hours later.

"Davey Moore was considered the best fighter in the ring today, pound for pound," Furillo wrote, while the fighter was still in a coma. "If the best are in danger of death, it can happen to anybody."

At the time of Moore's death, another high-profile fighter was six months into a coma of his own as a result of a Los Angeles fight. Alejandro Lavorante, loser to Muhammad Ali and Archie Moore, had gotten knocked out the previous September in the Olympic Auditorium by John Riggins. Lavorante died in April 1964.

California Governor Edmund G. "Pat" Brown had seen enough after the Lavorante fight. He called then for a ban on boxing in the Golden State. He renewed his demand after Moore died.

As the abolition movement gained momentum, Bud Furillo went so far as to call for a six-month national moratorium on boxing. He'd been a fight fan his whole life, and had covered some of the best ever. He'd been to the Garden, hung out with the real Rocky, and palled it up with the original Sugar Ray. But the Steamer said he felt "shaky and ashamed" as a boxing honk over Moore's death.

"Make a thorough study of the sport," he wrote, "which now finds your life on the line, as well as your title, like it was with Davey Moore."

•   •   •   •   •

The Steamer soon got over his reformer's impulse.

Following the ring death of one great featherweight champion, it was the rise of another that brought the L.A. fight game back to life.

Raul Rojas was a tough kid from the gang-heavy, inner-city streets a few miles south and east of downtown. He'd watched a pal die from a bullet to the head, gone to prison, earned his parole in December 1962, and took up boxing. He moved to San Pedro, got pretty good in the ring, and gained a following among the longshoremen. He debuted at the Olympic in March 1963 and headlined his first card in November. In December, he earned his first mention in The Steam Room. Bud Furillo called him "the most exciting young boxer to come on the local scene in many a season."

Rojas grew better and better against a string of opponents that got tougher and tougher. He won ten straight main events at the Olympic through the end of 1964. He built his record to 22-0-1 with sixteen knockouts and set himself up for a May 1965 title fight in the Coliseum against the great Vicente Saldivar of Mexico.

"Boxing would have perished completely in Los Angeles the past couple of years if it hadn't been for Rojas and the enthusiastic crowds from the waterfront who came to cheer him,'" Furillo wrote before the fight.

Rojas ran twelve miles a day leading up to Saldivar, and his good shape kept him going into the fifteenth round against the 12-to-5 favorite. But in front of 15,400, outdoors on a cold spring night, Saldivar dominated all the way and battered Raul until the referee stopped it, with only ten seconds to go. Afterward, somebody asked Jackie McCoy if the experience would benefit Rojas.

"Getting the hell beat out of you never does you any good," The Steam Room reported as Jackie's response.

It took Raul eight months to recover, but in his second fight back, in the Olympic Auditorium, he sparked what Bud Furillo called "a smashing comeback of the ring sport" in a single night. It would endure as one of the most talked-about fights in L.A. for the rest of the Steam Room era.

The opponent was Ricardo "Pajarito" Moreno, a Steamer favorite since 1957, when the Little Bird brought his wallop north from Mexico.

"The whole world loves a puncher, and few hit like Pajarito," Furillo gushed after Moreno debuted in L.A. with a knockout win."

Ring magazine sure thought so. In 2003, boxing's bible listed Moreno number seventy-six among the 100 Greatest Punchers of all-time, just ahead of number seventy-seven, Evander Holyfield. Joe Louis was number one.

Mexican fans liked popular Pajarito so much, they had to stage a couple of his L.A. fights in the ballparks. Unfortunately for Moreno, he lost them both, one to Davey Moore and another to Kid Bassey. The setbacks sent him back to the bushes of Mexico, where he fought in bullrings, border towns, and the mountain outback. Twelve straight knockouts re-stoked California promoters' interest in Pajarito. North of the border, he KO'd another nine in a row in Oakland, San Jose, and San Francisco.

The streak got him back to L.A. for the epic March 17, 1966, bout with Raul Rojas. The Olympic sold out in a hurry, so the promoters put the fight on closed-circuit television in the downtown Orpheum Theater. On fight night, a near-riot ensued when hundreds of shut-out fans massed on the sidewalks around the Olympic and demanded entry. They wound up missing one of the greatest fights in Los Angeles history, according to Bud Furillo.

From the opening bell, Rojas and Moreno tore into each other like Grant and Lee at Spotsylvania. In the first round, the pride of the docks opened a nine-stitch gash over the left eye of the beloved Little Bird of Mexico. Pajarito wailed back in the second with hooks to the body that hurt Raul so badly, "it looked as if he might retch," the Steamer reported. Moreno followed the body assault with head shots that had Rojas talking to himself when he retreated to his corner at the end of the round.

Moreno pressed the attack in the third, but Rojas refused to back up and "returned every blow" and then some, Furillo wrote, until he turned the fight in his favor. "He pounded Moreno's face into a bloody mask as the customers screamed," The Steam Room reported. "This was action like they hadn't seen for years."

At the end of three, Moreno led on points, but he couldn't see. Ringside physician Dr. Jack Useem told referee Joey Olmos that if it kept going, Pajarito would need major surgery to save his eye. Olmos stopped it, to the displeasure of Moreno, "the sweet-swinging Pajarito of Mexico," the Steamer said, who "sat on his stool, wiping away the blood from his left eye and growling at Rojas. Raul snarled back and waved his gloves, anxious for more after his three-round knockout."

Suddenly, the fighters' interest in Vicente Saldivar diminished. They wanted each other again. A capacity crowd of 15,700 filled the Sports Arena for the rematch, a night that turned into the greatest of Rojas's career. He got on top of Moreno in the first and knocked him cold in the second. It took the doctors ten minutes to revive Pajarito.

It was the last big fight for Moreno, who retired the next year. For Rojas, it was time for Saldivar again, but Vicente had since hooked up with Howard Winstone of the United Kingdom for three big-money fights. Vicente swept the series. Then he played a trick on everybody and retired.

While Saldivar was out of action, the World Boxing Association sanctioned a title fight to fill his vacancy. They set it for March 1968 at the Olympic in Los Angeles, between Rojas and Enrique Higgins, a Colombian with only eleven professional fights, and none of them north of the Caribbean.

Two days before the fight, Bud Furillo, working the political beat, reported that Rojas had received a key endorsement. Senator Robert F. Kennedy was campaigning on Olvera Street for the presidency of the United States.

"And I hope Raul Rojas wins the world featherweight championship next week!" he told his supporters, departing from his prepared remarks, according to the Steamer's story the next day.

"Rojas didn't even know that Bobby cared," the Steamer said.

Despite his inexperience, Higgins brought a nice jab up from Baranquilla, and he did a fine job sticking it in Rojas's right eye. He built up a lead in the middle rounds and held it into the twelfth, until a lightning left-right combination by Rojas knocked Higgins down.

"The smile went out of Higgins's eyes," the Steamer wrote. "Colombian coffee couldn't have gotten him going again after Rojas took charge in that round."

The caffeinated finish made Raul the first Los Angeles champion since Don Jordan, and he didn't even have to worry about Frankie Carbo or Blinky Palermo trying to steal his purse money.

Rojas celebrated the next morning with a walk on the docks.

"The longshoremen mobbed me," he told the Steamer. "They

kept shaking my hand until I thought it would fall off."

Furillo described Rojas as the Rocky Graziano of L.A., after the New York middleweight whom Paul Newman played in the movies. They were each maulers who did prison time and won their titles with one eye closed.

The two fighters had one other similarity: neither could successfully defend his title. Graziano lost the rubber match of his three-fight series to Tony Zale. The first time out for Rojas after the Higgins victory, Raul, in a non-title bout, lost in the Olympic to Shozo Saijo of Japan, a shocking upset.

Bud Furillo's explanatory reporting provided the backstory.

"You may recall," the Steamer pointed out, in a column before the rematch, "that Rojas tuned up for the non-title bout by sparring nightly with Jim Beam and Jack Daniels."

Jim and Jack had ruined many a fighter, and Raul was wise enough to distance himself from them the next time he fought Saijo, in September 1968, in front of 23,211 at the Coliseum, with his title at stake. Rojas probably could have used a shot afterwards.

Saijo, in the rematch, exhibited "a fluid boxing style that kept the bruising Rojas from working to his best advantage inside," the Steamer reported. The Japanese hero won the second fight more decisively than the first. Sho also showed that "they know a little about street fighting in Tokyo, too," Furillo wrote. "There wasn't a single occasion in the fight when [Rojas] was able to get the best of a toe-to-toe flurry with the rising fighter from the rising sun."

Just like that, it was all over for Raul Rojas. Booze maintained an upper hand in his life, and he never won another big fight. Sugar Ramos and Ruben Navarro beat him in the Olympic. For some reason, a promoter in Japan put up enough money to fly him to Tokyo, where he lost a super-featherweight title fight to Yoshiaki Numata.

Mando Ramos, a former stablemate and drinking buddy of Rojas, finished Raul's career with a September 1970 knockout.

In retirement, Rojas made the transition from fighter to full-time longshoreman. He overcame the booze, made it to age seventy, and died as the champion who saved himself from the streets and the L.A. fight game from extinction.

• • • • •

Every once in a while, big names from back East flew in for a Los Angeles payday. Fighters like Joe Frazier and Sonny Liston—and middleweight Rubin Carter.

"The Hurricane," as they called him, may or may not have been good for a robbery murder in Paterson, New Jersey. But because of it, he got more ink than any 27-12-1 middleweight in history who never won a championship.

Bud Furillo did his piece on the Hurricane in June 1964, the week before Carter fought Clarence James in the Sports Arena. This was years before Bob Dylan's terrific song rather presumptuously proclaimed that Carter "coulda been the champion of the world." Only 2,243 turned out to see the Hurricane blow away James in the first round.

"I don't want no trouble," Carter told the Steamer in their one-on-one interview. "Somebody on the street lays their hands on me, he's in trouble. I'll get a gun and shoot him."

This from a guy who had just gotten out of prison for armed robbery and assault, unrelated to the ruckus in Paterson that had caused him so much trouble.

With the interview going sideways, the Steamer straightened it out by informing the Hurricane that Carl Sandburg once said a man hasn't lived until he's been locked up for at least a little bit.

"Carter liked that," the Steamer wrote. "He laughed for the first time. The advantage was pressed with a ticket to a ball game."

The Hurricane scowled.

"It has your name on it," he said to the Steamer. "They'll say, 'You ain't Bud Furillo.' What am I going to say then?'"

Then the light bulb went on inside the Hurricane.

"I got it," he told the Steamer. "I'll say, 'Of course I am. What you got against Italians?'"

Furillo reported that "Rubin laughed again, and the eyes

were dancing to a tune of friendliness."

•   •   •   •   •

The best heavyweight to ever come out of Southern California
mystified the Steamer.

Jerry Quarry could knock you out with either hand. He
could move side to side, in and out. He was fast and tough. He
could take a punch—several, as a matter of fact. He fought everybody. In 1971, *Ring* magazine had him as high as number two in
the rankings.

So why did Quarry get booed whenever Olympic Auditorium ring announcer Jimmy Lennon invited him in to take a bow?
Why did a guy in Jerry's own bar once hit him over the head
with a pool cue? Why did Jimmy Cannon scream at the Steamer
the week of the Buster Mathis fight in New York, "The kid can't
fight, Bud!"

Quarry's 53-9-2 record with thirty-two knockouts, with
wins over ex-champion Floyd Patterson and top contenders like
Mathis, Ron Lyle, Mac Foster, and Earnie Shavers, proved Cannon wrong. Yet there was something infuriating about Quarry.
By his own admission, he spent too much time standing in the
middle of the ring "doing nothing" in big fight after big fight.
Then, when he should have laid back and counterpunched, he
bulled in on Joe Frazier and nearly had his head torn off.

"If Quarry listened more, he'd be better," Frazier told Furillo in an interview a few months after his June 1969 KO over
Quarry.

In the end, the glory and confusion of Quarry's career melted into the tragedy of his sport. His sixty-four professional and
237 amateur fights made him rich, but also produced pugilistic
dementia and early death. Bud Furillo never saw it coming, not
even on the night when Quarry endured enough punishment to
kill a horse.

In the seventh and final round of their first fight, Smokin' Joe
Frazier dropped sixteen bombs on Quarry's head, according to
my count from watching the video. He lacerated Quarry's right
cheek—eight stitches to the bone.

Yet the Steamer criticized Dr. Harry Kleiman, who was ringside, for recommending that the fight be stopped. He even called him "Dr. Milquetoast."

"Quarry came out of Orange County to die like a man, not be a party to a mercy killing," Furillo wrote.

Beatings like the one Frazier laid on him left Quarry unable to write his own name or walk around the block without getting lost. He died at fifty-three.

Once one of the most popular fighters of the Steam Room era, the L.A. fans turned on Quarry because he didn't flash the power often enough that got them so excited about him in the first place. Jerry tired of the disrespect and turned on his hometown.

"Nuts to the fans in L.A.," he told Furillo in 1968.

Yeah, the booing got to him.

"The fans would have gotten a helluva lot more out of me if they would have been in my corner instead of my opponent's," he told the Steamer.

Furillo saw the seedlings of future frustration in Jerry's first professional fight. Coming off his Golden Gloves triumph, Quarry debuted as a pro on the Coliseum undercard the night Rojas fought Saldivar. The opponent was a former middleweight named Gene Hamilton, who came in with fourteen straight losses and was knocked out in seven of them.

Quarry prevailed in a four-round decision.

"I held my breath waiting for Jerry to score a knockout . . . and turned blue," the Steamer wrote.

Over the next year, Quarry got better and became a Thursday night regular at the Olympic Auditorium. Promoter Aileen Eaton took him off TV in early 1966 and made the fans come out and pay money if they wanted to see him. An estimated 6,100 watched Quarry knock out former Muhammad Ali sparring partner Prentice Snipes, and the next thing Quarry knew, Rocky Marciano was expressing interest in buying a piece of his contract.

Jerry flew back to meet with Rocky in New York. While he was there, Quarry fought the tall, once-promising Tony Alongi in one of the last fights in the old Garden. Jerry knocked

Alongi down once, but only got a draw. They fought again in Los Angeles, to another draw, in which Quarry appeared to have regressed.

Marciano came out to L.A. for a final study on Quarry, against Eddie Machen at the Olympic Auditorium, before plunking down the $100,000 for half the kid's contract. Machen dominated the fight, and Rocky fled the building before the decision was announced in Eddie's favor.

When it was over, Quarry told reporters that he was thinking

QUARRY CAREER STALLED IN ANOTHER DRAW
MAY 28, 1966

It is inevitable in close fights, particularly draws, that everyone will assure you the underdog won.

I've learned to lean away from the underdog rooters. They didn't convince me that Tony Alongi deserved the decision over Jerry Quarry last night at the Sports Arena, where 5,444 folks forgot to leave town for the holiday weekend. . . .

But [Quarry] didn't impress anyone, particularly those of us who watched Joe Frazier belt out a couple of boys the last two weeks at the Olympic. . . .

. . . It appears that Frazier has roared by Jerry on the heavyweight express for contenders.

Quarry's career seems to be at a standstill, especially against six-foot-five-inch heavyweights. Jerry and Tony have gone twenty rounds now from coast to coast and neither boy has scored a decision. . . .

Alongi is a nice boy, but everyone knows he is going nowhere except back to Paterson, New Jersey, at the age of twenty-six.

Quarry, twenty-one, seemed bent on bigger things in boxing. But if anything, he looked worse struggling to a draw for the second time with Alongi than he did in their first fight. . . .

[He] needs a teacher who can develop a new style for him if he is to go any further than boxing draws with Alongi. . . .

"Jerry could be a great fighter," said [trainer Al] Silvani. "He can take your head off with that left hand. Tell that kid he has to learn to move his head and arms instead of standing up there like John L. Sullivan. He doesn't have to reach back to Chicago for that hook. He'll get just as much power by throwing it from the ribs. Jerry has the punch—he just needs the moves."

about enrolling at USC and studying mechanical engineering.

"It remains to be seen," Furillo wrote, "how much Marciano will pay for fifty percent of a mechanical engineer."

Quarry did come back to win six straight and pack the Olympic each time. Even though he won, the fans went home disappointed by his failure to put away a string of former contenders whose present states of disrepair made them easy notches.

The headlines over The Steam Room columns told the story of Quarry's career trajectory: "Jerry At A Standstill," "No Kayo So 10,400 Jeer Quarry," "Quarry Ponders Villain's Role."

Quarry opened a bar in Norwalk, a town over from Bellflower, and called it the Neutral Corner. With his career sent there, a patron walked in one night to shoot some pool. For some reason the fellow got into a beef with the owner and wound up smashing Quarry over the head with a pool cue.

The Steam Room reported: "'I don't understand people,' Quarry said, putting himself in a category with millions of other human beings. 'The customers expect too much from me. They figure I should knock everybody out because I'm a puncher.'"

It looked like Jerry found his way on the June 1967 evening he fought Floyd Patterson in the Coliseum, in front of 20,800 people. He knocked down the two-time champ twice in the second round. Then he failed to follow up and wound up lucky to get a draw.

Floyd and Jerry fought again in the tournament arranged by the World Boxing Association after it stripped Muhammad Ali of his title. Quarry won in a boring twelve-round decision. He made it into the tournament championship, but in the June 1968 finals in Oakland against Jimmy Ellis, he never fired. He lifted Jimmy off the floor with a right hand once in the thirteenth round, but failed to pursue, even though his man was hurt.

"Somehow, somewhere, he has misplaced his ability to move in and destroy his opponents," Furillo wrote after the Ellis loss.

In one of his better performances, Quarry came back to beat Buster Mathis the next year in New York. It qualified him for his June 1969 loss to Frazier in Madison Square Garden. Jerry battled back again in 1970 and wowed the Garden with a sixth-round knockout over the previously undefeated Mac Foster.

The win made him a viable foe for Ali's return to the ring. Quarry's two losses to the legend were all about Ali. Their second fight in 1972 could have been a killing, had Muhammad not stepped back in the seventh round to ask referee Mike Kaplan to please stop the fight.

Maybe Jerry was bummed, because it took several minutes to bring his younger brother, Mike, back to consciousness after his undercard knockout loss in a light-heavy title fight against Bob Foster. "Soul Brothers vs. the Quarry Brothers" is how they billed the doubleheader on the marquee.

Older brother Jerry sat motionless on his stool before coming out for the seventh and final round of the nightcap.

"He left his stool with less desire than a guy reporting for work on blue Monday," the Steamer said of Quarry. "Ali ripped him without return and motioned for the referee to step in and do his thing."

The Bellflower Bomber scored his victories over Lyle and Shavers and got one last substantial payday in his fifth-round knockout loss to Ken Norton in 1975. It was a year after the end of the Steam Room era, long after Bud Furillo and other pundits quit trying to solve the puzzle that was Jerry Quarry, and years before the fighter's brain became the subject of scientific study.

·   ·   ·   ·   ·

Emile Griffith fought three times in Los Angeles for the welterweight championship, and he was between his middleweight title-fight losses to Carlos Monzon when he came to Southern California in January 1972 and gave a boxing lesson to L.A. hopeful Armando Muniz.

"He's as accurate with his jab as Wilt is with his slam dunk," Jerry West told the Steamer ringside at the Anaheim Convention Center.

Otherwise, "Griffith punished Muniz inside, outside, and finally at the end of the ninth round rapped him on the fanny in a token of good show to the collegian from L.A. State," Furillo wrote. "It was the only place that Muniz hadn't been hit."

• • • • •

"Isn't it true you like to drink?" the impertinent Bud Furillo asked Ruben Olivares.

"Who doesn't?" the long-time bantamweight champion replied.

The interview took place in Mr. Rudy's, the Steamer's barbershop in Downey, conveniently located in the same little strip mall as the Lancer Lounge. The arrangement worked well for the Steamer and the salon proprietor, Mr. Rudy Flores. Steamer and Sons received free haircuts, and Mr. Rudy was poured free drinks and fight tickets, although his translation services were required on occasion, like the day the Steamer brought in Olivares for a trim a few days before the June 1973 Bobby Chacon fight.

With Olivares in the barber's chair and the Steamer firing questions, the champ tossed a counter-query back at the reporter.

"Do you drink?" Olivares asked.

The inquiry flummoxed Furillo.

"Socially, but I've virtually given up the real hard stuff," the Steamer lied. He'd no more given up Cutty Sark than Raul Rojas had abandoned Daniels and Beam before the first Sho Saijo fight.

It dawned on the Steamer that Olivares had trapped him in a corner.

He sought to punch his way out of it.

"Hold on, *señor*," Furillo said, turning the tables again on Olivares. "The Steamer is giving the test here. You're the one that's fighting. How long has it been since you've been on a toot?"

"More than two months," Olivares answered. "And I miss it. I miss the Bacardi and Cokes. You know Cuba libres?"

"*Si*," Furillo replied.

Going into the Chacon fight, Olivares had compiled a career record of 72-3-1, with sixty-six knockouts. No wonder they called him "Rockabye Ruben." Besides being great press, at least when confined to the barber's chair, Olivares, at the time of the interview with the Steamer, was the greatest single

box-office draw in Los Angeles boxing history. His fights attracted more cash than Sugar Ray Robinson, Muhammad Ali, Archie
Moore, Jerry Quarry—anybody.

His first two fights with Chucho Castillo, his destruction of
Lionel Rose to win the bantamweight championship, his loss to
Rafael Herrera in a non-title fight, and his victory over Jesus
Pimentel made for five of the ten biggest gates in California his-
tory at the time of his ninth-round knockout of Bobby Chacon.

Olivares fought twenty-four times in Los Angeles, mostly on
cards promoted by George Parnassus, the former Olympic Auditorium matchmaker under the banner of Cal and Aileen Eaton,
who made the family a lot of money bringing up fighters from
Mexico, from as far back as the mid-1950s.

The Steamer had loved the Mexican fight game in L.A. from
the time Parnassus first discovered Pajarito Moreno. He called

MONEY IS REASON PARNASSUS LIKES FOREIGNERS
MAY 22, 1969

The United Nations Boxing Club,
George Parnassus, president, holds
its monthly meeting tomorrow in
the Forum.

Among those gesturing for attention with their hands will be Ruben Olivares of Mexico City, Takao
Sakuraj of Tokyo, Arturo Lomeli
of Guadalajara, Frankie Narvaez
of San Juan, Puerto Rico, Antonio
Roldan of Acapulco, Shinichi (Fig)
Kadota of Osaka, and Genero Soto
of San Juan.

Incredibly, Jimmy Fields of
Los Angeles was asked to motor
in to Inglewood to take part in the
show. . . .

It doesn't really bother me,
but I can't understand why Parnassus scours the world for fighters to
show at the Forum. . . .

"I want to get money in the
house," he explained. "The foreign
fighters haven't let us down in our
first year at the Forum. They provided the action that keeps the people coming back." . . .

"Why do you have to go out
of the country to dig up fighters?"
Parnassus was asked. "There are
plenty you could dig up here."

"You've hit on it," said George.
"I tired of digging up fighters years
ago. I've tried to give boxing some
live ones."

the Mexican fans "the greatest in boxing." He celebrated with them when Jose Becerra knocked out Alphonse Halimi to win the bantamweight championship in the first event in the new Sports Arena in 1959. The Becerra-Halimi rematch two years later drew 31,836 to the Coliseum—still the largest crowd to see a boxing match in California, I believe.

Parnassus's success with Mexican fighters prompted him to ask Aileen Eaton for a bigger cut of their gates. When she turned him down, he split from her. Parnassus would then stage his international extravaganzas at the Forum in Inglewood, the new arena built by Canadian sports and media mogul Jack Kent Cooke.

On fight nights at the Forum, traffic stretched bumper-to-bumper along Manchester Boulevard, from the Harbor Freeway off-ramp all the way to the arena. Lines of over-heating, beaten-up Chevys with "Front, B.C." license plates led straight to the parking lot at Manchester and Prairie.

Parnassus's first big show at the Forum featured the ferocious Chucho Castillo. "Scary, mean-eyed, and hits like a shot of tequila," is how the Steamer described the bantamweight contender. In Castillo's first L.A. win, over Jesus Pimentel, Furillo said Chucho demonstrated a jab "that whistled into Pimentel's puss like a rubber ball bouncing into a paddle. Only the paddle got the worst of it. There were occasions where it rattled Pimentel seven or eight times before the perfect right cross. And then came the hooks."

Castillo's next Forum outing was for the bantamweight title against defending champ Lionel Rose of Australia. The aboriginal hero from the outback scored a split-decision victory that was met with quite a bit of disfavor by the majority of the estimated 18,000 aficionados. Many of them expressed their disappointment by setting fire to the lovely orange and gold drapery that decorated the arena's interior. Other Castillo backers flipped their switchblades to cut open the plush, theater-style seats, making it easier for the customers to ignite the stuffing with their cigarette lighters. Stars such as Kirk Douglas, June Allyson, Don Rickles, and Elia Kazan had to duck a bottle barrage

THE TRANSFORMATION OF MELVILLE HIMMELFARB
AUGUST 13, 1963

Harry Kabakoff took up failure as a career early in life. He became an overnight success at it the day he got a job as batboy for the St. Louis Browns. . . .

[Now] he's a fight manager. He adopted this vocation the minute word circulated that boxing was dead. . . .

Kabakoff grew up in the same Missouri neighborhood with Yogi Berra and Joe Garagiola. Only then his name was Melville Himmelfarb. It was too much for Yogi, who used to say, incredulously, "Melville?" . . .

Kabakoff says he used to do some fighting around Los Angeles. He walked into Babe McCoy's apartment in 1948 and tried to pry belief for this allegation from the late matchmaker.

"Do you remember me, Mr. McCoy?" asked Harry.

"Lay down, kid," ordered McCoy.

Kabakoff did a one-and-a-half kamikaze.

"Now I remember you," laughed McCoy.

In no time at all, Harry qualified himself with loyalty to front for McCoy's fighters. . . . He became prelim matchmaker for McCoy at the Olympic.

The rise in stature won him a kick in the ego from Jim Cox during former Governor [Goodwin] Knight's probe of boxing here. . . .

Kabakoff dropped out of sight after Cox changed the boxing picture in Los Angeles. He took up working for a living, for a while. . . .

He ran a bar in Santa Ana and toiled diligently to develop young boxing talent in the community.

Give the batboy his due. He's a first-rate trainer and proved himself a clever manager . . .

. . . Harry has done a tremendous job with his contender [Jesus Pimentel] for the world bantamweight title. Until signing for [Jose] Lopez, Pimentel never made more than $700. Harry wrangled him a $6,000 guarantee.

ringside. Rioters slashed tires, turned over automobiles and burned a couple, and smashed windshields.

"Police and ushers threw makeshift barricades of chairs and debris across aisles leading to Rose's dressing room as angry Castillo partisans attempted to storm the champion's sanctuary," the Steamer reported from the riot zone. "Rose, apparently oblivious to the action outside, calmly puffed on a pipe as he held court for a post-fight interview."

Rose went Down Under for one successful defense of his title before returning to America, where he knew he would give it up to the slugger from Mexico City who liked his Cuba libres.

Ruben Olivares came into the Rose fight with a record of 52-0-1, with fifty-one knockouts. Rockabye Ruben—number twelve on that *Ring* magazine list of the greatest punchers in boxing history, a notch behind Sugar Ray Robinson—took Rose apart in the fifth round. Olivares's KO win set the table for him and Castillo to fight for the heart of Mexico, in Los Angeles.

On the April 1970 day of the first of the three Olivares-Castillo wars, the Steamer tuned up with a poker game at home with a few of his pals. After four hours of drinking, they were off to the fights, where Furillo had assigned himself to cover the main event. Early in the fight, an exchange between the fighters sent Olivares to the mat for such a brief spell that he got up before referee George Latka started the count. The Steamer, on press row but semi-blind from the poker game, insisted that it was Castillo—not Olivares—who went down. *Herald Examiner* boxing writer Allan Malamud finally convinced Furillo that it was indeed Olivares who had suffered the knockdown.

Ruben recovered to win the easy decision, and Furillo sobered up enough to write his story.

"Olivares did it with rhythm, with lefts to the body, back to the head, back to the body and crossing with right hands," he wrote of the champ's artistic demonstration in the twelfth round. "It was symphonic for those who like rhythm, but not much fun for the catcher, who was Castillo."

Ruben suffered his first defeat ever in the rematch, when Chucho stopped him on cuts, but Olivares overcame a sixth-round knockdown to beat Castillo in the tie-breaker of their series.

"I couldn't believe it when Castillo bounced out of the ring after having been dribbled around it for ten minutes," said Furillo's main bar story after the third fight. "You couldn't get this muchacho's attention if you hit him with a sap. However, he left with plenty of marks indicating he had been involved in a disagreement."

At age twenty-seven, Castillo was more or less finished.

Only twenty-four, Olivares still had enough sock to rule the world's bantamweights through the end of the Steam Room era. Then came the string of losses to lesser fighters and a retirement that didn't last, only to be followed by more losses and no more offers for substantial paydays—the usual conclusion to a great fighter's career. Ruben, though, had saved enough to buy himself a soccer team, racehorses, a ranch in the country, and a fleet of expensive automobiles that he parked in his living room to make sure nobody could steal them—information available only in The Steam Room.

Furillo called Olivares "the best native-born fighter ever produced by Mexico," despite his "many long nights with cups." That statement held true until the arrival of Julio Cesar Chavez many years later.

I'm not sure if Julio sipped Cuba libres or anything else.

"Only one thing can get to you faster than drink," Olivares told the Steamer in Mr. Rudy's barbershop.

"What's that?" the columnist asked.

"Tougher guys," said Ruben.

•   •   •   •   •

Sugar Ray Robinson was too old, and Muhammad Ali was too young, but Jose "Mantequilla" Napoles was just right.

The Cuban native who moved to Mexico when Fidel Castro banned boxing in his island country gets the award of the Most Valuable Fighter in the Steam Room era. Napoles won all ten of his L.A. fights, including six where the world's welterweight championship was at stake.

In the middle of his reign, Napoles lost his title on the road in a TKO loss to Billy Backus in Syracuse, New York, near the challenger's hometown of Canastota. Backus, the nephew of the great former champ Carmen Basilio, consented to a rematch at the Forum in Inglewood.

One night, Billy's training table consisted of homemade

ravioli prepared at the home of the Steamer's mother in Downey. Basilio, who managed his nephew's career, had been a friend of Furillo's since the 1950s. On ravioli night, he showed the Steamer's kids how to throw a screwball.

Too bad Billy didn't throw some hard inside stuff to back Napoles off the plate when they got together again in the ring. Jose retrieved his championship in the June 4, 1971, slaughter that came to a halt when Basilio told referee Dick Young his fighter had had enough.

"The man Mexico calls Mantequilla because he's smooth as butter spread punishment evenly," the Steamer wrote. "Billy was chopped up like a Canastota onion, but on his feet after two knockdowns in the [eighth] round. He had all his strength and courage. All he lacked was a meat cleaver to even the score."

•　　•　　•　　•　　•

Only seventeen, Mando Ramos lied about his age so he could fight as a pro. Despite his presentation of a phony birth certificate, Ramos won seven straight on Olympic undercards. Then he moved up to main events and won five of those in a row before he had to register for the draft.

Bud Furillo broke the story that Mando had been kicking the crap out of grown men while still in his infancy.

"I had to fight or I would have been a delinquent," Mando told the Steamer in the columnist's exclusive report that hit the paper a couple months after the fighter's eighteenth birthday. "Actually, I was a delinquent. I started smoking when I was in the second grade. I was a chain-smoker by fourteen. I got into a lot of trouble before I started fighting for money."

Mando's terrific jab, solid right, and strong and precise footwork quickly established him as one of the best young lightweights in the world. His good looks made him a Thursday night TV favorite, especially with the chicks. Sportswriters dubbed him the golden boy of his generation. Mando fueled the characterization by wearing golden robes and trunks in his early fights, but he showed no appreciation for local ring lore when the Steamer asked the kid in the same January 1967 interview if he saw himself as second coming of Art Aragon,

"I'm a better fighter than Aragon," Ramos answered, accurately, with a slice of arrogance. "Why should I mimic him?"

A couple losses in his sophomore year, to Suh Kang Il and Frankie Crawford, should have chastened Mando. Maybe they did, but not enough to chill his appreciation for the nightlife. Mando liked to stay out late, and what better way to enjoy the afterhours than to share a taste with friends?

The post-midnight workouts affected Mando's day job. He developed an aversion to roadwork, a vital component of any fighter's conditioning program. Ramos's handlers found it wise to put the fighter under house arrest before big fights. McCoy and co-manager Lee Prlia would stash Mando in a hotel in San Pedro. It was unfamiliar territory for the young man from the other side of Terminal Island.

"To know Mando is to love him, particularly if you're a young girl addicted to good-looking, curly-haired fighters," the Steamer said. "It reached the point with Ramos that even the ones who didn't know him were falling for him. It helped his roadwork, picking his way through the field, sort of like the old tire drill in football. But running from the girls didn't help his approach to boxing any more than running after them will help you in any line of work."

Restricted to entertainment provided by *Ring* magazine and jazz radio, Ramos benefitted from the hermitage and set himself up for a September 1968 title fight with the new world lightweight champ, Carlos "Teo" Cruz, in the Coliseum the same night Shaijo beat Rojas the second time. Mando lost a close decision that merited a rematch with Cruz, and once again it meant solitary confinement for the challenger.

Ramos's adherence to the Spartan existence did not seem to be serving him well early in the second fight with Cruz. The native Dominican kept "popping him with sucker rights" through the first several rounds, the Steamer wrote, before Mando changed things in the eighth, blasting home a left-right combination that ripped open the champion's left eye. Ramos spent the rest of the evening successfully deepening and widening the incision.

"Cruz was blind in one eye and couldn't see much out of the other—except those jabs coming before the crossing rights," the Steamer reported from ringside. Teo "ceased to function . . . with blood pouring from the eye that seemed to have been punctured by a banderillo. The phlegm of nervous anxiety dripped from his nostrils. This bull knew the matador was winning. You'd be surprised how many of them don't."

Referee John Thomas stopped it in the eleventh round.

Mando was champ at age twenty. The celebrations lasted long into many evenings of drink.

He still won three easy fights over the next year, then went down to Panama to train for a defense against the lightning-quick Ismael Laguna.

Fight fans in the isthmus did not take to the handsome young champion the same way the girls did in the harbor region of Los Angeles. They harassed him when he did his road work, crank-called him in the middle or the night, and cheered for his sparring partner in his public workouts.

When Mando sustained a cut in training camp, manager Jackie McCoy found it a convenient reason to call off the fight. They then moved it from Panama City to Los Angeles, even though the relocation meant a pay cut for Mando. The Panamanian promoters had agreed to pay him $150,000. His wage in L.A. would only be $100,000. It was a $50,000 reduction well spent, in Ramos's estimation. No way would he ever again spend much time in Panama.

"The boxing fans in that country don't have any class," he told the Steamer.

Maybe not, but Laguna sure did, when Ismael and Mando finally met at the Sports Arena.

"When the bell went off, it tripped switchblades in the gloves of the challenger, a black beauty from Colon," the Steamer wrote the next day. "He spilled blood, sweat, and tears from the face and eyes of the young champion, whose cuts might have startled an army surgeon in the field."

Blood poured out of Mando's left eye as soon as the second round. McCoy clamped it down to a trickle as Ramos rallied to hurt Laguna with body shots in the middle of the fight. The champion had the Sports Arena crowd roaring "Mando! Mando!" when the fighters came out for the seventh.

"The yell swiftly went back to the Panama cheering section," Furillo reported, "as the Colon butcher went to work. He ground up some hamburger, and then sliced off some top sirloin."

Mando rallied again in the eighth, but when Laguna opened a cut over Ramos's right eye in the ninth, McCoy intervened, and that was it.

Five months later, Mando was back in the ring, and he won in a decision over Sugar Ramos—the same guy who killed Davey Moore—in one of the greatest fights in Olympic Auditorium history. Sugar opened cuts over both of Mando's eyes, each of which needed three stitches to close. Ringside physician Dr. Bernhart Schwartz, of Watts, made several house calls on Mando's corner, but allowed the fight to continue. Sugar's fans didn't appreciate the physician's judgment, or that of the judges themselves, who saw past the blood covering Mando's face to reward the courage pouring out of his heart and the power from his fists to correctly award him the fight. The outcome led to a Schlitz shower launched by Sugar supporters, who were also responsible for a two-alarm blaze in the back of the building.

Back at the Lancer Lounge, one-time *Herald Examiner* sportswriter Steve Harvey, later to write the popular column Only in L.A. for the *Los Angeles Times*, told The Steam Room, "Dr. Schwartz was called up to look at the fire. He said it would be okay to continue."

The lightweight championship had shipped to Central America with Laguna and then sailed to Scotland, when plaided challenger Ken Buchanan's toughness prevailed over the Colon butcher's speed in their title fight in San Juan, Puerto Rico.

Buchanan was supposed to defend in L.A. against Ramos, but Mando suffered what they called a "training injury" seventy-six hours before the fight. Ruben Navarro—East L.A.'s "Maravilla Kid"—stepped in on short notice and put in a respectable showing before losing to Buchanan. When Buchanan then chose to defend against Robert Duran instead of Pedro Carrasco, the

WBC stripped him of its version of the championship.

Fast-forward to Madrid and the night the columnist became a cornerman. Jackie McCoy, manager and trainer of champs such as Don Jordan, Raul Rojas, Ramos, Rodolfo Gonzales, and Carlos Palomino, ran the Steamer through a crash course in Cut Man 101. He showed Furillo how to wipe the brow, dab goop into a cut with a Q-tip, clamp it down with his thumb and forefinger, and hold on until the zebra ran him out of the ring.

The 1:00 AM post time for the fight in the Palacio did not seem to be a problem for Mando, "who has been up even later than that," the Steamer said of the fighter out of Long Beach who was known to close a few bars from Anaheim Street to Belmont Shore.

He came out sharp and knocked Carrasco down in the first round with a left hook. Mando put Pedro down again in the eighth with a shot to the liver, but the third man in the ring, Samuel Odubote, waved it off.

"The kindly referee picked [Carrasco] up, rested him, and said it was a low blow," the Steamer wrote.

Odubote couldn't do much to stop the Ramos barrage in the tenth round. A right hand accounted for one knockdown, and it looked like Carrasco was gone later in the inning after Mando planted the Spaniard on the canvas with a combination. Odubote counted to eight, then called time out to make sure that Ramos, who was already stationed in a neutral corner, stayed there. Instead of picking up the count once he was assured Ramos was safely at bay, Odubote took it from the top. By the time he ticked it up to eight again, Carrasco had recovered.

"He couldn't have gotten more rest or better care at a sanitarium," Furillo, reporting from Mando's corner, said of Pedro.

Earlier in the fight, Odubote had warned Mando against "throwing" Carrasco as if he were a tango partner. Odubote had consulted with officials from the Spanish Boxing Federation about this rules violation, and when he saw the egregious conduct repeated in the eleventh round, that was enough for the Nigerian referee. He stopped the action before the twelfth round and awarded the fight to Carrasco, which surely pleased the Franco regime.

Stiffed in the ring, the Ramos camp had another problem on its hands when it was over—the matter of the fighter's $50,000 purse. They had yet to see a penny of it.

The cash finally arrived at 3:00 AM, minus the Generalissimo's thirteen percent. McCoy stuffed the American denominations of hundred-dollar bills into a shaving kit. The Ramos contingent hustled out of the arena with the money, if not the WBC belt.

"McCoy carried," the Steamer wrote. "The rest of us blocked."

Perhaps for old-time's sake, McCoy once again invited Bud Furillo to work Mando's corner when Ramos and Carrasco met again in February 1972 at the Sports Arena. The columnist accepted, of course. It gave him a fine vantage point to watch another terrible decision play out when the scorecards favored Mando in a fight even Ramos thought he had lost.

"The guy beat me," Ramos said, coming back to his corner at the end of the fight.

The decision at the Sports Arena did not fool the L.A. fight mob. Fans who once roared on Mando's behalf booed him back to his dressing room. Mando's problem, according to The Steam Room, was that "he doesn't feel he has to train more than two weeks for a fight."

In the dressing room, Ruben Navarro helped splay Mando onto a rubbing table. Ramos told his friend the truth about the state of his career.

"I'm shot," the Steamer heard him say.

It was a rare moment of humility for Mando. If only he could have absorbed that reality for the long term, he may have avoided the beatings that were to come. Instead, hubris trumped humility.

Two days before Ramos's September 15, 1972, title defense against Chango Carmona in the Coliseum, *Herald Examiner* boxing writer Allan Malamud reported that Mando had stormed into Aileen Eaton's office, infuriated with the late starting time. According to Malamud, Ramos told the promoter he had to catch an 11:00 PM flight that night for his victory party in Las Vegas.

"I can't be late," he told Eaton.

"The nerve," Eaton told Malamud. Then she added another six-round preliminary to the card, to ensure that Mando's fight against Carmona would go on even later.

Carmona also believed Mando should have thought through his travel plans a little better. When Chango was through with him, they rode Mando out of the Coliseum in an ambulance, through the crowd of 20,311. Ramos, who had previously only been off his feet once, was knocked down four times by Carmona.

"Mando Ramos had wanted to beat a fast exit from his title defense to a victory party on the Las Vegas strip," Furillo reported. "But the emergency car was bound for a Boyle Heights hospital instead of the Tropicana."

In trying to escape Chango's onslaught, Mando "was cornered more times than Bonnie and Clyde," according to the Steamer. "His only chance was to punch back, and he did. Ramos hit [Carmona] with his best punches and got a few crooked smiles out of him, but that's all."

The fight was "one of the worst beatings I have ever seen," the Steamer said.

Eleven months later, Furillo was on hand the night of August 9, 1973, to ring out the era of the new golden boy—just as he had in January 1960, when the original, Art Aragon, fought his last fight in the Olympic.

Tury Pineda was a guy Mando "would have stiffened in a hurry two years ago," Furillo wrote. Instead, Mando finished the fight splattered in a corner.

"There was terror in his eyes," the Steamer said.

McCoy did his kid a favor and asked referee Dick Young to stop the slaughter. Young obliged. Mando was finished, his career ruined by his refusal to put in the work, and his weakness for the drink. The Steamer wrote that Ramos's mind "sent out the messages but the body ignored them because of what Mando had done to his body in the prime of his life." The fans cheered Ramos into the ring, but the enthusiasm couldn't counteract the years of hard boozing.

Against Pineda, "Mando pushed right hands in the manner

of a pizza man reaching into the oven without a pot holder,"
the Steamer wrote. "He spun Pineda's head around with the
once-classic jab a couple of times, but he couldn't land the right
that might have brought him back into the big money."

The former champ tried it some more the next year in Ger-
many, where he fought eight-rounders and beat a guy who came
in with an 0–10 record. In his last fight, he got knocked out in
the second round at the Silver Slipper in Las Vegas.

Like Mando told Ruben Navarro the night he beat Carrasco,
he "didn't have anything left."

The Steamer and everybody else in L.A. knew it, and Mando
was only twenty-four.

•   •   •   •   •

Rodolfo Gonzalez retrieved the WBC lightweight title for
Los Angeles with a November 10, 1972, destruction of Carmona.
The fight in the Sports Arena ended with Carmona on his chair,
refusing to come out for the thirteenth round, and "gulping his
own blood," The Steam Room reported. Carmona also had a
trickle of blood coming out of his left ear—"never a good sign,"
in the Steamer's medical opinion.

Gonzalez would be the last L.A. champ of the Steam Room
era.

Some really good ones were coming up, future champs like
Carlos Palomino and Bobby Chacon and Danny "Little Red"
Lopez. Danny would win nine straight featherweight championship fights before two losses to Salvador Sanchez induced his retirement. Chacon, however, stopped the previously undefeated
Danny in front of 16,027 at the Sports Arena the night of May 24,
1974—the last fight in Los Angeles sports history to be memorialized in a column by Bud Furillo.

"So Chacon is the city champ and now he'll move on to bigger things," the Steamer wrote. "He will go after the world of
126 pounders, which includes about two billion people. The other [two] billion are overweight, of course."

Chapter 11

LAKER BREAKTHROUGH

When the seven-foot center arrived at the Forum in his Bentley, he was able to open the door to let himself out. This was encouraging. In the dressing room, the Lakers gathered around for the great experiment. Wilt tried to grab a ball with his right hand, and he did it. What a shout. When he proved he could hold and pass the ball, coach Bill Sharman wrote his name down in the starting lineup. Then Wilt went into the game and proved he could rebound it, inbound it, shoot it, stuff it, and block it. He could have kicked it, too, but he doesn't like to show off.

—May 8, 1972

Wilt Doubtful Tonight," read the banner sports section headline in the *Herald Examiner* the morning of the biggest day in Los Angles Lakers history.

It was the Sunday of Game Five in the National Basketball Association championship finals, and the Los Angeles Lakers held a 3–1 lead over the New York Knicks. The Lakers and their fans were on the precipice of a championship that had very cruelly and inhumanely eluded them for a decade. A buzzer beater clanked off the rim in Boston in 1962. Balloons remained festooned in the rafters of the Fabulous Forum in 1969, when the Lakers' frantic fourth-quarter Game Seven rally against the Celtics fell short. And to the roar of a Madison Square Garden crowd in 1970, Willis Reed limped out of the locker room to sink a basket and beat them in the seventh second of the seventh game of their seventh straight NBA finals defeat.

This was supposed to be the Lakers' year, 1972. They had won thirty-three games in a row, a streak that still stood forty-four years later as the longest in big-league professional American sports history. They finished with a record of 69–13, the best in the history of the league as of then.

Only now, Wilt Chamberlain had two bad hands. The left, he had hyperextended in the first round of the playoffs against the Chicago Bulls. Bud Furillo reported that it had "swollen to the size of an ordinary man's calf." The right, Wilt had broken four months earlier. He had managed to keep the fracture quiet until he slammed it into the bottom of the backboard and doubled over in pain in New York on February 29—an occupational hazard for a seven-foot-two center. When Mitch Chortkoff of the *Herald Examiner* asked him about it afterward, Wilt confirmed the break. And he kept playing.

In Game Four of the finals against the Knicks, Chamberlain took a spill and broke his 275-pound fall by stretching out the same right hand that had been broken since mid-January. The team said Wilt suffered a sprained wrist. It was a lie. He had actually fractured the wrist.

The morning of Game Five turned into late afternoon and then early evening, and still nobody knew "the Dipper's" status. Observers got their first signal on Wilt's prospects for the evening when he cruised his Bentley into his parking space at the Fabulous Forum in Inglewood. Arriving in the flatlands from his Santa Monica Mountains hideaway, Will killed the engine and, with the assistance of no one, unlatched the door handle with his left hand to let himself out, according to Bud Furillo's reporting. Optimism grew when Wilt walked into the locker room and showed he could manipulate the ball with his hands.

Playing with them braced, padded, and wrapped in bandages, Wilt hit ten of his fourteen shots, grabbed twenty-nine rebounds, and blocked ten of the opposition's field goal attempts. The mummification of his extremities restricted his ability to pass the ball, so Wilt could only distribute eight assists—two short of what would have been a fairly astonishing quadruple double.

Wilt played for forty-seven minutes. He did not come out of the game until Sharman called time out in the final sixty seconds of the 114–100 win, and only then so that the Forum crowd of 17,505 could shower a city's joy on him and Jerry West, the star guard who had been traumatized for life by the decade of Lakers playoff failures.

The clock ticked away, and as the time passed, it muffled the clang of a Boston brick. It clouded the recollection of the balloons that never dropped, and quieted the memory of Madison Square Garden.

•　　•　　•　　•　　•

Over the next thirty-eight years, the Lakers would win a total of eleven NBA championships, nearly twice as many as any other team during that period. The Magic Johnson decade would be followed by Shaquille O'Neal and Kobe Bryant and Pau Gasol and Ron Artest. They would make the Lakers the most popular sports franchise in town.

What a contrast to the franchise's earliest months, when the Lakers moved to Los Angeles from Minneapolis and almost nobody cared. Soon enough, Elgin Baylor and Jerry West made the city's sports fans cognizant of the greatness on display—Elgin with the head bob and the explosion to the rim, and Jerry with the clutch stop-jumper going to his right. If only they could have done a little better at the end once or twice against the Celtics, the emotional damage to the city's sports psyche wouldn't linger as deep.

Bud Furillo climbed aboard with the Lakers from the beginning, after he overcame his early irritation with the owner who had brought the team to town and presumptuously expected to be treated in the fashion of Walter O'Malley and the Dodgers. Los Angeles officials worked it out for the baseball club to bulldoze a ravine above downtown for a new ballpark. Only Bob Short's men from the Minnesota winters did not capture the imagination of the country in the same fashion as O'Malley's boys of the Brooklyn summers.

The Lakers team that dominated professional basketball in the late '40s and early '50s had skidded into irrelevance with the retirement of George Mikan. The bespectacled big man could hook the ball into the hole from either side of the plate, righty or lefty, and defend the rim with such authority that basketball rule makers rewrote the game's regulations to prevent six-foot-ten fellows such as himself from standing underneath the hoop and jumping up at the last second to flick the ball away when the other guys' shots approached the iron. George Mikan was the father of goaltending.

Once Mikan quit, the fans stopped coming to the WPA-constructed National Guard Armory, where the Lakers played their home games in Minneapolis. Fans in the upper Midwest went back to ice fishing in the winter months.

Bob Short was a trucking magnate who later acquired the Washington Senators before he moved back to Minnesota in a losing effort to become a member of what used to be the world's greatest deliberative body. By 1960, he had given up on Minneapolis as a basketball town. Or maybe it was Minneapolis that had grown tired of him, or the Lakers. Either way, Bud Furillo wrote in The Steam Room, Short's team "seldom lures more than a few high-jumping muskies from the Minnetonka lakes chain" to its home games in the armory that has since been converted into a parking lot.

During the 1959–1960 season, Short decided it was time to long-haul the Lakers out of town. He showcased the team in Seattle and San Francisco, and then shipped it on overnight delivery to Los Angeles for a game against superstar center Wilt Chamberlain and the Philadelphia Warriors. More than 10,000 fans turned out to the newly built Los Angeles Sports Arena to see the novelty of professional basketball. It was a good number, the 10,000, but Short wasn't so sure the support was for real, so he scheduled two more Laker games for later in the month against Bob Pettit and the St. Louis Hawks. Ahead of the later matches, he notified Los Angeles fans through The Steam Room that they needed to step up their game to improve the city's chances of a permanent Lakers relocation.

"A large turnout on successive nights would put Los Angeles number one on the list of a new home for the Lakers if and when we decide to move," Short said in a prepared statement.

Bud Furillo did not much care for the implied threat

contained in Short's communiqué. The words from the boss trucker "smack of a hustle," the Steamer wrote, from a sport that for all its popularity in this modern day, wasn't worth the bait needed to catch a Minnetonka muskie during the Steam Room era's early period.

The Harlem Globetrotters were more popular. When their tour used to hit L.A., they sometimes had to play the game at the Rose Bowl.

"It would be nice to have an NBA team here, even if it has to be the Lakers," the Steamer sniped. "But let's stop the show-up-or-else routine."

The National Basketball Association then fielded only eight teams, and three of them were in Syracuse, Rochester, and Fort Wayne, Indiana. Not exactly Madison Avenue material. Meanwhile, Furillo reported, representatives of the Philadelphia and Syracuse franchises had been sniffing around L.A., too, along with Minneapolis.

"If business is so good in pro basketball," he asked, "why do three of the eight teams want to move here?"

L.A. wasn't about to give Short a ravine, but the city did have a brand new, 16,000-seat arena it had just helped build next to the Coliseum. Who couldn't use a new tenant? Short signed a lease, and the Lakers moved to L.A.

The town barely noticed. The Lakers drew only 4,008 for their first home game against the Knicks, and they finished their first season in L.A. with another losing record and crowd counts just as bad as they had been in Minneapolis. Only now, it was a much longer leap for those fish from Lake Minnetonka.

It wasn't much easier for the seven other teams in the league to get to L.A., either—or for the Lakers to get to them. They were all stationed north and east of St. Louis. It made travel an issue. The Lakers once played six games in eight days, in New York, Syracuse, Philadelphia, St. Louis, Detroit, and then another in Philadelphia. Then they flew home for their seventh game in nine days, arriving in L.A. at noon for a meeting that night against the Boston Celtics. The defending world champs had been in town a day already, and were well-rested for their game that night against the tired Lakers.

"This was the third time we've been asked to play a game at home after flying across the country all day or all night," Lakers coach Fred Schaus told the Steamer. "We've lost them all."

Then there was the occasion when a delayed flight made Wilt and the Philly Warriors almost two hours late for a game scheduled for 8:30 PM at the Sports Arena. With his team's plane sitting on the tarmac in Philly, Warriors owner Eddie Gottlieb called Lakers GM Lou Mohs.

"You better think of something to keep the customers in the joint until we get there," Gottlieb told Mohs, according to The Steam Room.

When the crowd arrived for the tip-off, it was entertained by Salesian High School playing a pick-up collection of prepsters from Roosevelt and Lincoln.

"It was surprising how many of the folks quickly sensed this wasn't the main event," the Steamer reported.

The Warriors dressed in the bus on the way to the game and beat the Lakers, 113–106. Wilt, after the unconventional quick change, scored forty-one.

In their first year in Los Angeles, the Lakers nearly achieved the impossible—by missing out on the NBA playoffs. This was at a time when the regular season eliminated only two of the eight teams in the league. Having lost thirty-one of their first fifty, the Lakers improved down the stretch to take seventeen of their final twenty-nine to make the post season. Then they beat Detroit in the first round and had a chance to knock out the Hawks in Game Six of the Western Conference finals and play for the NBA title.

Bud Furillo snuck off the Angels reservation to drive up from Palm Springs and watch the Lakers lose a heartbreaker in overtime to the Hawks.

"The long ride back gave me a lot of time to digest what happened," the Steamer wrote. The main takeaway was this: the record crowd of 14,841 left the Sports Arena with the kind of sports pain that only comes from being a fan. Losing a toughie is almost a precondition for a city to bond with a team, which explains Chicago's unexplainable love for the Cubs. Now the Lakers fans had gotten their taste of hurt, and there would be a lot more of it in the decade to come.

• • • • •

The Lakers brought one principal asset with them from the Midwest, in the form of the brilliant Elgin Baylor. A six-foot-five forward who had grown up in Washington, DC, and gone to college in Seattle, Baylor revolutionized the game, injecting it with the kind of soaring athleticism that came to mark the National Basketball Association's worldwide brand.

Before Dr. J and Michael and Dominque Wilkins, before Clyde Drexler and Jumpin' Joe Caldwell and Connie Hawkins—before any of them—there was Elgin Baylor. When John Wooden drew up his all-time basketball starting five nearly fifty years later, he included Baylor, along with Bill Russell, Oscar Robertson, Larry Bird, and Michael Jordan.

His first year in Los Angeles, Baylor averaged thirty-five points and twenty rebounds per game. Early in the season, he scored seventy-one on the Knicks to set what was then a new single-game NBA record. Bud Furillo proclaimed Elgin as "the greatest L.A. ever had in any team sport," and the Steamer never backed away from that statement in the fifteen years he wrote his column. Not for Sandy Koufax, Deacon Jones, or Nolan Ryan. Not for O. J. Simpson, Lew Alcindor, or even Eddie "The Jet" Joyal of the early Kings.

All over town, the Steamer saw signs that the Lakers, riding on Baylor's coattails, were catching on.

"The other day I passed a school playground where a group of youngsters were playing basketball," he wrote. "One of them jerked his head down on his right shoulder, darted to his left and scored with a layup."

The kid was imitating the head bob that everybody knew belonged to Elgin Baylor. Elgin couldn't help himself with the twitch—it was a nervous reaction that had been part of his game going back to his college days at Seattle University. Coming up the court on the dribble, he had no control over the jerky head motion. Pretty soon kids in pickup games were mimicking El-gin's nervous twitch.

Elgin told the Steamer that the whole thing was an accident.

"It used to drive me nuts," Baylor said to Furillo. "I went to doctors and finally a neurologist, who explained it was nervous reaction caused by tension. Nothing to worry about. It must be the tension of the ball game because I never twitch like that off the court."

Baylor got himself a superstar partner his first year in his new town.

Jerry West was a skinny rookie out of West Virginia. West went up and down in his first regular season before establishing his stardom in the playoffs, when he averaged twenty-four points a game. He got so good over the years that the NBA turned a likeness of his slashing figure on a left-handed dribble drive into the league's logo.

Early in his second season, West scored sixty-three points in one game. "Prince Jerry," the Steamer called him; over the

---

WEST IN HOSPITAL, LAKERS HURTING
FEBRUARY 28, 1963

PALM SPRINGS—Astride his trusty Impala, the Steamer stole out of Sheik Bel-Ali Rigney's desert camp yesterday to visit some sick friends in Los Angeles. . . .

The first stop was at Daniel Freeman Hospital to call on Lakers star Jerry West in Room 567. . . .

Two weeks ago, West rein-jured his left leg trying to pick up his son, David, age twenty-seven months, weight forty pounds. . . .

Since West was originally lost to the Lakers, the club barely kept at .500, with a 7–7 record. In thirteen games prior to Jerry's inju-ry, the Lakers were on a 12–1 high ride. . . .

The visit paid West came short-ly before the start of last night's Laker game in Syracuse. . . .

Jerry began to perspire. He said:

"This is the hardest part—waiting to hear how they make out. Gets me awful nervous. I miss be-ing around the fellas."

They miss you, too, Jerry. Look at the results.

next decade he would earn the nickname "Mr. Clutch" for his many game-winning, last-second shots. West could fly right past you and beat the big guys at the rim, or slam on the brakes to nail the high-dribble jumper going to his right. He could direct an offense. Nobody his size rebounded or defended any better. Furillo called Baylor and West "the most exciting one-two punch in basketball."

Four games into the 1961–1962 season, Furillo wrote that the Lakers "have a good opportunity to win it all in the West, even though they don't appear ready to dethrone Boston as the world champion."

The Steamer got it right on both ends. The Lakers improved their record by twenty-one games and won the Western Conference. They moved up in the attendance rankings, too, to second best in the NBA. Then they nearly shocked the Celtics in the playoffs. They took a 3–2 lead in the series when Baylor set an NBA single-game playoff scoring record in Game Five in Boston with sixty-one points. The mark stood for twenty-four years, until Michael Jordan broke it with sixty-three in a first-round, double-overtime loss in 1986 against the Celtics.

With a chance to win the championship at home in Game Six, the Lakers jumped out to an eight-point halftime lead. The capacity Sports Arena crowd stood and cheered when the Lakers ran off the floor at intermission. Too bad they had to play the second half, when the Celtics came back for the victory with six players in double figures, to outscore Baylor and West, who had thirty-four each.

Again sneaking away from Angels spring training, the Steamer sped to the Sports Arena to report that the Celtics "were majestic in a game they had to win." He described Bill Russell as looking like a "a high priest during the time of the Pharaohs." Russell played the game with bandaged fingers while Satch Sanders, Tommy Heinsohn, and Sam Jones wore knee braces.

Furillo gave the Lakers no chance in Boston.

"It boils down to the well-known fact the Lakers don't have enough talent to go with their super stars," he wrote in his column after Game Six.

At the end of regulation in Game Seven, Lakers forward Frank Selvy had a chance to prove the Steamer wrong. The Lakers had the ball for the last shot in a tied game, and Fred Schaus drew up a play that called for "Hot Rod" Hundley to find West. When Jerry couldn't get open, Hundley spun around and passed to Selvy, who was open from about eighteen feet to the left of the basket, toward the baseline. Selvy had plenty of room and got the ball off before Bob Cousy lunged at him in desperation. Selvy told the *Herald Examiner*'s Jack Disney that he thought Cousy had fouled him, but it sure doesn't look that way in the video. The ball bounced off the rim and the Celtics won it in overtime, 110–107. L.A. fans watched on television as their colleagues in Boston flooded the floor and Russell and Celtics coach Red Auerbach swam through the sea of humanity toward each other for a victory hug.

Hooked on the agony of the defeat, Lakers fans swarmed the Sports Arena over the next four years to marvel at the beauty and grace of Baylor and West. They became the best home draw in the league, while they lost in the championship finals one year after the next.

•   •   •   •   •

A devastating knee injury took Baylor out in the first game of the 1965 playoffs. A lot of people thought he was done the next year, especially when he finished the regular season averaging only 16.6 points a game.

He proved everybody wrong in the '66 playoffs, which he turned into a showcase for the wonders of reconstructive knee surgery. In one of the great comebacks by any athlete in any sport, Baylor scored forty-two points in Game Two of the Western Conference finals to beat the Hawks, on his way to a 26.8 average for the post-season.

"Baylor had his old racehorse speed, the stops, the starts, drives, hang shots, and double reverse moves to go with the game's best head fake," the Steamer wrote.

Talk about hops. Elgin, the first great superstar to bring the air game into the NBA, even banged his elbow against the backboard going up for a rebound.

"It didn't amount to anything," Baylor told the Steamer.

Nothing at all, unless you were there to gasp in amazement at the sight of a man who could jump so high, his elbows crashed into objects ten feet off the ground.

•   •   •   •   •

Jack Kent Cooke sold encyclopedias as a Canadian kid and acquired radio stations and newspapers before he turned thirty, owned a minor-league baseball team in Toronto, and then got into the L.A. media market in 1959 when he bought the Top 40 radio behemoth KRLA. In 1965, he paid Bob Short an astounding $5.2 million for the Lakers, which started him off on thirty-two years of professional intimacy with Bud Furillo.

Long after the Steam Room era ended, when Furillo was doing radio in Palm Springs, he conducted what may have been the last interview anybody ever had with the sports and media entrepreneur, who had also owned the Washington Redskins and was a major principal in TelePrompTer.

"Bud, I feel great," Cooke told the Steamer on the air.

Two days later, Cooke died of a heart attack.

The two may have been fond of each other, but boy, did the Steamer like to give a nice poke every once in awhile to Cooke, who needed it. Impossible as it was, Furillo tried to inject some humility into the affably arrogant Cooke—like the time Jack had the Steamer over for dinner at the Sports Arena. Cooke had only owned the Lakers for five months. He'd only recently acquired the L.A. franchise rights for the National Hockey League. And now he was talking to the Steamer about building a new arena to replace the one in town that was just seven years old.

"The effervescent Cooke tugged at my arm as he talked about the arena he plans to build as we walked to our seats in the Sports Arena," the Steamer reported. "'Won't it be wonderful when we have our own stadium?' he said."

Furillo thought about it a second.

"Looking around the Sports Arena," he wrote, "it occurred to me that we already had our own stadium."

The Steamer pulled out the needle again when the Lakers acquired Mel Counts, a skinny seven-footer from Boston with an effectively awkward shot.

Cooke told Furillo, "We strongly believe when we traded for Mel Counts that we acquired a young man who is going to be one of the outstanding centers in this league for many years."

"Jack said this in all sincerity," the Steamer deadpanned.

As Cooke's new sports palace in Inglewood took shape, he told Furillo, "I drive by it every morning and every night when I can. If you haven't seen it lately, you're derelict in your job. It is one of the most satisfying achievements in my life."

So the Steamer asked his readers, "How many of you have been remiss in your duty to go by the Forum this week to see how it is coming along?"

One time, when they were talking hockey on the phone, Cooke told Furillo he had improved the Kings because "we have extirpated ourselves of the bad apples."

"'Hold it,' I whistled," Furillo wrote. "'Where did you get that word?'

"'It's a regular word,' said Cooke.

"I put Jack on hold and asked [*Herald Examiner* handicapper and racing writer] Gordon Jones, our resident professor who used to teach at USC, if he had ever run into extirpate.

"'A long time ago and I can't remember the circumstance,' said Jones. 'Don't worry. I won't confuse you by using it.'

"'You better not,' I said, and plugged Cooke in again."

Despite the regular barbs directed at him in The Steam Room, Cooke invited Furillo up to Canada in the fall of 1967 to watch the first exhibition games to be played by the owner's new hockey team, the Kings.

"There's only one thing worse than sitting next to Jack Kent Cooke at a basketball game," the Steamer wrote. "It's sitting next to him at a hockey game."

When L.A. defenseman Dale Rolfe nailed a guy with a body check, the excited team owner, sitting at the glass with Furillo at the Guelph Memorial Gardens west of Toronto, mimicked the hit with a slam into the Steamer's ribs.

"I moved into the third row," Furillo wrote.

The next night, Cooke said he would like to see even more physicality on the part of his new club.

"Hockey is a game of beauty and brutality," he told the Steamer. "So far, we're only beautiful."

•　　•　　•　　•　　•

Cooke's Kings glammed it up in the '70s and '80s with Marcel Dionne and then Wayne Gretzky on the ice. They would gain enormous popularity a few decades later, when they captured a couple Stanley Cups.

But they were a mostly miserable bunch during the Steam Room era, missing the playoffs in four of its seven hockey seasons and winning in the preliminary round only once.

The Steamer had some fun with them in their 1974 Stanley

PEACENIK PLAY GETTING KINGS NOWHERE
FEBRUARY 28, 1969

It's great to be a fan. I like everything.

The knocks against baseball are actually a put on. I see more baseball games than anything else. Of course that can't be helped. Baseball season never ends.

Lately it is hockey that piqued my curiosity. You can't help but be curious of the Kings. . . .

Of all his enterprises, the Kings are [Jack Kent] Cooke's baby. But the kid gives him more trouble than a runaway. . . .

The other night against Boston, the Kings played the second period like they wanted to win. They played the third like Sonny Liston, sitting on his stool. . . .

There is more action in the pillow fights along USC's sorority row than there is in some of the Kings' games. They avoid the boards as if they were strung with barbed wire.

The team that belts the other team into the boards usually wins the game. Ron Sears, a friend of mine, observed:

"The Kings should paint a peace symbol on the puck. They should write on it MAKE LOVE, NOT HOCKEY."

If the Russians saw the Kings play, they'd be in Pasadena by Sunday.

Cup run, before the Chicago Black Hawks knocked them out in the first round in five games. On the road with the Kings, Furillo was first in the Chicago Stadium locker room after the Black Hawks' win to inform Stan Mikita he had just scored his fiftieth career playoff goal.

"I didn't know that," responded the four-time NHL scoring champion.

Furillo followed with an inquiry: "What was all that shoving between you and [Kings defenseman] Terry Harper?"

"Terry doesn't realize what the whistle is for," Mikita said, referring to Harper's propensity to jostle opponents when the play had stopped. "Mr. Harper may need a hearing aid."

"Did you tell him what the whistle is for?"

"It wouldn't do any good," Mikita said. "He wouldn't hear what I tell him."

In their early days, the Kings attracted a loyal and rambunctious following—just not a very large one. Cooke had the funny line about how L.A. had a huge population of Canadian expatriates, but that they had all fled south because they hated hockey. If the smallish gates bothered him, they contributed to a small fringe benefit for the players, as Steam Room attendees learned in a 1971 interview with Kings captain Bob Pulford.

"In Toronto, a hockey player can't go to dinner or to the theater without being recognized," the former Maple Leaf told Furillo. "My wife and I have enjoyed a lot of quiet dinners in Los Angeles."

Pulford peered into the future. He foresaw the day when successors such as Anze Kopitar and Drew Doughty best rely on room service.

"Someday it will happen," Pulford said to the Steamer. "The Kings will make it."

•   •   •   •   •

Cooke's basketball team made the finals in his first year of ownership, but lost in seven again to the Celtics in 1966. L.A.'s ostentatious first-year front office man made a serious rookie mistake in the finals. After the Lakers won Game Six at home to tie the series at three apiece, Cooke popped the cork on the champagne.

"Normally in a world championship, the bubbly is reserved until the best of seven series is over," Bud Furillo wrote.

Back home in Boston, the Celtics beat the Lakers for the championship, 95–93. Boston beat L.A. again in the '68 finals. When it was over, a forlorn Cooke asked the Steamer, "What's it going to take to win?"

Furillo had the right answer.

"Go get Wilt," he said.

CELTICS BETTER THAN LAKERS IN ANY SHIRT
APRIL 23, 1966

In one of the more believable upsets of the season, the Celtics overcame the favored Lakers at the Sports Arena last night to take basketball's world series back to Boston.

Of course it was going back to Boston anyhow. But with a 3–1 edge, the Celtics have the playoffs locked up in a bank vault enclosed in one of those cement silos used to bury Minuteman missiles. . . .

. . . Millions of non-bettors must be wondering today how the Lakers could be advertised as one-point favorites in the marketplace last night. . . .

Perhaps this was because the visitors took the court dressed like anything but a class outfit. All of them didn't wear the same kind of shirts.

Bill Russell, John Havlicek, and K. C. Jones had "Celtics" on the front of their shirts. Satch Sanders and Sam Jones advertised "Boston."

This was brought to the attention of Russell, in the hope that when he takes over the coaching duties for Red Auerbach next year he'll do a better job of dressing the boys.

Heroism in defeat is something the athlete shuns. But it would not be right to pass over the performance of Jerry West.

West tried to take on the perennial champs all by himself, and did, on numerous occasions. His shooting—forty-five points—and overall play was worth a twenty dollar bill to the true patron.

He will next be seen on television tomorrow morning from Boston. . . .

Don't miss him. It should be the last time Jerry will play basketball until September.

•   •   •   •   •

On April 9, 1968, the Lakers traded starting guard Archie Clark, center Darrell Imhoff, and reserve forward Jerry Chambers to the Philadelphia 76ers for arguably the greatest basketball player and one of the top five or ten best athletes of all time.

Wilt Chamberlain stood seven feet, two inches tall and weighed 275 pounds. Just as Mikan forced rule changes on the defensive end, Chamberlain did the same on the offensive side of the floor. There was no offensive goaltending rule until Wilt came along, and they had to expand the NBA key from twelve to sixteen feet in 1964 to cut down on Chamberlain's forceful inside presence.

The Steamer hit it off pretty well with "The Dipper" right from the start. Furillo called Chamberlain "the most accessible superstar in the world today."

"You dial his number and he answers the telephone," the Steamer wrote. "You ask for Wilt. 'Who's calling?' he will ask in a disguised voice. You identify yourself and he responds with, 'What's happening?'"

Wilt was probably the most criticized superstar, too. When he lit up the scoreboard, the wise guys said he should play more defense. When he focused on "D" and rebounding, they said he should shoot more. He was a loser because his teams only won two NBA titles. He was too Wilt-centric. He wasn't Bill Russell.

"It's a fact the public will build up a resentment to a star without really knowing why," the Steamer wrote after a visit with Chamberlain during the 1970 playoffs. "Rooting against Chamberlain was fashionable, and I did it, too. I'm sorry for that, now that I know him. He's a good fellow."

I don't think Wilt ever came out to Downey to troll for chicks at the Lancer Lounge, although it likely would have added to his astonishing estimate of 20,000 women laid. But he did have Furillo up to his pad a few times. Once, when Chamberlain was living in Trousdale Estates, the Steamer dropped in to report on Wilt's cooking talents. It was part of a *Herald Examiner* series on sports celebrities' personal recipes.

Barefoot and wearing a white chef's hat and coat, Wilt

invited Furillo into the kitchen. The Steamer likened the space to the NBA's enlarged three-second area, because the Dipper "is usually in it."

"This is Shrimp Barbara," Wilt offered, for the dish he had named after one of his six sisters.

"But we had a shrimp recipe last week from Jim Fregosi," the Steamer protested. "You just thought you had a shrimp recipe," Chamberlain assured Furillo. "Wait until you try this one."

Wilt's dish required loads of shrimp, lobster, minced meat, and diced ham, along with fresh tomatoes, green peppers and onion, dumped in a slightly-buttered saucepan and seasoned with a half-dozen spices simmered into chicken broth and tomato sauce. The Steamer instructed his readers to bake at 350 degree for half an hour and serve with optional rice topping.

"Now stuff yourself, like Wilt does a basket," he wrote.

In covering sports, Bud Furillo's seasonal rhythms usually

BASKETBALL FOR SCREAMERS
FEBRUARY 25, 1969

I am trying to work up the nerve to go see the Lakers play tonight but I can't. Everyone at the game reminds me too much of me.

They are all screamers.

The fans scream at the officials. The officials scream at the players and the coaches. The coaches and players scream at each other and the officials. Jack Kent Cooke groans. It's terrible.

One time when Dean Martin used to make all the games I asked him why.

"It's a great way to relax," he said. . . . "It's a great way to relieve yourself of your frustrations."

What frustrations? At the time of this explanation by Martin, he was having to play a kiss freak with Kim Novak in a picture called *Kiss Me, Stupid*. . . .

Basketball fans have to be a little dippy the way they go off their rocker when a foul is called. The officials of the National Basketball Association don't help matters with their circus calls. . . .

Frankly, by eight o'clock at night, I am all screamed out. However, I must admit that I am trying to pull myself together for the NBA playoffs, which is actually when the basketball season starts.

Oh, am I going to give it to that Mendy Rudolph.

didn't take him to Laker games until late January.

"Football season must be over," Chamberlain would growl when the Steamer made his first appearances at the Forum.

Sometimes, when the sports editor assigned himself to writing the main bars on the Lakers playoff games, he occasionally found an empty seat on the airplane next to Wilt. During the Chicago series in '73, Wilt confided to the Steamer on the flight east that he'd just about had it with basketball, but couldn't walk away from his $600,000 salary.

"I'd like to see the ski resorts of St. Moritz in the winter just once instead of in the summer," Chamberlain told Furillo. "But I can't take a year off, not at these wages."

The Steamer's first-hand reporting informed his readers just how hard it was at times to be the Big Dipper.

"Every airport in every city had guys like the one," he wrote, "who came up to him at the baggage circle at O'Hare and asked, 'Are you Wilt Chamberlain?'

"'Wish I was,' Wilt responded.

"'Cripes, you're tall,' the intruder observed. 'How tall are you?'

"'One question to a customer,' Wilt answered. 'You've had yours.'"

Wilt's size and celebrity confined him on occasion to meals in his room instead of the fine restaurants he would have preferred, like the time he stayed in at the Essex House on Central Park South, when the Lakers were in New York for the '72 finals.

"It's customary for the big fella to order dinner for four—for himself," the Steamer reported. "He is likely to place an order for tournedos of beef shashlik gaussienne, broiled fresh flounder, maître d'hotel, and fried chicken Maryland. Perhaps for a starter, the Icelandic matjes herring plate, escargots à la bourguignon, and Nova Scotia salmon."

The Dipper could never understand, though, why they hammered him on the room service fee.

"The service charge is one dollar per person," Wilt complained to the Steamer. "They charge me four dollars. I explain that I am the only one eating. Therefore, the charge should be one dollar. 'But you ordered dinner for four, sir!' they whine. I tell them to look in the closets to see where the other three people are. I never win. I have to pay the four dollar service charge.'"

•   •   •   •   •

The early returns on Jack Kent Cooke's investment in Wilt Chamberlain looked spectacular. The night of November 19, 1968, they beat the defending champion Celtics, 116–106, for their ninth win in a row. Wilt scored sixteen points and pulled down twenty-two rebounds, compared to six and twenty-one for Bill Russell—a statistical breakdown that excited Laker management.

"Wilt is doing exactly what I knew he would do for us," Cooke told Bud Furillo after the game.

The Steamer called the evening's result "encouraging, except that Russell didn't seem bothered by it." The Celtics center, in fact, drew some yuks from the Steamer and the rest of the press corps, as well as locker room visitor Bill Cosby, with some of his post-game remarks.

Asked how he felt at age thirty-four, the Boston player-coach replied, "I feel like I'm making more money than I ever did before."

"Everybody's laughing in November, but what's it going to be like in April?" the next day's Steam Room said. "The jolly green giant is too jolly for comfort."

The Lakers went on to win the Western Division with a record of 55–27, their best so far in L.A., but their regular-season success cloaked a serious problem. Wilt and first-year coach Bill "Butch" van Breda Kolff had a clash of personalities that made the Rams' Dan Reeves and George Allen look like Ozzie and Harriett. Van Breda Kolff, the Princeton coach when Bill Bradley took the Tigers into the NCAA Final Four in 1964–1965, preferred a wide-open, fast-breaking attack. So he was obviously the wrong guy to coach a team that just acquired a major power in the low post.

Herald Examiner beat reporter Doug Krikorian said the strain began to show the day of the Lakers' season-opening loss in Philadelphia.

"He's terrible, just terrible," VBK spouted about Wilt afterwards, according to Krikorian. "He didn't hustle. He clogged up the middle. I wish we never would have gotten that guy."

Wilt responded that in his opinion, van Breda Kolff was the worst coach he'd ever played for.

"I've been in the league for nine years and he's been in it for one, and he's trying to tell me how to play the game?" Chamberlain told Krikorian.

They kept the rift under wraps even through the playoffs, as the Lakers beat San Francisco in six and Atlanta in five to set up their sixth appearance in the NBA finals against the Celtics in eight years. Going into the series, it looked like the Lakers' best chance yet, and the town started to feel it when L.A. beat Boston the first two games at the Forum.

Jerry West scored fifty-three points and passed for thirteen assists in Game One, where Wilt grabbed twenty-three rebounds and blocked eleven shots, including five in the last five minutes of L.A.'s 120–118 victory.

West had forty-one more and Elgin Baylor scored the Lakers' last twelve points for a total of thirty-two in the second-game, 118–112, win, and Jack Kent Cooke, who should have known better, packed champagne for the trip back to Boston.

What a waste of fine wine. The Celtics won both games back East, 111–106 and 89–88.

Game Four was a wrist-slitter for Lakers fans. L.A. had the ball and a one-point lead with fifteen seconds to go, but lost the inbounds pass and then the game on a crazy shot by the Celtics' Sam Jones from the top of the key. It bounced off everything but the Old North Church before it slunk into the net, almost in embarrassment.

"Mr. Clutch," as they called West, pulled a hamstring but scored twenty-nine points when the Lakers came home and won the fifth game, 117–104. Then the Celtics tied it up in Boston, 99–90, on a night when Wilt, with West hurting, inexplicably took only five shots.

You'd be wrong to think the self-idolizing Cooke learned much from this embarrassment of drinking champagne too early in 1966. Three years later, he repeated the blunder. Before the seventh game against the Celtics, Cooke had his workmen fasten celebratory balloons in the rafters of the Forum. There they hung while Boston went up by twenty in the third quarter. Baylor and West shot the Lakers back into it, while Wilt grabbed every rebound in sight. Chamberlain snagged his twenty-seventh and final board with 5:20 to go in the game and the Lakers down by seven. In coming down with the ball, Wilt landed badly and wrenched his knee. He came out of the game to walk off the pain. Even in his absence, the Lakers kept closing the score— down to a single point.

With 1:17 to go, the Lakers' Keith Erickson knocked the ball away from John Havlicek, but it went right to Don Nelson at the free throw line, and the reserve Boston forward put up a shot "that would have struck oil if the iron on the hoop hadn't gotten in the way," Bud Furillo wrote. "The ball shot up for the rafters and came down straight and true for two, and the Celtics led by three points."

It wasn't over yet, but van Breda Kolff had already screwed his team by screwing Chamberlain, who had been demanding to be put back into the game.

"On the bench," the Steamer observed, "Wilt fought his coach, but the big guy was no match for Bill with his bad knee." Van Breda Kolff kept Wilt on the bench and the Celtics made it six straight finals losses for the Lakers, 108–106.

West scored forty-two in the game and averaged thirty-eight for the series, for which he was voted MVP of the series—the only time in NBA history the honor went to a player on the losing side.

"It's just hard for me to believe that they beat us," Jerry said in the locker room after the game, according to Doug Krikorian. "What makes it so hard is I know we had the better team. In other years, I could rationalize our setbacks. But this time, I can't."

Bud Furillo came up with a reason in his playoff post-mortem.

"The Celtics always play as a team," he observed. "The Lakers do it spasmodically."

Another might have been van Breda Kolff's failure to reinsert Wilt for the conclusion of Game Seven. The Steamer had already written before the playoffs that only a championship would have saved van Breda Kolff's job. When the Lakers came up short, so did Butch's time.

It ended when he stuck his head in the noose at a post-season Friars Club luncheon, with public remarks recorded and played in The Steam Room. With Deacon Jones in the house, van Breda Kolff told the Friars that the Lakers could use a tough guy like the Rams' defensive end.

"I don't imagine we'd be out-roughed if we had the Deacon," van Breda Kolff said. "I thought we had the guy we needed."

Five days later, van Breda Kolff was gone.

•   •   •   •   •

The Lakers put out a press release in late June saying they would soon have some news to report on their new coach.

Bud Furillo found the announcement about the announcement curious. He called Jack Kent Cooke for an explanation.

"We have to wait for the man to get here from Athabasca," Cooke said.

"Of course," Furillo replied.

It was never explained in the column what Joe Mullaney was doing in the tiny town in upper Alberta, but Furillo tracked down Wilt Chamberlain in Las Vegas for a reaction.

"The new coach is from Athabasca," the Steamer told the Dipper.

"Is that anywhere near Princeton?" Chamberlain asked.

"I'll have to check," Furillo said.

He called the owner and said, "Wilt wants to know where Athabasca is."

"I believe it's in the north of Canada," the owner answered.

"That could be anyplace in Canada," the Steamer said. "Everything is north. Can you pin it down?"

"Try Cookie Gilchrist," Cooke said. The former 1,000-yard man for the Buffalo Bills had initially played for Canadian Football League teams in Hamilton, Saskatchewan, and Toronto, as well as for the Sarnia Imperials and Kitchener-Waterloo Dutchmen of the Ontario Rugby Football Union. There was no record available of Gilchrist ever having played in Athabasca.

Mullaney, meanwhile, had been coaching college ball at Providence. He eventually made it to L.A. from whatever he was doing in Athabasca. Like every Lakers coach before him in L.A., Mullaney got the Lakers into the NBA finals.

It became more of an uphill task for the new coach when Chamberlain, who had taken to wearing a headband, crumpled to the floor while running down it in the third quarter of a November game in Phoenix. Wilt had ruptured a tendon underneath his right kneecap, the first significant injury of his career. Teammates Bill Hewitt and Mel Counts helped him off the court. He wouldn't return until the last week of the regular season.

Without Wilt, the Lakers finished in second place in the Western Division, behind Atlanta. With him, they found themselves down 3-1 in the first round of the playoffs against the Suns. Then Chamberlain decided to stop favoring the knee. In Game Five at the Forum, "The long gentleman blocked nine shots," the Steamer pointed out.

Wilt blocked twelve more when the Lakers tied the series in Phoenix. One of the rejections sent back a shot attempt near the basket by the Suns' Connie Hawkins who, according to the Steamer's estimation, had soared four feet into the heavens.

"Inability to jump has been Chamberlain's biggest problem since he came back from Centinela Valley Hospital," Furillo wrote. "He's jumping again."

Before Game Seven, the Steamer was down in the Lakers' locker room when the Suns' Paul Silas walked in to get a basketball for the Phoenix shootaround.

"Chamberlain rose to his full height and sounded the voice of doom," the Steamer wrote. "'We're going to kill you, Silas,' said Wilt. That was seven o'clock. One hour and thirty-eight seconds later, Elgin Baylor machine-gunned the first three baskets from his trigger fingers and the Lakers were on their way to Atlanta for the Western Division finals."

A surprising sweep over the Hawks meant another trip to the championships for the Lakers and Wilt, this time against the New York Knicks, who had the best record in the league and would replace Boston as L.A.'s eastern tormenter in 1970.

The colors had changed—Knicks orange and blue instead of Celtics green and white. So did the faces—Willis Reed, Walt Frazier, Dave DeBusschere, and Bill Bradley instead of Russell, the Joneses, Havlicek, and Cousy. But the pain of defeat in seven games to New York felt about the same as it did in the six championship losses to Boston. Maybe worse.

Even one of the most wonderful moments in Los Angeles sports history turned to dust. Jerry West, the Steamer said, "looked like one of the Flying Zucchinis coming out of a cannon" when he launched his sixty-four-foot swish to tie Game Three, before the Lakers lost in overtime.

Things looked really good for L.A. in the fifth game of a tied series when Willis Reed went down with a debilitating hip injury. The Lakers built up a thirteen-point halftime lead in the Garden. Then they turned the ball over nineteen times in the second half and lost.

"Like George Allen says, the fumbles will kill you," the Steamer wrote.

After the game, basketball pundits wondered why Wilt hadn't scored more against the smaller DeBusschere and Dave Stallworth, the Knicks' inside guys who helped the perimeter defenders in denying the ball to the low post. The result: Chamberlain only took three shots in the second half.

The Lakers figured out the Reed-less Knicks defense in the sixth game. They got the ball to Wilt in deep, and he hit twenty of the twenty-seven shots, most of them dunks and finger rolls at the rim. He finished with forty-five points.

"Wilt Has the Range Now," the *Herald Examiner* headline said the next day.

The Steamer's story asked the question that had puzzled everybody in the basketball world: Why didn't Chamberlain and the Lakers turn it on like that in Game Five?

"Like he says, it's not that easy," the Steamer wrote. "Gosh, nobody wants to get this thing over with quicker than Wilt. As he has pointed out several times, he is losing a fortune in the market and his tan at the beach."

Chamberlain and the Lakers then went on to lose Game Seven in New York when Willis Reed hobbled out of the chute to a maddening roar to join his teammates for the pre-game warmup. Then he hobbled down the floor and into position on the Knicks' first possession after a missed Laker shot. In transition, Reed hit from the left elbow, and the game was over, 2-0.

The Steamer said the Garden fans all but ended it during the pregame introductions with the ovation for Reed.

"The Lakers went to pieces," Furillo wrote. "Oh, they tried. Why, they had the game tied at zero for the first seven seconds. But then the one-legged Reed limped down to take a shot that went in, of course. The Garden went crazy for the second time. Now you may wonder where Wilt Chamberlain was when Reed made that first shot. Well, it was not always easy to find the seven-footer. But he shouldn't have to take the rap. His teammates were even less effective."

Up twenty-seven points at halftime, the Knicks threw what Bud Furillo called "the final psychological punch" when Chamberlain prepared to jump center in the third quarter against Nate Bowman.

"Frazier appealed to the officials to wait for Willis. He would be along in a bit," the Steamer wrote. Then Reed came out on the floor and brought the house down again. "Out he limped, after two more injections of carbocaine and cortisone. The Lakers could have used some of the carbocaine to kill the pain of their humiliation on national television."

Reed dragged his leg up and down the floor and leaned on Wilt hard enough to hold him to ten points for the twenty-seven painful minutes Willis was on the floor.

"The hurt in Reed's eyes inspired the incredible Knick showing," the Steamer wrote. "His lips were drawn in a thin line as he stiff-legged it around the court. It's a good thing he isn't a horse. He might have been shot."

A few days after the Lakers lost the series, the Steamer got a call from Bill Cosby. The comedian informed the columnist that for the second straight year, the Lakers had won his On Paper Award, professional basketball division.

"The signing of Wilt created a dynasty," Cosby told Furillo.

Cosby then named the Steamer vice president of the On Paper Awards and asked him to please handle the mail while he went to Lake Tahoe for a double engagement at Harrah's with Ray Charles. Between shows, Cosby said he and blind soul man Ray planned to play plenty of dominoes.

"Now on paper," Cosby told the Steamer, "I should win."

•   •   •   •   •

Joe Mullaney lasted two years before the Lakers dumped him in favor of a long-time Steamer favorite.

Bill Sharman had roared out of Porterville to star for the USC baseball and basketball teams in the late '40s before teaming up with fellow NBA Hall of Famer Bob Cousy in Boston to form one of the game's best backcourts ever. When he finished playing, he coached the L.A. Jets, the L.A. Stars, and L.A. State. He did a little announcing in St. Louis and coached some more for the San Francisco Warriors when they made it to the finals and lost to Wilt's 76ers of '67.

Sharman had developed a reputation along the way as a conditioning freak.

"The first time Sharman had the Warriors run wind sprints, we had guys keeling over on the floor," former Laker and San Francisco forward Rudy LaRusso told the Steamer. "I thought I was having a heart attack."

When the Lakers reported to Honolulu for what Furillo described as their "customary vacation" of a pre-season camp, they learned there would be no time for luaus under the Sharman regime.

"The plane landed at four o'clock," the Steamer wrote. "Sharman . . . had them on the court at six o'clock."

Sharman hired on with a Lakers team on the verge of major transition. Jerry West suffered a knee injury late in the 1970–1971 season that kept him out of the playoffs. He knew his end was near.

"It's going to be the hardest decision of my life when the day comes I have to give up basketball," he told the Steamer. "I know it can't continue forever."

Wilt bounced back from his knee injury to put up impressive numbers in 1970–1971, although his 27.3 points and 18.4 rebounds per game were merely mortal for him. He could still call on his super powers here and there, but he had only a couple more years left himself.

The third member of the group had reached the end of the line. Elgin Baylor played in only two games in 1970–1971 due to an Achilles injury. He gave it a shot the next year, but Elgin had lost the explosiveness that made him the first high-flying star in NBA history. He had scored 23,149 points in his career—third best in recorded history, as of that time. His 11,463 rebounds ranked fifth, even though Elgin, at 6-5, was several inches shorter than the four men ahead of him—Wilt, Russell, Bob Pettit, and Walt Bellamy.

The Steamer suggested Elgin as sixth man, but Baylor didn't want any of that. On November 4, 1971, he retired.

"I wanted to have one more good season but it just wasn't being fair," he told the *Herald Examiner*'s Mitch Chortkoff.

The next day, the Lakers won a game, 110–106, over the Baltimore Bullets, in front of 11,168 fans at the Forum. Baylor's replacement, Jim McMillian, the second-year man out of Columbia, scored twenty-two points.

The streak had reached one in a row. They beat Golden State the next night in Oakland, and won a few more without a loss to make it five straight.

•　　•　　•　　•　　•

Bill Sharman, the practice and conditioning freak, had instituted a new regime of game-day practices, and they were not universally well-received. In fact, they slightly irked the large man who played center for him.

Wilt Chamberlain had a reason to be mildly irritated. He had just moved into the relative wilderness of the Santa Monica Mountains, and he rather enjoyed his new three-acre estate. The rustic stone-and-wood Frank Lloyd Wright design that he lived in featured twenty-foot ceilings and a retractable bedroom ceiling, kind of like the ballparks in Milwaukee and Phoenix, and almost as big. He named the crib Ursa Major, after the constellation that contained the starry shape that gave him his nickname, the Big Dipper. The serfs down in the flatlands of Van Nuys always knew when the king of hoops was home because they could see smoke coming out of the chimney of his mountaintop castle. Why would anybody want to leave this paradise to make an extra trip to Inglewood, and on the day of the game? Wilt sure didn't, but his was a relatively minor gripe.

"Bill has this fetish about muscle memory," he said of coach Sharman.

Wilt didn't feel his muscles needed their recollection refreshed, but he went along with the schedule, and the team continued to win. They made it eighth straight at home on November 14 against the Celtics. With the retired Bill Russell in the Forum, Wilt blocked thirteen shots, grabbed thirty-one rebounds, and didn't take a shot.

"It was a mighty fine imitation of the way Russell brought eleven titles to Boston," Chortkoff wrote.

The Lakers and defending-champion Milwaukee Bucks each carried ten-game winning streaks into their November 21 game at the Forum. The Lakers came out of it with theirs at eleven and the Bucks' at zero. Wilt snatched twenty-six rebounds away from Milwaukee third-year center Kareem Abdul-Jabbar, and a sixth man named Pat Riley hit eight of eleven off the bench for the winners.

In their thirteenth straight, Wilt scored thirty-one and retrieved thirty-one rebounds in a rout over Detroit.

"Chamberlain played like he was in his second childhood," Pistons center Bob Lanier said afterwards.

L.A.'s fourteenth in a row was another romp, over Seattle.

"Not one of these fourteen games could have gone the other way," Wilt said. "Most of them were so one-sided that it scares me. And it's all happened because we're playing great team ball. It's Sharman's game."

West, coming off an ankle sprain, scored forty-five in a win at Boston, and Jim McMillian, who was coming off the flu, had forty-one in Philadelphia.

"I don't feel pressure to score twenty-seven points every night like Elgin did," McMillian said. "My job is to move the ball, play good defense, and shoot when I'm open."

The Lakers reached twenty-one straight at home on December 12 against Atlanta, by a score of 104-95. It set an NBA record. They ran the streak to twenty-five on December 19 at home against Philadelphia on a night when Wilt scored thirty-two, rebounded thirty-four, and blocked twelve—"his best game in several seasons," Chortkoff said. Then they flew across the country to beat the Buffalo Braves, where fellow Overbrook High alumnus Walt Hazzard made an interesting observation about the more prominent product of the Philadelphia school.

"When Sharman took over the job, I had one fear," Hazzard said. "I was afraid he was going to teach Wilt how to win."

The victory in Buffalo tied the Lakers with the 1916 New York baseball Giants for the longest winning streak in American professional team-sports history. They broke it the next night in Baltimore, 127-120, in a game that was televised in Korea and Vietnam.

"It's almost unbelievable," said West, who scored thirty-seven.

They ran it up to thirty-one in Boston, where Bill Russell commented modestly in a TV interview that the Lakers were winning because "they are finally playing Bill Russell-type basketball."

Two more wins, in Cleveland and Atlanta, extended the streak to thirty-three before the Lakers traveled to Milwaukee on January 9 to try and make it thirty-four against the defending champs. One of the largest audiences to ever watch an NBA game tuned in on national TV.

Milwaukee came into the game angry, and so was the Bucks' coach, Larry Costello, who had grown sick and tired of having to keep reminding people that it was his team that was the incumbent champion. To stop the streak, Costello installed a defensive scheme to slow down the Lakers' fast break. It called for Abdul-Jabbar to hang back after the Bucks missed a shot and harass the Lakers rebounder to deny him the outlet pass. The Lakers still hung in for most of the game, but a late 12-0 run by the Bucks broke it open and Milwaukee won, 120–104, to stop the streak at thirty-three.

Kareem had one of his best games ever, scoring thirty-nine points, grabbing twenty rebounds, blocking ten shots and passing for five assists. He also got whistled for punching Lakers power forward Happy Hairston.

In the span of the forty-eight-minute loss, it felt like the winning streak never happened at all.

Mitch Chortkoff wrote: "A defeat somewhere was inevitable, but when it came to the world's champions, twenty million television viewers must have thought the same thing collectively: 'Here we go again.' The old stereotypes are alive. The Lakers could win the next thirty-three in a row, but it wouldn't mean much. The only remaining proving ground will be in the playoffs in April and May."

· · · · ·

For a decade, the Steamer said, Laker fans had been made to feel like "rubes in a shell game," when it came to the NBA title.

"Every time they thought the pea was under the Los Angeles shell, it wound up in Milwaukee or New York or Boston," he wrote.

They would finally flip the right nut in 1972, with a team that transcended its superstar parts. Wilt, for one thing, had become something of a role player. They were big roles, rebounding and defending. But he didn't have to carry the ball every play anymore. Jerry West, coming off knee surgery, could still do everything, only he didn't have to do as much of it. Gail Goodrich, the UCLA great who was back in his hometown after spending a couple years in Phoenix, took a ton of pressure off Jerry in the scoring department. The shortish lefty could flip 'em in from anywhere and loop his layups over the big guys in the lane on his drives to the hoop. Goodrich led the team in scoring with 25.9 a game. West was right with him at 25.8 and Jerry also averaged 9.7 assists, best in the league and the highest mark of his career, in an offense that featured ball movement. Mc-Millian, the small forward who replaced Baylor, averaged 18.8

on forty-eight percent shooting, mostly from outside. Wilt was able to focus more on defense because power forward Happy Hairston had his back on the boards, averaging 13.1 a game and scoring just as many points with an effective mid-range jumper. Flynn Robinson gave them quick points off the bench. Pat Riley could defend and score at small forward and shooting guard. Long, tall, and fast Leroy Ellis could defend on any of three positions. John Q. Trapp lent mean-eyed intimidation to the mix; he averaged 6.2 fouls per thirty-six minutes to easily lead the team, and whenever the Lakers played in his hometown of Detroit, he was especially tough in front of his pals, who were known to pack heat into Cobo Arena.

The Lakers finished the season with a 69–13 record—the best in NBA history, until Michael Jordan's Chicago Bulls won seventy-two in 1995–1996.

But like Mitch Chortkoff said, the Lakers knew their thirty-three-game winning streak and won-loss record wouldn't mean anything unless they won it all, and they knew Milwaukee was the team they had to beat to get there.

Bud Furillo called it "the glamour series of the NBA playoffs."

The year before, the Bucks had won sixty-six games. They finished 1971–1972 with sixty-three.

Kareem Abdul-Jabbar, in his third season, had become the best player in the league. He led the NBA in scoring with 34.8, and his 16.6 rebounds per game was his second highest total ever. Oscar Robertson battled abdominal injuries but still threatened to triple-double anybody on a given night, while playing backcourt defense with the best. Bobby Dandridge could score. Lucius Allen, Kareem's old college teammate, was beginning to get the league figured out. Jon McGlocklin provided firepower from range. Curtis Perry could even muscle the likes for Wilt for a rebound.

Yep, you could forget about the winning streak and having the best record in this matchup. And after the first game of the series, you could forget about the home-court advantage, too. The Bucks demolished the Lakers in Game One at the Forum, leading by thirty-one in the fourth quarter before settling for a

93–72 win. The Lakers shot a miserable twenty-seven percent for the afternoon.

Some commentators, including the Steamer, blamed the American Broadcasting Company for the team's inability to put the ball in the basket, by putting in new floor lights for national TV. As early as Saturday's practice before the Sunday game, Goodrich had noticed an uncommon glare.

"Coach, what are they doing to the lights?" he asked Sharman.

About an hour and a half before the game, Jack Kent Cooke ordered his lieutenants to have the new light banks removed.

NBA officials overruled him.

"This must be the one time that the owner of the building didn't have his way," the Steamer wrote.

Milwaukee didn't seem bothered. It was just the Lakers who were affected, a malady that Furillo said extended from their eyes to the insides of their heads.

"The Lakers felt they were going insane," he wrote, "somewhat like Ingrid Bergman did in *Gaslight*, with Charles Boyer making the adjustments to drive her nuts."

ABC tinkered with the lights a bit for the second game, and they sure enough improved the shooting touch—of the Bucks. They shot sixty-one percent, but lost. The Lakers shot twenty-one more free throws, and won. By one point.

The game turned on two huge calls in the last fifteen seconds. With the Lakers up 133–132, Abdul-Jabbar jumped out to the mid-court stripe and trapped West.

"I've never been covered like that in my life," Jerry told reporters later. "I felt like Jabbar was eight feet tall."

Under Kareem's harassment, the ball came free, but it bounced off referee Manny Sokol and Jerry retrieved it legally on the Lakers' side of the fifty-yard line. The Bucks howled for a back-court violation. They didn't get it. West then snapped a pass to Hairston on the baseline and Happy streaked to the hoop and laid it in without putting the ball on the floor. The Bucks screamed for traveling. Didn't get that one, either. Final score, Lakers 135–134, and we go to Milwaukee tied at one.

The first two games in L.A., Kareem scored thirty-three and forty points, so the Steamer called on Wilt to exercise extreme measures to cut down on the great center's offensive production. First, the Steamer wanted the Dipper to get angry, to lean on Abdul-Jabbar in an effort to knock him off the spot where Kareem liked to begin his swing to the basket with the sky hook.

"Everybody leans on Wilt," the Steamer wrote. "It's about time he leaned on everybody."

On offense, the Steamer advised Wilt to stop dribbling the ball when he got it, to just take it straight to the rack with some attitude.

"Abdul-Jabbar would move over if Wilt swung an elbow," the Steamer said. "So would Russia and possibly China."

Furillo wrote, "God didn't put the Big Dipper on this earth to dribble the ball. He is supposed to stuff it down the basket's throat."

Wilt didn't do much stuffing in Game Three, after he reinjured his hyperextended left hand. He also took a shot to the testicles from Kareem just before halftime, an unintentional but painful consequence of going up to block the taller fellow's hook. Gingerly, Chamberlain struggled to the locker for the halftime break. Then he came out and finished the job of stifling Abdul-Jabbar. Wilt blocked ten shots, including a Kareem dunk, and held Milwaukee's big to fifteen field goals in thirty-seven attempts in the Lakers' 108–105 win. It was a game the Lakers decided to play tough. Pat Riley threw a punch at Bobby Dandridge, West banged a knee off Kareem, and the Lakers twice belted the hot-shooting Lucius Allen to the floor.

Milwaukee out-rebounded the Lakers 75–43 in the fourth game to win in a rout, 114–88, but the Lakers regained control of the series with a crusher of their own in the fifth, 115–90. Wilt did the job on Kareem again, forcing him to miss twenty of his thirty-three shots. Twice, Wilt skied above Abdul-Jabbar to block his shots, one of which triggered a third-quarter fast break that drove the usually somnolent Forum crowd wild.

"They weren't so blasé," West told reporters.

The energy didn't dissipate on the road. Wilt wouldn't let

it. Nine days earlier, he had told Bud Furillo, in regards to the Bucks' series, "We will win it in six or find a way to lose in seven."

So before Game Six in Milwaukee, Captain Chamberlain called his team together.

"We've had a fantastic season," he told them, according to The Steam Room. "It won't mean a damn thing if we don't win this playoff. Everybody will say, 'Same old Lakers. Can't win the big ones.' We can end this thing today. Why should it go on any longer?"

Nobody could give Wilt a good answer, except the Bucks, who built a ten-point lead in the fourth quarter. That's when Wilt, who had focused on defense and rebounding through the first forty minutes, turned on some offense in the final eight. At one point he stole the ball from Kareem, passed it ahead, ran the floor, and finished with a dunk. The Steamer said it took Wilt about six steps to make it from rim to rim.

Abdul-Jabbar outscored and out-rebounded Wilt in the game. Furillo said the numbers lied in the Lakers' 104–100 series clinching victory, that Wilt "gave his finest performance in thirteen National Basketball Association seasons." In willing the Lakers to the win, he said, Wilt, for a single contest, "may have been the best man who ever played the game."

•   •   •   •   •

The Lakers were about to become the kings of the basketball world, but the Knicks delayed the coronation a little bit in the finals when they shot seventy-two percent in the first half of the first game. Bill Bradley and Jerry Lucas bombed away from outside to give the Knicks a thirty-point first-half lead. Bradley failed on only one of twelve shots.

"He missed more questions than that on the Rhodes Scholar test," the Steamer said of the Princeton-educated sharpshooter, who, unlike Bob Short, later became a U.S. senator, although he was elected from New Jersey and not Minnesota.

The 114–92 victory represented the end of the Knicks' run against the Lakers. In the second game, Gail Goodrich scored thirty-one on 14-of-18 shooting and Wilt overcame a bad night's sleep beneath the stars in Ursa Major to score twenty-three and grab fourteen rebounds in the Lakers' 106 -92 win.

"Yes, it is Wilt who is Mr. Universe, not Arnold Schwarzenegger," the Steamer wrote. "What chance would Herr Schwarzenegger have going one-on-one with Captain Wilt?"

After the eleven-point Game Three win in New York, Furillo said, "Mayor Lindsey has summoned the immediate family to Broadway."

Still smarting from the Knicks' fantastic outside shooting in the first game, the Lakers played defense "as if they were protecting the honor of their wives," the Steamer said. Furillo noted that "square shouldered Phil Jackson" of the Knicks, who would later become the NBA's all-time championship coach with the Bulls and the Lakers, "played well in relief with twelve points. Only Phil looks odd doing it. His right hip seems to be out in front of him."

The Lakers needed overtime to win the fourth game and move up 3-1 in the series.

"Dip is determined to win this thing," Furillo said of Chamberlain. "He and Jerry are through with the taste of ashes."

When Goodrich went to the free-throw line to seal Game Four in the final seconds, West began to laugh and wave his hands, according to the Steamer's observations.

"I feel fantastic," Jerry told the press. "I'm shaking."

Looking ahead to Game Five back in L.A., West added, "We are quite anxious to play that game."

Jack Kent Cooke had the good sense to not hang any balloons in the rafters, and nobody knew where he stashed the champagne.

Trepidation over the wrist Wilt broke in Game Four gave way to what Alan Greenspan might call irrational exuberance the moment Chamberlain completed his ball-holding experiment.

Wilt's performance in the championship-clinching victory earned him a Dodge station wagon as the series MVP, but the Dipper knew the man of the moment was the one who had suffered the most for half a generation. Jerry West had been in a shooting slump for nearly the entire playoff season. He broke out of it in the final two games of the Knicks series, scoring twenty-eight in the fourth and twenty-three in the fifth. His ten points in the third quarter of the finale helped the Lakers break open a tie game, and they extended their lead in the fourth to win it, 114–100.

"This makes up for all those summers trying to explain why we didn't win the whole thing," Furillo quoted the teary-eyed West afterward.

Beating the Knicks and winning the title was nice for West and Wilt and the Lakers and Los Angeles, but not much more than nice. Better than losing, yes. It could only have been the work of Beelzebub, had the Lakers not won the championship in the year they won thirty-three straight and compiled the best record, up to then, in NBA history.

Did it make up for the taste of ashes? Not even close, and Jerry West himself said as much in his 2011 book.

"Those losses scarred me, scars that remain embedded in my psyche to this day," he wrote. Sorry, he said, if "I sound like a permanent victim when I say this," but "it is true and it haunts me still."

Magic and Kobe and Shaq and Gasol and Artest got a lot of it back and those championships felt great—and none of them will ever erase the painful memories from the Steam Room era, of Selvy's rim shot or the balloons in the rafters or Willis Reed hobbling up the floor in the Garden.

•   •   •   •   •

The Lakers barely even enjoyed their long-awaited first Los Angeles championship. The night of their victory party at the Forum Club, they squabbled with Jack Kent Cooke over who was going to pay the coaches' share of the championship money, the players or management.

Jerry West left after the cocktail hour and didn't sit down for dinner. Wilt Chamberlain and Cooke exchanged words before the center "stalked away" from the owner, as Bud Furillo reported.

The party started at 8:00, and at 9:30, the Steamer went to

the bar to order a Campari and soda.

"That will be two-fifty," the bartender informed him.

"I'm with the party," the Steamer answered.

"The party's over," the keeper said.

•   •   •   •   •

The Lakers had the home court advantage in the next year's finals, too, against the Knicks, but age hit the tape ahead of Wilt and hamstring injuries slowed down West in the last couple games of the series. Happy Hairston didn't play at all. It was a different team, a different feeling. They lost in five. It was their eighth loss in the NBA finals in twelve years.

West gave it a shot in the final year of the Steam Room era, but injuries restricted him to thirty-one games in his last season, 1973–1974, before he retired.

Wilt quit the Lakers for San Diego, where he coached the ABA's Conquistadores—on the nights he showed up.

Bud Furillo went to the Forum for his last Lakers column in February 1974, to note the passing of the greats—Baylor to TV color commentary, West to injury, and Wilt to another league.

He took his seat in the Forum's press area, halfway up the arena, right behind the roost of Naismith Memorial Basketball Hall of Fame broadcaster Chick Hearn.

"The players ran up and down the court," the Steamer wrote. "I checked the numbers and tapped C-Baby on the shoulder.

"'Where's Elgin?'

"'Tending the popcorn machine for CBS,' said Hearn.

"'Where's West?'

"'That's him on the end of the bench, the skinny kid in the sweater.'

"'Then where's Wilt?'"

Chick didn't have an answer for that one. The question marks remained about the Lakers, too, until they got Magic six years after The Steam Room's end of watch.

Chapter 12

MCKAY'S BEST TEAM

In one respect, the Trojan landslide outdid that of the president's reelection. Even Massachusetts went for Southern California.
—December 3, 1972

f all the teams in Los Angeles, the one closest to Bud Furillo's heart played football for the University of Southern California. He never liked the Trojans more than in 1972, when they won all their games and were declared national champions.

The '72 Trojans still rank as one of the greatest in college football history. They never trailed in the second half, and no team came within nine points of them all year. They beat the other guys by an average score of 39–11. They intercepted twenty-eight passes and recovered twenty-five fumbles. They beat six teams that were ranked eighteenth or higher. They didn't give up a run from scrimmage longer than twenty-eight yards. They had five All-Americans. They were the unanimous number-one pick in both the AP and UPI polls.

In the estimation of Bud Furillo, it was a more impressive performance than Richard Nixon's defeat of George McGovern in the presidential election the same year, forty-nine states to one and 520 electoral votes to seventeen. USC achieved its monument, however, without the benefit of any third-rate burglaries or the laundering of any campaign cash.

Of course, the Trojans faced impeachment proceedings of their own in the 1950s, the 1980s, and the 2010s for assorted mishaps in complying with the complicated rules that govern college sports. But the scandals that occurred in the Steamer's lifetime did not bother him greatly, and I'm fairly confident that he would have overlooked the Reggie Bush-related sanctions imposed in the years after his death. Hell yes, he was a Trojan honk.

"Only in Los Angeles," Bud Furillo once wrote, "could you have a sports editor who admits to being a fan. Why not?"

Nobody ever gave him a good answer for why he couldn't, so the Steamer fell in deep with the Trojans—right about the time a cigar-smoking jokester from Shinnston, West Virginia, became the head coach.

John McKay's teams gave one of college football's best programs fifteen of its best years. He won five Rose Bowls and four national championships and produced two Heisman Trophy winners. In a conspiracy with his close friend and fellow coaching legend Paul "Bear" Bryant, McKay also helped integrate football in the Deep South.

McKay and the Steamer hit it off from the start—an easy thing to do in an era when coaches still liked and hung out with the writers who didn't consider such friendships some sort of journalistic crime. The Trojan head man regularly cultivated the press at Julie's, a bar and grill across the street from the USC campus. Once a week, or more, McKay got together for a taste or two with the Steamer and *Herald Examiner* beat writers like Steve Bisheff and Jim Perry and other charter members like John Hall of the *Times*, Bud Tucker of the *San Gabriel Valley Tribune*, and Loel Schrader of the *Long Beach Independent-Press Telegram*. They'd huddle up in the coach's booth at Julie's while McKay gave them the inside dope on the Trojans.

Bud Furillo wasn't always so giddy about USC. As a babe in industrial Ohio, he grew up indoctrinated into the cause of Notre Dame football. Among the earliest images in his sports memory were those of his father buying a new line of Studebaker called the Rockne in 1931, named for the Irish's fabled coach and manufactured in South Bend, Indiana, hometown of the Notre Dame campus. The old man drove the six-year-old Steamer around Youngstown in the Knute-mobile and taught him the words to the Victory March.

Although his father had a very fine voice, "he couldn't make car payments very well," the Steamer reported. "[The Rockne] disappeared mysteriously, about the time the second payment was due."

In 1938, the Irish were having their best season of the Steamer's adolescence. They rolled over Kansas and beat the Techs, Georgia, and Carnegie. The service academies fell, and so did the Big Ten—Illinois, Minnesota, and Northwestern, anyway. Only USC remained on the Notre Dame schedule, and even though the Trojans won the Pacific Coast Conference and were on their way to the Rose Bowl, the Steamer figured them for barely a bump. Notre Dame would kill the Trojans, he surmised, and finish undefeated and ranked number one.

Unbelievably, the Irish faked a punt from their own thirty as a scoreless first half wound down. The play fooled nobody. USC cashed in the blunder on a touchdown pass from Ollie Day to Al Krueger and went on to score the upset of the year, 13-0, to break the heart of the thirteen-year-old subway alumnus listening on the radio from his home on South Avenue in Youngstown.

Bud Furillo's emotional pain carried into Los Angeles when his family moved there a couple years later. In his new town, he strongly favored UCLA over the Trojan curs. He dug in deeper with the Bruins in later years, when he became a sportswriter and shared sips with the Bruins' terrific coach, Henry "Red" Sanders.

Over time, he grew to appreciate USC's standing in the local sports culture. The Trojans arrived on the national map when they beat Penn State in the 1923 Rose Bowl. A couple years later, they tried to hire Rockne away from Notre Dame. Fat chance that Knute would leave South Bend. But Rockne did recommend a coach to the Trojans in Howard Jones, a Yale man by way of Iowa. USC hired Jones and over the next fifteen years, "The Head Man," as they called him, turned the Trojans into a national power. He won four national championships, defeated Notre Dame six times, and scored huge intersectional victories over the likes of Pittsburgh, Tulane, and Tennessee in the Rose Bowl.

The Steamer locked in with the USC program when he took it on as a beat in 1957. Two years into it, McKay zoomed down from Oregon to work as an assistant, and he got the head job in 1960. A star athlete from West Virginia coal country only 167 miles down the road from the Steamer's Youngstown homeland, McKay had learned to smoke cigars as a tail gunner in the Army Air Corps and played college ball at Oregon with Norm Van Brocklin, another close contact in the Steamer network of friends and idols. Not at all thrilled with L.A., McKay thought about blowing town himself when the alumni turned up the heat on his predecessor, Don Clark. McKay reconsidered his relocation plan when the USC administration offered him the job.

Going into his first year, *Playboy* magazine put the pressure on McKay. The skin sheet made USC its 1960 pre-season number one. The Trojans responded by losing their first three games.

"It only proved that *Playboy* knows a good deal more about the female formation than it does about the T formation," McKay told Furillo.

•   •   •   •   •

McKay's first two USC teams finished with losing records, and it took some pleading with the USC administration from Bud Furillo and other L.A. writers who liked their new drinking buddy to keep the bosses from firing him. In 1962, McKay's third year on the job, he proved the writers correct. His team began to click. The Trojans won their first five games and climbed to number three in the rankings.

People didn't pay much attention, though. They were more consumed by the possibility of nuclear war with Russia.

McKay and his staff didn't have time for petty distractions such as the Cuban Missile Crisis. At the height of the naval blockade of the island regime, USC was scheduled to pay undefeated, ninth-ranked Washington. Holed up in their campus offices, the Trojan brain trust broke down film and looked for openings in the Husky defense—oblivious to the Soviet shootdown of one of our U-2s over Cuba.

"Wives of the Trojan coaches have implicit instructions not to bother them unless Castro starts shooting," the Steamer wrote.

Furillo, however, broke through for a word with the USC command.

"We're in for trouble," McKay told the Steamer.

The coach said the thinking from the bunker was that the Trojans would not be able to run the ball on Washington's more physically dominant defensive front.

"Unless we throw, we won't move the ball at all," McKay told Furillo.

The Steamer interrupted the nervous coach.

"John," he said. "The books have your team a two-and-a-half-point favorite."

"We're what?" McKay said.

Such disingenuity. And this talk about throwing the ball—it was part of a McKay misinformation campaign. Apparently, Washington had been reading the Steam Room communiqués. The Huskies, worried about an air attack, installed a four-deep secondary for the Coliseum conflagration.

McKay's feint worked. With Washington laying back, he punched them in the gut, his ground forces marching for 247 yards. The running game paced a huge, 14-0 victory.

After Washington, USC handled Stanford, 39-14, and the United Press International voted the Trojans number one. It was the first time in the history of wire service polling that the Trojans ever topped either of the lists.

They got the Associated Press vote a week later when they beat Navy, 13-6, despite a 126-yard running day by Midshipmen quarterback Roger Staubach, who won the Heisman Trophy the next year.

Only UCLA stood in the way to muck it up for the Trojans. The Bruins were down in '62, but they were good enough to take a 3-0 lead into the fourth quarter. The Trojans, growing desperate, finally moved into position to take the lead. They advanced the ball to the UCLA twenty-four, but it was fourth-and-eight when USC quarterback Bill Nelsen let one fly on a windy day. The ball looked like it was headed for Vermont Avenue. But tailback Willie Brown, who had lined up outside, skied over the middle of the field and made an acrobatic catch.

"Willie went up a ladder of air to make one of the finest catches in the history of this great series," Furillo wrote of the game-turning play. "He came down on the two-yard line and [fullback] Ben Wilson came down in the end zone on the next play."

The Trojans scored again and won, 14–3, and clobbered Notre Dame the next week, 25–0, their biggest margin of victory up to that point in the thirty-six-year history of the series with the Irish.

When Wisconsin flew out for the Rose Bowl, the Badgers were ranked second in the country, but favored to beat number-one USC. In the Trojans' first Rose Bowl appearance in ten years, the co-starter at quarterback, Pete Beathard, threw four touchdown passes and USC led, 42–14, in the fourth quarter. As the sun went down behind the poorly lit Arroyo Seco stadium, USC's pass defenders got lost in the dark in search for the Badgers' receivers. Wisconsin quarterback Ron Vander Kelen had no trouble finding them. He threw three fourth-quarter touchdown passes and accumulated 401 yards through the air for the game. They were nice numbers, but not enough to overcome the Trojans, who held on for a 42–37 victory.

The Wisconsin comeback was all anybody wanted to talk about afterward. Except in The Steam Room.

"Good show, Badgers," Furillo wrote. "There is plenty of space available for you today. But not here."

•　　•　　•　　•　　•

It had been five years since Notre Dame had even had a winning season when the Irish hired Ara Parseghian away from Northwestern in 1964 to spark up the best years of college football's greatest intersectional rivalry.

In the eleven seasons McKay and Parseghian presided over the USC-Notre Dame series, at least one of the teams went into the game undefeated ten times. All eleven had a significant impact on the national championship. Five times, the winner finished number one.

Parseghian had a pedigree that appealed directly to the Steamer's roots and sense of history. Ara was born in Akron, just fifty-one miles from Youngstown. He played at Miami of Ohio under Sid Gillman, and then in the military and the pros under Paul Brown. Ara coached on Woody Hayes's staff at Miami, then got the head job at his alma mater before moving on to Northwestern and then to Notre Dame.

In Parseghian's first year, the Irish had won their first nine games by the time they arrived in L.A. for the season finale. On a sunny Coliseum afternoon in front of 83,840 fans, Notre Dame built up a 17-0 halftime lead. It looked like the Irish were going to win the national championship, until USC scored a couple of second-half touchdowns and moved the ball deep into Notre Dame territory with less than two minutes to go.

On fourth-and-goal from the Irish fifteen, USC flanker Rod Sherman lined up wide left. He cut to the middle while quarterback Craig Fertig rolled left, still inside the pocket. Here came Notre Dame's great sophomore tackle, Alan Page, crashing through the middle. Page slammed Fertig to the ground, but the Trojan quarterback got the ball out first. Fertig's pass found Sherman over the middle at the three, and Rod caught it in front of the Notre Dame safety, Tony Carey, who slipped to the turf as the USC receiver slipped into the end zone.

Thousands stormed the field to celebrate the Trojans' 20-17 victory, while Irish priests wept outside the Notre Dame locker room.

"In the ancient house of football thrills on Figueroa Street, the tunnels echoed the belief this might have been the greatest game ever played in the Coliseum," the Steamer wrote. "It's the best one I've ever seen."

That night, USC students—who sat on their hands through most of the turbulent '60s—finally found an issue to inspire protest. They found it unacceptable when the Athletic Association of Western Universities, successor to the shambled PCC, had voted to send Oregon State to the Rose Bowl instead of the Trojans.

Roaming bands of Tab Hunter lookalikes set bonfires on USC's Fraternity Row. Bud Furillo played to the mob and called for a breakup of the AAWU. With Saturday night's embers still putting off heat, he wrote: "The AAWU knows less than the WCTU about selecting a team for a football bowl game."

Oregon State proved the Steamer right, getting killed by Michigan in the Rose Bowl, 34–7.

•   •   •   •   •

In 1965, Mike Garrett stamped the USC tailback position as one of the glamour spots in college football when he ran for 1,440 yards, broke Ollie Matson's career NCAA rushing record, and won the Heisman Trophy. But an otherwise terrific team failed against its two principal rivals to ruin Iron Mike's big season.

The Trojans were undefeated when they took the field on a windy, rainy, thirty-nine-degree day in South Bend. It was the famous "Remember Game," in which Irish fans wanted revenge on USC for depriving them of the national championship the year before.

On this day of cold remembrance, the Trojans inexplicably forgot to bring their parkas. Even without proper outdoor gear, they stood in the cold and wet and waited twenty minutes for Notre Dame to make its way to the Irish sideline, through a human tunnel of students who carried banners promising death and destruction to the visitors.

Notre Dame won the toss, took the wind, and chose to kick off. USC chose to accept it—as much a mistake as forgetting the parkas. The Trojans should have just gone home right there. Instead, return man Mike Hunter received the kickoff at the fifteen and fell flat on his face.

"Christ," McKay said on the sideline, amid the bedlam. "They shot him."

Notre Dame mauled USC with four consecutive pulverizing drives that concluded with short touchdown runs by Irish fullback Larry Conjar in the 28–7 Irish win. Conjar told the Steamer afterward that he had worked out over the summer as a railroad track repairman in his hometown of Steelton, Pennsylvania, swinging a pick and ramming a jackhammer and hauling railroad ties and thinking about the previous year's upset loss to USC.

"Conjar remembered 20–17," the Steamer wrote. "Wow, he remembered. How every Irish player remembered. How every student remembered. The question now is will they ever forget?

If you watched on television, you saw one of the most vicious beatings any football team ever got."

Following the devastation of South Bend, the Trojans rallied for impressive wins over California and Pittsburgh. They still held on to a number six ranking coming up to the UCLA game, against the surprise team of the year under new coach Tommy Prothro, whose arrival on the Westwood campus was made far more enjoyable by the impending eligibility of quarterback Gary Beban. As a sophomore, Beban had run and passed for more than 2,000 yards. UCLA got better every week, and the Bruins came into the USC game undefeated in conference and ranked seventh in the country.

Bud Furillo tabbed the more physically imposing Trojans, but advised caution at the betting windows.

"The Bruins have become tougher to defense every week," he wrote. "Prothro feeds formations constantly into the minds of his smart young men. They absorb the information and their bodies respond to it with computer precision and intelligence."

With 94,085 stuffed into the Coliseum for the Rose Bowl decider, the Trojans gave up an early touchdown on a forty-nine-yard run by Mel Farr, but spent the next fifty minutes smashing the Bruins with what the Steamer called "a record number of nine-count knockdowns." USC fumbled, however, on the UCLA one, the twenty-one, and the twenty-three. The Trojans also screwed up a first-and-goal from the UCLA seven before the end of the first half. Still, they had the ball and a 16–6 lead with just over four minutes to go.

They appeared to be in total control until, almost in succession, there came four of the most horrific plays in cardinal-and-gold history. USC quarterback Troy Winslow lost a fumble at his own thirty-four. Next play, Beban threw a touchdown pass to Dick Witcher. UCLA's Dallas Grider recovered an onside kick, and one play after a USC sack of Beban, the quarterback got up to hit Kurt Altenberg with a fifty-two-yard touchdown pass. Bruins win, 20–16.

In a final indignity, UCLA drove deep into their territory before easing up on the Trojan two-yard line.

"Refusing to pour it on, the UCLA Bruins extended sympathy to Southern California and ran out the clock," the Steamer wrote.

UCLA followed up the Trojan win with a stunning upset over undefeated and number-one-ranked Michigan State in the Rose Bowl, 14–12. Just like they did to USC late, the Bruins zapped the Spartans early. They turned a fumbled punt into a touchdown. On the ensuing kickoff, Dallas Grider became the undisputed onside-kick recovering champion of the Steam Room era when he grabbed another dribbler. A Beban zinger to Altenberg put the ball on the Spartan doorstep, and the Bruin quarterback broke in from the one. Early in the second quarter, it was 14–0.

Michigan State wore down the Bruins for two scores in the fourth quarter and went for a two-point conversion for the tie with thirty-one seconds left. Coach Duffy Daugherty called for a pitch to fullback Bob Apisa around right end, but UCLA safety Bob Stiles, who stood five foot nine and weighed 175, plugged the six-foot-one, 212-pound ball carrier at the one. Apisa staggered Stiles senseless with a knee to the chest, but the smaller defender held on and got him on the ground a yard short of the goal line as UCLA fans swarmed the field.

"UCLA is one of the smartest teams I've ever seen," the Steamer wrote the next day. "Lucky? The heck they are. They force the other guy into the mistake and make the most of it. Their alertness is a tribute to Prothro and his entire staff. The Spartan offense looked messy in comparison to the bag of tricks the Bruins showed in Pasadena yesterday."

•   •   •   •   •

UCLA didn't need a late fumble or an onside kick to beat USC in 1966. The Bruins simply had the better team, even without Beban. He missed the city championship due to a broken ankle. UCLA still had the best quarterback when backup Norman Dow led the Bruins to a 14–7 win.

"Regrettably, Norman Dow played his final game of 1966 Saturday," Bud Furillo wrote in his game story. "It was also his first."

Dow won the game with his legs, gaining ninety-nine yards in nineteen carries, including twenty-six on a second-and-twenty-seven to set up the tie-breaking touchdown in the fourth quarter.

UCLA finished 9-1 and USC fell to 7-2, but the AAWU botched another one by naming the Trojans as the conference's "most representative" team and sending them to the Rose Bowl.

Like USC's two years earlier, UCLA students protested. Angry Bruins even blocked the San Diego Freeway for awhile. But it was USC that got run over—by Notre Dame.

A week earlier, the Parseghians had departed East Lansing with a 10-10 tie against Michigan State. Bud Furillo thought it was the greatest Notre Dame team ever, but the Irish didn't show it when they not only failed to beat the Spartans, but didn't even try. Getting the ball on their own thirty with 1:24 to play, they ran the ball four straight times. The Living Room A.C. booed them off the field.

Ranked number one in both wire service polls going into Michigan State, Notre Dame came out of it number two in the eyes of the United Press International—just USC's luck. With the Spartans' season finished, Notre Dame had one last chance to impress the electoral college in the season finale against USC.

The Irish made the most of the opportunity, with second-string quarterback Coley O'Brien throwing for 255 yards in a rout of the number-ten Trojans, 51-0.

"Notre Dame excelled in all departments," Furillo wrote in his game story the next day. "But it was the pass, the weapon the Irish refused to use in the final minute of last week's 10-10 tie with Michigan State, which stripped the Trojans of their dignity."

The Steamer added, "The shocking win over a USC team which lost only two previous games by ten points should bring Notre Dame its first national championship since 1949." The Irish in fact wound up number one in both polls.

After the game, John McKay gathered his team in the locker room before the press swarmed in, to put the embarrassment into perspective.

"Forget it, guys," he told them. "Do you realize there are

IRISH WOULD HAVE BLED TO DEATH TO BEAT TROJANS
OCTOBER 28, 1973

SOUTH BEND—Notre Dame football, which had grown increasingly suspect, regained its credibility with a display of old-time fury Saturday which must have returned that crooked smile to the ghost of Knute Rockne.

[Notre Dame] hadn't beaten USC since 1966, and the Trojans had become the most hated enemy in all the years since a young priest named Edward F. Sorin first rang the bell for class at Notre Dame in 1842.

The Fighting Irish captured one of the most violent college football games ever played, 23–14 . . .

[USC quarterback Pat Haden] took a fearful beating from the Irish throughout the game. . . .

He had to come out one time. . . .

The collisions in this contest rattled the vital organs of the young men playing in it . . .

Notre Dame lost two fullbacks . . . Tackle Steve Quehl of Cincinnati was another casualty and safetyman Tim Rudnick was knocked out once.

But the Irish didn't care if they bled to death so long as they won this one. I have never seen a team more emotional.

---

seven hundred million Chinese who didn't even know the game was played?"

These days, a peasant farmer can look up scores on his cell phone. Back then, he had to rely on the Xinhua news agency, which, during the days of Cultural Revolution, did not carry college football scores.

Xinhua missed another one when it failed to report McKay's decision to go for two in the Rose Bowl against Purdue. The attempt failed, and USC lost, 14-13.

"In a season in which it was fashionable to play football for ties—one team did and won the national championship—John McKay, the ol' blackjack player, hit on thirteen and went broke in the Rose Bowl," the Steamer wrote.

•   •   •   •   •

After two years of Bruin dominance, it was pretty clear to everybody in town: Tommy Prothro was smarter than John McKay.

The Trojan coach closed the IQ gap in 1967, when he landed San Francisco City College transfer O. J. Simpson to carry the ball for him. Every week, McKay got smarter and smarter as he gave the ball to Simpson more and more, while O. J. led the Trojans to win after win. Genius move.

Bud Furillo got his first look at the kid the second week against Texas. O. J. gained 158 on thirty and the Trojans beat the Longhorns, 17–13.

"[Simpson] appears to be everything we have heard from San Francisco, where the reports on their outstanding people are never sketchy," the Steamer wrote. "You could see him get better as O. J. and the game got older."

A week after Texas, the Trojans beat Michigan State in East Lansing and elevated to number one in the rankings. It made for a very interesting afternoon when they traveled to South Bend in the middle of October to play Notre Dame. USC hadn't won back there since the Trojans broke the Steamer's heart in 1938.

The Irish began the season where they left off the year before—ranked number one. Purdue, however, popped them in the second week. They needed to beat USC to reclaim a credible position in the national championship conversation.

McKay's memory still simmered from 51–0, the dumbest day of his life. He also recalled how his team had stood in the rain and cold for twenty minutes before the "Remember Game" disaster. The coach made it clear that he would not allow his team to endure such shabby treatment again.

"We won't go out until they do—and the students get off the field," McKay told the Steamer beforehand. "I don't care if it takes until midnight. I guess 59,000 people are going to feel mighty foolish sitting in that stadium if they don't get to see a game."

Sure enough, the referee walked into the Trojan locker room beforehand and told McKay it was show time. McKay told the zebra his team wasn't going anywhere until Notre Dame took the field first.

Fine, the ref said. That'll be a 2–0 forfeit.

"That would be the best deal we've ever gotten in this

stadium," McKay told him.

The sit-down worked. The Fighting Irish were first out of the tunnel.

Notre Dame was also first into the end zone and led 7–0 after thirty minutes. But the Irish fumbled the second-half kickoff and USC tied it up when O. J. sailed in for the score on fourth-and-one. A few minutes later, when USC got the ball back, Simpson ran thirty-six yards for a touchdown, right past all those Notre Dame students with the good memories. USC intercepted seven passes, four of them by linebacker Adrian Young. O. J. scored his third touchdown from point-blank range, and the final score was 24–7. As of then, it was one of the four biggest wins in USC history.

"It had been a tradition for Trojan teams to come back to Indiana and be pantsed before the usual sellout crowd of 59,075 that comes to laugh at them," the Steamer wrote from the Notre Dame press box.

He pointed out that USC was now halfway to the national championship, which prompted a comparison from McKay between the '67 and '62 teams.

"They are very similar," McKay said. "Both of them were 5–0 at this point."

•   •   •   •   •

Meanwhile, the Einstein on the other side of town who carried a briefcase onto the field before every game had his team going good, too.

Tommy Prothro never said what was in the briefcase, but whatever it was, it had UCLA undefeated after its first six games, and the Bruins climbed in the rankings to number two behind USC.

Gary Beban was still the star of the show. In one of the biggest plays of the year, he snaked twenty-seven yards to score the winning touchdown late in the opener and beat a tough Tennessee team at the Coliseum.

A late-season tie with Oregon State knocked the Bruins down a few notches in the rankings, but Beban turned in one of the best performances of his career a week before the USC game, when he threw for 239 yards and three touchdowns and ran for forty-four and another score in a smashing 48-0 victory over Washington.

"The Bruins Saturday were the best college football team I have seen this year," the Steamer wrote from the Coliseum press box. "Beban makes them the best—and it may be that the senior from Redwood City is just reaching his peak."

As good as Beban was against the Huskies, the 46,368 in the Coliseum tuned out the rout and switched their transistors to the USC game up in the mud pits of Corvallis, Oregon. The stormy week of the USC game, the Oregon State grounds crew opted not to tarp the pitch, and the field turned into a primordial ooze. The Beavers kicked a field goal early, before the field deteriorated. The Trojans couldn't get untracked, and Oregon State held on, 3-0.

With the city championship a week away, UCLA was now number one in the country. USC fell to number three, behind Tennessee. But thanks to that terrific Beban run against the Vols, it was likely that the winner between the Trojans and Bruins would be voted national champion. The game also would give Beban and O. J. Simpson, the nation's top two Heisman Trophy contenders, one last whistle-stop in their campaigns. And the Rose Bowl would be on the line—for real, this time. No more voting by the AAWU.

If the L.A. writers needed another angle, they found it in the face-off between the intellectual capacities of the two coaches.

"We've got to prove we're not stupid," McKay told Furillo.

A more accurate quote would have been for McKay to say that he had to prove *he* wasn't stupid.

"Yes, John has heard how Tommy Prothro supposedly has the pink slip on the Trojan horse, with McKay up," the Steamer wrote. "This was McKay's first acknowledgment of the saloon topic: Prothro vs. McKay."

The day before the game, McKay told a Rotary luncheon for the two coaches that his wife had figured out how to make him at least look as smart as Prothro.

"[She] went out and bought me a briefcase," he told the crowd, according to The Steam Room report.

When the game got underway, the USC coach proved how dumb he was when the ball slipped off the side of his punter's foot and gave UCLA possession on the USC half of the field. The Bruins scored on a thirteen-yard run by Greg Jones and UCLA took the lead, 7–0.

McKay removed his dunce cap for a moment later in the first quarter when one of his defensive backs, Pat Cashman, intercepted a Beban pass and ran it back all the way. Scholars nodded in approval on USC's next possession when McKay reversed to Earl McCullough, and the world-class hurdler sprinted deep into UCLA territory. O. J. blasted through half the Bruin team from the thirteen to get into the end zone and give the Trojans the lead.

Beban hit a couple of touchdown passes to put UCLA back on top in the second half, but you had to wonder about Prothro's mental acuity when his kicker, Zenon Andrusyshyn, missed an extra point, hooked a field goal attempt, and had two other three-point tries blocked. On the other hand, maybe McKay wasn't such an idiot after all. Andrusyshyn kept a low trajectory on his ball, so McKay stationed the tallest guy on the team, six-foot-eight defensive end Bill Hayhoe, on the line. Damn if he didn't block a couple.

With the Trojans down 20–14 and facing a third-and-eight from their own thirty-six, McKay earned a nomination into Mensa International when his quarterback, Toby Page, called an audible. Toby handed the ball to Simpson, and O. J. ran sixty-four yards for a touchdown. Kicker Rikki Aldridge's extra point made the score 21–20, and that stood as the final tally when USC's defense beat the hell out of Beban for the next eleven minutes.

"This one was for blood, honor, the Pacific-8 championship, possibly the national championship—and an end to the myth that Prothro can out-coach McKay on any given Saturday," the Steamer concluded. "For two years of Bruin domination, people persisted that USC had better players but that Prothro could make up for it with his coaching brilliance."

Steamer didn't like the emphasis on the coaches' brains.

"Football players win games," he wrote, "not coaches."

Reporters asked McKay what was going through his head when O. J. broke free on his long touchdown run.

"I was thinking," he said, in Allan Malamud's sidebar, "that a lot of people in this town will say I'm smarter than I was the last two years."

•   •   •   •   •

Gary Beban won the Heisman Trophy, but the Trojans won the national championship. They finished off the season with a 14-3 snoozer over Indiana in the Rose Bowl. Their guy would win the Heisman the next year, but he first had to make it through a night out with the Steamer.

After downing a platter of ribs at the Gala Cellar on fight night, O. J. Simpson was Furillo's ringside guest at the Olympic Auditorium. They took in a terrific main event, with Ernie "Indian Red" Lopez scoring a TKO over Hedgemon Lewis, one in a series of terrific battles between the two talented welterweights

Simpson told the Steamer that boxing was his second love of sport, and that he had thought about taking it up for a living. There was just one shortcoming, though.

"Fighters don't wear face masks," said "The Juice," sensibly.

O. J. still got nailed with a couple of shots during his night out with the Steamer at the Olympic. After an action-packed prelim, the fight fans roared their approval and backed it up with cash money that they threw into the ring from every corner of the auditorium. A twenty-five-cent piece bounced off O. J.'s head. At the end of the main event, when referee John Thomas stopped the Lopez-Lewis fight, a flying cup of beer drenched the Juice.

"A guy could get hurt here," Simpson told the Steamer.

Before the season got underway, Furillo telephoned Frank Leahy in Portland to get the legendary Notre Dame coach's take on USC's extremely impressive tailback. Leahy had been in South Bend the year before to see Simpson's touchdown hat trick.

"I can't think of any runners in intercollegiate football of the past who were any better than O. J.," Leahy told Furillo. "I feel he is a combination of Gale Sayers and Jim Brown."

In 1968, the year he won the Heisman, O. J. did his best to prove Leahy correct, almost every time out. In the opener against Minnesota, he carried thirty-nine times for 236 yards and scored four touchdowns. He caught fifty-seven yards' worth of passes, returned kickoffs for seventy-two more, and brought the Trojans back from a fourth-quarter deficit to win going away. The next week, he carried thirty-eight times for 160 tough yards against Ted Hendricks and Miami. O. J. beat Jim Plunkett and Stanford almost all by himself—forty-seven carries for 228 yards and all three USC touchdowns.

A year and a half into O. J.'s career, Bud Furillo began to notice a trend. Simpson ran for 151 of his Stanford yards after halftime and 120 of his total against Miami after the break. He would later gain 136 of his 238 yards in the Oregon State game in the fourth quarter alone.

"Simpson hits the holes and the people in them sharper and with more determination after halftime," the Steamer said. "Nobody can stop Simpson when he is determined to make five yards."

USC went into the Rose Bowl with a 9-0-1 record and a number two ranking in the polls, right behind the Trojans' Pasadena opponent, number-one-ranked Ohio State. A few days before the game, the Steamer ate breakfast with his old pal Woody Hayes, whom Furillo re-introduced to Southern California as "the most successful unpopular coach in America."

One Rose Bowl tradition in those years was for the two teams to compete in the Beef Bowl, a meat-eating contest at Lawry's prime rib joint on La Cienega Boulevard. Woody, however, didn't like the celebration of gluttony, so he held his team out of the competition. With Ohio State refusing to come out of its corner, USC won the Beef Bowl, 278 pounds to nothing.

"However," the Steamer said of the Trojans, "they remain three-and-a-half-point underdogs."

Early in the game, it looked like a good price for Trojan backers when USC jumped to a 10-0 lead, six points coming on an eighty-yard run by Mr. Heisman. Then the Trojans turned the ball over five times, with Simpson responsible for two of the fumbles. The stronger Ohio State team made much of the holiday gift packages, turning them into seventeen second-half points and winning the fifty-fifth Rose Bowl, 27–16.

When it was over, the Ohio State coach couldn't leave the ballpark without adding to his reputation for Rose Bowl rudeness. Upset because USC scored a meaningless touchdown on the last play of the game, "Woody didn't bother to visit with USC's John McKay for the traditional handshake," Bud Furillo wrote. "McKay stood like a faked out cornerback as Woody ran a square out away from the Trojan coach into the Ohio State locker room."

O. J. WANTS SAYERS-SIZED SALARY; BUFFALO WARY

AUGUST 3, 1969

While O. J. Simpson's advisors have made it clear that they will never permit their client to perform for sweatshop wages of $50,000 a year in Buffalo, they should be advised that Bills owner Ralph C. Scrooge Jr. has adopted a harder line as well.

Scrooge Jr. checked with Scrooge Sr. in Chicago the other day. Papa George Halas informed that he is paying Gale Sayers $70,000 a year. It has been learned from Cleveland that Leroy Kelly is earning $75,000 for leading the National Football League in rushing.

It is only in jest of course that liberties are taken with the name of the Bills' Ralph Wilson, a decent fellow who hardly fits the role of King Midas. . . .

He has taken the position that until Simpson proves himself to be a better player than Sayers or Kelly, O. J. shouldn't be in a higher tax bracket than they are.

At this stage, I am beginning to feel for Simpson, who is being shopped like a carnival act by Sports Headliners Inc. I suspect that any day now it will be announced that they are considering an offer for Simpson to strip in Tijuana—or at least open a chain of automobile seat cover shops there.

Since he left USC, the Heisman Trophy winner has been reported to be on his way to the Canadian League, the Continental League, the Texas League, the Barnstorming League, and the Pineapple League.

I find this to be degrading to a classy fellow like Simpson.

•   •   •   •   •

In the year man landed on the moon, one big question emerged in college football: How in this world would USC do without O. J. Simpson?

The answer was 10-0-1, another Rose Bowl victory and a season that ended with the 1969 Trojans ranked third in the country.

Film director Sam Peckinpah scored a big hit that year with *The Wild Bunch*, a gloriously violent movie about a band of desperadoes on the prowl in Texas and Mexico. Most memorable, of course, is the scene at the end when Ernest Borgnine, Bill Holden, and the boys shoot up a Mexican border town with a Gatling gun.

With USC's defensive line laying waste to opposing offenses, defensive tackle Al Cowlings nicknamed the five-man unit "The Wild Bunch." Then somebody gave Bud Furillo the idea to dress up the players in cowboy get-ups, take their picture, and publish it in the paper.

It was the greatest posed publicity shot since Notre Dame saddled up the Four Horsemen and outlined Miller, Stuhldreher, Layden, and Crowley against a blue-gray October sky. USC defensive end Jimmy Gunn looked a lot like Jimi Hendrix, with his hippie headband and his rifle cocked lefty, the same way the guitar man held his axe. Defensive tackle Tody Smith wore desert boots instead of the cowboy variety. In the background, out beyond middle guard Bubba Scott, defensive end Charlie Weaver and Al "A. C." Cowlings (who would later gain fame as O. J.'s chauffeur the night of his arrest for murder), somebody parked what appeared to be an Oldsmobile in the background.

Nobody would have remembered the Wild Bunch, probably, had the Trojans not come from behind about every other week to win games late in the fourth quarter.

A 10-3 win over Michigan in Pasadena concluded the first decade of John McKay's career at USC, and the Steamer thought it was time to put the coach's recent accomplishments into perspective.

McKay's record over the previous three years stood at 29-2-2. Since the opening of the '67 season, the Trojans had never

EVEN PROS PICKING AT MCKAY'S BRAIN
MARCH 28, 1965

Is John McKay the smartest offensive coach in football?

Evidence continues to mount for this verdict.

The Trojan coach is a much sought after professor at football clinics around the nation. He gives private lessons, too.

A recent visitor at USC was the Army coach, Paul Dietzel. Army intends to install the "Hungry I" formation next year.

The Steamer calls it the "Hungry I" because McKay gets backs and ends running in all directions, like a pride of famished lions eager to feast on yardage any way they can. . . .

McKay borrowed pro-type ideas and exploits them better than the professionals. He instills confidence in his players. He has them believing they could score on the Cleveland Browns on a day when the Baltimore Colts couldn't.

The USC style of football has been copied by many of the professional teams, with Norman Van Brocklin's Minnesota Vikings emerging as the best imitators. The Colts use a lot of McKay's stuff, too. . . .

Why has McKay advanced to the head of the class in coaching? He doesn't believe this is the case, but explains:

"We believe in the wide open aspects of the game which people like to see. My philosophy of life is the same as that of John Wooden—do something different. Of course John has himself in a rut. All he does is win the national championship every year."

been ranked lower than seventh in the thirty-nine Associated Press polls. They were ranked number one in fourteen of them and finished the three seasons listed at first, fourth, and third. All three teams made it to the Rose Bowl, and two of them won it. Going back the full ten years of the McKay era, the Trojans had won three of the five Rose Bowls they played in, two national titles, and two Heisman Trophies. They had eighteen players named All-American.

A few days after the Rose Bowl win, the Steamer put a headline over his column that read, "McKay: The Best in the Business."

He did not entertain arguments on behalf of Bear Bryant,

Ara Parseghian, Woody Hayes, Darrell Royal, or anybody else.
"The case," he said, "is closed."

•   •   •   •   •

The night before USC played Alabama in a friendly to open the
1970 season, they held a reception at the Vestavia Hills Country Club outside Birmingham, Alabama, where Crimson Tide
football coach Paul "Bear" Bryant played host to his friend and
counterpart, John McKay.

Bryant and McKay sat at a fairly large, round table, in a
group that included Bud Furillo. In front of the Steamer and a
few other writers from L.A. and Alabama, Bryant asked McKay
about the backgrounds of a couple of his players, including Trojan tailback Clarence Davis.

The year before, Davis had led the Pac-8 in rushing with
1,351 yards. McKay told Bryant they'd be happy to know down
south that Clarence Davis was born in Birmingham, not far from
Legion Field, site of the next day's game. Yet Davis, like every
other African American kid in Birmingham, in Alabama, and in
the entire Old South, never got a recruiting sniff from the Tide.
All Bryant could do was shake his head and mutter, while McK-
ay listed several other black kids on his team or in the recruiting
pipeline with connections to Alabama and the South.

Bryant looked at McKay, paused for effect, and cracked up
the table with a single-word accusatory description of his guest
from California: "Carpetbagger!"

They all laughed, and the next day USC beat Alabama, 42–
21, in a game that helped take Jim Crow off the rosters of big-
time college football programs in the South.

Bryant had been plenty successful with all-white teams, winning national championships at Alabama in 1961, 1964, and
1965. But he knew his program was slipping and he felt he got
screwed out of a national championship in '66, when his undefeated and un-integrated team finished the season ranked third
behind Notre Dame and Michigan State. It didn't help that Alabama didn't play anybody during the regular season west of Oxford or north of Knoxville, or that the Crimson Tide had become

a pariah in polite college football company.

"Our 1966 team was the finest college football team I've ever seen," the Bear told the Steamer, in a column ahead of the somewhat historic game that Bryant had shockingly scheduled with USC for the night of September 12, 1970, at Legion Field. "But it wasn't recognized because of criticism of our schedule. And rightfully so. We were limited in the people we could schedule because of the segregation problem."

The Alabama coach said he went to work on "the segregation problem" as soon as his second year in Tuscaloosa. When the administration wasn't looking, Bryant scheduled the Tide to play Penn State in the 1959 Liberty Bowl, which in those days was held in Philadelphia.

Alabama's Klan-backed governor, John Malcolm Patterson, must have fallen asleep at the switch to allow Alabama to play a team with black players on the roster. Patterson, after all, had defeated George Wallace for the Democratic gubernatorial nomination in 1958 because Wallace wasn't racist enough. Wallace, of course, was the guy who later stood on the front steps of the Alabama campus to keep African American students out of it.

The Tide's 7–0 loss to the Nittany Lions in '59 mattered hardly at all to Bryant. More importantly for him, he scored a major victory by establishing a precedent for Alabama to play integrated teams in bowl games. The Penn State game, he told the Steamer, "was the start of getting us out of the woods."

As the 1960s came to an end, Alabama, as a state, hadn't exactly become a place where the Huxtables might relocate, but at least it was no longer acceptable to murder little girls in churches. As times changed, Bryant found a way to insinuate the idea among Alabama football thinkers that if they wanted their program to remain relevant, they damn well better eliminate "the segregation problem."

"Eventually, he was able to convince Alabama that if his teams could play integrated teams in bowl games it should be granted the same privilege in the regular season," the Steamer wrote.

Having accomplished this important breakthrough, Bryant

felt it was time to take the big step with the public. It helped that he had grown friendly over the years with John McKay. In February 1970, the two of them got together to play golf in Las Vegas and put together a home-and-home series—1970 in Legion Field and 1971 in the Coliseum.

Looking at USC's three years of dominance and its expectation to have a very strong team again in 1970, Bryant told the Steamer, "I'm not sure it was a smart move to get USC on our schedule."

It was a nice try on the coach's part to make himself look dumb. But the Steamer was convinced Bryant knew exactly what he was doing. Bryant knew the Tide was in for a severe beating and that Southern football fans needed to absorb it, Steamer's theory held.

On a steamy night in Birmingham, McKay, with a team made up almost entirely of black players, stomped all-white Alabama.

"The hospitable folks of Alabama began to leave Legion Field with eleven minutes to play between the Crimson Tide and USC Saturday night," the Steamer wrote in his opening paragraph the next day. "And some may have been wondering if it might be a good idea to search for some black running backs."

USC sophomore Sam Cunningham stole the show. At six foot three and 215 pounds, Cunningham, according to McKay, could have played twenty different positions on the football field. That night in Birmingham, Sam stuck with fullback and blew down Alabama with twelve carries for 135 yards and two touchdowns.

"Cunningham explodes through the line almost as fast as O. J. Simpson," the Steamer wrote, "and mercy does he have power when he gets his 215 pounds moving."

Clarence Davis, the Birmingham kid, added seventy-three on thirteen, Lou Harris contributed sixty-one on thirteen, and Mike Berry had sixty-four on eleven.

"All are black," Furillo pointed out, in case nobody noticed.

As the 72,175 fans emptied Legion Field in the fourth quarter, some of them must have known that Bear already had recruited his first African American scholarship player: running back Wilbur Jackson. Bryant signed three more black freshmen the next year, and he also ripped off a JC transfer from the recruiting list of his good buddy McKay. The Trojan coach got a lead on a very fine defensive end named John Mitchell, a Mobile, Alabama, native who played JuCo ball at Eastern Arizona. McKay thought he had Mitchell in the bag, and couldn't help but chortle to Bryant during the off-season about how he had stolen another one from the heart of Bear territory.

The cunning Bryant moved quickly. He put word out to his staff to find this Mitchell kid and make him an offer. Mitchell switched from USC to Alabama, and it probably came as a surprise in the Coliseum in September when McKay looked up and saw the kid lining up on the other side of the ball when his team had it.

Alabama shocked the heavily favored Trojans, 17-10. The Tide then went 11-1 on the year—and 109-16-1 over the next eleven years under Bryant, finishing in the top ten in the Associated Press poll nine times.

It wouldn't be long before African American players dominated the rosters on Alabama and every other team in the south—and in major college football, and in the National Football League, their abilities helping make the amateur and pro games the most popular sports in the country.

•   •   •   •   •

The promise of Birmingham melted into a mediocre couple years for the Trojans, but going into spring drills in 1972, McKay appeared optimistic when he had Bud Furillo and the rest of the favored over to Julie's.

Cunningham returned for his senior year, and he would be joined in the backfield by brash sophomore Anthony Davis, who promised to "put this school back on the map." Trojan quarterback Mike Rae had showed enough promise as a backup the previous year that a lot of people on the team thought he should have been the starter. The offensive line that had been learning on the job for two years was now a solid veteran unit. Rae had a smorgasbord of receivers: Charles Young, still the best tight end in program history; sprinter Edesel Garrison, who owned times of 20.4 in the 200 and 45.1 in the 400; McKay's kid, Johnny, who contributed as a sophomore; and the best of them all, Pro Football Hall of Famer Lynn Swann.

Defensively, the experienced front line featured All-American John Grant. As a group, the back end picked off those twenty-eight passes. In the middle, sophomore linebacker Richard Wood would become the first three-time All-American in school history.

At Julie's, McKay told the writers he had a plan to cut down on a fumbling problem that had plagued the team in 1971.

"I've decided not to play guys with arms shorter than the football," he said.

•   •   •   •   •

McKay knew he'd know a lot more about his club after the first week on the road in Little Rock, against Arkansas, which was ranked fourth in the country. Hogs quarterback Joe Ferguson had been mentioned as a preseason Heisman Trophy candidate, and they were favored by six points.

With the game scheduled for the evening, Furillo swung by McKay's hotel suite during the day to get read on the coach. The mood was giddy.

"Start the season!" McKay bellowed as they flipped on the TV to watch a little bit of Georgia Tech-Tennessee.

Under the lights at War Memorial Stadium, the world learned why McKay exuded such enthusiasm. Rae threw for more yards than the Heisman Trophy candidate. The Trojan doctors had fixed up Rod McNeill, the starting tailback who had broken his hip the year before, well enough for him to gain 117 yards. Taking the blanket off the young defense, McKay unveiled a fast band of attacking raw talent. Richard Wood turned out to be scary good. He dropped thirteen Razorback runners all by himself and intercepted a pass.

"Wood, the eighteen-year-old from Elizabeth, New Jersey, hits so hard that the runners have to check their hole card when they get up," the Steamer wrote.

The 31–10 victory shot the Trojans to the top of the Associated Press poll. They followed it up with KOs over Oregon State, Illinois, and Michigan State, to set up a blood match in Palo Alto with undefeated and fifteenth-ranked Stanford. The two-time defending Rose Bowl champions had beaten the Trojans back to back, after having lost to them for eleven straight years. The manner in which the Stanfords celebrated their success, however, deeply upset the Trojans.

McKay and his African American players said the verbal abuse directed at them by a bile segment of Stanford partisans after the 1970 loss in Palo Alto far exceeded anything they'd heard in the lands of Bull Connor or Orville Faubus. It outraged McKay so much that in the 1972 game, he was throwing for a score on the last play of the game in the Trojans' 30–21 victory. When Stanford coach Jack Christiansen expressed his displeasure afterwards, McKay said his only regret was that the Trojans didn't win by 2,000 points.

"Street fights aren't tidy," the Steamer mentioned in the first paragraph of his game story. "These bitter rivals went at it as if the game were being played in a prison yard."

Sophomore tailback Anthony Davis began his PR campaign on behalf of the obscure USC football program by scoring a touchdown from a yard out late in the first half. Kneeling in the end zone, Davis "did a dance that will earn him a cup at the prom," Furillo's story said.

Davis made a larger impression two weeks later against Washington, scoring on runs of forty-four and fourteen yards. A week later, in an Oregon rainstorm, A. D. broke open a scoreless tie in the third quarter with touchdown runs of forty-eight and fifty-five yards.

The week of the Washington State game is when Davis actually made the remarks about putting USC on the map, reported in The Steam Room. Indeed, the Trojan tailback attracted some attention for the university when he gained 195 yards on thirty-one carries against the Cougars, scored three touchdowns, and returned a kickoff sixty-nine yards.

For the fourth time in seven years, the city championship

showdown with UCLA was for the Rose Bowl. But the personal stakes for McKay weren't what they used to be. Tommy Prothro had blown out of UCLA to take the Rams job, so it was no longer a matchup between him and McKay to see who was dumber. That competition ended in a 3–3 tie.

In the Bruins' second year under Pepper Rodgers, they shot up in the rankings after beating top-ranked Nebraska in their opener, and UCLA was still ranked number eight in the country coming into the USC game.

Under Rodgers, the Bruins ran a wishbone offense directed by Mark Harmon, son of Tommy, the Heisman Trophy winner out of Michigan and former broadcast partner of the Steamer with the Los Angeles Chargers. "Old 98" knew early on that his kid—later to become a huge TV star—was a pretty good athlete. When Mark was only fourteen months old, "He went off the diving board and swam the length of the pool," Tommy told the Steamer in an interview conducted in the backyard of his Brentwood home.

Against the Trojans, UCLA's game plan appeared to be to keep the score down, and the Bruins did a fine job of achieving respectability. They only lost 24–7.

"Fullback Randy Tyler got the ball seventeen times" for the Bruins, the Steamer reported, "probably because he was open."

Only Notre Dame remained on USC's regular-season schedule, and Anthony Davis, batting leadoff, ran the opening kickoff ninety-seven yards for a touchdown. In the end zone, Davis slid to his knees and repeated the little jig he'd first broken out against Stanford. He gave five repeat performances in the afternoon, none more meaningful than after Notre Dame scored a couple of times in the second half to sneak dangerously close to the Trojans.

"There was 1:19 left in the third quarter as Cliff Brown kicked off" for Notre Dame, the Steamer wrote. "His kick went out of bounds. Then he kicked again. This was a mistake. Davis took the ball on his four-yard line and his 190 pounds were bunched into cement as he hit the wedge up the middle and broke to his left. He beat two potential tacklers going down the south sideline and was looking back after his second touchdown return of a kickoff."

Following the afternoon's knee-dance recital, only Woody Hayes and his Ohio State Buckeyes stood between USC, its greatest season ever, and John McKay's 100th career victory.

The emotionally unpredictable Ohio State coach arrived in Pasadena as irritable as ever, although the Steamer, as usual, was happy to see him. They went out to breakfast, but if you had Woody and the Buckeyes showing up for the Beef Bowl, you lost. A foodie Woody wasn't.

"We all dig our graves with our teeth, anyhow," he told the Steamer.

The largest crowd in Rose Bowl history showed up for the game: 106,869. Early arrivals who sat behind the Ohio State bench were treated to one of Woody's most spectacular emotional eruptions, almost as good as when he slugged the kid from Clemson in the '78 Gator Bowl. Woody's punch-out in Jacksonville had cost him his job, but it wasn't as big a deal when he went on the attack at the Rose Bowl on New Year's Day in 1973. In Pasadena, he only hit a photographer, not a football player.

L.A. Times shooter Art Rogers had been working the Ohio State sideline a few minutes before the game. Rogers's lens had Woody in its sights when all of a sudden, it was the coach who snapped. He bolted toward Rogers, grabbed the camera and shoved it into the photog's face.

"That ought to take care of you, you son of a bitch," Hayes told Rogers impolitely, according to the photographer's account, which he gave to the Pasadena police.

When a reporter at the post-game press conference asked Woody about it, Hayes spiked the microphone and stalked off.

"Woody never stops hitting," the Steamer observed.

Rogers filed a criminal complaint, but Woody never did any time behind the rap.

Ohio State hung in with the Trojans for a half, but Lynn Swann, the smooth-as-silk Trojan flanker, found the soft spots in the Buckeye secondary after intermission and quarterback Mike Rae found him six times for 106 yards.

The passing opened up the running for Anthony Davis, who gained 157 yards, much of it behind the devastating lead blocking from fullback Sam Cunningham, who dominated his position that year unlike anybody in any slot for USC before or since. Sam turned linebackers into dust, sometimes taking out two or even three defenders on a single play.

Cunningham, who had launched his career with the spectacular game against Alabama two years earlier, launched himself into end zone four times from short distance to earn Rose Bowl MVP honors. Just before Sam's last dive, McKay could be seen on the sidelines hailing Woody Hayes, pantomiming the Buckeye coach how Cunningham was about to go over the falls again.

The 42-17 win convinced the suspicious, the cantankerous, the paranoid, and the proud. That is, it convinced Woody Hayes.

"It's the finest football team I've ever seen," he told the Steamer.

Chapter 13

WOODEN, WALTON, AND OTHER BRUINS

You wonder if Bill Russell's USF team would have done much better against the aroused Bruins. Russell and Walton would have matched up pretty well as collegians. There was a determination on Walton's part to score in this game. He's an unselfish player. But he seemed ready to explode with his eagerness to do it all as the streak moved to fifty-eight in a row.

—January 20, 1973

ohn Wooden had known Bud Furillo for twenty-four years, so the teacher/coach trusted the columnist to take care of one of his prized students on an interview date in the spring of 1972.

The last time Furillo had gone out on the town with the best college player in his sport, future Heisman Trophy winner O. J. Simpson had to dodge a beer shower at the Olympic Auditorium and rub a knot out of his head after somebody bounced a twenty-five-cent piece off it. Instead of the bloody, smoky halls of the downtown L.A. fight palace, Bill Walton only had to deal with autograph freaks the day the Steamer escorted him to the Cockney Pride Restaurant in Beverly Hills for lunch.

It was two months before Walton's arrest in an anti-Vietnam War protest in front of the UCLA administration building, and it had yet to become public knowledge that Walton had been hypnotized into the psychedelic groove of the Grateful Dead. There had been no publicity about his transcendental meditation, or his vegetarianism—probably because Walton hadn't paid $400 for his mantra yet and because he still ate meat. Walton was only the best college basketball player in the country, and nothing more, the day he downed a platter of steak and eggs with the Steamer and *Herald Examiner* beat writer Doug Krikorian.

His 1971–1972 UCLA basketball team was also making a case it just might be the best in the history of the college game. It was a year of Los Angeles winning streaks. The Lakers ran off thirty-three straight and USC's football team also won twelve in a row in 1972. In this period of consecutive victories, the most impressive of them all—the one that still stands as the lengthiest in any major American sport—was in the middle of its making.

UCLA had already won fifteen in a row by the time Walton made the varsity. By the end of his sophomore season, it grew to forty-five. Walton finished his junior year with the streak at seventy-five. It reached eighty-eight in his senior season, before a back injury to the Bruin center allowed Notre Dame to beat the Bruins.

John Wooden always said his favorite championship team was his first, in 1964—the one with Walt Hazzard and a bunch of small and fast guys who ate up the opposition with their full-court zone press. For pure dominance, no single player exercised more of it than Lew Alcindor during his three-year UCLA career.

Everybody moistened up when UCLA won the title in 1975, Wooden's last season. But when it came to the pure joy and beauty of basketball, there was no edition of the Bruin dynasty that matched the John Wooden creation of 1971–1972, the one that attained perhaps the closest earthly manifestation to the game's Platonic ideal. Massive individual talent, meshed into selfless, synchronized movement—this was a band beyond description. Basketball purists took warmth in how the boys enacted the vision that sprang from the imagination of the modest but demanding genius who guided them.

Walton, in the middle of the unit, made the whole thing work. As a sophomore, the tall, red-headed nineteen-year-old could pluck a rebound off the defensive board, whip his body around in mid-air, and snap off a perfect chest pass forty feet down the court to hit a sprinting teammate in perfect stride going the other way—before his feet ever touched the floor. If somebody challenged him in the lane, Walton elevated in perfect time to a perfect coordinate to slap the shot into abject harmlessness, or, oftentimes, redirect the pitiful attempt to an awaiting teammate, who swung the action in the opposite direction at breakneck pace.

Walton swirled in constant, controlled motion when UCLA dropped into a half-court set, in conjunction with the actions of every other member of his team, a beautiful dance of five moving as one. When the coaching wizard's design called for Walton to receive the ball deep in the hole with his back to the basket, he sprang pinpoint passes to teammates cutting free or touched them off with a flick so quick none of the collapsing defenders ever saw them coming.

At the top of the key, he threw passes over defenders to teammates at exactly the right spot on the floor for them to hit their open bank shots, according to the Wooden plan, or to proceed to the hoop for easy lay-ups. He hit open jumpers at a high percentage out to eighteen feet, so defenders couldn't just ignore him out there when he didn't have the ball. Their mistake. Soon as they came out on him, or if they left space unattended around the rim, Walton flashed to the unguarded spot and timed his leaping arrival with a teammate's high-arching pass to drop the coin right into the slot.

He made you pay if you didn't think he could jump into a passing lane and dribble the length of the floor for a lay-in. Defenders also might have thought they had done their job if they forced him deep into the baseline. What goofs. He'd squeeze around them with a dervish spin under the iron and kiss the apple off the glass and into the rim.

Walton emerged onto the national sports scene at a time when Tom Seaver dominated National League hitters and nobody could stop Kareem Abdul-Jabbar in Milwaukee. Nicklaus and Palmer were still knocking them in the hole, and Bill Shoemaker and Laffit Pincay could get them home under the whip. Willie Stargell had just hit forty-eight home runs for the world champion Pirates, which was one better than Hank Aaron's

forty-seven for Atlanta. Ali and Frazier had made boxing relevant again, and the L.A. fight scene was never hotter than it was
with Mando Ramos on top and Danny Lopez and Bobby Chacon
coming up. Nobody looked prettier than Otis Taylor or Paul
Warfield catching footballs, and very few athletes in any sport
played theirs as well as Bobby Orr did hockey in those days for
the Boston Bruins. A swimmer named Mark Spitz was also warming up for Munich.

Bud Furillo appreciated all of the artists of athleticism. But
as the calendar turned into early 1972, he realized he was witnessing perhaps the single greatest athletic accomplishment in
the golden age of all L.A. sports.

It revolved around a six-foot-eleven sophomore basketball
player barely ten games into his career, who was already being
mentioned as one of the greatest of all time. Watching the Bruins
in 1971 and '72, Furillo knew he was witnessing something special congeal around Bill Walton, the astonishing young center
who would later be voted into the Naismith Memorial Basketball
Hall of Fame and named as one of the fifty greatest players in the
first fifty years of the National Basketball Association, despite a
professional career that was severely constricted by injuries.

At the end of a notes column that bounced from Senator Alan
Cranston's fifth-place finish in the previous week's Sunkist Invitational senior-division sixty-yard dash, to unfounded rumors of
an O. J. Simpson trade from Buffalo to the Rams, to reports that
the previous year's Kentucky Derby winner, Canonero II, would
not be racing in Santa Anita's winter meeting, the Steamer concluded his January 26, 1972, column in the *Herald Examiner*
with an announcement.

"My current favorite athlete," he wrote, "is Bill Walton."

•   •   •   •   •

UCLA's streak had reached thirty-eight, and it had three
more regular season games to go when Bud Furillo and Doug
Krikorian, his UCLA beat man, drove out to Westwood on
March 1, 1972, as the Bruins were wrapping up their Pac-8 season before their next championship playoff run.

"The jolly red giant met Doug Krikorian and myself in the athletic department office in Westwood where Coach Wooden introduced us to his hard-working player," the Steamer wrote.

Furillo's story that ran in the *Herald Examiner* five days after the interview gave the world one of its earliest mainstream-media glimpses into the Walton worldview. It demonstrated that there was more to the guy than his outlet pass. In the first opening Steamer gave Walton on a controversial issue, the big guy took it to the rack.

"How do you feel about things?" Furillo asked.

After talking about his upbringing, his friends, and his lack of concern for material possessions, Walton zeroed in on an item that was still of some concern in a nation emerging from Jim Crow and urban riots—a country not yet past its racial divide.

"I think one of the reasons I'm getting so much publicity is because I'm white," Walton told the Steamer. "I think the biggest problem is racism."

The remarks reported in The Steam Room were among the first to suggest that Walton was not your conventional six-foot-eleven, 225-pound gym rat. The Steamer identified him as the son of a district director in the San Diego County welfare department, which the columnist said might explain a few things about Walton's "strong feeling for the underprivileged." It was the view of the thoughtful college student that some people "have gotten it into their heads that because they're white, they're right." Maybe it was the white man who flew to the moon, Walton said, but that didn't make them better than anybody in the African bush.

"Maybe they never had any desire to go the moon," Walton said of the folks in the jungle.

As for himself and his own skin color, Walton said, "It's been a long time since there's been a big white player who makes people say, 'This guy's good.' You have to realize that people who support basketball are white, upper middle class. So the white fans dig on me because I'm white."

In his conversation with Walton, the Steamer felt perfectly comfortable engaging in the subject of race, and he moved ahead into the dangerous testimony. The Steamer's remarks very well could have gotten him into trouble in a later age, along the lines of the verbal missteps that swallowed up Jimmy "The Greek" Snyder and Al Campanis. Civil rights activists savaged the oddsmaker and the Dodger GM for their ill-considered discussions, on, for instance, the theory of natural selection and how it pertains to African American athletic success and also how black people don't have the "necessities," in Campanis's ill-chosen words, to swim or coach third base.

"I'd be a damned liar," Furillo told Walton, "if I didn't think it was important to me that you're white." Being white, he said, "doesn't mean you're bad."

The Steamer went on to say in his conversation with Walton that, in a day of "emerging prides," there was "no reason for white people to lose theirs."

Discussions of white pride are usually reserved for Ku Klux Klan conventions, or for the Aryan Brotherhood caucus in any state or federal prison. The Steamer probably would have been on safer ground had he confined his ethnic identification to being a proud Italian American. In the racially and ethnically mixed melting pot of Sharon Line, his old neighborhood in Youngstown, Ohio, the young Steamer had known black people as just folks. They were no different, in his view, than the other poor, tough, and hard-working steel townies whose families struggled like his own during the Depression.

Throughout his life, Furillo had delved deeply into black culture and music. He was a Zoot Suiter. He took dates to Central Avenue jazz clubs. When he first started out in sportswriting, he rather clumsily sought to draw attention to the African American pioneers in all sports by reminding his readers that they were black.

In their conversation, Walton helped educate the Steamer to the sensitivities of an increasingly multicultural society. The UCLA star politely agreed that people should take pride in themselves. He just didn't think his own accomplishments should be viewed through a racial prism.

"If I was black, I wouldn't be getting as much publicity,"

Walton said. "I would just be another big black center who does things well."

Moving beyond race, the Steamer reported that Walton was "a young man devoted to his family and to his coach." Bill told Furillo that John Wooden had helped his "total life."

"'He coaches you as a human being, which in turn helps you as a basketball player,'" the Steamer quoted Walton as saying.

At the end of their long lunch, Walton offered to chip in to pay for the check, "to take care of an extra dollar needed on the tip," the Steamer wrote. The Steamer fly-swatted the buck away, like Walton rejecting a shot in the lane.

"Someday, I'll be sorry I didn't take that dollar," he wrote. "It would have been nice to frame above the fireplace and tell the grandchildren it came from one of sport's finest young men."

He told Walton, "Thanks so much for giving us this opportunity to learn something about you."

"You're welcome," Walton said. "I enjoyed the meal."

•   •   •   •   •

It took the Steamer a while to break through for an interview with one of Walton's more prominent predecessors. A New Yorker by birth, the young Lew Alcindor did not take well to Los Angeles in the early years of his tenure at UCLA, or to its media. Nor did he care much for the college of his choice, according to interviews he gave to New York journalists.

"Most of the people I've met out here don't strike me as being for real," Alcindor told one national magazine. "This isn't much of a campus. It's beautiful, but there's not that much going on. I couldn't take those dormitories. It's too loony around there."

He told United Press International that UCLA students "seem out of it. They don't seem to know what's going on around them. . . . They have a limited point of view, as opposed to the people of New York City."

If he had to do it all over again, Alcindor said, he would have gone to Stanford. Or Cal. Or Michigan.

John Wooden and Alcindor's UCLA teammates defended Big Lew and said the magazines set him up for the negative portrayals. Local writers put in their interview requests to clear the matter up. Alcindor wasn't interested.

"As you may know," Furillo wrote in 1967, "Alcindor is the most unreachable young man in the history of sports, and it isn't because of his height."

The Steamer reported how one local columnist—he didn't say who it was, or even if it was himself—had asked the UCLA sports information department whether Alcindor could spare a few minutes of his time.

"Alcindor said he can't make it," a UCLA press agent said.

"Did he say why?" the columnist asked.

"He isn't the sort of fellow you ask why," was the response.

"What would happen if you did ask him why?" the columnist persisted.

"He would ignore me," the publicist said.

Lew did most of his speaking with his skyhook and, in his first year of college ball, before they outlawed the dunk, with his assaults on the rim. In UCLA's 73-58 semifinal win over Houston in Alcindor's sophomore season, Lew scored nineteen points on only eleven shots. Furillo commented that Alcindor "was as completely unselfish with the ball as he isn't with his time off the floor."

The next night, UCLA beat Dayton, 79-64, to finish Alcindor's rookie season as the undefeated national champion. The Steamer reported that his UCLA beat writer, Mitch Chortkoff, had spotted Alcindor in the Louisville airport the next day, catching a flight home to New York.

"Thanks for all your cooperation," Chortkoff had remarked rather sarcastically to "The Big Fella."

"Don't mention it," Alcindor had replied.

It was one down and two to go for the player for whom anything less than three straight national championships would have been considered a disappointment. The next year, the Steamer remained slightly miffed as Alcindor continued his arm's-length relationship with Los Angeles and its sporting press.

Furillo didn't let it get in the way of appreciating Alcindor's greatness, however—and basketball greatness rarely ascended to the level it attained in the Los Angeles Sports Arena on March 22, 1968, when UCLA played Houston again in the NCAA semis. Earlier in the year, Houston and its star big man, Elvin Hayes, had snapped a 47-game UCLA winning streak by defeating the Bruins, 71–69, in front of 52,693 fans in the Astrodome. The loss occurred nine days after Alcindor nearly had his eyeball scratched out against Cal.

His visual health restored for the playoffs, Lew scored nineteen in the 101–69 wipeout of the Cougars. All the UCLA starters hit double figures, with guards Mike Warren and Lucius Allen pulling up for mid-range jumpers on the break and forward Lynn Shackleford dropping in high-arching, left-handed twenty-five-footers from the corner.

"You can finish a cigar waiting for Shack's shots to come down," the Steamer observed.

More importantly for UCLA against Houston, Alcindor "played defense like a National Football League cornerback, intercepting passes all over the place," Furillo wrote. Lew also shut down "The Big E," as they called Elvin Hayes. The Houston big man scored thirty-nine in the Astrodome, but not quite as many in the Sports Arena.

"The Cougars got balanced scoring from 'The Small E,'" Furillo wrote, "five in each half."

"This was easily the best Bruin performance of the Alcindor Era," the Steamer continued, "and most of the 15,742 who watched it, including the Big E, would have to conclude that Big Lew never played better. He's had a tendency to loaf on defense but the seven-footer from New York City didn't even coast to the bench for timeouts. He was emotional the way a charged-up athlete should be as he raised the first finger of his right hand to let everyone know who was number one."

Houston coach Guy Lewis called the game "the greatest exhibition of basketball I've ever seen."

UCLA beat North Carolina in the anti-climatic final, 78–55.

The next year, Lew lightened up, and the Steamer finally got to interview him.

"Alcindor found himself thrust into the role of travel critic as soon as he arrived at UCLA from New York City," Furillo said. "Magazines outdid themselves publishing his diatribes on Southern California."

It was kind of a misunderstanding, Alcindor explained—writers who had it in for L.A. were using him to crack on the town.

"Nobody ever asked me what I thought was good about UCLA or Los Angeles," he said. He cited John Wooden, his University of California education, and the weather as upsides of his move to Los Angeles.

The Steamer found a news hook for the column. Boston

BRUINS READY TO ROLL BRONCOS
MARCH 14, 1969

Whew, I thought it would never end. But now that the Bruins have snapped out of their slump, they should go all the way again as college basketball's best team.

Santa Clara should be no problem tomorrow afternoon in a quarter-final at Pauley. The Bruins probably defeated a better team than the Broncos last night when they handled a slick New Mexico State team, 53–38.

The Amazing Aggies played it close for half the game, trailing UCLA by only four points, 21–17, in one of the lowest scoring halves since the old Pitt-Fordham football games of the late '30s. They played three scoreless ties for those of you who came in late.

The Aggie slowdown seemed to dull the senses of the Bruins for awhile, but Lew Alcindor and his associates must have gotten some group therapy from Dr. John Wooden in the dressing room.

UCLA rubbed out the Aggies within a few minutes of the second half and Alcindor even got physical. He returned the shoves of the Aggies who tried to intimidate him.

Wilt Chamberlain, for one, wonders if Lew can be physical enough to dominate the NBA. But then you should hear what Lew has to say about Wilt's ball-handling. . . .

Alcindor turned an ankle, but he'll be back to match up with Santa Clara's Dennis Awtrey. Lew wouldn't miss that one for the world. . . .

You never like to see a great one hurt. But it won't decide the Western Regional final. Lew could take care of Santa Clara playing with a crutch.

Celtics general manager Red Auerbach had spouted off back East about Alcindor, saying that Lew "extends himself only when he wants to."

Furillo took issue with Red, pointing out that Lew "has gotten the Bruins out of more jams on the court this year than F. Lee Bailey has accomplished in courtrooms."

"I don't know why he would say something like that," Alcindor said of Auerbach.

In 1969, Alcindor no longer had Mike Warren and Lucius Allen in the backcourt to take some of the pressure off of him. The Bruins actually lost a game at home, to USC—their first setback in Pauley Pavilion since they opened the place in 1966.

"It has been a little tougher this year," he said, "but it makes the victories sweeter."

Alcindor finished his career with thirty-seven points and twenty rebounds in UCLA's 92–72 championship win over Purdue.

He had met his burden of monumental expectation.

•   •   •   •   •

John Wooden was not the sort of guy who did Julie's. He didn't drink, which was proof that no man in this material world is perfect. Unfortunately, Wooden's failure to indulge in cups circumscribed his relationship with Bud Furillo. Too bad for the Steamer.

On his own, Furillo had internalized much of the "Pyramid of Success," Wooden's blueprint for daily living and achievement. The Steamer fully believed in "competitive greatness," the top rung of the pyramid, putting on his game face every day he walked into the office to publish the best sports section in town. But he could have used a little more self-control and patience. Forget about the building block of "condition," where Wooden pointed out that "rest, exercise, and diet must be considered" and "moderation must be practiced." A lover of vice, the Steamer never slept well, was always out of shape, and ate and drank to excess.

Bud Furillo's sportswriting career began just a few months before UCLA hired Wooden in 1948. The Steamer first wrote about Wooden in 1949, in a *Herald Express* Sports Chatter column on the coach trying to recruit a local kid. Furillo stayed in fairly close contact with Wooden over the next decade, when his winter and spring duties included helping out on coverage of L.A.'s college basketball teams.

"Master cage chef Johnny Wooden intends to serve the Washington Huskies a platter of defeat tonight as his UCLA Bruins turn on the speed and gas in their pressure cooker gym in Westwood," Furillo wrote in March 1952, when UCLA was gunning for its fourth straight conference title. He called Wooden "the miracle man."

In those days, American business didn't shut down for a few weeks every March while people across the country filled out their bracket sheets and minimized work to watch the college basketball playoffs. There was no madness in March—especially in L.A., where the Bruins played their home games in a tiny on-campus gym, or at the Pan Pacific Auditorium near Gilmore Field in the Fairfax District, or even at Venice High School.

It would be a while before college basketball mattered much outside of Oklahoma, Kentucky, and New York City. It was starting to catch on in the Bay Area, though, and the Steamer got to see why when he witnessed a matchup of future legends on December 11, 1954, when the University of San Francisco came down to play UCLA. He observed that USF was "a high class club that should go far this season, mainly because of Bill Russell, a six-foot-nine-inch center who is All-American material."

The Dons did go far—all the way to the NCAA championship, with a 28-1 record. The night they played the Bruins in December, Wooden constructed what Furillo called a "specially designed collapsible defense" to constrain Russell. The Bruins held him to fifteen points, but "Russell's all-around performance was marvelous," Furillo wrote. "He controlled the boards, knocked down at least eight sure points when it looked like the ball would drop in, and just made himself a general nuisance."

The Steamer covered a little bit of UCLA again the next year, when they won another Pacific Coast Conference championship. In the NCAA tournament, Wooden's PCC champs lost to Russell's USF squad in the first round, the Bruins giving the Dons their toughest game of the post-season before succumbing to the back-to-back champs who won all twenty-nine of their games. Pete Newell's great Cal teams in the late 1950s delayed the ascendancy of the UCLA dynasty.

In those years before his deserved canonization, Wooden was just another hard-edged basketball coach who was not above haranguing the refs and opposing players. Sitting at the end of the Bruin bench, Wooden rolled up a program in his hand and used it to shield his mouth from public view, much the way modern baseball players talk from behind their mitts so nobody can read their lips. Wooden may have looked gentlemanly from afar, but behind the rolled-up program, he gave everybody the business.

"Remind me some day to do a column on how Johnny Wooden badgers officials," the Steamer wrote in 1960. "There isn't a bench jockey in basketball that compares with the loquacious Wooden during a game. I just love Johnny's routines."

The next year, the Steamer took his own advice and wrote a full piece on Wooden and his two assistants, Bill Putnam and Jerry Norman, ragging on the refs during a win over USC.

"The Bruin trio picks on the officials from start to finish in every game," he wrote. "Wooden is basketball's Leo Durocher."

In 1962, the Steamer smacked Wooden again in what had become an annual ritual, this time after another Bruin spanking of fifth-ranked USC. Now Furillo was saying that Wooden could even give Durocher a few tips in the art of bench antagonization. He got on Wooden for picking on the Trojans' Ken Stanley "until the latter was so bugged he came to the Bruin bench and asked the Bruin coach to 'lay off' during a timeout." The Steamer also noted a nice rip Wooden laid on Jim Tunney, a basketball ref and high school principal who would later become the National Football League's zebra-in-chief.

"It's all part of his 'win' psychology," the Steamer wrote. "And he does win."

The day after the column ran, Furillo gave the coach equal time in The Steam Room. Wooden said, "I've never cursed an official, opposing player, or a coach. You have never seen me shake a fist, grab a chair, or take off my coat and dash it to the floor, have you?"

True enough, that. Wooden said his whole idea was to make sure his team knew he was behind it.

"I tell my kids to let me do the battling on whistle-calls," he said. "Their job is to play ball—not get riled up by the officiating."

Wooden also let the Steamer in on the secret behind the team's impending success: Just make the kids play as hard as they absolutely could. Don't think about the scoreboard. Play your best and give everything you have. Nothing else matters.

It was an approach that took the pressure off his boys. It was the secret behind the calm—the poise—that the Bruins demonstrated year after year, when they won ten NCAA titles in twelve years.

"Many times I have been more pleased by the way our kids have played in games they lost than by a winning performance," Wooden said. "I never want it said our team was outfought. Outplayed, yes. Coaching can't conquer that. It's my job to keep them from letting down. Before the SC game, I told them no matter what the final score, they would leave the court with their heads held high if they hustled."

The win over the Trojans was the Bruins' fourth in a row to start conference play, and it would get them going toward a conference title and their first-ever appearance in the Final Four.

"It would be best," Furillo wrote, "if I ignored Wooden's whoopings for the time being to pay more attention to his amazing ball club."

•   •   •   •   •

Caught up in the optimism of the Belinsky Spring, the Steamer's observation of the 1961–1962 Bruins was limited to his spotting the emergence of the first superstar of the Wooden championship era.

Walt Hazzard may have been the most important recruit John Wooden ever landed, because he's the one who was most responsible for the Bruins winning the first of their ten NCAA titles in twelve years. The coach had found out about the Philadelphia kid from Willie Naulls, a former Bruin All-American who was playing for the New York Knicks at the time. Wooden told the Steamer that Naulls received a tip from Woody Sauldsberry, a buddy on the Philadelphia Warriors. Woody told Willie to come check out Walt when Hazzard was still an underclassman at the famed Overbrook High School, alma mater of Wilt Chamberlain and others.

"Willie liked what he saw and sold the boy on UCLA," Wooden said, just before the Steamer departed for the desert. "I had never heard of Hazzard until I received a letter from him and another from Naulls."

As a youngster, Hazzard had played on the same Overbrook team as Wayne Hightower and Wali Jones. It has to be one of the few high school teams in world history that featured three future NBA players on its roster. Talent scouts had showed lots of interest in Hightower and Jones, but not as much for Hazzard, so he'd moved west and enrolled at Santa Monica College. Walt improved his scholastic standing and transferred to UCLA for his sophomore year. His playmaking skills made an immediate impression on the coach.

"The finest compliment Wooden can pay a player is the one he reserves for Hazzard," the Steamer wrote, going on to quote the coach's praise: "He's an unselfish player.'"

According to Wooden, Hazzard studied the pass-first styles of Oscar Robertson and Bill Russell and based his philosophical approach to the game on those same two examples of American basketball exceptionalism—both of whom the coach later included on his all-time team.

"Walt has good vision, which is essentially behind his sharp passing," Wooden told the Steamer. "There are those who can't see to pass off. There are others who can but won't."

Then there are those whose flash with the pass can leave their teammates blinded. Early in his sophomore season, Hazzard snapped a no-looker to a teammate who dropped it. Wooden then lowered his rolled-up program and yelled at Hazzard from the bench loud enough for Bud Furillo to hear from press row.

"No more of that Hundley stuff," Wooden shouted, in reference to the Lakers' colorful "Hot Rod" Hundley.

Walt directed UCLA into the Final Four in 1962, where it lost a thriller to Cincinnati. Two years later, his leadership and skill, combined with the killer zone press designed by UCLA assistant coach Jerry Norman, helped fashion the Bruins' first NCAA title. By the time Hazzard was a senior, Furillo called him "the best collegian I've seen in seventeen years on the sports beat."

Hazzard was more than a playmaker, Furillo wrote. He knew when to sacrifice unselfishness and get the ball into the most talented pair of hands on the court—his own. Then he'd just take over the game and do all the scoring, driving to the hole or hitting from distance.

The Steamer was still covering the Angels beat in the spring of '64, when UCLA was on its way to its first national title. He watched the Bruins' toughest game of the tournament from one of his favorite Palm Springs bars, the Metropole. The other Angels beat writers joined Furillo at the bar for UCLA's second-round game against the University of San Francisco. Grimness set in when the Bruins fell behind the Dons by thirteen points, but Furillo, even watching on TV, could feel Hazzard's poise.

"His gestures to his teammates pack the assuredness of John Huston directing a movie," Furillo wrote.

Walt scored twenty-three, and UCLA foreclosed on USF's plan to upset the undefeated Bruins, wiping out the large deficit and winning, 76–72. The next weekend, Steamer watched the Bruin wins over Kansas State and Duke from the Living Room A.C., where my mom served him margaritas in a chair he pulled up close to the television set. He had been called home from Palm Springs after the sports editor of the *Herald Examiner*, George T. Davis, died of a heart attack in Vero Beach, Florida.

John Wooden won his first NCAA championship as the Steamer raised a salted-rim drink in toast. A couple weeks later, the paper promoted Bud Furillo to executive sports editor. He had achieved the dream job he had set in his mind from the day he began work at the old *Herald Express*.

• • • • •

Pneumonia and sarcoidosis knocked the Steamer out of action in early 1965, keeping him from writing much about UCLA's repeat championship or anything else. The Zone Press put out another twenty-eight winning editions for UCLA, including an easy win over Michigan for the NCAA title. In the featured matchup, the Bruins' Gail Goodrich outscored Michigan's Cazzie Russell, 42–28, which more than accounted for the winning margin in UCLA's 91–80 win.

Then came the Lew and Wooden titles—numbers three, four, and five—before the '60s gave way to Sidney Wicks and Curtis Rowe, who presided over the sixth and seventh NCAA flags for Wooden and the Bruins. It was during their tenure that the streak began.

Wicks and Rowe were young men from south and southwest L.A. whose Afro hairstyles and tough inside play gave the Bruins more of an inner-city look. They were complemented by the outside jump-shooting ability of Steve Patterson, the center from the coastal plains of the Santa Maria Valley, and some very fine guards in Henry Bibby, fighting out of Franklinton, North Carolina, and John Vallely, a shooter from the island of Balboa. But for two years, Sidney and Curtis were the faces of franchise—especially Wicks, who first had to endure an in-game admonishment from the coach.

It was the last game of the 1969–1970 regular season, and the Bruins were coming off an 87–86 loss the night before against USC. Early in the first half of the rematch, the Trojans built themselves a substantial lead, and it looked extremely possible that they would send UCLA into its NCAA title defense with two consecutive losses. Unhappy with Wicks's effort, Coach Wooden sat Sid down next to him.

"You're going to sit here the rest of the night and you may sit next to me during the tournament, too," Wooden told Wicks, according to Mitch Chortkoff's reporting in the *Herald Examiner*.

After four minutes of that, Wicks was begging Wooden to put him back on the floor. Satisfied that his star's fire had been lit, the coach gave Wicks another chance, and Sidney led the

Bruins to an impressive comeback win, 91–78.

"He played his greatest game," Wooden said of Wicks.

In the NCAA finals, Wicks played even greater. Even at six foot eight, he seemed to tower over the seven-foot-two Artis Gilmore of Jacksonville, who also had a much more developed Afro. Wicks blocked five of Gilmore's shots and made him miss on twenty of twenty-nine as the Bruins won, 80–69. Sidney scored seventeen points and collected eighteen rebounds, most of them off Gilmore misses.

UCLA beat Villanova for the championship the next year, 68–62, in an odd circumstance by modern standards because the second-best team in the country didn't make the tournament. The Bruins' cross-town rival, USC, finished 24–2, but the NCAA only allowed conference champions into the tournament in those years. It was not like the present day situation, in which the NCAA affords invitations to everybody but the campus washerwomen.

The most impressive winning streak ever in the world of sports stood at one in a row the night UCLA went across town to play number-one-ranked USC in early February of 1971. Bud Furillo poached the lead story on what still stands as the most memorable basketball game in UCLA-USC history. The top two teams in the country played on a night, in a point of time, when the tide of basketball history in Los Angeles appeared to have shifted toward the school on the South-Central side of town. Alcindor and Hazzard were gone, and the Westsiders had actually lost three games in two years. The Trojans were undefeated, and their best player, Paul Westphal, who reminded people of Jerry West, had chosen USC over UCLA.

In the capacity-packed Sports Arena, Dennis "Mo" Layton, Westphal's teammate in the backcourt, hit a left-handed jumper at the halftime buzzer to lift Trojan fans out of their seats and USC into a one-point lead at the break. Layton filled the basket some more after intermission and the Trojans led by nine, with nine and a half minutes to go.

With the pressure on the Bruins, the Trojans cracked. They didn't score another basket the rest of the game, and UCLA systematically cut the lead, took it for their own with five minutes to go, and sealed it with twenty seconds left when Wicks hit two free throws. Final score: UCLA, 64–60.

"I always tell my players to keep everything in balance, mentally, morally, and physically," Wooden told Krikorian. "Balance is the key to life and also to athletic achievement. When we were behind, I told my players not to hurry, to play their own game. If you try to catch up too quickly, then all you do is fall further behind. I always emphasize to my team that winning is not the most important thing in the world. Ideally, I'd like a player to react to winning the same way he does to losing. As long as he's doing his best, that's the most important thing. He should keep everything in proper perspective and take the victories in stride."

•   •   •   •   •

Walton was unbelievable in his sensational sophomore season, but he had a pretty decent rhythm section behind him.

Tough and experienced, Henry Bibby, a three-year starter at guard, banged home the fifteen-foot Wooden banker as well as anybody. Henry would play nine years in the NBA and average 8.2 points a game. Greg Lee and Tommy Curtis manned the point and fed fellow sophomore Walton in the post. On the fly, they found a smooth and skinny forward with a slingshot jumper that he lofted off his right ear and that he could sink from anywhere inside twenty-five feet. Keith Wilkes, who changed his first name to Jamaal in the pros, played on three NBA championship teams and gained selection to the Naismith Memorial Basketball Hall of Fame. Wilkes shot fifty percent for his pro career and averaged 17.7 points a game. Power forward Larry Farmer protected the board when Walton roamed off the block, and he could also run and score. Larry Hollyfield added points and flash off the bench. Walton always said that UCLA backup center Swen Nater gave him more trouble in practice than any other big man did in the games. Nater averaged 12.4 and 11.6 in an eleven-year pro career that included invitations to two American Basketball Association All-Star games.

Bud Furillo didn't get out to Pauley Pavilion much. It was

the only joint in town his kids couldn't crash, because his comps to the Bruin home games paid doctor and car bills. So his kids only got to see UCLA live when they played on the road at USC. Because Pauley was an impossible ticket, a local TV station, KTLA Channel 5, replayed all the Bruin home games at 11:00 PM on Friday and Saturday nights. They were the best show in town, and it was never better than in 1971–1972, when some teenagers, I'm told, used to conduct pot parties in their parents' absence to ooh and ahh at the displays put on by Walton's Bruins. UCLA was so good that they not only beat everybody they played, they also out-pointed *Tonight Show* host Johnny Carson in the local TV ratings.

Sportswriters called it "the Walton Gang," and the team showed itself right away as a terrifying bunch. The 1971–1972 Bruins scored 105 or more in their first seven games and more than doubled the other team's point total in three of them. Their average margin of victory over that spread was forty-seven. Of the early slaughters, the one that brought the most warmth to the UCLA bosom had to be the 114–53 annihilation of Notre Dame. The year before, the Fighting Irish had been the last team to beat the Bruins.

The nation's college basketball community gulped when it saw the result of UCLA's eighth game of the year, a thrashing of sixth-ranked Ohio State, 79–53. The Buckeyes' high-scoring guard, Allan Hornyak, who averaged twenty-one points a game on the season, didn't make a shot. Walton had unnerved him early, blocking three of his first four attempts.

Wooden began to think this might be his best team ever. Even so, he told the press afterwards, "We will get better."

For the Bruins' twenty-sixth straight win, Walton authored a stat line as gorgeous as a sunset looking coastward from the hills of Westwood. He played twenty-seven minutes in UCLA's 118–79 win over Stanford and hit fifteen of eighteen shots for thirty-two points, snatched fifteen rebounds, blocked nine shots, and passed for five assists.

Writers again asked Wooden if this was his best team.

"I think right now, this is the most balanced team I've ever had from every point of view," he told Krikorian. "It does so many things well."

Walton painted another masterpiece in the Bruins' thirty-nine-point win over Washington, when he scored twenty-seven, rebounded twenty-four, and blocked fifteen. Poor Husky center Steve Hawes. Walton force-fed him his first three field goal attempts, and Hawes scored only four points in the game. And this was a man who would go on to play ten years in the NBA.

When the Bruins stretched the streak to thirty-eight, Wooden said, "I'd have to say at this stage this team certainly is as good as any I've had at UCLA. If we go on to win the title, I'd have to rank this team as stronger than any I've ever coached." He told Doug Krikorian that on the subject of the Bruins' red-haired center, "It's inconceivable to me that anyone has even come close to dominating games like Bill has this season."

The Steamer wintered in New Orleans in early 1972, where he hung out with his idol, New York–based columnist Jimmy Cannon, at the Super Bowl and then at Joe Frazier's heavyweight title defense on the Mississippi crescent against Terry Daniels. Cannon lived near Central Park, a major mugging zone in its day, so the California writer asked his colleague from the rival coast a friendly question.

"Have you taken to carrying a gun yet?"

"Yes," Cannon replied, "to protect myself against earthquakes."

Home from New Orleans, the Steamer reported on the Rams' trade of Deacon Jones to the San Diego Chargers, and then he worked Mando Ramos's corner again in the rematch with Pedro Carrasco. The night Danny Lopez knocked out Tury Pineda in four wild rounds at the Olympic, he pronounced Little Red "the best nineteen-year-old fighter I've ever seen." Then he took Walton to lunch and turned his attention to the Bruins.

UCLA qualified for the Final Four with a Western Regional victory in Provo, Utah, over Long Beach State, a team that had nearly KO'd the Woodens the year before. With UCLA's defense in lockdown mode this time, the Steamer said it appeared on television that Long Beach "went out onto the floor looking as if they were wearing tight shoes." Before the game, a film crew captured 49ers coach Jerry Tarkanian showing his big men what they needed to do to control Walton.

"It seemed sound the way Tarkanian explained it," Furillo wrote. "But the solution grew increasingly difficult when the six-foot-eleven Walton replaced the five-foot-eleven Tarkanian, who had been imitating him in the drill."

The NCAA championships returned to the Sports Arena in L.A. in 1972, so Furillo commanded a seat on press row to watch his current favorite athlete win his first ring and the Bruins' gather their sixth straight championship and eighth total under Wooden. Again, Furillo exercised his authority as sports editor to steal the game stories from Krikorian.

UCLA routed Louisville in the semis, 96–77. Walton's thirty-three points, twenty-one rebounds, and six blocked shots toppled the Cardinals. Furillo compared Walton's performance to the fine effort shown by the leadership of the striking International Longshoremen and Warehousemen's Union, which at the time employed a zone press of its own to shut down every port on the West Coast, from San Diego to Seattle.

"Because Bill Walton controls college basketball the way [legendary ILWU president] Harry Bridges does the West Coast waterfront, the UCLA Bruins are favored by sixteen points to defeat Florida State tomorrow afternoon," Furillo wrote.

Walton showed a longshoreman's toughness in the win over Louisville. The Steamer wrote that the six-foot-eleven sophomore took a punch and numerous elbows, and survived a couple of knockdowns during the win. Early in the game, Walton returned some of the rough stuff when he bumped the Cardinals' Mike Lawhon while the two ran down the floor. Lawhon, who later became doctor, didn't show a very good bedside manner when he took a swing at big Bill.

"Henry (The Enforcer) Bibby saw it," Furillo reported. "Lawhon did penance as a blocking dummy for Bibby."

Referees closely monitored the aggressive Bibby the rest of the way, and whistled him into foul trouble. Wooden inserted Tommy Curtis into the Bruin lineup in Bibby's absence, and although the fast little backup guard couldn't shoot with the precision of the starter, the Steamer wrote that he was so quick he "could penetrate Fort Knox."

The game was close for a half. When UCLA took it over in the second, Louisville "turned its attention to the upcoming ninety-eighth running of the Kentucky Derby," the Steamer said. Two days later, the Bruins completed their own wire-to-wire ride as the number-one team in the country. Florida State won the first eight minutes of the game and outscored UCLA in the second half.

"However," the Steamer wrote, "the stylish Bruins raised enough hell along the way in the forty-minute game to win their sixth consecutive national collegiate basketball championship."

The final score was 81–76. It was only the second time all season UCLA failed to win by double digits. It was also UCLA's third undefeated season in eight years. Up to then, only two other teams in the history of the NCAA had ever accomplished the feat even once. One of them, the Steamer wrote, was "the University of Bill Russell at San Francisco" in 1956. The other was the North Carolina team that beat the University of Kansas at Wilt Chamberlain in the final the next year.

Bud Furillo's game story reported that Bill Walton took no great joy in the defeat of the tough Seminoles. Walton, he said, "was embarrassed. He didn't feel that he played well. He scored twenty-four points, rebounded twenty times, and blocked four shots. For this, it isn't likely he will be shipped on the next plane from Westwood to Ulan Bator."

The UCLA center "appeared to be tight at the start as the Seminoles shot their way into a six-point lead at 15–9 after five minutes," the Steamer said. Keith Wilkes, with twenty-three on the afternoon, and Bibby, with eighteen, kept the Bruins close until Bill loosened up. Furillo, meanwhile, continued to be fascinated by the quickness of "Tallahassee Tommy" Curtis, as he called him, "who is from the same town as Florida State, but not the same campus."

"T. C. can drive people crazy," the Steamer said of the backcourt backup. "He knocks on the front door. By the time you answer it, he is in through the back."

A twelve-foot turnaround by Tommy halfway through the first half bounced into the bucket and gave the Bruins their first lead. The basket started a run UCLA built to sixteen points before the Florida State gunners got hot again late to shorten the lead to seven with four minutes to go. All of the Louisville and North Carolina fans in the Sports Arena fell in with the Seminole rooters. Los Angeles never sounded more like Tallahassee.

"But the Bruins killed them and the clock by introducing the stall, which isn't their style," said the Steamer. "They were adequate enough at keep-away to run their lead back up to nine points with twenty-seven seconds remaining."

The streak reached forty-five. Captain Henry Bibby cut down the nets beneath a banner in the UCLA rooting section that read, "Welcome to the Sixth Annual Bruin Invitational."

"UCLA is now accepting reservations for hotel rooms in St. Louis," the Steamer wrote. "That's where the Seventh Annual Bruin Invitational will be held next year."

•   •   •   •   •

Thirty days and thirty nights of basketball spread over four months meant another thirty wins in a row the next year for UCLA.

Without Bibby, the Bruins weren't quite as good. Their average margin of victory fell from thirty to twenty-one, and they had one close call on the road at Stanford. Still, the streak reached seventy-five when Bill Walton played the greatest game in basketball history. It came in the NCAA championship against Memphis State. He hit jumpers from outside and spun inside for layups on lobs from his buddy at point guard, Greg Lee. Walton connected on twenty-one of twenty-two shots, and finished with forty-four points and thirteen rebounds—and he did it on a bad night's sleep. He'd had to change hotel rooms in the middle of the night before the game because his bed was uncomfortable.

Walton limped to the Bruin bench with 2:50 to go, with the eventual 87–66 victory secured. Memphis State's high-point man,

Larry Finch, assisted Walton, who had sprained his ankle. Even Memphis State fans joined in the one-minute standing ovation.

"They were appreciative of what they had just witnessed," Krikorian wrote, "just like the fans who saw a Koufax no-hitter or a Louis knockout or Ruth calling his shot."

Furillo stayed in Los Angeles to put out the paper. He also was between columns on a young fighter named Roberto Duran making an appearance in L.A. and Bill Shoemaker preparing for the Santa Anita Derby. The race was won by Sham, with Laffit Pincay up. The two of them would spend the rest of the spring chasing Secretariat.

The Steamer caught up with John Wooden a month later, courtside at the Forum, where the national AAU team was playing the Soviet Union. Wooden's appearance at the game may have been motivated by the presence of his center in the Americans' starting lineup. Bill Walton and the red, white, and blues beat the Soviets, 83–65. The United States rejoiced in the drubbing of the team that had stolen the 1972 Olympic gold medal from us.

Never really a Hollywood guy, Wooden nevertheless watched the game with former UCLA quarterback and film producer Mike Frankovich and film director Billy Wilder, a friend of Frankovich's.

"There are too many Aleksanders on the Russian team," Wilder pronounced. "There are five Aleksanders. Who turns around when somebody yells 'Aleksander?'"

The Aleksander with the last name of Belov was the player who had scored the winning basket against the U.S. in the '72 Olympics. He attracted Wooden's interest. The coach told the Steamer that Belov was "one player I'd go after if he were in this country." At six foot seven, Belov would have made a fine replacement for Larry Farmer.

Playing against the Soviets the month after Memphis State, Walton twisted a knee in the first half, but showed Wooden and the 17,505 in the Forum that he was okay to start the second when he lifted up in the key to knock a shot away.

"They've never seen that," Wooden said of the visitors.

"You're awfully fond of him, aren't you?" the Steamer asked the coach.

A conservative from the Midwest, Wooden replied that in spite of his differences with Walton—a guy who, by then, was out of the closet with his antiwar politics and his castigation of what he viewed as a racist society—he certainly was fond, and proud.

"He's an outstanding young man," the coach told the Steamer. "People wonder about him because he's so outspoken. But he lets you know where he stands. For instance, Bill and I disagree on a number of things. But we have no disagreements."

Walton and the Bruins ran the streak to eighty-eight the next year, until Notre Dame beat them in South Bend on January 20, 1974, by a score of 71–70. Walton had injured his back and missed three games in a row before he paid a visit to Notre Dame's Athletic and Convocation Center. His mobility was restricted, and he tired late.

"He'll feel better next week," Wooden told the press after that one.

A couple days before the rematch a week later, Bud Furillo's lead art on the sports page was a picture of the gas chamber at San Quentin. The caption suggested that this was the fate that awaited Notre Dame. Against the Irish in L.A., Walton felt better enough to score thirty-two and rebound eleven as UCLA dropped the pill on Notre Dame, 94–75. When Walton fouled out with five minutes to go and the Bruins up twenty-five, he returned to the bench "amid one of the biggest ovations ever accorded anyone in Westwood," Krikorian wrote.

UCLA may have avenged the loss to Notre Dame, but the team never got a chance to make up for their defeat to North Carolina State in the Eighth Annual Bruin Invitational. A loss to David Thompson and the Wolfpack in the NCAA semifinals deprived them of the title, just a couple months before another run was about to come to an end.

Chapter 14

THIRTY

As the score mounted against the Dodgers the Steamer stared with disbelief at the word pictures of Jerry Doggett on the radio. "There's more to this than meets the eye," I said to myself, perhaps one of my biggest listeners. Finally . . . Doggett explained that someone had left the sound system on outside the poolside rooms at the Chase Hotel until eight o'clock in the morning. Now you can understand why the Dodgers hit into five double plays yesterday afternoon in St. Louis. They were walking in their sleep. . . . Now nobody likes music more than the Steamer, who will remain a devoted Duke Ellington fan until the day I die. But it can wear you down if you try to sleep with it on down by the pool. I know how that is. After George Foreman knocked out Ken Norton, he played "Love Train" by the O'Jays all night. Or somebody in his party did. We were staying at the same hotel. After I had listened to shouts and screams for the thirty-fifth time, I began to scream as well. Nobody was alarmed. They figured it was part of the arrangement. What else could I do, go down and tell Foreman to knock it off?

—May 28, 1974

Eras come and golden ages go. New teams take shape in old uniforms as decades unfold. New superstars bring new legacies, and their stories continue to be told through new technologies that reinforce memories in new ways.

Bud Furillo adapted to the early stages of the revolution. In the spring of 1974, he went multimedia when the biggest talk radio station in town asked him to try out for its afternoon sports show. He gave it a shot and landed a gig that paid him more than twice his newspaper salary.

These days, sportswriters all over the country parlay their columns into radio and TV work, and newspaper managers love the exposure. It wasn't always that way, at least not at the *Herald Examiner* in 1974, when the newspaper was seven years into a nasty strike. Forget that Bud Furillo had suffered a heart attack a month into the strike and had to be wheeled to the ambulance through an angry mob of pickets. So what if he got death threats in the middle of the night. It didn't matter that he had rebuilt the *Herald Examiner*'s sports staff and maintained the paper's journalistic viability while readers threw the rest of the rag into the street.

The only thing that counted for the top brass at the paper was that, in June 1974, Sears, Roebuck and Company had cancelled a $50,000 advertising contract with a paper that had bled red ink due to a secondary boycott that organized labor called on the *Herald Examiner*. The big bosses at the paper went nuts when Sears began to sponsor Bud Furillo's radio show at the same time it was dumping the paper. They told Furillo that he had to quit the radio show or he would be fired. It was a Friday, June 14, and they gave him the weekend to think about it.

The Steamer was making $345 a week as sports editor. The radio station paid him $800. There really wasn't much to think about. Furillo went up to talk about it with the publisher, George Randolph Hearst Jr., grandson of the real-life "Citizen Kane," William Randolph Hearst, the founder of the media empire. George, who was worth $1.9 billion when he died thirty-eight years later, offered Bud Furillo a raise of twenty-five dollars a week. The Steamer turned it down.

On Monday, June 17, 1974, the paper informed the Steamer that, after his twenty-eight years of service, he was fired.

The Steam Room era was over.

•   •   •   •   •

No, the games did not end with Bud Furillo's forced separation from the *Herald Examiner*, and neither did he. He stayed on the L.A. sports beat and worked it for another thirty-two years, mostly with a microphone.

The Steamer was still around when the Lakers became a basketball dynasty with a nickname: "Showtime." A new pro football team came to town, won one of the biggest prizes in sports, and then left. A beloved old team, the first professional outfit in the city, moved to the suburbs and then all the way to the Mississippi River. Old sports withered away and new ones took their place. A racetrack closed and a new sports showcase opened downtown and turned what used to be a dead zone into "L.A. Live," one of the most popular entertainment venues in the city.

When the Steamer left the paper, his new employer, KABC 790, served as the Dodger flagship station. It tightened him up with the club that would win seven divisional titles, five National League pennants, and two World Series titles over the next fourteen years. He went to Florida with the Dodgers every spring that he was with KABC, and came up with funny stories—like the time utility man Mickey Hatcher, upset that he'd been traded to Minnesota, snuck into the Dodgers locker room, stole Tommy Lasorda's clothes, and ran them up a flagpole. The Steamer took up causes on behalf of players such as Jay Johnstone, whom Lasorda once fined $250 because his valuable left-handed pinch-hitter was late to the plate after dragging the infield between innings. Johnstone then proceeded to hit a two-run homer. The sympathetic Steamer asked Dodgers fans to help pay Jay's fine, and they came up with $1,500 for him and pitcher Jerry Reuss, who also joined in on the grounds crew prank.

The Lakers slipped into mediocrity in the late '70s, even after they acquired Kareem Abdul-Jabbar. Then Jerry Buss traded Gail Goodrich to the New Orleans Jazz for a draft pick who turned into Magic Johnson. The Lakers won five NBA titles in the '80s. The Steamer hung on for Shaquille O'Neal—the single coolest athlete he'd ever met, he told me.

Besides keeping tabs on Bill Walton, the Steamer never took to the Clippers when they moved to L.A. from San Diego. Who would have ever believed that by 2014, the Clippers would be better than the Lakers—or that the Kings would win two Stanley Cups, not to mention the one secured by the Anaheim Ducks?

Down in Anaheim, the Angels floundered through many a
horrible tragedy. The Steamer, through his business relationship
with the Dodgers, grew estranged from them. But he came back
to take a bow when they finally won a divisional championship
in 1979. By the time they won a World Series, Furillo was out of
radio and not even living in L.A. anymore.

USC continued to win a few football games, and the Steamer
remained very much a part of their picture. He was gone from
the paper when they won their last national championship under
John McKay in 1974, but he more or less worked for the school
that year when he hooked on as the color man paired with the
great play-by-play man Ray Scott on the Trojan TV replays. The
season was highlighted by possibly the most electrifying eighteen minutes in college football history. They began when the
Trojans were down 24-0, just before halftime against Notre
Dame. By early in the fourth quarter, USC had scored fifty-five
straight, unanswered points, shaking the Coliseum. McKay
then completed his collegiate eligibility and turned pro. Furillo
fell in with the new head man, John Robinson, who won three
Rose Bowls and one national championship, and produced two
Heisman Trophy winners in seven years. The Steamer spent the
Robinson years watching games from the USC sidelines, at the
coach's invitation. In 2004, the university inducted Furillo into
the USC Athletic Hall of Fame.

John Wooden won his tenth and final national championship
in 1975, with the Steamer off in Florida with the Dodgers. The
coach, whom the Steamer used to rag for ragging the refs and
opposing players, later gave Furillo a championship ring from
the 1972 season.

Although the Steamer rooted for USC on the air, he'd always liked UCLA. He grew very close with Terry Donahue, who
coached the Bruins to three Rose Bowl wins and four top-ten fin-
ishes and won more Pac-10 games than any coach in the history
of the conference. One afternoon in 1976, after Donahue had
just landed the job and was driving down the San Diego Freeway and listening to his car radio, he heard oddsmaker Danny
Sheridan trashing the Bruins on Bud Furillo's show. Donahue

called the station for equal time, and the Steamer put him on the air with Sheridan. Donahue kept in touch with the Steamer and invited him to get rid of his cardinal-and-gold sweaters and come on down to Bruin land every once in a while, maybe even spend some time on his sideline. The Steamer accepted the invitation, and the two remained friends for the next thirty years.

Steamer pal Chuck Knox erased the Hollywood image and shaped the Rams into one of the toughest, most physical teams in the NFL, but he never could get over the Minnesota or Dallas hump in the playoffs. Carroll Rosenbloom fired Knox and replaced him with Ray Malavasi, who took the Rams to Super Bowl XIV against Pittsburgh, which they lost. Tragically, Rosenbloom died before the Super Bowl season, drowning at a Florida beach. The coroner ruled it an accidental death, but the Steamer and plenty of others—including the producers of a PBS *Frontline* documentary—thought something stunk about it.

With Rosenbloom's death, the team was taken over by his wife, Georgia. The grieving widow soon took up with musical composer Dominic Frontiere, who became her eighth husband. Frontiere got in a jam when he scalped several thousand Rams tickets to the Super Bowl. He did a little prison time behind it, before Georgia dumped him. Under her tenure, the Rams moved to Anaheim. She hired John Robinson, who drafted Eric Dickerson and made the Rams competitive—until they weren't. In 1995, Georgia moved the team to her hometown of St. Louis, where they won the Super Bowl four years later.

When the Rams abandoned the Coliseum for Orange County, an old Steamer acquaintance sought to fill the football void in South-Central. In 1979, Al Davis, the managing general partner of the Oakland Raiders, announced that he was moving the club to L.A., and Furillo championed the franchise shift. When the Raiders came to Los Angeles to play the Rams that year, the Steamer even had a friend tape a banner to the Coliseum press box that read, "Welcome Home, L.A. Raiders." The National Football League refused to approve the move, so Al Davis took them to court and won. During the antitrust trials, the Raiders' legal team hustled copies of the daily transcripts to the Steamer, who gave his radio listeners a blow-by-blow account of the court-room happenings. In 1982, the Raiders moved into the Coliseum and won the Super Bowl in the 1983 season over Jack Kent Cooke's Washington Redskins. The Raiders drew big crowds to the Coliseum for three years after the Super Bowl win and made the playoffs twice. Then they started to lose, the crowds fell off, and by 1995, Al Davis had suckered Oakland into taking him back. The Rams, meanwhile, blew the O.C. for the riches of St. Louis and won Super Bowl XXXIV. Then the team faltered on the banks of the Mississippi and attendance declined. In January 2016, they moved back to Los Angeles.

As the Olympic Auditorium roared into the '80s, Carlos Palomino won the welterweight championship, Danny "Little Red" Lopez locked up the featherweight crown, and Alberto "Tweety" Davila killed a man in the ring to win the bantamweight title. The Steamer's appearances fell off when he went into radio, but he had done enough over the year to merit his induction into the California Boxing Hall of Fame. Oscar de la Hoya fought at the Olympic Auditorium in 1994 and tried to promote there into the 2000s, but the sport went dead on him. At last check, the Olympic had been turned into a Korean church. George Parnassus died in 1975, and that was it for the big, international Forum boxing shows. Cage fighting has since surpassed boxing as America's blood-sport of choice.

In the racing business, bicycles became bigger than horses, even though you can't bet on them—and who would want to, given that everybody's doped up? Santa Anita and Del Mar are hanging in there, but Hollywood Park went down in the fall of 2013. The last Hollywood Gold Cup attracted 6,493 to the oval, to what used to be one of the biggest sporting events in town. Owners of the property had planned to build an upscale housing development, until Rams owner Stan Kroenke announced in early 2015 his plans to build a football stadium on the old Hollywood Park site and move his team there. Later in the year, the Chargers and Raiders disclosed plans to build and share a stadium in Carson. The NFL rejected them.

•   •   •   •   •

Bud Furillo applied a newspaperman's mentality to the airwaves. He worked the production end and mapped out talk over time, much like he did with print space when he dummied the pages for his sports section. He still reported the hell out of the L.A. sports beat, working clubhouse scrums all over town. He had a tendency to dominate press conferences, turning them into personal conversations with Tommy Lasorda or John Robinson or Chuck Knox while everybody else took notes. He maintained his A-list of contacts. He broke stories on the air, stoked the sports conversation, and gave fans a voice, keeping them connected to their teams, the players, and each other. He banged out a commentary every day that he called *The Steam Room*. He made money he'd never dreamed of, getting into six-figures at a time when $100,000 bought you something.

Still, it wasn't an easy transition, moving from the newspaper to the radio station. The Steamer was a natural-born newspaperman, and now, the occupation he identified himself with was gone. No more "getting our teeth into this paper," as George T. Davis liked to say, from edition to edition. No more working a big game and assigning his staff to cover every angle of it and splash it right for the next day's layout.

Furillo liked radio, but he loved the newspaper. The radio gave him a voice, but the newspaper gave him a sense of being.

Maybe there was a way he could have worked out a deal to do both. But there was no way he would walk away from a doubled salary. There was no way he would grovel to George R. Hearst Jr., and there was no way Hearst was going to grovel to Furillo. He didn't get to become one of the richest men in the country by bowing to the whims of refugees from the Sharon Line.

Right after he went into radio, the Steamer told everybody around him about another drawback to the job switch.

"I've lost my juice," he said.

Oh, he could still call up any team in town—any team in the country, really—and get a pair of tickets to a game. As late as 1993, the Steamer and I were in New York City for the confirmation of one of his grandsons. The day of the sacred rite, we

noticed that Buddy McGirt and Pernell "Sweet Pea" Whitaker had a fight scheduled that night in Madison Square Garden
for the welterweight championship. The Steamer made a phone
call and we got a couple of very fine seats to a terrific fight, won
over in twelve rounds by the speedy, hard-to-hit Whitaker. Afterward, we attended the press conference in the Felt Forum. The
Steamer took notes.

But he no longer controlled the dozens of Rams tickets he
used to get. He couldn't put the Los Angeles County district attorney on the fifty-yard line anymore. He said goodbye to those
eight ringside tickets at the Olympic every Thursday night.
Teams and tracks no longer remembered him during the holidays. No more flying the kids to the Indy 500 or to the USC-Notre Dame game in South Bend. Las Vegas stopped giving him a
booth to the best show on the Strip, with the champagne on ice.
He still had his friends in the restaurant business, but he couldn't
just walk in anywhere and get the best table in the house. They
listened to the radio, all right, but how do you cut that out and
put it in a frame on the wall?

Graft was coming to an end, anyway. With Watergate and the
newspapers taking down the president, the press had to clean
up its own act, and that mainly meant cutting out the goodies
that went to sportswriters.

The day of the last crooked sports editor was over.

At the same time newspapers were hosing corruption out
of their sports departments, a new emphasis on professionalism
was taking hold in the industry. Newspapers paid more and
brought in fine writers and essayists to cover sports as social
phenomena. They wrote lengthy profiles that delved into every
aspect of the players' lives and their environments. Sportswriting moved beyond the locker room, examining issues like racism, the psychology of performance, and the politics of sport.
Editors de-emphasized game stories, and a new kind of sports
journalist emerged.

Jimmy Cannon, in his interview in Jerome Holtzman's oral
history of sportswriting, *No Cheering in the Press Box*, called
these sports journalists "chipmunks." According to Cannon, a

chipmunk "wears a corduroy jacket and stands in press boxes with other guys wearing corduroy jackets and they only discuss what they've written. They don't watch the game." Not only that—they hated the games, and the people who played them, Cannon told Holtzman. This new wave of sportswriter, Cannon said, lived for the rude question. "They regard this as a sort of bravery," he added.

Toward the end of the Steam Room era, the "shaky trust between player and scribe" had already begun to break down, according to *New York Times* columnist Robert Lipsyte in his memoir, *An Accidental Sportswriter*. Lipsyte wrote that writers like the Steamer lost their access because they could no longer offer what Lipsyte called "the promise of protection."

They sure enough couldn't. How can a writer protect anything in a twenty-four-hour multimedia environment, where TMZ tracks athletes into the same kind of night spots where they used to hang out with Bud Furillo?

Monopolization, meanwhile, shrank the newspaper business and ran out a lot of the hacks from the old days. Almost every city became a one-paper town. Then advertising changed. Newspapers no longer printed money. A brutal economy turned some of those one-paper towns into no-paper towns. Big media companies like ESPN took over everything, from game coverage, to round-the-clock highlights, to radio, to local website coverage that scooped the papers. Their talking heads blabbed so much, the hot air drove out insight and analysis.

Everybody got everything there was to get at the same time, with more adding up to less. Coaches stood at podiums in front of background screens decorated with corporate logos and answered questions like politicians running for office, sometimes showing their contempt for writers, their fear palpable that they'd say something the opposition would splice into attack commercials. Cameras jammed players into their lockers and athletes spoke off talking points that all boiled down to: "At the end of the day, it is what it is—we've got to make plays."

Intimidated and isolated, sportswriters were frozen out of the action by athletes who didn't trust them. They were hounded by editors who all but ordered them not to write anything about the great things happening on the field or on the court—readers already knew the score and had already seen the highlight reel. Spin it forward. Your team just won the title? We already know that. How will they do next year?

Today, with everything on TV or radio or the Internet all the time, writers' access no longer matters. Some of the most popular sportswriters in the country even brag that they don't want or need it. Others use what access they do have to make coaches and athletes look stupid. It's all served to make sports sections quite a bit different than they were during the Steam Room era. In some ways, they're better, as long as you don't miss the absence of the drama of the game in prose that used to be as good as any writing in the country. Just ask Ernest Hemingway, who said that, when properly inspired, Jimmy Cannon would "leave writing dead on the floor."

The public absolutely has a right to know when a football coach on the public payroll drops dead of a heart attack in a hotel room with a hooker, like Red Sanders did with Ernestine Drake. Readers need more information, not less, about concussions in football and the use of performance-enhancing drugs that have made athletes ride their bikes faster and hit baseballs farther. College football recruiting scandals need to be exposed. So do football players who murder their girlfriends, commit suicide in front of their coaches, and drive drunk and kill their teammates in car crashes.

Sports sections sure are different, all right. But they're not as much fun. For the hard-core sports fan, they're no longer crucial, either.

Television now dominates sports. National networks, conference networks, and the teams' own networks put every game in every sport on television—and sometimes control other reporters' access to players and coaches. The ones they don't broadcast, they stream on computers. Who needs to read the paper when you can watch any damn game you want, and get the results in real time on your phone?

In the decades since the Steam Room era ended, sports talk

has become a twenty-four-hour enterprise. There used to be one three-hour sports talk radio show in Los Angeles in the middle of the 1970s. Last time I checked, there were three sports talk stations running around the clock. With everybody talking all the time, nobody has any time to read.

On the Internet, athletes can control their own images via social media. They don't need the writers to reach their fans anymore.

And the old audience—the readers—have become writers, too, posting their own opinions and accounts of the games in their social media networks, or in the comment sections on newspaper websites, or on fan sites. Some of them can write as well as the people who get paid for it, even if they don't have to put their names on their stuff, which poisoned the conversation.

In 1962, the Steamer didn't have a cell phone camera, but if he had, I'm sure he wouldn't have used it on his pals. But what about Joe Blow Fan with his camera phone in the nightclub? You don't think he's going to snap you downing shots of tequila and doing the twist, the night before you're supposed to pitch?

• • • • •

As the sports editor of the *Herald Examiner*, the Steamer exercised almost total control. He very much adhered to the thinking of Al Davis, as expressed in a 1972 Steamer column: "You've got to be dictatorial," said the Raiders managing general partner. A guy who worked for Furillo once said he'd had an easier time in a North Korean prisoner of war camp.

Lack of control became a problem for the Steamer in the radio business, where ratings went up and down, fads flashed in and out of style, and station managers tried to ride the wind. Unbelievable to the Steamer, they tried to tell him what to do. His resistance to management led to twenty-six years of tumult in his relationship with it. He'd been in radio barely a year when he got mad at his KABC bosses and decided to look around for other work.

He moved over to soft-rock KIIS and worked out a sports talk show he broadcast from a high-rise near Sunset and Vine. He appreciated that KIIS management pretty much left him alone, but he returned to KABC in 1979 as the station solidified its relationship with the Dodgers. For the next eight years, the Steamer served as an on-air Dodgers cheerleader. He also rooted hard for USC and UCLA and the Raiders, Rams, Lakers, Kings, and everybody else.

In his spare time during his radio days, the Steamer raised enough money for charity to earn himself a dinner put on by the City of Hope, a major-league cancer research center in the L.A. area. Sports stars such as Tommy Lasorda, Howie Long, Deacon Jones, and Freddie Blassie lauded him for his humanitarian work. Furillo also spent more than thirty years trying to help out a Lynwood High School football player named Shawn Powell who had suffered a paralyzing injury on the field. The Steamer visited the kid regularly in the hospital and spent the rest of his life being his friend and father figure. Powell later changed his name to Shawn Powell-Furillo. He called the Steamer "Dad."

But radio being what it is, KABC fiddled with its lineup in 1987 in a fashion that did not please the Steamer, who was only growing more bombastic with age. KABC told Furillo, who was sixty-two years old at the time, that the station was taking him out of the afternoon/early evening drive-time slot and replacing him with Stu Nahan, a long-time L.A. television personality. The Steamer would be relegated to his *Dodger Talk* shows before and after the games. He would also keep doing his *Steam Room* commentaries. A commensurate cut in pay accompanied the reduced on-air time.

Well, the Steamer showed them. He quit KABC and hooked up with a "brokered" outfit—for half the money he would have received, had he stayed at the big station.

His new show was broadcast off the Redondo Beach pier. It was a beautiful location, and his show was good. He lassoed Caesars Palace to pay his nut. But few advertisers followed him from KABC, as he mistakenly anticipated. You could barely pick up the station east of the San Diego Freeway.

A few years later, Furillo flubbed a tryout with a new sports talk show booming out of San Diego into L.A. Tired of the brokered radio arrangement on the pier, he signed up with a network out of Las Vegas. Once a guy who used to swagger up and down the Strip, the Steamer found himself sleeping in a creepy side-street joint. He became depressed and soon moved home to his condo in South Gate, where he'd been living since 1978. He did fill-in gigs for **WFAN** in New York City, but they never became permanent. In 1992, he moved to Sacramento to host a two-hour talk show, until a better opportunity came along a couple years later in Palm Springs. He jumped on it, in one last push to regain his position in the big time. It didn't happen.

Six years of that was enough. In 2000, the Steamer retired from radio—but he wasn't quite done yet.

· · · · ·

Along with the heart attack, the Steamer had a long career of physical ailments. He'd suffered through pneumonia and sarcoidosis and had two quadruple bypasses. His gut had busted open once while he was on vacation in Catalina, and the peritonitis nearly killed him.

In 1996, Furillo came down with a bad back. He visited some screwball doctor in Palm Springs, who ordered surgery. The procedure did little to alleviate his discomfort, but he did come out of it with a new fascination for pain killers. By the end of the twentieth century, the Steamer was gobbling a murderer's row of pharmaceuticals. He had found doctors all over Palm Desert to write him prescriptions. Somebody was always in pocket. He'd also developed a lively co-dependency with new friends and acquaintances, and even had one move in with him.

The Steamer added a morphine patch to his prescription repertoire. The patch was supposed to last thirty days, but pretty soon, it was running out of gas at twenty-nine. Then twenty-eight. When the patch gave out, Furillo worked his legitimate connections in the medical industry. If no Dr. Feelgood was available, he consulted other experts, without portfolio. Most of the time, they came through on a timetable to the Steamer's liking, which was usually Right Now. Sometimes he wouldn't get the meds mix right, or he'd wash it down with booze.

The kids tried to intervene, admitting him to a thirty-day treatment program in Pasadena. He didn't last one night.

The Steamer wound up in an assisted living facility in Palm Springs, with a new taste for sedatives. Combined with the drinking and the other drugs, they tore his insides out, and the internal bleeding nearly killed him. He spent a month in Eisenhower Medical Center, where Ike's people put his innards back together.

Furillo's oldest daughter found him a nice little spot in a beautiful independent living home at the base of the Topatopa Mountains in Ojai, about ninety miles north of Los Angeles. The Steamer grumbled about the joint, because they kept very close tabs on his medications. But he liked the food and the company at Table 10, where he took his meals with a retired Air Force colonel, a college professor, and a woman who had been a Berkeley radical in the '30s.

If the joint was a lifesaver for the Steamer, so was a contact his daughter made for him to do a column for the *Ojai Valley News*. Twice a week, he wrote about anything he wanted. His sports pieces were historical and contemporary, local and national, and mostly about L.A. He went to lunch with the mayor. He made characters out of local bartenders and other new buddies. His pal, ESPN poker analyst Norman Chad, came up from Los Angeles and took him out to lunch once a month.

Along with the column, the Steamer worked on his memoirs.

"I felt Durocher was the best ever between the lines even if his record didn't accentuate that," he wrote.

He had been with Walt Alston the day the Dodgers skipper was selected to the Hall of Fame, and remembered that the manager "broke down and wept" when he got the news.

He was also with Johnny Podres when the pitcher, hitting on a chick in a bar in 1958, told her he'd won the seventh game of the '55 World Series, to which the doll replied, "So?"

The last time he saw John McKay, in Palm Springs, the coach made the Steamer cry like a baby when he told him, "Bud, what I did at SC—you were part of that."

Annette Funicello, he wrote, "called me once to see if I could arrange a date for her with Sandy Koufax. I don't believe I ever passed along the information."

When he wore one of those ghastly, early-'70s leisure suits on a visit to stroke-ridden Jimmy Cannon in New York in 1973, the columnist told the Steamer, "You look like a Milano pimp."

Warming up over coffee with Red Smith one spring training morning in Pompano Beach, the great sports columnist told Furillo, "Bud, I have nothing against Los Angeles. I like Los Angeles. Just tell me one thing, where is it?"

Of Pete Carroll, the Steamer said, "He is the most dynamic speaker I've heard in a lifetime of clocking football coaches."

Furillo, of course, was sorry when Jimmy "The Greek" Snyder died, and for good reason. "He still owes me $300," he wrote.

The Steamer forever recalled something Willie Stargell once told him: "Nothing positive comes from negative thought."

On the Saturday afternoon of July 8, 2006, Furillo attended a baseball game at Dodger Stadium for the last time and dropped in to say hello to everybody in the press box.

"He was frail now, his skin translucent, his step showing the wear from eighty hard years," Steve Dilbeck wrote in a column later for the *Los Angeles Daily News.* Not too many people recognized the Steamer anymore, but "the eyes still sparkled, the hair gray but thick, the mind still sharp."

"It was," Dilbeck continued, "the last chance most in the Los Angeles sports scene would have to pass a moment with a man once a giant in this town."

The last time I talked to my dad was eight days after his trip to the ballpark. He was in good spirits. Italy had just won the World Cup, and we had a couple of good yuks at Zidane's expense. He sounded great. But so had Jack Kent Cooke in his last interview with the Steamer, two days before he died.

Forty-eight hours later, I got the news from Ojai. When they let us in to go through his room, the *L.A. Times* sports section was still on the bed. I found a five-by-seven yellow notepad on his nightstand. One of his last notations read, "Umpires Too Fat."

He worked it to the end.

THE STEAM ROOM COLUMNS

A DOZEN OF THE AUTHOR'S FAVORITES

ARAGON LIKE OLD FOOTBALL; COULDN'T BE PUMPED UP

JANUARY 22, 1960

Those who hadn't been seen at a fight in years came to witness the "execution." But that's the way it always has been in boxing. The game's members faithfully attend "funerals" for one of their own.

The old pros who were there knew inside that Alvaro Gutierrez, a common brawler, would "bury" the thirty-two-year-old Art Aragon at the Olympic last night.

But they came to give him one last rousing cheer. And stand in sobbing requiem as Referee Tommy Hart held the Golden Boy straight for a second to tell him "it's all over" at 2:22 of the ninth round. The massacre came with Aragon helpless against the ropes.

Before the bout started, the old pros hoped beyond hope some of the old snap might return to his punches, even though it hadn't been observed in two years.

PAY LAST RESPECTS

Those who spat out against him publicly in past years, came to pay their last respects. Fighters of the same era, like Enrique Bolanos, Cisco Andrade, and Freddie (Babe) Herman, once an Aragon stablemate. Lauro Salas, too.

Jimmy Roche, who managed Art in his most glorious days, was there. So was Joe Stone, the referee who quit that post after one of the controversies which normally followed an Aragon fight.

Outside of Salas, the retired fighters I mentioned, seldom are at ringside. But they came to see the man they envied as the biggest drawing card the town has ever known.

Guys who brought their dolls saw a few of them run up to Art's corner during the fight to shriek encouragement. The Olympic ushers and police, who refrain from emotion, shouted for him as they knelt in the aisles.

Every time Art swung, the joint rocked, but the cheers weren't enough to spur the 150-pound body in the faded and sagging gold briefs.

Nothing was going to help and ▶

that was obvious from the beginning when a first-round left hook catapulted him to the canvas.

Between rounds, his seconds fed him pure oxygen from a tank.

It reminded me of the neighborhood kids trying to pump up an old football which has sprung a leak. But soon as you kick it, the bounce is gone again.

BOLANOS CRIES FOR ART

Tired himself and comfortably ahead, it seemed that Gutierrez was content to loaf it out for the decision. But when Art reached into that big heart to launch a rally at the start of the ninth, Gutierrez walked through his punches to set him up for a thirty-second battering before Hart jumped in.

Ten years ago in the same ring, Aragon wrote finis to a brilliant Bolanos career. Last night, Bolanos wept openly as he limped up the aisle next to Jim Healy. He sobbed:

"A couple of years ago, Art would have knocked him out in two rounds. It happens to all of us. We all quit later than we should."

Bolanos was the only visitor allowed in Aragon's dressing room for more than five minutes. At first, Art would not live up to the promise of retirement he had made before the fight, in the event he lost.

"Give me a couple of days to think it over," he said.

Perhaps a calculating look at his torn, bleeding face brought the truth home. Two hundred fans remained to cheer him when he climbed out of the Olympic catacombs forty-five minutes later. The proud man jumped up on a beer case and spoke:

"I'm telling you fans you'll never see me again. This is my last fight."

Goodbye, and good luck.

MOORE'S DURABILITY AMAZES RING VETS

JUNE 12, 1961

NEW YORK—Archie Moore claims he's forty-four. His mother says he's forty-seven.

Mickey Walker believes Arch and his kindly mother are both hedging. I walked away from ringside with the famed "Toy Bulldog" after the indestructible Moore baked Giulio Rinaldi's face in an oven of gloves for forty-five minutes to convert it into a pizza—heavy on the sauce. Walker shook his head, which must have been full of compressed awe for the ageless wonder. Mickey let it out a little at a time, in praise of the light-heavyweight king, who successfully defended his title Saturday night. He said:

"He's an encouragement for old age.

"Let me tell you something about Mr. Moore. He's fifty-four if he's a day. He has to be. He was a sparring partner in my camp in 1927. And he could fight like the devil then."

Before Walker, Gene Tunney did the head shake in tribute to Moore. Tunney assessed:

"You have to go back to Fitzsimmons to find a fighter who successfully defied age the way Moore does. He's an absolute marvel."

SPARRING PARTNER THIRTY-FOUR YEARS AGO

Walker's sparring partner thirty-four years ago confounded a lot of experts with the boundless energy he used to turn the legs of his twenty-six-year-old opponent into something resembling those of a woman scaling the seventy-ninth row of the Coliseum.

Odds favoring Archie once high as 3–1, dipped to 8–5 after the weigh-in because Moore looked so emaciated making 174½. He weighed 200 for a tune-up fight in Manila less than three months ago. Hollywood's movie queens should be so lucky to lose weight as rapidly as did the old mongoose.

Every time out though, and he's been to the post 213 times now, the ranks of those who doubt his longevity are swelled. Rocky Marciano joined them Saturday night at the Garden. He turned to Toots Shor after the seventh round and observed:

"Moore's all through."

Toots turned the other way to Don Ameche and barked:

"Double our bet. I never saw a fighter who knew anything about fights."

ARCH TOSSES MEAN SPEECH, TOO

Archie's pseudo-scholarly delivery of a speech would make you think he knows everything about his trade. Boxing's elder statesman spoke to the press like a valedicto-rian after riddling Signor Rinaldi.

He was grateful to me for ap-pealing to my fellow animals to step away from the rubbing table so that everyone could hear what the ring's Baruch had on his mind. Ar-chie stood on the table and began his phony eloquence:

"I was boxing along conven-tional lines. When Rinaldi got rough as he had in Italy when I discovered him over there, I said to him:

"'You shouldn't hit me on the back of the head as that can cause severe brain injury.' Too bad he doesn't understand English.

"I was determined to give this young man a lesson because of what happened in Italy last Novem-ber. When he went home to Anzio, they rang church bells all night long. They kept me awake."

"Arch," I interrupted. "You heard church bells in Rome?"

"That's right," he answered promptly, aware that I might have an idea more than 125 miles sepa-rate Rome and Anzio. Then he fed a carny man's pitch:

"Rome is quite a distance from Anzio, but there is a valley which runs between the cities, through which sound traverses. And I sleep with my windows open."

SHOWS SPORTING BLOOD

Who am I to disbelieve Moore's extra-sensory powers along with his other attributes? One of these was the sporting manner in which he refused to hit Rinaldi for ten seconds in the final round when the challenger turned his ankle. Moore explained:

"I have never extended any leniency myself. But this man is a visitor and wanted him to feel at home."

Moore asked the writers if they were satisfied with his per-formance. The room got so quiet I almost thought I heard the bells of Anzio. Archie re-phrased the question:

"Were you satisfied with the performance of an old man of for-ty-dum and up?"

The naughty old tease pur-posely garbled his age. The writers responded affirmatively.

Moore carved up a rank ama-teur in Rinaldi, who was a year old when Archie had his first profes-sional fight recorded. But the vet-eran butcher used a dull cleaver.

If age has robbed Moore of anything, it could be his punch. The man who has knocked out more people with his fists (130) than anyone in history, couldn't spill the wobbling Italian. Even though he blasted him repeatedly with his best left hooks and straight rights.

Dick Sadler, one of his sec-onds, had an answer. He claimed Moore hurt his right hand in the fourth round and his left in the seventh.

What if some of the sting is gone? What if Arch does use hair dye to disguise his mat of grey?

There's still plenty of spring in "Mr. Machine." Before the fourteenth round he did a knee bend exercise and danced through the final minute of the fifteenth.

Archie Moore may not go on forever. But those who bet against this possibility turn their prosperity into well-kept graves.

BATTING CAGE DIDOES STACK GRIST FOR PRESS BOX MILL

MARCH 22, 1963

PALM SPRINGS—A day at the batting cage:

Willie Mays rushed in with two bats.

He took three swings with one of them and sprayed singles to left, center and right. Then, baseball's best player exchanged the lumber. He socked a cloud-scraper to left-center Missouri.

"Think that one's going out of here?" Harvey Kuenn asked of Rocky Bridges, his old roomie from Detroit days.

Bridges shifted his chaw and drolled:

"It's out of the parking lot on the other side of the fence."

Willie bounced around the cage like a most happy fella. He said in a voice slightly higher than the one Shirley Temple used to sing her way to fame and fortune in *Little Miss Marker*:

"I brought my long bat today. In Phoenix you can hit 'em out with short bats. This is a bigger park."

WAGS SUBJECTED TO NEEDLE

Mays asked Leon Wagner to shag balls for him while he hit a few to the outfielders. Willie McCovey needs practice catching the balls. Wagner snorted:

"What's wrong with you? I ain't your caddy anymore."

Mays screeched a few insults which put a smile on Daddy Wags's face. He went back to caddying for Willie.

Albert Gregory Pearson passed behind the cage. Mays looked at him. Then he said to Wagner:

"My that Albie's small. He ain't big as my glove."

The mighty mite of the Angels wheeled to shout:

"I heard you, Willie. It's not so bad being a midget centerfielder. I get a lot of work during the winter riding horses at Santa Anita."

Orlando Cepeda waited to hit in the cage. To pass the time, he jingled some money in his pocket. The sound made general manager Chub Feeney of the Giants wince.

"You should have seen Cepeda and Juan Marichal on the plane coming over here. They sat together and talked about how they outsmarted me."

Between them, the crafty Caribbean holdouts held up Feeney for $73,000.

Looking at Cepeda, I thought to myself the Giant writers better find a new nickname for him. Baby Bull doesn't fit anymore. He's full grown.

Feisty Bill Rigney rasped at Wagner:

"Haven't I told you to stop fraternizing with the opposition? You're liable to pick up some of his bad habits."

"What bad habits I got, Skip?" queried the soprano slugger.

"Lining singles to left field after you've been knocked on your hip pocket by a pitch."

WILLIE CROSSED 'EM

Mays giggled. He remembered what Rigney was talking about. A year ago to the day, the Giants played a game at the Springs. First time up, the Angel pitcher thought Willie would look better down.

In came a fastball which would have spun Mays's cap. Willie hit the deck faster than Floyd Patterson.

But he reached up with the "long bat" and singled one-handed.

Coach Del Rice showed Mays a scar on his leg.

"That's what you did the time you slid in and broke it."

"What you mean I broke your leg? I only fractured it," grinned the basket catcher.

A groundskeeper tapped the Steamer on the shoulder.

"Thanks a million for holding up the batting cage for us. But we'd like to move it now. Why don't you hurry off to your sentry duty on Palm Canyon Drive?"

From the batting cage I moved up to the squirrel cage—the press box—where the typewriters have been known to break down.

THE BOMBERS WENT IN FEARING KOUFAX
OCTOBER 3, 1963

YANKEE STADIUM, N.Y.—The Yankees were taking their cuts before the curtain went up for the big show yesterday and Joe Pepitone was standing outside the cage singing an awful song.

It was one of those things your kids play on the stereo that drive you insane.

"I'm singing to get my mind off Koufax," said the Yankee first baseman, and he gave me another chorus of:

"I wish I was home where I belong because I'm just a lonesome teenager."

As it turned out, Koufax made unwanted children of the Yankees with a pitching performance I'll remember for the rest of my life.

AN UNFORTUNATE
I'm one of the American League unfortunates who doesn't get to see him very often, you know.

"If you have any influence at all, please keep him in the National League," said Bill Rigney, shaking from the thought of his little Angels having to face scary Sandy.

The Steamer has to think the Yankees went into the series opener fearing Koufax. They justified this view by his fifteen strikeout performance.

Tony Floria is the handsome teen-aged batboy of the Yankees who enjoyed a day off when he should have been working. It is Tony's job to return the bats to the rack after the players hit the ball.

Tony toted very little lumber with fifteen of the fellas bringing back their own bats after strike three to slam them into the racks.

Through the first half of the game when Koufax dominated like a supreme being, the only thing the Yankees could hit was their fists against the dugout wall. Their helmets took a vicious beating, too, especially the one Mickey Mantle slammed when he was called out on strikes in the second inning.

And how did his scowl for umpire Joe Paparella light up your television screen?

The player who will be remembered most outside of Koufax as time makes a classic of a chilling series opener will be Harry Bright.

Harry knocked around baseball for seventeen years before he got to the Yankees. He played for clubs in Fond du Lac, Twin Falls, Independence, Houma, Sioux City, Clovis, Topeka, and Janesville.

Those of us with Coast League memories recall when he was with Sacramento. Pittsburgh gave him a big league tumble and then sent him to one of the closest places to a return to bushville with an assignment in Washington.

Harry is a nice guy, but he was getting as much out of baseball as Joe Valachi was as a soldier in sordid Cosa Nostra.

Bright was a loser in the game until he hit the twin double, the 5–10, and the Irish Sweepstakes. The Yankees took him figuring Harry might pinch-hit for somebody in the Series and make a little history.

Which is what he did in the ninth inning with a man on base in the first game against the Dodgers. The Yankees were behind 5–2 but the sun was going down.

That's when the Yankees are most dangerous. They don't call them the sundowners for nothing.

Once in a while this year Harry Bright hit a home run for the Yankees in this situation.

When he stepped into bat for the pitcher, Harry was looking to do something like that. Only the odds were 69,001 against him. The crowd and Koufax.

"He threw me a fastball," said Bright. "I knew it was coming. It was no surprise. But what the hell could I do?

"There were 69,000 people yelling for me.

"They were yelling for me to strike out."

Harry Bright didn't disappoint them.

BAYLOR AT PEAK AS LOS ANGELES LAKER

MARCH 8, 1965

Los Angeles didn't know what a superstar was until Elgin Baylor came to town. The year was 1960. Don Drysdale and Sandy Koufax weren't in full bloom yet.

What's Baylor like five years later? The question was put to his coach last night after Jerry West won the game as usual with a bucket in the last eight seconds. The Cincinnati Royals were the 106–104 victims. Fred Schaus didn't hesitate to register his opinion.

"Baylor is playing better than he ever has in Los Angeles. He had the shots when he came here but it's his defense that is vastly improved. You take into consideration that he still plays in pain and you conclude he's fantastic," said Schaus.

Elegant Elg brought out most of the shots in his voluminous play book to score thirty-eight points against the Royals.

There is no man in the history of the game who ever laid the ball up on the iron any softer than the Lakers captain. It seldom caroms off wildly as it does for other players. For Elg, the ball hangs on the iron until it gets enough gravity going to fall through the net.

THE BEATINGS HE TAKES

He showed off bank shots that would draw envy from Cisero Murphy, the pocket billiards champ.

Baylor shot better than anybody else on the floor from the outside, too. Remember that Oscar Robertson, West, and Jerry Lucas were on the floor.

When Baylor drives, it reminds you of films of the young Indian brave who catches hell and has to run the gauntlet for letting Gary Cooper escape. Elgin takes a terrible beating trying to dodge whales like Wayne Embry, Bill Bridges and Zelmo Beatty to unload reverse layups.

It shows all over his body. He's carrying an ugly bruise on his right biceps from a Saturday session with Bridges in St. Louis.

The knees that failed him last year still ache enough to tax his sleep. But he forgets 'em to rebound under both baskets and play as if he was twenty-one instead of thirty-one.

The Steamer has never seen Baylor play any better than he did last night. But then I don't get out to see the Minneapolis Basketball Corporation as much as I should.

"He's been playing that way all year," said Schaus. "The man has pride. He remembers last year."

The calcified knees reduced Baylor to an ordinary NBA performer last season. The Lakers finished third. The old pro is hungry to prove his club should be on top in the Western Division.

A division title means $13,000. There's an additional $14,000 available in the divisional playoffs and a total of $50,000 if the Lakers go all the way and upset the Celtics. That kind of money stimulates one's pride.

Baylor was the last one out of the dressing room last night.

"The knees are sore," he admitted. "We played three games in different cities on consecutive nights. I'm glad we don't have to play tomorrow. That's when the misery will set in.

"I'm getting some injections in the morning. Shots don't bother me anymore. I don't even feel the needle."

TIME FOR OIL CHANGE

Baylor got a cortisone lube job this morning. Before each game, towels are heated in a machine known as a hydrocollator and applied to Baylor's knees.

"We've found that with moist heat I don't have to warm up very long. It saves wear and tear on the leg," he said.

Walt Hazzard is in charge of packing the hydrocollator from city to city. It's his job to make sure it goes everywhere Baylor goes.

"It's the price I pay for being a rookie," said Hazzard. "I hope there's a rookie on the club next year. I'll buy a hydrocollator for him to carry for me. That Baylor really works me out."

Baylor was asked why he has to take a pounding to shoot on the drive.

"The officials seldom call the other side for fouling me when I drive," he said. "I guess it's because I always get the shot off. Other players don't, and the foul in the act of shooting is more obvious."

If a team in the NBA knows it can foul a man and get away with it constantly, he goes through the wringer. That's the situation with Baylor, who also may be getting the business in the hope by the other side, that one of those knees will give out.

The opposition may be out to wreck Baylor, but it's only because he is still held in such high regard.

The players paused from clotheslining him, elbowing, tripping, and holding him long enough the other day to pick him as a forward on their own All-NBA team.

"I was honored," said Baylor, as he limped through the door to the street.

STENGEL HEEDS HIS PITCHING COACH
APRIL 21, 1965

Implementing the "isolated sportswriter," the *Herald-Examiner* caught a conversation between Casey Stengel, seventy-four, and his pitching coach, Warren Spahn, forty-four, at a very critical ninth inning moment in Dodger Stadium last night.

Why Stengel would listen to someone thirty years his junior is anybody's guess—probably because Spahn was pitching at the time.

The Amazin' Mets were doing their level best to throw away a 3–0 lead and were two-thirds of the way home when Stengel called time. The score was 3–2, nobody out, and runners on first and third.

Casey wobbled to the mound, crossed in front of it and said in a voice best suited for calling trains:

"I got McGraw and Ribant down in the bullpen. Which one of those fellas should I bring in?"

Spahn didn't see the logic of bringing in Frank McGraw or Dennis Ribant to relieve a 356-game winner in the major leagues who had the Dodgers shut out until the last inning. Spahn kicked the dirt.

"How do you feel?" Stengel inquired.

"I feel good," Spahn assured. "Let me pitch to the next kid."

"You may feel good," said Stengel, "but a few of those balls they've hit off you have been pretty lively, although I guess the first basemen helped out."

Stengel reconstructed, with that last sentence, what had finally brought an opening night Dodger crowd of 36,161 to life.

HE HELD ONTO BALL

Wes Parker singled to open the ninth with L.A. behind 3–0. Willie Davis hit a double play ball to first baseman Ed Kranepool, who entered the game at the start of the inning for defensive purposes. Kranepool accepted the ball and then in the manner of a quarterback trying to run out the clock, held on to it.

Two singles later, Spahn was in the position where Stengel asked him who should come in to pitch.

Casey went with experience. McGraw and Ribant learned something if they paid attention. Spahn struck out Jim Lefebvre on screwballs. Ron Fairly bounced the ball back to the game's all-time southpaw winner, who trapped Tommy Davis off third. Warren wound it up by fanning John Kennedy on screwballs.

The screwball is a pitch Spahn came up with ten years ago when it appeared to him he would need something extra if he intended to pitch in the bigs for another decade.

The screwball got him his first win as a Met after nineteen years with the Braves, and, as Spahn pointed out:

"It's my first win for Casey in twenty-three years."

Stengel was Spahn's first big-league manager back in 1942—in Boston before the Braves became a road show.

"I only pitched once or twice for Casey that season, then I went into the service," Spahn recalled in front of his locker.

Yogi Berra, a younger man in the locker next to him, said to Spahn:

"If you pitched to everyone like you did the last three batters we wouldn't be here this late."

Spahn smiled. So did Yogi, who has learned a new cheer.

"Let's go Mets," he shouted, in a Yankee accent.

Yogi explained why Spahn is with the Mets. Everyone knows why Berra left the Yankees.

"Warren told me his screwball wasn't good last year," said Berra. "That's why the Braves let him go."

The Boston-Milwaukee-Atlanta club gave Spahn to the Mets just to pay his salary, which is only $65,000. They "gave" him away because Spahn fell fourteen short of his normal twenty wins.

Bobby Bragan, the Braves manager, took to poor-mouthing Spahn after the deal, and Spahn did not lead any cheers for Bobby. Spahn was asked how he felt Bragan might feel about his route-going clutch win over the Dodgers.

"No comment," said Spahn. "I just hope he reads the papers."

RECORDS 2,500TH STRIKEOUT

It was called to Spahn's attention that he recorded his 2,500th strikeout while knocking the Dodgers out of first place. He even went one better than that.

"I never had a bigger one in my life than that last one," said Spahn.

"I threw some good pitches to the last three hitters, but I had some eager guys up there, too.

"I didn't tire. If anything, I got careless. I gave John Roseboro a pitch that was too good."

Someone wanted to know if Spahn could remember the first man he ever struck out in the majors. He couldn't, but denied that it was Abner Doubleday.

"It was before the war," he said.

"I think it's great to have confidence going for you on the bench. I just had to break my back after Casey left me in there like he did."

Stengel merely went along with the advice of his pitching coach.

JUAN FEELS AWFUL, PITCHES GREAT
JUNE 13, 1966

SAN FRANCISCO—The 1966 winner of the Cy Young Award is certain to be a very sick man.

The only candidates at this stage are eleven-game winners. On the left, there is Sanford Koufax, with the arthritic elbow, and on the right, Juan Marichal.

Marichal has elbow trouble, finger trouble, rib trouble, back trouble, nose trouble, and ankle trouble. Many believe that all of these ailments stem from Juan's head trouble.

They claim he's a hypochondriac. But Marichal doesn't share that view.

Things are so bad for Juan he can't kick anymore, and that's an important part of his game.

Perhaps you noticed that Marichal wasn't at his high-kicking best even though he salvaged a win for the Giants against the Dodgers here in Candlestick yesterday. Juan beat the world champions, 3–2, on a four hitter.

"I am afraid if I kick my leg in the air I will fall down or fly away," Marichal said. "The wind was too strong. I never did see it that strong before."

"You always pitch good with a strong wind," someone said to Juan.

"You think so?" Marichal asked. "You never see me turn my back so many times, huh? There is too much dust.

"One time I threw a fastball to Willie Davis over the middle of the plate—the ball almost hit him. Another pitch I throw off speed to Tommy Davis—I thought it was going to come back to me instead of go up to him."

BEST SINCE SIR FRANCIS
The wind was furious as usual in Cyclone Park on the most beautiful weekend in San Francisco since Sir Francis Drake sailed into the bay several hundred years ago. It was beautiful everywhere but Candlestick—the only ballpark in the world where the usherettes wear parkas in June.

Howling right along with the wind were the crude customers who insist on booing John Roseboro. They haven't forgiven him for hitting Marichal's bat with his head last August.

The booing of Roseboro annoyed Marichal.

"I don't go for that," Juan said.

"He will never forget what happened. I won't forget that either. But the people should forget. They should not boo."

Marichal rubbed his left side.

"I have pain in my ribs," he said. "It was bad. I have to take pills in the third inning. I don't know what is trouble."

"What else is wrong with you?" I asked.

"I have a pinch nerve in my elbow. I hurt it in Cincinnati," Marichal said. "I throw curve too hard. Oh boy, it hurts."

Juan the Patient moved on to other miseries.

"I cannot breathe good all the time. The doctor say it is allergy. It is always worse in Houston.

"I feel good in L.A. in the nighttime. It is the best for my allergy. But I like to pitch in San Francisco. I am always strong here because it is cold. I come from hot country, but I don't like to pitch where it is hot."

Marichal looked at his right ankle.

"Two years now I have trouble with it," said.

He compared index fingers.

ONLY ONE THING RIGHT

"See how swollen it is," he said, poking out his right hand.

The second knuckle was twice the size of the matching knuckle on his left hand.

"How long has it been since you felt good?" I asked.

"Hmmm, 1963," Marichal answered. "I feel pretty good in 1963."

Juan won twenty-five games that year at full strength.

Marichal wheezed, rubbed his aching side, and gazed at his swollen finger.

"Is *anything* all right?" I asked.

"I like your suit," he said.

SANTA ANITA HANDICAP TO FAVORITE

FEBRUARY 27, 1967

Pretense is described by his owner as a "big, strong country boy." A sentimentalist he isn't.

The big boy refused to be taken in by the applause for Native Diver in the walking ring and again in the post parade.

Pretense, only four years old, knocked off Native Diver, the Archie Moore of racing, to win the thirtieth running of the $145,000 Santa Anita Handicap in Arcadia Saturday.

Native Diver is twice the age of Pretense. But he was still good enough to be second best in the Big Cap, staged before 51,709 on a cool but comfortable afternoon—particularly for those who backed Pretense down to 8–5 favoritism.

The Diver led the first mile of the way, but the last quarter belonged to Pretense and Bill Shoemaker, the stakes chairman of the board.

Pretense had three lengths on Native Diver at the finish, with O'Hara third and somebody named Damelo II fourth.

Drin, winner of the Strub Stakes, never got out of a gallop and wound up fifth as the second choice. Then came the girl, Natashka, Quicken Tree, Fleet Host, and Moontrip in the field of nine.

The form players collected $5.40, $3.40, and $3.20 on Pretense. Native Diver, now eligible for Social Security, returned $6.20 and $4.80 for the fans who have grown old backing him. O'Hara paid $6.60. Time of the race was a credible 2:00 4/5.

THE HUNDRED GRANDER

It was the third straight visit to the winner's circle for Pretense at Santa Anita and his fourth of the meeting. This one will buy a lot of hay.

The Big Cap score netted $100,000 for his owner, Liz Tippett, who doesn't appear to need it. One of her divorce settlements brought her $3 million.

She is the wife of Colonel Cloyce Tippett, of Ocala, Florida, who owns an aircraft company and a few mines in Peru.

Liz, who heads up Llangollen Farm, has been to the winner's circle in the Big Cap before. She was there with Corn Husker in 1957, but she was Mrs. Richard Lunn then.

Before that she was Mrs. John Hay Whitney and Mrs. Cooper Person. She started out as Mary Elizabeth Altemus of Philadelphia and she was one of the world's leading horse show performers at one time.

There is nothing to indicate that Liz comes from great wealth except that she wears full length mink coats and carries a poodle named Killer in her purse. Killer is one year older than Pretense, but she can't run as fast.

Native Diver was third choice in the betting, but you would never have known it from the manner in which he was received by the players, who are noted for showing compassion for geldings.

The Diver was cheered in the walking ring and responded with a dance. Naturally, many were taken in by this and raced for the windows.

The Diver got a tremendous hand in the post parade, again at the start—and it carried him a mile. He ran most of it in the middle of the race track with Donald Pierce on his back. The Diver runs out because he can't stand to have horses by to his right.

SHOE HAD ROOM

So Shoemaker brought Pretense inside of him on the turn for home.

"Pierce gave me a lot of room to get through," said Shoemaker, thirty-six, who won the Big Cap for the sixth time.

Shoe's statement shouldn't be construed as a hint that Pierce did a bum job of riding Native Diver. The Diver runs in the middle of the track for everybody, including his regular boy, Jerry Lambert, who was sidelined by a suspension.

"I got the feeling that once he got to the front, Pretense wanted to loaf," Shoemaker said, "so I hit him a couple of times. He had

something left at the end."

It was Shoemaker's only winning ride of the afternoon. It was also his twelfth stakes triumph of the meeting, a Santa Anita record. There are only eight jockeys on the racetrack who have won as many total races this season as Shoe has stakes. Over the years, Shoe has been on 104 stakes winners at Santa Anita.

Pretense broke second behind the hustling Diver who led by as much as 3½ lengths with a half mile to go. Then the son of Endeavor II made his move and rolled by with the ease of a sports car going by a semi truck and trailer.

"It didn't break his heart, though," Pierce said of Native Diver. "He never gave up but the winner is just too good now.

O'Hara, with Milo Valenzuela, made a big move on the turn. "But he didn't have the punch to catch the first two," said Milo.

Second place was worth $20,000 to Native Diver, which should keep him off Skid Row for a few more years. A square shooter even though he is a gelding, the Diver doesn't appear to be the type who'll become a lush when he falls out of public favor. Third place money brought $10,000 to the O'Hara people while Damelo II earned $5,000 for fourth.

THE FILLY FLOPS

Natashka, the first filly entered in the Big Cap since Silver Spoon in

1960, was up there with the top two until the stretch. But then her mind must have switched to the things that females regard as important, such as settling down and raising a family. After all, Natashka is four. Next year she'll be a mare.

While Native Diver did the dancing in the walking ring, Liz Whitney Tippett did it in the winner's circle, which has come to be known as Shoemaker's Half Acre.

She gave Santa Anita president Bob Strub a big kiss—after Pretense got same—and threw the blanket of anthuriums over her friend Connie Dinkler, who, as everybody knows, owns the Palm Bay Club on the other coast. Connie was still wearing Pretense's flower blanket a half hour later in the press box, where Liz challenged Buckpasser.

"This is the greatest horse I have ever bred," she said. "Now we want to tangle with Buckpasser. We're ready—he better be ready."

Buck was out of earshot. He was back in the barn with a sore foot.

PRETENSE DUCKED BUCK

Had Buck been able to run in the Big Cap, it might not have been so big from a field standpoint. There would have been more like five instead of nine horses in the race, although Pretense would have been one of them even though beaten by Buck in both of their meetings.

It was surprising to hear Pretense's owner shouting challenges, considering that trainer Charlie Whittingham ducked Buckpasser last month.

When it looked as if Buckpasser would go in the Strub Stakes, Whittingham dropped Pretense into the San Pasqual Handicap two days earlier.

Then Buck got sick. So did Charlie.

"I'm the only one who has never been scared of Buckpasser," said Mrs. Tippett, a rightfully happy owner who added:

"Winning a race like this is much more exciting now than it was ten years ago because I'm so much older."

You can imagine how Native Diver would have felt.

ROCKY: THE NO. 1 ITALIAN HERO

SEPTEMBER 2, 1969

Those who saw Rocky Marciano fight suspected it would take something like an airplane crash to keep him down. Punches couldn't do it.

He was the invincible man in the ring. Out of it, he became an underdog like the rest of us in the game with fate, which ended his life before he could enjoy a full one.

The shock of his death makes it difficult to write about him. There is the tenacious urge to be maudlin because that's how I feel. But the champ wouldn't want that.

In my world of heroes, he was number one. Nobody else ever came close.

He meant as much to the Italian-Americans in this country as Joe Louis and Jackie Robinson have to the Negroes, what Muhammad Ali represents to the militant young blacks—or the sense of pride the Irish and Indians get from identifying with Jack Dempsey.

Son of an immigrant cobbler, Rocky made it the way every kid in all the poor neighborhoods of America dream of making it. Anyone who hasn't put together a vision of what it would be like to be champ has missed something in daydreams.

Fighters, more than other athletes, feel a sense of duty in being polite to people. Marciano was

undefeated in this respect, too.

He understood the feeling Italian-Americans had for him. I can see the people beaming now on North Broadway the first time the champ made the rounds at Little Joe's, Costa Grill, and stood in front of Dario's Delicatessen on Ord Street in the company of Otto Basso, to meet the good people of the neighborhood. They loved it.

CLOSED CIRCUIT DEBUT

Rocky's challenge for Joe Walcott's championship was the start of boxing on closed circuit in the Los Angeles theaters.

The Orpheum was packed that September night when Rocky made his bid even though the title fight wasn't shown live.

You have to remember that those were the carriage days of 1952. L.A. still had street cars, although not all of them were horse-drawn.

Mushy Honek, king of the ushers before he moved into the travel agency business, grabbed my arm and said: "Want to know who won?" The fight was over and he knew the winner.

He could have saved me a few heart attacks, and [boxing writer] George Main a sore arm from the pounding he got when the fight was over and Rocky was the champ.

Rocky made a lot of people happy and wealthy as well.

There was Jimmy Sinelia, the eastern tomato king they called Jimmy Tomatoes. They say he won more than a hundred grand on Marciano. When Rocky retired, they went into the frozen food business and took a bigger beating than Walcott did.

The most anxious moment Marciano fans ever had was in his second fight with Ezzard Charles. Rocky's nose was split. It was impossible to control the flow of blood.

After the seventh round, the referee told Rocky that he would not let the fight go beyond the eighth round. "You'll bleed to death," he said.

Marciano knocked Charles out in the eighth and went to the hospital.

The story of the friendship between Marciano and Allie Columbo in the march to the title was a lesson in the importance of a buddy.

Boyhood pals in Brockton, Massachusetts, they went into the Army together, and, when Rocky decided that fighting for a living beat digging ditches for the gas company, he asked Columbo to be his manager.

Allie agreed. However, realizing his shortcomings in a cruel business, Columbo asked Al Weill to take Rocky over.

Weill did a masterful job of managing the remainder of an undefeated professional career of 49–0 for Marciano. Rocky lost one fight as an amateur—a decision to Coley Wallace, who was a contender for a while, but realized his greatest purse portraying Joe Louis on the screen.

Marciano could have been champion for at least five years after he quit. He realized it and often regretted the decision.

We were together the nights before and after Ingemar Johansson knocked out Floyd Patterson for the title Rocky gave up. The champ kicked himself for quitting.

Stories continued to appear throughout the decade that the Rock was coming back. He encouraged them and permitted them to linger before the inevitable denial.

"I need the publicity," he told me.

Marciano never lost his enthusiasm for boxing.

He managed Tony Alongi for a while and once tried to buy Jerry Quarry's contract. The Rock saw something in Jerry early in his career at the Olympic, where the Rock used to come with his cousin, Jimmy Cione, who lives here.

"He was in the ring the night I fought Buster Mathis," Quarry recalled yesterday from Oakland. "He told me, 'You can take this big fellow.'

"I can't even think about my fight because of this terrible thing that has happened," Quarry said.

Jerry fights Brian London

tomorrow night in a bout which doesn't necessitate a whole lot of thought on his part.

COMPUTER CHAMP

Marciano won the computer heavyweight championship two years ago by "defeating" Jack Dempsey in the finals. Results were determined by feeding the records of all the former champs into the electronic brain.

Rocky didn't put much stock in the computer. He thought Dempsey and Louis were better than he was.

The computer didn't think so. Neither will a lot of people who will increase his stature in death.

It would be so much better to have him alive.

WHO'S GREATEST? FRAZIER, OF COURSE
MARCH 9, 1971

Muhammad Ali, the prophet from Islam, vowed to straighten out the heavyweight mess, but he didn't.

Joe Frazier did that by beating Ali into poor health over fifteen rounds. He did it with a left hook that transformed the right side of Pretty Boy's face into a blown-up profile of the Hunchback of Notre Dame.

Ali was rushed to a hospital for X-rays of his jaw to determine if it was broken at the Fight of Champions last night at Madison Square Garden. The preliminary report was that his jaw was not broken, but Lord have mercy on us all, it is extremely difficult for him to talk this morning.

The Fight of Champions was more like a waltz between two babbling clowns through most of the middle rounds.

But Smokin' Joe saved the show with a lunging left hook that blasted Ali flat on his back forty seconds into the fifteenth round for a mandatory eight count. He got up at the count of four.

The fact that Ali finished the round and the fight dispelled for all time the notion that he couldn't take a punch. He took a few hundred.

Several other old wives' tales were aborted from this overcrowded world as well.

In the first place, Ali isn't the greatest. Frazier is so far as fighting is concerned because he is still unbeaten and Ali isn't. However, Cassius Clay is. He never did lose under his slave name.

Secondly, Ali looked anything but beautiful after Frazier hooked him as the latter used to go after sides of beef in a Philadelphia slaughterhouse. It was Kosher beef that Joe used to snag with his meat hook. This should come as a relief to Ali, who only eats Kosher cattle.

Frazier didn't look much better at the finish with an egg boiling over his left eye. Like Ali, he bled from the nose. But Joe doesn't mind.

He never boasts about looks. Hooks are his ego.

The unanimous decision was close only in the eyes of the referee, Arthur Mercante, who voted for Frazier 8–6–1. Judge Arthur Aidala stretched it to 9–6 for the twenty-seven-year-old Frazier while the other judge, Bill Recht, fell in love with Joe, 11–4. My card favored Frazier, 9–5–1.

It would have been wider for Frazier under the California scoring system in which a fighter can get more than one point in a round. Frazier had a couple of two-point rounds which he didn't get credit for in New York's unfair round system.

Joe seemed to have Ali on the way out in the eleventh and twelfth rounds. Muhammad actually went down in the eleventh, thirty seconds into the round.

But referee Mercante called it a slip. A man has to be poleaxed before Arthur will conclude he's down.

Ali staggered around the ring and they would have pinched him for sure if he had been walking in that manner around the Bowery. He held on as if Allah depended on it and perhaps it was prayer that saved him. Nothing else seemed to be working.

Ali was hurt so badly in the eleventh that Mercante summoned a doctor into the ring. Ali told Dr. Harry Kleiman that he was all right.

Frazier came out swinging from side to side with the scent of a twelfth round knockout in his nasal passages.

If nothing else was clear to Ali at this time, he seemed to understand he was being punished for the $2.5 million he received in his thirty-second fight, the same guarantee given Frazier for his twenty-seventh.

The twelfth round was sheer agony for Muhammad who still had the trace of smelling salts in his nose.

Frazier kicked the living hell out of him in that round and the crowd of 20,455, paying $1,352,961 into the live gate to go with the anticipated $25 million from closed

circuit outlets, couldn't understand what was holding Ali up.

His legs buckled several times and he would fall into the ring ropes which held him up. Now the suspicion creeped into some minds that Frazier was punched out.

The eyes of trainer Angelo Dundee and Bundini Brown widened as they saw the egg taking shape over Frazier's left eye. They thrust more smelling salts into Ali's nostrils and water all over him.

"You got to win," Bundini cried. "You got God on your side."

Ali shook his head. He suspected that and had turned toward Mecca for prayer before the first round.

He came out and speared Frazier with jabs. Suddenly the timing was there. The defrocked Muslim minister ducked hooks and dropped rights on Frazier.

But Joe caught up with him right over the ringside photographer, Frank Sinatra, and the hooks brought a terrible look of pain from Ali. I believe it was here that Frazier did whatever he did to Ali's jaw.

The egg had grown to a golf ball on Frazier's face and Ali was inspired to trade with Joe in the fourteenth round. Frazier laughed and poured back the punishment to Charlie Humble.

The crowd, which had chanted for Ali and gave him a tremendous ovation, suddenly found a new hero after the fifteenth round knockdown. They pleaded with Frazier to knock Ali out because all but close friends had wanted to see this happen for years.

But the clever fellow who has eluded the government's draft evasion conviction for 1 1/2 years was able to keep away from Frazier for the last two minutes. This he did with great courage.

He was through. He couldn't fight anymore because Frazier's early body shots had brought the hands down to make the jaw a lantern that was lit and ready to be shot out.

The decision brought no boos. Some taunted Ali. A black woman at ringside called him Clay and screamed: "Crawl on your hands and knees over to Joe like you said you would."

Muhammad didn't keep this promise either.

His litany at the weigh-in that saw him hit 215 to 205 1/2 for Frazier was: "I am going to straighten this heavyweight mess out. Joe Frazier is clumsy and ugly."

It was carny but Ali had always admitted there's a lot of that in him which he picked up from watching the put-ons of the late wrestler, Gorgeous George.

The showboat steamed merrily down Seventh Avenue from the time Ali entered the ring until he began to tire as early as the third round.

Despite his bravado beforehand which included a prediction that he would win by a sixth-round knockout—another broken promise by the politician—he seemed nervous. He kept wetting his tongue, which is a sure sign of being uptight.

He danced around the ring before the action began, bumping into Frazier and threatening him.

Ali's incomparable jab and right that dropped over missed hooks won the first and second rounds comfortably.

When Joe landed, which wasn't often in the opening rounds, Ali would shake his head to inform the audience that Joe hadn't hurt him and couldn't punch.

The laughing and talking between them disgusted referee Mercante who ordered Ali and Joe to knock it off.

The customers ate it up for a while but even those who had paid $150 for a seat got tired of the clowning.

They loved-tapped each other on the head and the tummy as Ali rested on the ropes. The crowd booed them vigorously for this in the eighth and ninth rounds.

The boos spurred Frazier. He grabbed Ali in the ninth round and threw him in the middle of the ring.

"Get out here where I can hit you, sucker," laughed Joe.

Maybe he shouldn't have said that. Ali stunned Joe immediately afterward with a right cross that put a shimmy in Joe's right wheel. He needed smelling salts between rounds. That ninth round right was Ali's best punch of the fight.

The fans screamed for Ali and even the roving bands of several thousand outside the arena atop Penn Station must have figured that Ali was making his move. He did, but flattened out like a tiring race horse by the eleventh.

At twenty-nine, Ali doesn't dance like he did at twenty-five. He was flat-footed after a couple of rounds and never got back on his toes with his white-tassled shoes.

Because this one miraculously went to a finish, the fighters will have to do it all over again. This shouldn't sorrow the promoters, Jack Kent Cooke and Jerry Perenchio, who have the rematch set for the Forum.

Some will say that Ali will take Frazier now that he has this tough fight under his draft-skipping belt.

The way he stood up to Frazier's smoke and pressure made it plain he has the heart for anything. Maybe even soldiering.

MYSTERY OVER MACHEN'S DEATH
AUGUST 8, 1972

The mystery surrounding the death of Eddie Machen coincides with his life.

It should have been a lot better, maybe not as clear as a High Sierra stream, nor as muddled as it turned out.

A polished boxer with a punch, he was talented, personable, and handsome. It was difficult not to like him.

But he kept falling on his dentures, either by his own doing, associations, or four years of frustration while the heavyweight champions ignored him. He was the world's No. 1 contender from 1959 until 1963.

Machen, forty, fell for the last time yesterday in San Francisco. He was found dead in the driveway of the Mission Street apartment house where he lived with a girl named Sherry who was away at the time.

Police aren't sure if he jumped, fell or was pushed from a second-story fire escape.

The coroner said he died of liver damage.

Friends say he was a doper on and off as well.

The real cause of his death may be as tough to solve as that of Sonny Liston, who took the longest count under mysterious circumstances in Las Vegas. Both graduated from prisons to make remarkable strides in prize fighting.

Sonny beat Eddie in a twelve-round decision before he won the title and everyone thought they should have done it again.

They didn't, and now they are dead.

Thus, Machen accomplished what he set out to do ten years ago.

He was picked up by the highway patrol near Crockett in the winter of 1962 with a loaded pistol in his lap and a suicide note to his wife and three children.

THREE YEARS AT SOLEDAD
Three bullets had been fired into a mud bank.

"I wanted to make sure the gun worked," Machen told the patrolmen.

He was committed to Napa State Hospital where he scored two knockouts his first night there before other attendants and heavy sedation overpowered him.

Eddie, who left Redding early in life, made Soledad when he was twenty-two and had three birthdays there for stickups which netted him $150.

Like Liston, it was in the slammer that he learned to fight by Marquis of Queensbury rules. But the purses when Eddie got out weren't much better than the take from the stickups.

Boxing was cruel to Machen, who was snubbed by Floyd Patterson and Liston during their terms as heavyweight president of the united states of earth.

It didn't get any better when Cassius Clay became Muhammad Ali. Finally, Eddie stopped training and ran out the string, winning here and losing there until he quit in 1967.

He underwent shock treatment and enough forms of psychiatry and therapy to straighten out a regiment.

But he went off the fire escape anyway and it doesn't seem right.

Machen was a hot fighter around Los Angeles in 1966. I got to know him fairly well in some Downey refreshment stands, where we had a taste.

He knocked Joey Orbillo and Jerry Quarry out of the undefeated ranks at the Olympic Proving Grounds. And it appeared he might run the table when he had Joe Frazier crawling on his hands and knees in the same year.

But Frazier stopped him in the final round.

He had a lot of managers who liked him and tried to get him a title shot. It never happened, but Eddie smiled except for that night near Crockett and yesterday.

Undefeated in twenty-five fights, he was knocked out in one round by Ingemar Johansson.

"He caught me with a sucker right," said Machen. "It only happened twice in my life.

"The other time was at Soledad. A big redhead in the yard belted me in the mouth and broke my upper plate in half."

THE SOLEDAD FIGHT

"I took the plate out and got up. He grabbed my jacket, pulled it over my head and kicked me where the legs come together.

"Now it was my turn. I got my jacket down and flattened him.

"He tackled me and the guards broke it up.

"We each got a day in the hole."

Then the heavyweight champions put him in solitary.

He lost only four times in eight years before he got into the habit of seeing the other guys' hands raised. At the end, his record was 50–11–3, including twenty-seven knockouts.

One night at the Sports Arena early in 1966 [matchmaker] Don Chargin looked him in the eye. Chargin, a close friend of Machen's, told him:

"This is it, Eddie. You stink out one more arena and it's fights in San Jose."

Machen lost a split decision to Manuel Ramos that night after winning the first seven rounds. Then he blew the duke at a restaurant in the company of a girl named Shary and was arrested for drunk.

But Eddie wasn't finished. He came back to win three in a row from Orbillo, Quarry, and Scrap

Iron Johnson.

He made Frazier quiver like a sloop in a monsoon before Joe smoked him out in the final round.

It's too bad Eddie couldn't have gone the distance.

AND YOU WERE JIMMY CANNON

DECEMBER 9, 1973

You were Jimmy Cannon and you picked up the chronicle of Broadway where Damon Runyon set it down.

You outlived Broadway if that was any comfort to you. But coming up on sixty-four, a stroke which you said was "like an earthquake in your body" finally put you down for the count.

You checked out this week after giving illness the kind of fight you wrote about so many times when courageous guys like Braddock and Zale stood up as long as they could.

You battled for a year and a half in and out of several hospitals.

They took you into surgery last year. You looked up at everyone wearing masks except you and you said, "What the hell is this, a stickup?"

You tired of the hospitals and you demanded to go home. "The hell with that," you said from your apartment overlooking the East River. "I'm going to make my stand here. This is where I live."

•

Writing in the second person was one of your styles. There were many others. Your one-liners had the impact of a police revolver. You made people laugh until they cried from enjoying "Guaranteed to Happen," "Nobody Asked Me But" and "What He Really Meant."

Your street corner philosophy was Plato to the mob.

Your idol was Hemingway and he said to you: "I don't know anybody who takes his job more seriously, or with more confidence. Cannon is able to convey the quality of the athlete and the feeling, the excitement."

You were incorruptible. Nobody bought Jimmy Cannon's space.

You made a lot of enemies. You were an abrasive person. But you were liked by those who wanted to take the time to understand you.

Put you on the scene and your fresh material had the zing of wild strawberries.

You liked to walk the streets of New York late at night and did until it wasn't safe anymore. You were a night person.

You came to California for a visit and I asked you if you carried a gun when you went out in New York. And your machine-gun answer was: "Yeah, to protect myself from earthquakes." Touché.

Oh but you were quick. I walked in to see you last spring in your apartment which had become your prison, but you came out of the blocks like O. J. Simpson at the sight of my California casuals. "You look like a Milano pimp in that outfit," you said.

You came up the way ghetto kids do today. You ran off and joined a newspaper after less than a year of high school. Your first big job as a frightened cub reporter was the funeral of Chauncey Depew, elegant wit and financier of the '20s. You sat next to Gene Fowler in a Western Union office terrified. Finally, you asked the most famous reporter in New York to look at your copy. He did and Fowler handed it to the operator. "File it, kid," he said. "It's better than mine."

One of your first efforts after replacing Bill Corum in 1959 with Hearst Newspapers was a column which blew up golf. It appeared in the *Herald Express*. The paper apologized for it for weeks to the golfers. I loved the piece. I played it across the top of our front sports page and my boss, George Davis, nearly killed me for it. You wrote:

"Golf is a form of solitaire played in a meadow. Croquet demands the same concentration and poise, but that is ridiculed as lawn cribbage and ignored by sports editors. If golfers are athletes, so are mail men."

You walked more than seventy-two holes covering the Third Army for Stars and Stripes as a master sergeant during World War II. You had a press row seat for the Battle of the Bulge which is maybe why you could put football in its right perspective.

You ran off to Korea when that thing broke out because of your feeling for the foot soldiers. You always said: "I believe that the bravest man in the world is an infantry soldier."

•

You never married but you almost made it. You were thrown out at the plate in the courtship of a Broadway showgirl.

You rated the greatest spectacles in sports as the Kentucky Derby, the World Series, the Super Bowl, and a heavyweight championship fight.

Your closest friends in sports were guys named Joe—DiMaggio and Louis.

You could describe a guy like Leonardo could paint 'em. Of Charlie Dressen's lovable ego, you wrote: "He speaks of himself as if praising a dear friend who had just left the room."

But you had the same kind of ego. I asked if you wanted me to mail the daily paper and you said: "Only if my stuff is in it."

You took special interest in Eddie Pope in Miami, Dave Anderson in New York, and the Steamer.

You were Jimmy Cannon and to me you were the best.

BIBLIOGRAPHY

Allen, Jennifer. *Fifth Quarter: The Scrimmage of a Football Coach's Daughter*. New York: Random House, 2000.

Allen, Maury. *Bo: Pitching and Wooing*. New York: The Dial Press, 1973.

Bisheff, Steve. *John Wooden: An American Treasure*. Nashville, TN: Cumberland House, 2004.

Bisheff, Steve, and Loel Schrader. *Fight On: The Colorful Story of USC Football*. Nashville, TN: Cumberland House, 2006.

Cannon, Jimmy, Jack Cannon, and Tom Cannon, eds. *Nobody Asked Me, But . . .* New York: Holt, Rhinehart and Winston, 1978.

Cherry, Robert. *Wilt: Larger Than Life*. Chicago: Triumph Books, 2004.

Curran, Bob. *The $400,000 Quarterback: Or, the League that Came In from the Cold*. New York: The Macmillan Company, 1965.

Deford, Frank. *Over Time: My Life as a Sportswriter*. New York: Atlantic Monthly Press, 2012.

Fowler, Will. *Reporters: Memoirs of a Young Newspaperman*. Malibu, CA: Roundtable Publishing.

Fowler, Will. *The Young Man From Denver: A Candid and Affectionate Biography of Gene Fowler*. Garden City, NY: Doubleday, 1962.

Halberstam, David. *The Breaks of the Game*. New York: Ballantine Books, 1981.

Harris, David. *The League: The Rise and Decline of the NFL*. New York: Bantam, 1986.

Holtzman, Jerome. *No Cheering in the Press Box*. New York: Henry Holt, 1973.

Izenberg, Jerry. *Through My Eyes: A Sports Writer's 58-Year Journey*. Haworth, NJ: St. Johann Press, 2009.

Krikorian, Doug. *Between The Bylines: The Life, Love and Loss of Los Angeles's Most Colorful Sports Journalist*. Charleston, SC: History Press, 2013.

Leavy, Jane. *The Last Boy: Mickey Mantle and the End of America's Childhood*. New York: HarperCollins, 2010.

Leavy, Jane. *Sandy Koufax: A Lefty's Legacy.* New York: HarperCollins Publishers Inc., 2002.

Linkon, Sherry Lee, and John Russo. *Steeltown U.S.A.: Work and Memory in Youngstown.* Lawrence, KN: University Press of Kansas, 2002.

Lipsyte, Robert. *An Accidental Sportswriter.* New York: HarperCollins Publishers, 2011.

Mailer, Norman. *King of the World.* New York: Signet, 1971.

Murray, Jim. *Jim Murray: The Autobiography of the Pulitzer Prize Winning Sports Columnist.* New York: Macmillan, 1993.

Newhan, Ross. *The Anaheim Angels: A Complete History.* New York: Hyperion, 2000.

Ortiz, Johnny. *My Life Among the Icons.* Baltimore, MD: Publish America, 2009.

Perry, Jim. *McKay: A Coach's Story.* New York: Atheneum, 1974.

Reid, David, ed. *Sex, Death and God in L.A.* Berkeley and Los Angeles: University of California Press.

Remnick, David. *King of the World.* New York: Random House. 1999.

Remnick, David, ed. *The Only Game in Town: Sportswriting from the New Yorker.* New York: Modern Library Paperbacks, 2011.

Robinson, Sugar Ray, with Dave Anderson. *Sugar Ray.* New York: The Viking Press, 1969.

Shoemaker, Bill, and Barney Nagler. *Shoemaker: America's Greatest Jockey.* New York: Doubleday, 1988.

Smith, Walter Wellesley "Red," and Daniel Okrent, ed. *American Pastimes: The Very Best of Red Smith.* New York: Literary Classics of the United States, 2013.

Starr, Kevin. *Embattled Dreams: California in War and Peace 1940-1950.* New York: Oxford University Press.

Starr, Kevin. *Golden Dreams: California in an Age of Abundance, 1950-1963.* New York: Oxford University Press, 2009.

Underwood, Agness. *Newspaperwoman.* New York: Harper & Brothers Publisher, 1949.

Wagner, Rob Leicester. *Red Ink, White Lies: The Rise and Fall of Los Angeles Newspapers, 1920-1962.* Upland, CA: Dragonflyer Press, 2000.

West, Jerry, with Jonathan Coleman. *West By West: My Charmed, Tormented Life.* New York: Little, Brown and Company, 2011.

Woodward, Stanley. *Paper Tiger: An Old Sportswriter's Reminiscences of People, Newspapers, War and Work.* Lincoln and London: University of Nebraska Press, 1963.

THE STEAM ROOM COLUMNS USED IN THIS BOOK

"Herald-Express Grid Cup Awarded to Santa Monica," December 15, 1947.
"Brown Tells All, Would Break Up Cleveland Club," October 12, 1949.
"Van Spots Weakness; Marks Rams to Title," December 24, 1951.
"Huskies Favored to Beat Bruins in Cage Opener," March 7, 1952.
"Reeves to Decide Stydahar's Fate Tomorrow," September 29 1952.
"Stydahar Out; Pool New Ram Coach," September 30, 1952.
"Haney Set as Pittsburgh Manager," December 3, 1952.
"Pittsburgh to Trade Ralph Kiner," February 14, 1953.
"Sports Chatter," June 4, 1953.
"The Red Sanders Story: Rides to Fame on Single Wing and a Prayer That
    Was Answered," December 7, 1953.
"Satchel Paige Huddles With Veeck Over Bid to Join L.A," January 30,
    1954.
"Even Art Ashamed of Win," February 19, 1954.
"Charles Has Chance, Says Robinson," June 2, 1954.
"Miracle Man Newest Nickname for Stormy Leo," October 5, 1954.
"Bruins Go North for Cage Tilts," December 13, 1954.
"We're Better Than Bruins, Says Hayes," December 23, 1954.
"Miffed Bucks Head For Home," January 3, 1955.
"Sports Chatter," January 6, 1955.
"Rams Coach Prep Star With 'Biggie' Munn," January 29, 1955.
"Rocky Glad British On Our Side; Praises Game Stand," May 17, 1955.
"Heat Hurt Señor," May 19, 1955.
"Marciano Would Like to Quit For Family: Rocky Forced to Fight," October
    27, 1955.
"Ring Probe Waste of Taxpayers' Money, Contends Cal Eaton," March 22,
    1956.
"Ray Dreams of Vacation," May 19, 1956.
"Tab Air Force 1½Point Choice," November 8, 1956.
"Latin Ring Star on the Rise: The Pajarito Moreno Story," February 14, 1957.
"Moore's 'Diet' Makes Bulky Folks Rejoice," September 4, 1957.
"Sputnik's Pal Is Escort," October 24, 1957.

"Outspoken Hayes Silences Cry for Brown's Return to Ohio State,"
　　December 27, 1957.

"Dodgers Get Top Expert Coverage," March 11, 1958.

"Dodgers' Drysdale Has Aaron Baffled," March 12, 1958.

"Frightened, Bashful Youth Top Prospect," March 13, 1958.

"Coliseum Has Podres OK," June 5, 1958.

"Rams Decide on Younger Next Week," June 19, 1958.

"Gifford Going Back to Giants," July 24, 1958.

"Akins Wants Don, Art in One Night," December 4, 1958.

"Rags to Riches for Jordan," December 6, 1958.

"Bears Regain TV Privileges," November 2, 1959.

"Snider's Lemon Crop Nets $4.25," November 27, 1958.

"If Moon Shines Dodgers Could Climb NL Ladder," February 23, 1959.

"Dodgers Toil Convincer That They Mean Business," March 6, 1959.

"Roseboro Man Inspired Under Campy's Coaching," March 12, 1959.

"Reformed Drysdale Curbs Temper, Set for Comeback," March 27, 1959.

"Play Me or Trade Me Says Furillo," April 22, 1959.

"The Case For and Against Dodgers' Walter Alston," May 13, 1959.

"Isn't It Time to Call On Carl Furillo Again?," June 17, 1959.

"Oops There Goes the World Bantam Crown," July 8, 1959.

"Moon Calls Shot to Aid Koufax Win," September 1, 1959.

"Bud Furillo's Steam Room," September 30, 1959.

"Dodgers Lost in Big Park," October 2, 1959.

"Charlie Neal Woke Up 'Sick' Yesterday," October 3, 1959.

"Son Wins Bet on Furillo's Big Hit," October 5, 1959.

"Tired Sherry Has One Inning Left," October 6, 1959.

"Rams Just One Big Troupe of Prima-Donnas," November 10, 1959.

"Salary War Over Meredith" (subhead), November 24, 1959.

"Rams Threatened Player Revolt if Gillman Stayed," December 14, 1959.

"Billy Cannon Real Man" (subhead), December 8, 1959.

"Fine Print Baffles Cannon" (subhead), January 2, 1960.

"Houston Ruined Boyhood Dreams of Billy Cannon," January 5, 1960.

"Waller Would Welcome Chance to Play for Sid," January 7, 1960.

"Make Big Pitch for L.A. Cage Team," (column note), January 19, 1960.

"Aragon Like Old Football, Couldn't Be Pumped Up," January 22, 1960.

"Series Starts on Aragon and Ends in One Column," January 23, 1960.

"Shoemaker, Arcaro Know How to 'Ride' Golf Ball," January 26, 1960.

"Rozelle Proved Worth Handling Ram Owners," January 27, 1960.

"Lakers Ask Angelenos to Prove Selves Again," February 9, 1960.

"Archie Moore 'Nervous Wreck' Over NBA Ban," February 15, 1960.

"Arena Would Be Crowded," (subhead), March 21, 1960.

"Dundee's a Ring Tutor Who Knows His Business," April 7, 1960.

"Losing to Celtics Isn't Disgraceful for Lakers," April 17, 1962.

"Maybe Cannon Was Going to Play Ball at Parties," April 28, 1960.

"Be Back to Haunt Us" (subhead), May 16, 1960.

"Ired Bavasi Gives Furillo Release," May 17, 1960.

"Jack Kemp Won't Muff Big Chance in Football," July 13, 1960.

"If Rams Are Playboys, They're Well Conditioned," August 10, 1960.

"Fans Will Come Later if Chargers Keep Up," August 12, 1960.

"Cannon Super Service Stations Under Construction," September 21, 1960.

"Title for Chargers Would Buy New Noses," September 26, 1960.

"Night Club Activities Kept Chisox Too Busy," September 27, 1960.

"Waterfield's Challenge May Finally Curb Halas," October 11, 1960.

"Getting the Game Ball in Denver Can Be a Problem," October 17, 1960.

"Rozelle Gives Views on NFL AFL Co-Existence," November 2, 1960.

"Troy Has Same Chance Albania Did in War," November 17, 1960.

"Van Brocklin Will Have to Find New Backfield Coach," November 21, 1960.

"Kemp's Day Cause for Charger Defeat," November 21, 1960.

"Nothing Goes Right For Lakers at Home," November 28, 1960.

"Chargers Should Drop Prices for Final Games," November 30, 1960.

"Robinson Over Fullmer by TKO in Ten Rounds," December 2, 1960.

"Title Team Costs Hilton $700,000," December 12, 1960

"San Diego Woos Club After 50–43 Thriller" (subhead), December 19, 1960.

"Gillman, Rymkus Friendly As 'Ike' and 'Mr. K,'" December 26, 1960.

"AFL Hopeful of Brighter Future," January 1, 1961.

"NBA Scheduling No Help to L.A. Lakers," January 4, 1961.

"S.D. For Chargers Like L.A. Was for Dodgers," January 10, 1961.

"Podres Gets Treatments Daily at Santa Anita," January 20, 1961.

"Basketball's Newest Nickname is Argue-Ball," January 26, 1961.

"Laker Ace LA's Top Star," February 6, 1961.

"Lakers Shouldn't Alibi–They Beat Themselves," March 30, 1961.

"Attention Shoemaker: Please Be My Partner," February 10, 1961.

"Fed Up With Basketball, Says' Celtics Bob Cousy," February 22, 1961.

"Bilko Wins Early 'OK' From Rigney," February 27, 1961.

"Ike Dyed-in-Wool Baseball Devotee," March 2, 1961.

"Piersall More Interested in Baseball than Writing," March 17, 1961.

"Angels Lose to Bosox, 10–5," March 18, 1961.

"Halas Gives Steam Room Safe Passage at Poolside," March 16, 1961.

"Talkative Cerv Recalls Jaw Injury," March 19, 1961.

"Maglie Says Drysdale His Own Worst Enemy," March 21, 1961.

"Halas Pressing Charger Suit," March 24, 1961.

"Groucho Declares Himself, Says He's an Angel Fan," March 28, 1961.

"Second Guessing Dykes" (column note), March 29, 1961.

"Awesome Power Makes Mantle Real Standout," April 21, 1961.

"Wagner Wrecks Yankees," May 8, 1961.

"Louis, Bonomi Unalike in Regard for Gibson," June 2, 1961.

"Angels, Bosox in 2nd Twin Bill," June 9, 1961.

"Moore's Durability Amazes Ring Vets," June 12, 1961.

"Maris Happy Again Now that Bob Cerv's Back," June 13, 1961.

"Houk Theory on Ford Differs From Casey's," June 27, 1961.

"Bavasi Man Behind Dodger Climb to Championship," July 21, 1961.

"102 Men Bat in Angel Rout," July 22, 1961.

"Mantle Would Rather Capture Triple Crown," August 8, 1961.

"Maris Bunt Typifies Yankee Spirit," August 8, 1961.

"Mantle, Maris Won't Discuss Ruth HR Mark," August 9, 1961.

"McBride Defeat Leaves Red Faces," August 17, 1961.

"Maris Balks at Naming New Offspring Homer," August 23, 1961.

"Stengel Says Both Maris and Mantle Will Break Record," August 24, 1961.

"Rigney Picks Faltering Yanks to Win A.L. Flag," August 25, 1961.

"Rams Out to Trade Away Complete All-Pro Teams," August 29, 1961.

"Angels, Athletics Duel in Matinee," September 1, 1961.

"L.A. Raves About Chargers, Now That They're Gone," September 14, 1961.

"Trojans Plotting Course for Surprise Bowl Visit," September 19, 1961.

"Maris Tells of Home Run Tension," September 21, 1961.

"Recognition at Last For Tracy Stallard," October 2, 1961.

"What if Baylor Broke Mark on Anniversary?," November 5, 1961.

"Bad Rap By Michaels" (subhead), November 8, 1961.

"UCLA-SC Game this Town's Main Sports Event," November 27, 1961.

"To Coughlin, Who Taught Me How to Be One Myself," January 28, 1962.

"Rigney Gives His Views on Alston as Dodger Manager," January 30, 1962.

"Leave It to Wooden to Cast Spell Over Trojans," February 3, 1962.

"Wooden Claims Bench Barbs Show Bruins He's Battling," February 5, 1962.

"Angel Rookie Another 'Goofy' Gomez?," March 2, 1962.

"Southpaw May Quit, Go Home," March 5, 1962.

"Giants Beat Out Braves to Mays by Investing $4000," March 16, 1962.

"Cassius Checks in Long Distance" (column note subhead), April 16, 1962.

"Trenton Swings Late, and Bobo Calls His Dad," April 19, 1962.

"Epitaph for McCoy—Fights On Level Were Good Ones," April 22, 1962.

"Mr. Confidence Doesn't Impress Old Patriarch," April 24, 2962.

"Belinsky Tosses No-Hitter," May 6, 1962.

"Here's How No-Hit Ball Earned $1060 for Bobo," May 10, 1962.

"Belinsky Eyes TV Series," May 12, 1962.

"Marilyn Adds Gentle Touch to Program," June 2, 1962.

"Bo, Chance Fined for 5 a.m. Frolic," June 14, 1962.

"Angels, A's in Earthy Brawl," June 21, 1962.

"Now It Can Be Told: Angels Rewarded Bo Big," June 28, 1962.

"When in Washington—Look for New Kefauver Probe," July 2, 1962.

"Angels Take Loop Lead; Nab Two, Soar to Top Spot," July 4, 1962.

"Gleeful Angels Whoop It Up," July 5, 1962.

"Box Office Greed, Belinsky Bravado Undermined Angels," July 7, 1962.

"Belinsky Draws Final Warning for Tardiness," July 13, 1962.

"With Bowsfield Pitching, Might See The Fight, Too," July 20,1962.

"Friends, Foes, Countrymen, We Must Listen to Cassius," July 21, 1962.

"Koufax Finger On Mend; Can Sign in Guests at Motel," July 27, 1962.

"O'Malley Not Czarring" (subhead), August 13, 1962.

"Nobody's Ready for Angel Flag—Except Angel Players," August 27, 1962.

"What Would a Sociologist Make of This Dream?," September 1, 1962.

"Lunacy Reigns as Angels Prepare for Big Showdown," September 2, 1962.

"All Gloom For Dodgers," October 4, 1962.

"Piersall Able Actor, Tests for Role as TV Cowboy," October 21, 1962.

"Blame Players With Rest for Rams Football Debacle," October 22, 1962.

"So You Wanna Be A Coach? No Thanks—Hours are Rough," October 29, 1962.

"Afternoon Session With Moore at Shugrue Hall," November 12, 1962.

"Clay Was Indeed Great—But Where Was Moore?," November 17, 1962.

"Troy Walks on Wild Side," November 25, 1962.

"'Million Years From Now,' Troy's Win Will Be Sweet," January 2, 1963.

"Michaels Another Ex-Ram Not Sorry About Trade," January 15, 1963.

"Chance Isn't Taking Any By Serving 'Fat' Pitches," February 23, 1963.

"UCLA Playmaking Star Not a Ball-Hogging 'Hazzard,'" February 1, 1963.

"Will Boxing Be Banned In the Olympics, Too?," March 23, 1963.

"Bo Has 'Fine' Day," April 1, 1963.

"How the Bruiser Wrecked Alex Karras' Detroit Bar," April 24, 1963.

"It's Good-bye, Good Luck To An Old Angel Friend," March 14, 1963.

"Rigney's Woes Are Just Beginning—And Now This," May 18, 1963.

"Aloha! Belinsky Sent to Hawaii," May 20, 1963.

"Stuart Overmatched in His Proposed Fight With Houk," July 4, 1963.

"Man Off His Rocker Picks Patterson in Big Upset," July 15, 1963.

"A Busy Buzzie Says He'll Recall Richert This Week," July 22, 1963.

"Battered Angels Heading for Home," August 1, 1963.

"Belinsky is a Cinch to be Elsewhere in '64," September 3, 1963.

"It Gets Late Early in Left Field" (subhead), September 6, 1963.

"A Warning: Yankee Pitching So Good Terry In Bullpen," September 23, 1963.

"New King of Yankees Want This Series Win Most of All," September 26,

1963.

"Crosetti's Greatest Thrill—Cashing His Series Checks," September 29, 1963.

"Howard the Yank to Fear," October 2, 1963.

"The Bombers Went In Fearing Koufax," October 3, 1963.

"Yankees Still a Proud Team And Dodgers Respect Them," October 4, 1963.

"Maybe Yankees Guilty of Clinching Flag Too Early," October 6, 1963.

"Yankees Can Offer No Protest Over Losing Championship," October 7, 1963.

"Les Richter Deserves a Day and He's Getting One," October 24, 1963.

"Parnassus, 68, But Still Going Strong in Boxing," December 1, 1963.

"Belinsky Declares War on Hitters, Girls," January 24, 1964.

"The Collegian With The Poise of a 10-year Veteran," March 16, 1964.

"'Bruiser 'Kook Club' Qualifier,'" April 11, 1964.

"Quick Steam and a Rub," April 25, 1964.

"Rookie N.Y. Pilot Has Firm Hand," June 7, 1964.

"The Hurricane's Really a Zephyr," June 21, 1964.

"Well Hello, Jack," August 19, 1964.

"Willie Won't Let Giants Quit," August 26, 1964.

"Why Dean Throws at the Records," August 30, 1964.

"McKay Football Genius of '60s," November 29, 1964.

"Isn't Tommy Prothro Coach the Bruins Really Want?," December 31, 1964.

"Jacinto's Act Ruined by Supplementary Steed," March 7, 1965.

"Angels Debate Bunning, Sandy," March 16, 1965.

"Dodger Fans: Be Optimistic," April 3, 1965.

"Stengel Heeds His Pitching Coach," April 21, 1965.

"Captain Wills Pulls Dodgers Together," April 26, 1965.

"The Feather Eats Like A Heavy," May 2, 1965.

"Saldivar a Good Champ," May 8, 1965.

"K.C. Vows Revenge for Mule," May 9, 1965.

"Cleaning Up on the Horses," June 6, 1965.

"A $5 Million Day," July 6, 1965.

"Purple Heart Juan," June 16, 1965.

"The 2,000-Year-Old Sports Expert," July 24, 1965.

"The $100,000 Pitcher," August 11, 1965.

"It's No Sport When Bats Become Weapons," August 23, 1965.

"Koufax Controls Emotion," September 11, 1965.

"Lefebvre Falls Into Slump," September 25, 1965.

"I Wanted That Record," September 26, 1965.

"Ferrara Dodgers' Unsung Hero," September 27, 1965.

"Willie D. Perkin'," September 28, 1965.

"Hungriest Dodger of 'Em All," September 29, 1965.
"Saturday Flag Day?" September 30, 1965.
"Big D Worth $100,000 Too," October 1, 1965.
"We Went Dead—Wills," October 2, 1965.
"Proudest Flag Winners," October 3, 1965.
"Allison Almost a Dodger," October 8, 1965.
"Do We Need The Series?," October 12, 1965.
"They Dominate Baseball Now," October 15, 1965.
"A Football Game Dictated by Hate," October 24, 1965.
"Tommy Prothro's Moment of Truth," November 15, 1965.
"Bruins Dominated It," November 21, 1965.
"Bruins—A Team With Character," January 2, 1966.
"The Dodger Profit: $2 Million," February 3, 1966.
"Dinner at Cooke's," February 19, 1966.
"Marciano Wants to Manage LA's Quarry," February 20, 1966.
"Spring's First Beanballs," March 14, 1966.
"Sandy Willing to Negotiate," March 16, 1966.
"Bird Stopped By Rojas, Doc," March 18, 1966.
"Wags' Heart in L.A.," March 22, 1966.
"Zaleechee People Issue a Warning," March 27, 1966.
"Koufax Drills, Defends Big D.," March 29, 1966.
"Koufax Highest Paid Ever," March 31, 1966.
"The Baylor Ballet Still Best in Town," April 4, 1966.
"Champagne Before 7th Game," April 27, 1966.
"Halas Best at Saving Footballs," May 1, 1966.
"Houk's Secret: Psychology," May 7, 1966.
"Juan Feels Awful, Pitches Great," June 13, 1966.
"Sandy's Night in San Francisco," June 11, 1966.
"Regan: Meet Me in St. Looey," July 11, 1966.
"Machen Blitzes Quarry," July 15, 1966.
"How Much Longer for Sandy?," August 21, 1966.
"The Rams Will Miss Baker," September 3, 1966.
"You Can Call 'Em Fighting Rams" (column note), September 4, 1966.
"Just Another 'Vulch' for Regan," September 6, 1966.
"Bear Allen Ignites Dixie's Rage," September 12, 1966.
"George Allen—The Spellbinder," September 17, 1966.
"George Allen: Worrier," September 18, 1966.
"Terms of Allen, Bass Agreement," October 2, 1966.
"Dodgers Get Big Break," October 7, 1966.
"A Pattern That Suggests Decay," October 10, 1966.
"The Night Sandy Had to Yield," November 19, 1966.
"USC Goes Upside Dow . . . n," November 20, 1966.

"USC Votes Irish No. 1," November 27, 1966.
"Sweetan Feared by Allen," December 1, 1966.
"Just Business, Says O'Malley," December 2, 1966.
"Are The King and Rick Next?," December 4, 1966.
"Quarry Ponders Villain's Role," December 11, 1966.
"Was Gamble Worth It?," January 3, 1967.
"Unbeaten Ramos Was Under Age," January 10, 1967.
"Green Bay Will Win, 31-17," January 14, 1967.
"Ten Per Centers Collect on Buck," January 15, 1967.
"The Difference Was Starr," January 16, 1967.
"Coaching Dull—Russ," February 16, 1967.
"A Final Supper With Jack Cooke," February 18, 1967.
"The Twins, Giants in the Series" (subhead), February 19, 1967.
"They Fly Very Low at Daytona" (column note), February 25, 1967.
"Santa Anita Handicap to Favorite," February 27, 1967.
"Dean Sends Out World Series Invites," March 15, 1967.
"Burdette Can't Stop Running," March 7, 1967.
"Supporting Cast Needed by Lew," March 25, 1967.
"Don't mention it" (column note), March 27, 1967.
"NFL Humiliated by Dirty Dozen," August 7, 1967.
"Quick Steam and a Rub" (subhead), August 2, 1967.
"The Right Team Left Town," August 28, 1967.
"The Kings Opening Game," September 19, 1967.
"Jumbo Joe Would Love The Kings," September 20, 1967.
"Trojans Have Some Horses," September 24, 1967.
"Rams: A Haven for Baldies," September 28, 1967.
"Will Trojans Show Up for Notre Dame?," October 12, 1967.
"The Young Generation—Defense," October 15, 1967.
"Beban Clinches Heisman Trophy," November 12, 1967.
"Can McKay Snap Prothro's Streak?," November 17, 1967.
"Millions Await 'Biggest' Game," November 18, 1967.
"Trojans Should Be No. 1," November 19, 1967.
"How to Beat the Anita Tab," March 20, 1968.
"Yanez: It Was Pineda's Fault," March 22, 1968.
"Can the Big E Make Mexico?," March 23, 1968.
"RFK Pulling for R. Rojas," March 27, 1968.
"Rojas: The New Graziano," March 29, 1968.
"LA's 14th Champion," March 31, 1968.
"The Night Quarry Got Hurt," April 21, 1968.
"Ellis, Frazier Fight Not In Sight," April 29, 1968.
"Somebody Quits in Corner—Not Sonny," May 24, 1968.
"Rigney Won't Tell What's Wrong," May 28, 1968.

"Dooley For Papa?," May 28, 1968.
"Pressure Subsides for Don Drysdale, Shutout," June 10, 1968.
"Bavasi: A Farewell Address," June 12, 1968.
"Pimental Plastered in Forum Feature," June 15, 1968.
"Mando Prisoner of His Manager," June 19, 1968.
"Where'll LaSorda Wind Up?," June 23, 1968.
"It's Time to Toast Rig Again," June 24, 1968.
"The Allen Approach," July 9, 1968.
"49ers Have Shot At Simpson," July 22, 1968.
"Rams Recover Brilliantly, 23-21," August 10, 1968.
"Autry's Song Getting Old," September 3, 1968.
"The Fight Camp," September 5, 1968.
"Frank Leahy Battles Leukemia," September 11, 1968.
"Pardee vs. Kelly," September 25, 1968.
"Saijo Breezes Past Rojas for 15-Round Win," September 28, 1968.
"Where's the Rockne?" (subhead), October 8, 1966.
"Two Halves of Simpson," October 17, 1968.
"Trojans Win Thriller From Huskies, 14-7," October 19, 1968.
"Hooray for Hollywood," November 3, 1968.
"Gabe Saves Ram Tech From Destruction," November 18, 1968.
"Biggest Game: Only in L.A.," November 19, 1968.
"Russell Isn't Worried—Not Yet," November 20, 1968.
"Riot At The Forum," December 7, 1968.
"Not The Same Without The Old Man" December 8, 1968.
"Some Players Back Allen," December 27, 1968.
"8 Rams Threaten to Quit; Players Will Take Protest to Dan Reeves,"
    December 27, 1968.
"Woody Hayes . . . The Importance of Being No. 1," December 29, 1968.
"Colts Choice By 17 Over Jets," December 30, 1968.
"Bucks Too Smooth for Sloppy Trojans," January 2, 1969.
"Reeves Wants Allen Back," January 2, 1969.
"Reeves-Allen Summit Today for a Decision," January 4, 1969.
"Rams Rehire Allen," January 6, 1969.
"Rams Physician Saved Allen," January 7, 1969.
"Will The Generals Get Lew?," January 19, 1969.
"Cosby For Little Guys," January 31, 1969.
"The New King of 135s," February 19, 1969.
"Alcindor: Reflections, Projections," February 23, 1969.
"30 Second Clock Not Far Off Now," March 14, 1969.
"Quarry Back Right Where He Started," March 24, 1969.
"Nixon is Wilt's Kind of Man," April 25, 1969.
"Why Did Lakers Freeze? Five-minute Sleep Aided Celts," May 6, 1969.

"Will Lakers Go After Deacon? VBK Wants a Policeman," May 15, 1969.

"One More College Game for 'Starved' Football Fans" (column note), May 11, 1969.

"Quarry Stopped By Doctor," June 24, 1969.

"Meet the Man from Athabasca," June 29, 1969.

"How Can Rams, Troy Do This To Us?," October 13, 1969.

"Allen's Way is the Right Way," October 14, 1969.

"Sid, We'll Miss You," November 11, 1969.

"Bruins Almost In Bowl . . . But along Came Jones (And Sam)," November 23, 1969.

"The Rams Waive Extradition," December 23, 1969.

"It's Ram Weather in Minnesota," December 25, 1969.

"Tailspin Makes Miami Last Stop for Angelenos," December 28, 1969.

"McKay: The Best in the Business," January 4, 1970.

"Chiefs Prove AFL is Equal—NFL Should Return $18 Million," January 12, 1970.

"Con is Over—Everybody Equal," January 13, 1970.

"How Allen 'Soothed' Lombardi," January 22, 1970.

"Frazier Still Heavy Choice," February 16, 1970.

"One Champ Now—Frazier," February 17, 1970.

"The New Master," February 25, 1970.

"Why Baltimore Colts Tapped Klosterman," January 8, 1970.

"LA Caught With Super Pants Down," January 13, 1970.

"Ramos Eager to Flatten Laguna," March 1, 1970.

"Blood, Sweat and Tears for Mando," March 3, 1970.

"A Knock At Shoemaker," March 9, 1970.

"Frazier: Smokin' Singer," April 1, 1970.

"Lakers Back In It—But For How Long?," April 6, 1970.

"Lakers Celebrate Like College Boys," April 8, 1970.

"Lakers Fly From Phoenix Ashes," April 8, 1970.

"Wilt Was Voice of Doom," April 10, 1970.

"It Goes 15, But Olivares Wins," April 19, 1970.

"Reed May Play 6th Game, But Will Lakers?," May 5, 1970.

"Wilt Has The Range Now," May 7, 1970.

"Lakers Wilt, Now It's Up To Stars," May 9, 1970.

"Ruben Navarro's Pre-Round Prayer," May 12, 1970.

"Bill Cosby For Lakers On Paper," May 13, 1970.

"Uncle Wiltie's Recipe," June 28, 1970.

"Ring Doctor Stirs a Controversy," August 9, 1970.

"Reeves Congratulates Allen," August 17, 1970.

"Bear Told: Walk Underwater," September 9, 1970.

"USC Runs Away from 'Bama," September 13, 1970.

"Los Angeles-Kansas City Super Bowl," September 13, 1970.
"Who Will Be Out: Allen or Cosell?," October 29, 1970.
"Los Angeles-Kansas City Super Bowl," September 13, 1970.
"Kings Out of Bad Apples," October 13, 1970.
"Who Will Be Out: Allen or Cosell?," October 29, 1970.
"Ali's Rhyme: Quarry . . . Sorry," October 20, 1970.
"Sharman Draws A Crowd At Last," October 22, 1971.
"Cut-Up Jerry a Loser in 3," October 27, 1970.
"Steamer's Hotel Full of Rumors," December 29, 1970.
"Mr. Allen Goes to Washington," January 7, 1971.
"The Case For Smoking (Joe)," March 7, 1971.
"Who's Greatest? Frazier, Of Course," March 9, 1971.
"La Pelea, Poker and Pinot Noir," March 31, 1971.
"No Butts This time—Olivares," April 3, 1971.
"Dan Reeves Dies," April 16, 1971.
"Cosell Is Reviewed by Cosell," May 5, 1971.
"Super Night By Napoles," June 5, 1971.
"Spanish Translation for Caliente is Hot," August 7, 1971.
"Thomas Observed, Seems Okay," August 15, 1971.
"Floor Plan at Ruben's House," August 18, 1971.
"Wrestling Taken in by Coliseum," August 26, 1971.
"Return of the '40s and Boley," September 23, 1971.
"Mando Passes Drug Test, Fight Is On," November 5, 1971.
"Incredible Loss By Ramos," November 6, 1971.
"Look Who's In Mando's Corner," November 7, 1971.
"Allen Gets Football But Not In Mouth," December 14, 1971.
"Haystack Is Holding Own, January 12, 1972."
"Griffith to Sign for Lopez Match," February 1, 1972.
"Quick Steam and a Rub" (column note), January 26, 1972.
"Mando's First Reaction: Thought He Lost," February 20, 1972.
"From Brandeis To The Lakers," February 21, 1972.
"Walton Just Plain Bill," March 6, 1972.
"Ali at 30: I Talked Too Much," March 15, 1972.
"Long Beach Was Just Overmatched," March 19, 1972.
"A UCLA-Florida State Final: Bruins Favored by 16 Points," March 24, 1972.
"UCLA Still Doin' Its Thing," March 26, 1972.
"Looks Like Oklahoma, Says McKay," April 7, 1972.
"Did Extra Lights Confuse Lakers?," April 10, 1972.
"Wilt's Muscles Urgently Needed," April 14, 1972.
"Are Buck-Laker Crowds Getting Too Much Credit?," April 19, 1972.
"Lakers Kareem Bucks," April 23, 1972.
"Basketball Clinic at Forum; Knicks Teach Lakers the Game," April 27, 1972.

"Fregosi Sneaking Back Into Anaheim," April 28, 1972.

"L.A. Gives N.Y. Heart Trouble," May 1, 1972.

"Knicks Sink, Call Family," May 4, 1972.

"Lakers Romp, 115-90—Just One More," May 6, 1972.

"Chamberlain's Problems Multiple," May 7, 1972.

"It's A Laker World," May 8, 1972.

"Lakers Run Out on Party," May 9, 1972.

"Allen Through Eyes of Tanner," May 30, 1972.

"Bobby Fischer Held In Check By Reykjavik," June 6, 1972.

"Ali: I'm Better Than Ever," June 28, 1972.

"Canton Flashes: Belinsky Joins Palookaville," August 24, 1972.

"Why USC Plays Big Openers," September 9, 1972.

"UCLA, USC 1-2 in One Poll," September 11, 1972.

"A Fast Ride Mando Hadn't Figured On," September 16, 1972.

"Trojans Fumble But Hold Onto Number 1," October 8, 1972.

"Hernandez Legacy: Cougar II," October 12, 1972.

"Gorilla Stalls, Slows Down Troy," October 15, 1972.

"Raiders Named For Al Davis," October 29, 1972.

"The Time Gonzalez Had Cancer," November 2, 1972.

"Rodolfo Does to Chango What Chango Did to Mando Ramos," November 11, 1972.

"No. 1: Six Touchdowns by Davis As Trojans Win U.S. Title," December 3, 1972.

"Different Look At Woody," December 21, 1972.

"USC World Champions," January 2, 1973.

"Valentine Is Still Smiling," April 24, 1973.

"Shoe Fit for Tennis, Horses," March 27, 1973.

"Finish Line Table For Golde, Please," April 5, 1973.

"What The Future Holds For Wilt," April 8, 1973.

"Wooden Would Have Coached U.S.," April 29, 1973.

"Ryan Got Boost from Jack McKeon," May 17, 1973.

"Frankel Doesn't Talk To Horses," May 20, 1973.

"Bo Belinsky New Author In Town," June 5, 1973.

"Eagles Lighten Gabriel Bid," June 8, 1973.

"Ruben Fasting—No Rum Or Coke," June 19, 1973.

"Rules Same for Great John L.—Or Mando Ramos," August 10, 1973.

"New York Won't Be The Same," September 23, 1973.

"Is Mark Harmon Underrated?," November 20, 1973.

"Troy Has The Roses, No. 1 Still Challenge," November 26, 1973.

"Ballad of the Horseplayers," December 27, 1973.

"A Night for Ali's Revenge," January 29, 1974.

"276 By Dave Wins L.A. Open By Two Shots," February 18, 1974.

"Lakers Only Need Wilt, West, Elg," February 23, 1974.

"Serfas in Better League Now" (column note), February 25, 1974.

"A Hundred Grander Full of Contention," March 8, 1974.

"Foreman Still For America," March 13, 1974.

"Battle of Wounded Knee," March 27, 1974.

"Foreman-Ali Set for September 24," May 14, 1974.

"Chacon Told By Corner That Red Was Set To Fall," May 25, 1974.

"Imagine How Nickel Beer Night Was," June 6, 1974.

INDEX